Twentieth-Century Europe

Twentieth-Century Europe

1900 to the Present

FOURTH EDITION

Michael D. Richards
Paul R. Waibel

WILEY Blackwell

Published by John Wiley & Sons, Inc., Hoboken, New Jersey.
Published simultaneously in Canada.

For general information on our other products and services or for technical support, please contact our Customer Care Department within the United States at (800) 762-2974, outside the United States at (317) 572-3993 or fax (317) 572-4002.

Wiley also publishes its books in a variety of electronic formats. Some content that appears in print may not be available in electronic formats. For more information about Wiley products, visit our web site at www.wiley.com.

Library of Congress Cataloging-in-Publication Data applied for

ISBN 9781119878735 (Paperback)

Cover Design: Wiley
Cover Image: © olrat/Getty Images

Set in 11/13pt Dante by Straive, Pondicherry, India
Printed and bound by CPI Group (UK) Ltd, Croydon, CR0 4YY

C9781119878735_061223

Contents

Preface

The fourth edition, like those before it, is meant to be not only brief but also readable and accurate. That it is relatively brief allows for some outside readings and other assignments. That it is readable is of great importance. It is important for students and instructors to have as much common ground as possible. This helps class sessions to be informed exchanges of questions and opinions. Lastly, accuracy is fundamentally important. We have worked to create a text that provides a reliable introduction to Europe from 1900 to the present and places Europe when appropriate in a global context.

The approach is largely chronological but there are, as well, some major themes. One theme is the slow unraveling of European dominance of the world. Another is the emergence of the United States as a major influence in terms of politics, the economy, and both popular and high culture. A third would be the postwar urge to find ways to cooperate, even while retaining a variety of approaches on the national level to political, economic, and social questions.

The book is divided into four parts with each part containing three chapters. The first two parts cover the period from 1900 to the end of World War II in 1945. The third and fourth parts cover developments from the end of World War II to the present. An "Overview," summarizing the main themes of the period, serves as an introduction to each part.

Maps, tables, and illustrations are meant to assist the reader in gaining a more thorough understanding of the information provided by the text. Four maps show national boundaries at key points during the last 120 years. The tables provided may either clarify key events (such as the German inflation of 1923) or offer an overview of a key development (e.g., the development over several decades of the European Community/European Union). Photographs, some from our own collections, are featured in every chapter to provide visual references. Each chapter begins with a brief chronology to orient the reader and to serve as a reference. The appendix contains a list of abbreviations and acronyms, which in this bureaucratic world grows longer with each edition. An extensive index, a useful if often overlooked feature, rounds out the resources supplementing the text.

This book has its own history. More than 40 years ago, Michael D. Richards, a young assistant professor at Sweet Briar College, published *Europe: 1900–1980: A Brief History*. Several years later, Paul R. Waibel, who had been using that original edition and had become acquainted with Professor Richards, joined with him in the creation of a new text. It was modeled on the original book but differed in some important aspects, in particular in an increased attention to intellectual and cultural trends. This edition offers an extensive revision of all chapters, in particular those chapters dealing with the twenty-first century.

We have each taught large numbers of students during careers several decades in length. To those students, to colleagues, and to our own teachers, we owe unpayable debts. This book is in some large part the product of countless conversations inside and outside the classroom. Our hope is that it will allow us to continue those conversations in some fashion with colleagues and students.

Every book is the work not only of its authors but also of the many dedicated employees of the publishing house. We would like to thank those who played a role in seeing the fourth edition to completion. We begin with Sophie Bradwell, who approached the authors more than a year ago to determine if we would be interested in a fourth edition. We were, of course, interested, and we began working with her. After she received a promotion, which we were most happy to hear about, she turned the project over to the capable hands of Anya Fielding, Rachel Greenberg, and Liz Wingett. As we worked through the revision of the manuscript, we were fortunate to have the help of Vijayalakshmi Saminathan and

Manju Subramanian in securing new illustrations for some of the chapters. Ed Robinson helped with the selection of the cover illustration and design. He and Sarah Milton handled other details of the cover and back cover. We also owe a debt of gratitude to the anonymous reviewers whose advice warned us away from potential several missteps. Radhika Raheja Sharma reviewed and accepted the manuscript. Shyamala Venkateshwaran headed the essential task of project management. Straive India copyedited this book, and Alison Waggit contributed to the preparation of the index. Belle Mundy contributed a much-needed professional proofreading of the manuscript and index. We would also like to thank Rachel Greenberg and Ed Robinson for guiding efforts to market the book.

As always, there are so many people who have contributed in one way or another to making this book possible. Mr. Richards wishes to thank Peter N. Stearns for generous editorial assistance with the original text. We both also want to recognize the assistance of Andrew Davidson for his work with the first, second, and third editions of the revised text. Mr. Richards also wishes to thank Nancy D. Potter for her support and encouragement over the years.

Mr. Waibel wishes to thank Darlene Waibel for her ever-present encouragement and assistance.

It is our sincere hope that readers will not only find this book informative but also enjoyable.

Michael D. Richards
Paul R. Waibel

Part 1

Overview: 1900–1919

THE TWO DECADES FROM THE DAWN of the twentieth century to the end of World War I form the era during which European civilization peaked. It was also the period in which the very foundations of European civilization began to crack beneath the weight of inner contradictions and new challenges.

In 1900, Europeans could have said, perhaps paradoxically, that Europe was the world and the world was Europe's. By 1914, "Europeans" controlled 84 percent of the world's land surface. Only Japan, which since 1871 had been pursuing a self-conscious policy of Westernization, was accepted as a "civilized" although non-Western nation.

Europeans' sense of superiority seemed confirmed by history. The Scientific Revolution, Enlightenment, and Industrial Revolution had given the West a scientific-technological advantage over the non-Western world. By the end of the nineteenth century, the lion's share of the wealth of the world flowed into Western nations.

In Europe itself, the remnants of the old aristocracy still occupied thrones and, in some countries like Russia, Germany, and Austria-Hungary, possessed real or potential power. But the period from the end of the Napoleonic wars to the outbreak of World War I or the Great War in 1914 was the golden age of the middle class, the

Twentieth-Century Europe: 1900 to the Present, Fourth Edition.
Michael D. Richards and Paul R. Waibel.

bourgeoisie. They were the self-confident children of modernity, the Enlightenment tradition. Their ideology was classical liberalism, both political and economic. Their social status and, in some countries like Great Britain and France, political power derived from their growing wealth.

This Europe of Strauss waltzes and middle-class outings captured in impressionist paintings was being transformed even as it neared its fulfillment. Forces that had their origins in the nineteenth century were about to topple centuries-old dynasties and with them their archaic nobility. Likewise, the middle class, the real pillar of the existing order, was under serious attack, challenged politically and economically by the emerging working class, itself organized in increasingly powerful labor unions and political parties.

The Great War changed the course of European history. Beginning as a localized crisis brought on by the assassination of the heir to the Austro-Hungarian Empire, it rapidly escalated into a world war. Each participant believed it was fighting to save its homeland from an aggressor. All felt that the war would be brief and glorious, concluding in time for them to be home for Christmas. All were disappointed. The enthusiasm that greeted the outbreak of war in August 1914 soon changed to frustration and disappointment.

Since no one had expected war to break out in 1914, none of the participants were prepared for what war actually brought. By 1916, the war had become one of attrition, each side trying to bleed the other to death. Necessity drove governments to assume a broader and more direct role in their economies and in the private lives of their people. Scarce economic resources vital to the war effort were rationed, as were consumer goods. Government-sponsored propaganda and censorship were used to mobilize "human resources." Civil liberties often received only a polite wink as the need to combat defeatism grew.

1917 was a momentous year. In February, the German High Command persuaded the Kaiser to authorize the resumption of unrestricted submarine warfare. This move, intended to bring Great Britain to its knees, instead led to the United States coming into the war in April, a development that meant Germany's eventual defeat. In March, revolution broke out in Russia.

As Lenin noted, Russian soldiers had voted against the war with their feet when they deserted in large numbers. The liberal Provisional Government failed to respond to the demands of the time and in November the Bolsheviks seized power. Their efforts to hold on to power would become one of the most important themes of twentieth-century European history. Fresh American troops tipped the scales in favor of the Allies on the Western Front. American intervention (and also in some cases failure to intervene) became another important theme in twentieth-century European history.

Allied armies broke through the Siegfried Line in July 1918. The Central Powers began to collapse. Revolution broke out in Germany. On 9 November, the Kaiser abdicated and went into exile in the Netherlands. On 11 November, Germany signed an armistice and the "guns of August" were finally silenced.

Germany had signed the armistice expecting to participate in the peace conference, but neither it nor Russia were invited to take part. The victors who gathered in Paris to bring an end to the war fought to end all wars were divided between new-world idealists and old-world realists. The treaty with Germany was a "victors' peace" that poisoned the future. A second world war was not inevitable but, unfortunately, likely.

1

Europe and the World Before the Great War, 1900–1914

Chronology

1899–1902	Boer War
1901	Death of Queen Victoria
1904–1905	Russo-Japanese War
1905	Revolution in Russia
	Tsar Nicholas II issues the October Manifesto

Twentieth-Century Europe: 1900 to the Present, Fourth Edition.
Michael D. Richards and Paul R. Waibel.

1906	Algeciras Conference
	Great Britain launches HMS *Dreadnought*
1908	Austria-Hungary annexes Bosnia and Herzegovina
1914	Assassination of Franz Ferdinand

If a member of "generation z" could somehow be transported back to the turn of the twentieth century, after the initial shock from the lack of modern technology, he or she would notice many similarities between the two periods. Both were periods of rapid change in every aspect of life. The pace of discoveries in the natural sciences was accelerating, providing new knowledge of how the universe machine operated. The new social sciences claimed to apply the scientific method to studying how people interacted with society. For many, the twentieth century promised an improved quality of life for all. While most saw peace and prosperity continuing, others saw dark clouds gathering over the horizon.

What would appear most different to our imaginary time traveler would be the international order. The twenty-first-century global village with its great diversity from which our time traveler came would not exist. Instead, with a virtual monopoly on certain kinds of scientific and technological knowledge, Western Civilization was able to exert imperialistic force all over the world by the end of the nineteenth century. Some of the more ancient civilizations—e.g., India, China, the Middle East, and North Africa—managed to retain their distinctive cultures while benefiting from Western science and technology. In some cases, Western influences were resisted by force, as in the Boxer Rebellion in China (1899–1901). Japan avoided becoming a victim of the new imperialism by embracing Western scientific, economic, military, and political practices while preserving its distinctive culture.

Europe and the World

Remnants of the overseas empires established during the Age of Exploration and Discovery (c. 1450–c. 1650) remained, but interest in overseas empires had waned by the mid-nineteenth century.

Those early outposts of Western influence around the globe mainly originated for economic reasons. According to the then-accepted economic theory (mercantilism), a fixed amount of wealth existed. The goal of a nation was to increase its share of the wealth, usually measured in precious metals, for example, gold and silver. International trade was one means by which a nation could either increase or decrease its share of wealth. A favorable trade balance increased a nation's share of the wealth, whereas an unfavorable balance of trade decreased its portion.

The new seaborn trade birthed a commercial revolution and the rise of capitalism (sixteenth to eighteenth century). The Scientific Revolution (1543–1687) provided a mechanical model of the universe governed by cause-and-effect natural laws. The intellectuals of the Enlightenment who followed the Scientific Revolution tried to find similar natural laws that governed society. Economic thinkers such as Adam Smith (1723–1790) believed they could identify the natural laws of economics. This new understanding of economics, often referred to as *laissez-faire,* free-market capitalism, or classical liberal economics, helped stimulate the Industrial Revolution that led to the new age of imperialism in the late nineteenth and early twentieth centuries.

The new economic theories that fueled industrialization required free access to raw materials and markets but did not require control of the areas that provided the raw materials or markets for finished goods. Most European leaders as late as 1870 believed that apart from a few exceptions, colonies cost more than they were worth. Why be burdened by tracts of overseas territory that were expensive to administer and provided little benefits? The lack of interest in colonies shifted quickly to a fast-paced and dangerous competition for colonies during the last quarter of the nineteenth century.

The New Imperialism

There were a variety of motivations behind the new imperialism, and they were not different from those that fueled the Age of Exploration and Discovery. Some, including Christian missionaries and humanitarians, wanted to bring the benefits of modern civilization to remote parts of the world. Some sought to explore unknown lands and people groups to satisfy curiosity and further knowledge of the non-Western world. Christian missionaries and humanitarians often built orphanages, hospitals, and schools for boys and girls, introduced agricultural technology, and tried to defend the native people from colonial exploiters. However, the two primary motives were first economic gain and, second, the role that colonies played in the ongoing struggle for power between the Great Powers in Europe.

The rapid industrialization in the West increased the demand for raw materials, some of which, like petroleum and rubber, were necessary to modernize existing industries and create new ones. As the standard of living increased for the working classes, there was an increased demand for items from distant parts of the world, such as coffee and tea. Mass production and distribution of manufactured products required reliable supplies of raw materials and new and expanding markets for finished goods. The seemingly insatiable need for new markets was due in part to the unequal distribution of wealth in the industrialized nations of the West. The concentration of wealth in fewer hands, combined with the inability of the working classes to purchase the ever-increasing quantities of goods they produced, drove the investment of excess capital abroad.

Governments of turn-of-the-century industrialized nations abandoned free trade in favor of neomercantilism to protect the profits of existing and emerging industries. The result was the creation of colonial empires that served as large, worldwide trading communities. Tariffs on imported goods, combined with restrictions on competition within the colonial empires, helped protect the upper classes' luxurious lifestyles while providing limited improvements in the working classes of the imperial powers. Except for the British Empire, however, the economic model fell short, as the cost of colonies often surpassed any economic benefit they provided for the mother country. More important, therefore, was what colonies meant in terms of national prestige and rivalry among the great powers.

Before the emergence of air power after the Great War, naval power determined a nation's rank among the great powers. Colonies required navies to protect them, and navies required coaling stations. Possessing overseas territories and navies to protect them became a sign of great power status. The interrelationship between seaborne commerce, large naval forces, and imperial expansion was the subject of a series of lectures by US Admiral Alfred Thayer Mahan (1840–1914), published in 1890 as a book titled *The Influence of Sea Power Upon History: 1660–1783*. He argued that sea power was the key to a nation's military strength and economic growth. Mahan argued that Britain's control of the seas accounted for its imperial dominance.

The Influence of Sea Power Upon History greatly influenced the development of modern navies. After reading Mahan's magnum opus, Germany's Kaiser Wilhelm II (1859–1941) invited Mahan to lunch aboard his yacht, *Hohenzollern*, then ordered copies of the book placed aboard every ship in the German Navy. Mahan influenced the imperialist foreign policies of US Presidents Theodore Roosevelt (1858–1919) and William McKinley (1843–1901), and the powerful influencer of American foreign policy, Senator Henry Cabot Lodge (1850–1924). Inspired by Mahan's study, the United States began building a navy capable of operating in the Atlantic and Pacific oceans. It became the "big stick" of American foreign policy at the turn of the twentieth century.

In defending America's annexation of Hawaii (1898), Mahan argued that sea power was critical in determining a nation's position and prosperity. Big navies, seaborne commerce, economic prosperity at home, and foreign colonies were all bound together. Behind it all lay the influence of Social Darwinism. According to Social Darwinism, the greatness of a nation or a people was determined by struggle, ultimately a struggle won or lost on the battlefield. The argument went that the "fittest" people would naturally triumph in any such conflict for the betterment of both parties. To bring the supposition to its ironic—and ultimately tragic—conclusion, progress would stop if peace prevailed, and Western civilization would stagnate.

The colonial peoples were mere pawns in the high-stakes power struggle between the great powers. Westerners viewed the occupants of the world's underdeveloped areas through lenses colored by theories of evolution and Social Darwinism. They presented a picture of the native peoples as childlike and backward, souls in need of "uplifting" from the darkness in which they seemed to exist and an introduction to the benefits of civilization, whether or not they wished such.

Most Westerners were caught up in the romantic image of colonialism portrayed by popular authors like Rudyard Kipling (1865–1936). Tales of explorers opening up the interior of Africa, still labeled the "Dark Continent" on many maps, or encounters with the mysterious ancient civilizations of Asia fed the popular imagination. One well-known example of how widespread support for imperialism was encouraged, or even manufactured, was the highly publicized search to find the Scottish missionary and explorer David Livingstone (1813–1873), who was reported missing somewhere in Africa. Sir Henry Morton Stanley (1841–1904), himself an explorer, convinced the *New York Herald* and London's *Daily Telegraph* editors to sponsor his search for Livingstone. The editors hoped to increase their newspapers' daily circulation; Stanley sought fame and fortune. Both were successful.

At the beginning of the twentieth century, Europeans and Europeans living abroad in North America and elsewhere took pride in the fact that the West's faith in progress and optimism was about to triumph over ignorance and darkness and usher in a new era of universal peace and prosperity. The humble peasant or laborer took pride in knowing that their country's flag was worldwide, on the high seas, and in the far corners of the globe.

The "Positive" Side of the New Imperialism

Europeans before the Great War divided the world into "civilized" and "uncivilized" peoples, much as we today speak of "developed" and "developing" nations. To be considered among the civilized nations meant being "Westernized," which in turn meant accepting the worldview and lifestyle of Europeans. "Westernized" peoples included more than the residents of Europe itself. The United States and Canada in North America and Australia and New Zealand in the South Pacific Ocean were also included. "European" and "civilized" were often used interchangeably.

Westernization offered more than a few benefits. Westerners were better housed, fed, and clothed than people anywhere else in the world. They lived longer, and their infant mortality rate was lower than in the non-Western world. Nearly 100 percent of the population of northwestern Europe was literate, whereas, in much of the non-Western world, the literacy rate was barely above zero. Europeans no longer lived in fear of unseen forces. Scientific knowledge gave them mastery over nature, showering them with a cornucopia of material blessings. They also governed themselves, while virtually the entire non-Western world was subject to the more advanced Europeans.

By 1900, the "relics of barbarism," such as slavery, infanticide, blood sports, and torture, were no longer allowed in the European nations. Even women, who were still denied the vote and full equality with men in employment and education, possessed the same human rights as every other human being. And where human rights clashed with cultural or religious practice, human rights were deemed superior. European Women were not subject to such barbaric practices as genital mutilation or *suttee*, burning a Hindu widow on her husband's funeral pyre. Nor were they condemned to a lifetime of illiteracy and unquestioned submission to the arbitrary will of father or husband. This message of universal and inalienable human rights went, if not always practiced, wherever the might of European imperialism was felt.

Whatever benefits the colonial people gained from Western influence must be viewed along with the negative impact of imperialism that continues to disturb world peace in the twenty-first century. Political instability in Africa, for example, is partly because the borders of the African nations today remain largely those of the former colonies, borders that were established without regard to centuries-old tribal boundaries. Thus, the post-colonial African countries are plagued by internal conflicts between cultural and religious minorities that undermine efforts to create national unity.

There were, of course, other civilizations in the world whose ancestry reached further back than Europe's. China, India, Japan, and the Middle East all possessed civilized characteristics, for example, a socioeconomic class structure and systematic philosophical thought. However, by the mid-1800s, all of the great non-European civilizations were but shadows of their past glory and vulnerable to the industrialized West in need of markets and resources to fuel its rapid development.

The Dark Side of the New Imperialism

There was a not-so-romantic reality to the new imperialism, the best-known example of which was the Belgian King Léopold II's private rubber plantation in Central Africa. Léopold II promoted his exploitation of the Congo Basin as a purely philanthropic and humanitarian effort to promote the end of slavery and the introduction of civilization to Central Africa: "To open to civilization the only part of our globe which it has not yet penetrated, to pierce the darkness which hangs over entire peoples, is, I dare say, a crusade worthy of this century of progress" (Hochschild 1998, p. 49). With the help of Henry Morton Stanley, Léopold laid claim to 905,000 square miles (2,343,939.24 km^2) of Central Africa with a population believed to have been around 30 million, which he named the "Congo Free State."

Because the Congo was recognized internationally as Léopold II's personal property, there were no legal restrictions on how he chose to exploit the Congo or its people. The methods employed by Léopold's agents to extract the Congo's natural resources—gold, ivory, and rubber—stand as one of the most shocking examples of how brutal imperialism could become. During the 23 years in which the Congo was Léopold's private property, the native population decreased by an estimated one-half due to the ruthless use of forced labor.

Léopold's Congo Free State was divided into districts. Each district and each worker were given near-impossible quotas of, for example, rubber that each district and each worker was required to produce. To enforce his demands and subdue the native people, Léopold established a military and police force (*Force Publique*) of white mercenaries and Africans recruited or drafted into its ranks. The officers were recruited from Europe, the British Empire, and the United States. When workers failed to meet their quotas, either they or their wives or children suffered the amputation of a hand or foot, an arm or leg. As proof that they performed their duty, labor gang bosses delivered their superiors' baskets of severed limbs, primarily hands.

When reports of Léopold's barbarism began to appear in Europe, people found them hard to believe. Sir Arthur Conan Doyle (1859–1930) provided descriptions and photographs of the atrocities in *The Crime of the Congo* (1909). Joseph Conrad (1857–1924) published *Heart of Darkness* in 1902, a novel based on his experiences as a steamboat captain on the Congo River. Mark Twain published *King Leopold's Soliloquy* (1905), a fictional monologue of Léopold defending his exploitation of the Congo. In November 1908, Belgium's Parliament yielded to popular and diplomatic pressure and ended Léopold II's personal rule. Ownership was transferred to the Kingdom of Belgium, and its name changed to the Belgium Congo.

The Congo Free State will forever stand as an extreme example of the horrors of imperialism, but there were others. When the Herrero, a native pastoral people in German South-West Africa, revolted in 1904, German forces suppressed the revolt and reduced the Herero population from an estimated 80,000 to an estimated 15,000. Similarly, in German South-East Africa, the Maji uprising of 1905–1907 was put down at the cost of between 80,000 and 100,000 African lives. During the Boer War in South Africa (1899–1902), British forces under Lord Horatio Herbert Kitchener's (1850–1916) command employed a "scorch earth" campaign to defeat the Boers. "The British forces systematically burned crops, destroyed farms, homesteads, and even raped Boer women and children as young as ten" (Pitzer 2017).

Many Americans are surprised to learn that the United States was an imperial power with colonial possessions at the turn of the twentieth century. The United States was, from its founding in 1783, an imperialist nation. Like Russia, the United States built a transcontinental empire stretching from the Atlantic to the Pacific Ocean. In some cases, the territory was added by purchase from other imperialists, for example, the purchase of the Louisiana Territory from France in 1803 or Alaska from Russia in 1867. In other cases, the territory

The German crown prince Wilhelm stands over a tiger he shot in a big game hunting trip to Ceylon, c. 1912, a fitting symbol of European dominance in the world before the Great War. © ullsteinbild/TopFoto.

was acquired by conquest, as in the Mexican–American War (1846–1848) and the Spanish–American War (1898). Hawaii (1898) and the Panama Canal Zone (1903) were acquired by dubious means, including intrigue, revolution, and annexation. The United States claimed more than one hundred uninhabited and unclaimed islands under the Guano Islands Act of 1856. The islands were a significant source of guano—bird poop—consisting almost entirely of nitrogen, phosphate, and potassium. Before the development of chemical fertilizers, guano was very much in demand for agriculture.

The United States asserted a kind of informal sovereignty within the Western Hemisphere. With the Roosevelt Corollary (1904) added to the Monroe Doctrine (1823), the United States claimed the right to, and at times did, intervene at will in the affairs of any Latin American state where American interests were threatened.

The traditional great powers of Europe, joined by the United States, were the masters of the world on the eve of the Great War. But the colonial empires could not last first because colonialism is finite. Eventually, as was the case by 1914, every bit of land and every island was claimed. Also, the introduction of modernism, including Western values, necessary for the profitable exploitation of the colonies, led to national liberation movements and the end of colonialism.

The Great Powers

Italy was considered by many in 1900 to be a great power, but, as the events of the Great War were to demonstrate, this was more a clever ruse on Italy's part than an accurate assessment of its resources. At least on the surface, the five European great powers in 1900 were the same five great powers in 1815, Great Britain, Germany (Prussia), France, Russia, and Austria-Hungary (Austria). In fact, there were only three great powers since Russia and Austria-Hungary lagged in those areas vital to maintaining great power status into the twentieth century. Both resisted the modernist ideas that came out of the Enlightenment, especially liberalism. There were signs of industrial development in the Austrian portion of the Habsburg lands and Russia. Still, both remained predominately agrarian states of a few fabulously wealthy landlords and a multitude of poverty-stricken peasants.

Great Britain (United Kingdom)

Great Britain possessed the world's largest empire and the world's largest navy to protect it. Although its economic growth rate was slipping behind Germany and the United States, especially in the critical steel, iron, and coal industries, Great Britain nevertheless lay at the center of world trade, with vast, highly profitable foreign investments. Also, London remained the financial capital of the world.

Great Britain possessed a stable, two-party parliamentary system. The trend throughout the nineteenth century had been in the direction of steady, if at times slow, social and political reform. With the Great Reform Bill of 1832, the Reform Bill of 1867, and the Franchise Bill of 1884, Parliament gradually extended suffrage until virtually every adult male could vote. By 1900, it appeared that Great Britain would make a smooth transition to democracy.

The Liberal Party, which came to power in 1906 and remained in power until after the Great War, actually presided over the transition from aristocratic conservatism to popular democracy and the first signs of the emergence of a welfare state. In 1909, David Lloyd George (1863–1945), chancellor of the exchequer and leader of the radicals within the Liberal Party, presented a budget that proposed a revision of the tax system, placing the burden for financing the new social legislation upon the wealthiest classes. It was a radical new departure that foreshadowed the future British welfare state. The proposed budget led, not unexpectedly, to a showdown between the two houses of Parliament.

The outcome came in the form of the Parliament Act of 1911. The House of Lords lost the power to veto bills that originated in and were passed by the House of Commons. The Lords could delay the passage of money bills for only one month and all other bills for up to two years. They could suggest amendments to money bills but could no longer veto them. The power of the House of Lords was severely curtailed, making the House of Commons unequivocally the center of political affairs in Britain.

The Liberals remained in power between 1906 and 1914, partly through agreements with the Labour Party and the Irish delegation to Parliament. By 1914, the Labour Party was increasingly dissatisfied with its alliance with the Liberals. Working-class militancy increased between 1911 and 1914. The idea that change would come only through direct action gained ground. There was a series of strikes in 1911 and 1912. During the spring of 1914, transport workers, railwaymen, and miners formed a "triple industrial alliance" beyond the control of the Labour Party and the union officials.

In 1914, the House of Commons passed the Government of Ireland Act 1914, also known as the Home Rule Act. Opposition to the Home Rule Act in the House of Lords was overcome when the Liberal Government invoked provisions of the Parliament Act of 1911. Ireland would receive home rule within the British Empire without any special provision for predominately Protestant Northern Ireland (Ulster). Civil war seemed possible when many in the British army indicated they would not enforce Irish Home Rule. A militant women's suffrage movement added to the labor unrest, and Irish home rule created an atmosphere of "domestic anarchy" in Great Britain on the eve of the Great War.

Germany

Germany, after 1900, was the dominant power on the continent and Great Britain's leading global rival. On the eve of the Great War, Germany produced nearly a third more pig iron, as much steel as Great Britain, and only slightly less coal. Having industrialized much later than Great Britain, German industry was able to take advantage of new power sources and techniques. Hence, its electrical and chemical industries flourished. German industry produced far more than could be consumed within the Reich. After 1880, Germany rapidly increased its share of world trade. By the outbreak of war in 1914, its merchant marine was the second largest in the world, behind Great Britain's.

Germany's surge to world-power status was not due only to its industrial development. Germany led the world in scientific development. Although no longer simply the land of "poets and philosophers," it still held a commanding lead in intellectual and cultural affairs. Its educational system, from elementary schools to graduate universities, was the model for, and envy of, all other developed counties. The number of German university students in 1911 was nearly twice that of students enrolled in universities in any of the European great powers.

In other areas, too, Germany appeared to be the most progressive nation in the world. Under Otto von Bismarck's leadership as the first chancellor (1871–1890) of the German Reich, Germany was the first nation to develop a social insurance system. The system provided accident and sickness insurance, old-age pensions, and unemployment benefits. English workers would have to wait until 1906–1914, and American workers until Franklin Roosevelt's New Deal (1933–1939) to receive such benefits.

But Germany was far from being a democratic country in the same mold as Great Britain and France. Political liberalism was defeated in Germany in the revolutions of 1848. After that, German liberals expended their energies on developing economic liberalism. Conservatives carried out the task of achieving national unity in 1871 with the enthusiastic support of the masses. Consequently, Germany emerged from the nineteenth century as one of the world's great industrial powers, but with a governmental system that one might best describe as pseudo-constitutional absolutism.

Outwardly, Germany appeared as a constitutional monarchy, but that was only an illusion based upon the fact that the *Reichstag*, or parliament, was elected by universal manhood suffrage of all citizens over the age of 25. In fact, the *Reichstag* possessed little power other than refusing to pass the federal budget. However, past experience in the Prussian parliament (1862–1867) left the liberals convinced that this one "real" power was best left untested in the *Reichstag*.

The German Reich was a federal union of individual German states in which real power was divided between Prussia, the largest state, and the *Bundesrat*, or federal parliament. The constitution vested sovereignty in the *Bundesrat*, presided over by the Reich chancellor, appointed by and accountable to the Kaiser (the King of Prussia). The delegates were appointed by their governments. All significant measures required approval by Prussia. Fourteen votes could defeat any attempt to amend the constitution in the *Bundesrat*—and Prussia had 17 votes.

The period from 1890 until Germany's defeat in 1918 is referred to as the "Wilhelmian era," for it was the Kaiser who determined the course of events in Germany. In foreign policy, Wilhelm II (1859–1941) chartered a "new course" meant to achieve Germany a commanding role in world affairs or, as he put it, a "place in the sun." Wilhelm II's new world policy, or *Weltpolitik*, brought Germany into conflict with France and Great Britain, especially the latter.

The "new course" meant colonies, and colonies meant a great navy capable of a commanding presence throughout the world. For Germany, the greatest military power in Europe, building a fleet capable of challenging British naval supremacy was a direct challenge to Great Britain. It was to prove a dangerous and ultimately disastrous course. The perilous situation for world peace was that, unlike Russia and Austria-Hungary, Germany possessed the economic power and national unity to make the Kaiser's wildest dreams possible. As in Russia and Austria-Hungary, the German emperor had real power. Whatever the constitutional trappings, Wilhelm II ruled Germany. Without responsible leadership, the German Reich was a real threat to the peace of Europe.

France

France, too, was an industrialized nation, although, on the eve of the Great War, it lagged behind Germany, Great Britain, and the

Nine of Europe's sovereigns gathered for a group picture while attending the funeral of Britain's King Edward VII. Standing fourth from left is Kaiser Wilhelm II. Seated in the middle is Britain's George V. World History Archive/ Alamy Images.

United States. France was a nation of small farmers, businessmen, and manufacturers, a country of the petit bourgeoisie rather than giant industrialists. More than half of the French still made their living from agriculture.

Of the great powers, France was the most democratic. Like Great Britain, it had a parliamentary system, but members of the upper house, or Senate, were elected in France. Also, unlike Great Britain with its two large political parties, French politics found expression in numerous small parties. The proliferation of parties meant that every government was a coalition, often only briefly in office. Between 1890 and 1914, a period of only 24 years, France had 43 different governments and 26 premiers. At the turn of the century, French politics and society were plagued by a sharp polarization between the left and right. In part, this was historic. Those on the left saw themselves as the heirs of an anticlerical, democratic revolutionary tradition reaching back to 1789. Those on the right were conservatives, who, from their base within the church and army, called for more order while blaming France's decline in power on too much democracy. In short, the Third Republic, a republic born out of France's defeat in the Franco-Prussian War of 1870–1871, was divided between those who favored a republican form of government and those who desired restoration of the monarchy but were unable to determine the "rightful" monarch.

French society's divisions deepened due to the Dreyfus Affair between 1894 and 1906. In 1894, Captain Alfred Dreyfus (1859–1935) was accused of selling military secrets to the Germans. Antisemitism and the need to defend the perceived honor of the French army played a prominent role in the twice-tried and twice-convicted Dreyfus and his being sentenced to life imprisonment in the infamous penal colony on Devil's Island. Believing Dreyfus was innocent, a group of noted politicians and intellectuals waged a public campaign for his release. Dreyfus was finally vindicated in 1906, but the army's image was tarnished, and France was more deeply divided. The Dreyfus Affair revealed a growing antisemitism in French society that was increasing throughout Europe and the United States on the eve of the Great War. France had a functioning democratic government in 1914, so long as not too many demands were placed on it.

Russia

Russia's status as a great power in 1900 rested upon its immense size—it stretched across Eurasia from the eastern border of Germany to the Pacific Ocean. Like Austria-Hungary, Russia was an old-fashioned agrarian state. The Romanovs, who ruled Russia since 1613, devoted their energies to maintaining autocratic rule. The current Tsar, Nicholas II (1868–1918), upon ascending to the throne in 1894, promised: "I shall preserve the principle of autocracy as firmly and undeviatingly as did my father" (Sulzberger 1977). Nicholas II dismissed the ideas of the Enlightenment, especially any thought of liberal political reform, as simplistic nonsense. He was handsome and devoted to his family but weak-willed and easily dominated by those around him. His goal was to leave an unchanged Russia to his son and heir. He was not well suited to rule Russia in the troubled years before the Great War.

From 1900 to 1914, Russia experienced economic troubles, strikes, peasant disorders, and acts of terrorism. Defeat in the Russo-Japanese War in 1904 further exposed the inability of the autocratic government to address the economic suffering of the masses resulting from the war. A peaceful procession of workers before the Winter Palace in St. Petersburg on 22 January 1905 was met by soldiers firing on the demonstrators. The event known as "Bloody Sunday" resulted in Nicholas II issuing the October Manifesto authorizing the election of a Duma, or parliament, by a very restricted franchise. The Duma could debate and advise the Tsar, but no more.

Pyotr Stolypin (1862–1911), the interior minister between 1906 and 1911, carried through an important series of measures that allowed a peasant to claim his land from the village commune as a unified, independent holding. The idea behind the measure was that the peasants would be more conservative politically if they had their own property. Furthermore, if they farmed as independent farmers free of the restrictions of the commune or mir, they would be more productive.

Failure to modernize meant that the demands for justice from the workers and peasants continued to fester. The small educated class felt increasingly alienated from the government. The increased suffering that would come with Russia's failures in the Great War would bring about a revolution with unforeseeable consequences for Europe and beyond.

Austria-Hungary

Austria-Hungary often called the Dual Monarchy, maintained a cumbersome government with separate parliaments for Austria and Hungary. Common to both halves of the empire were ministries for war, finance, and foreign affairs. Uniting the vast multinational realm was the emperor, Franz Joseph (1830–1916), who had come to the throne in 1848 and would stubbornly resist death until 21 November 1916. Like Queen Victoria, Franz Joseph was the much-beloved symbol of a great historical tradition. The House of Habsburg was the oldest and most prestigious dynasty in Europe. But unlike Queen Victoria, Franz Joseph was committed to and lived in a world that no longer existed.

Austria-Hungary did not possess an overseas empire. It was a multicultural land empire held together by soldiers, bureaucrats, parades, and a living symbol of past glory. It was being torn apart by nationalism. Poles, Czechs, Slovaks, Serbs, Croatians, and Ruthenians were only the most numerous of the minorities that inhabited the Habsburg lands. Fifty-one million inhabitants in 1911 spoke at least ten different languages. Among them were Roman Catholic and Greek Orthodox Christians, Jews, and Muslims.

Habsburg foreign policy had three primary goals: maintain and expand the empire at the expense of Turkey; prevent the spread of Russian influence in the Balkans; and combat the growth of nationalism among the South Slavs, especially the Serbian desire to create a Great Serbia.

One solution to the problem of appeasing so many minority populations was a triple monarchy with the organization of an autonomous Yugoslav (South Slav) state from portions of Austria and Hungary. Another was a federal state composed of several largely autonomous units. The obstacle to any of the various solutions proposed was Magyar intransigence. Magyar elites dominated Hungarian politics and opposed any reorganization of the empire. Many contemporary observers felt that only the aging emperor held the empire together.

The United States of America

The twentieth century is often referred to as the American century, just as one often refers to the nineteenth century as the *Pax Britannica* (British Peace). Both terms are allusions to the *Pax Romana* (Roman Peace), roughly 100 years when the Roman Empire enjoyed hegemony over the Mediterranean world. During the nineteenth century, Great Britain was the dominant power on the world stage. The British Navy ruled the oceans, and London was the world's financial capital. Little happened in international affairs without consulting Great Britain. The United States of America enjoyed a similar role after the Great War and particularly after the Second World War. One cannot understand the history of the twentieth century without considering the part played by the United States.

Before the Great War, the United States emerged as a significant power in world affairs. Its population stood at 76 million in 1900. Thirteen million immigrants, including one million Jews, were added before 1914, mostly from Central and Southern Europe. The immigrants provided an energetic and willing labor force for the burgeoning northeastern industrial complex, rapidly becoming the most productive in the world. Between 1900 and 1914, manufacturing replaced agriculture as the nation's chief source of wealth. The great captains of American industry and finance, like J. Pierpont Morgan (1837–1913), Andrew Carnegie (1835–1919), and John D. Rockefeller (1839–1937), were every bit as worthy of note as any of Europe's aristocracy. Blessed with abundant natural resources, a democratic and business-friendly environment, and a vision of America's destiny, the United States was becoming the world's leading industrial power.

America's rising status was not due solely to its industrial growth. The belief in "Manifest Destiny" that drove America's expansion across the continent from the Atlantic to the Pacific oceans was thrusting the United States onto the world stage during the late nineteenth and early twentieth centuries. That spirit of nationalism that drove Europe's great powers was propelling the United States to establish its place in the sun.

When Theodore Roosevelt became president in 1901, following the assassination of President William McKinley (1843–1901), he took every opportunity to make America's presence felt in world affairs. In 1905, Roosevelt offered to mediate between Russia and Japan and hosted the peace conference at Portsmouth, New Hampshire, that ended the Russo-Japanese War. The following year, Roosevelt was instrumental in persuading his admirer, Kaiser Wilhelm II, to agree to an international conference at Algeciras, Spain, to relieve tensions over the Moroccan crisis. In 1907, he sent the new American Navy on a cruise around the world to show the flag. It was standard TR theatrics, a bit of bluster perhaps, but with a serious purpose.

A booming industrial plant, a large navy, and the acquisition of overseas colonies, euphemistically referred to as territories, were signs of great power status or aspiration for such status. The United States was emerging as a great power before the Great War but was not yet a member of the club. In 1917, it entered the war to decide its outcome in favor of the Allies but afterward retreated into isolation. Not until the second Great War, World War II, would the United States reenter world affairs. During the Cold War that followed World War II, the United States would be the dominant power in the West.

The Class Structure

The class structure of Europe before the Great War was still a pyramid, with a handful of very wealthy at the apex and a great multitude of poor at the base. At the turn of the century, the ruling aristocracy was a union of the old landed wealth and the new industrial wealth. Titled, land-owning families with pedigrees that stretched back for centuries formed marriage alliances of convenience with the wealthy new plutocrats of commerce and industry. This new elite shared a familiar pattern of education and consumption and similar economic and political views. Generally, the greater the nation's industrialization, the more closely tied was the upper middle class to the government. Peers of the realm and the giants of industry and commerce often had the same values, political interests, and condescending attitudes toward the propertyless classes at the base of the pyramid.

The middle class was beginning to set the tone for all of society. The activities of the aristocracy, particularly the royal families of Europe, were still of great interest to many, but increasingly, standards were set by the new elite drawn from both the upper-middle class and the aristocracy. With its vast wealth, the upper class became an important source of patronage for the arts and significantly influenced fashion and style.

In later decades, the middle class viewed the era before 1914 mainly as a golden age, *les bon vieux temps*, "the good old days" in Europe, or the "Gilded Age" in American history. One measure of middle-class standing was the ability to employ one full-time servant. A prosperous middle-class family with an annual income of $10,000 (£7,308.15) could hire a staff of 10 full-time servants for only one-quarter of that income.

Economic opportunities abounded, political influence increased, and even social prominence rose for the middle class. The possibilities of achieving a comfortable income and a commensurate status were good, especially in Western Europe and America. The changing economic structure offered few options for individuals or families to own and control their enterprises, but this was compensated for by expanding management and civil service positions. Wider educational opportunities also made it possible for many to enter the professions or the upper reaches of government bureaucrats.

The middle class was not a unified group. The views of one group of businessmen often conflicted with those of professionals or other business groups. Nonetheless, the middle class was a formidable political power in states with well-established parliamentary governments. Politics was increasingly the preserve of elected and unelected professionals, and the middle class supplied more and more of these people. At the same time, the middle class furnished the leadership of most of the political parties in Europe and America. The same was true even of some socialist parties, in which renegade middle-class members formulated most policies and interpreted doctrine for the rank and file. Governments were increasingly sympathetic to middle-class views, as demonstrated by the trend toward protective tariffs and other legislation favorable to business.

The lower middle class was not a unified group. The independent lower middle class of shopkeepers, merchants, and artisans had long been a part of European and American society. It emphasized familiar middle-class ideals of family, property, and respectability. A second largely dependent component was a product of recent structural changes in the economy. As the distribution and sales of industrial goods increased and the complexity of industrial and business organizations became more complex, there was an increased demand for clerks, salespeople, and technicians. Governments also began to require increased numbers of clerical and technical personnel.

Both the independent and dependent elements of the lower middle class had in common a sense that they were distinct from the working class in terms of status and behavior. However, regarding income, the lower middle class no longer earned a great deal more than the working class. Lower middle-class people spent their money differently, buying or saving mainly for items connected with social status, such as a piano; the working class tended to spend on immediate pleasures. The intense consciousness of status was reflected not only in the behavior but also in the politics of the lower middle class, which was usually conservative, antisocialist, and sometimes anti-Semitic. In politics, the lower middle class favored parties like the Radical Party in France or the Christian Social Party in Austria, which catered to the "little man" and stressed the importance of order, property, and attachment to the nation.

Like the middle class, the lower middle class enjoyed the era's good times before 1914, including a new measure of prosperity, status, and political power. Living close to the lower classes, the lower middle class tended to take the good times less for granted than the middle class and remained more anxious about any developments that might threaten their societal position.

Most of those at the pyramid's base were better off in 1900 than at the beginning of the century. At least, this was true for those living in the industrialized nations of Great Britain, France, Germany, Belgium, and the United States. For them, the quality of life was improving. Not only had real wages risen, but purchasing power had almost doubled in the decade before 1914. Even so, poverty was a reality for most Europeans, even those in the most prosperous nations.

Out of a population of 44.5 million in Great Britain before the war, 15.3 million earned less than £50 a year. That was when the "poverty line" was estimated as £55 a year for a family of five (Tuchman 1966). One study of London households in 1899 revealed that almost one-third of the inhabitants of the world's most prosperous city lived in poverty. Poverty was even more pervasive in the unindustrialized areas of Eastern and Southern Europe. Life expectancy in the Balkans and Spain remained at less than 35 in 1900 (Carr 1979).

Politically, the laboring classes were attracted to ideologies that, in contrast to liberalism, emphasized the equality of reward over the equality of opportunity. The two most attractive political ideologies were anarchism and Social Democracy (i.e., Marxism). Anarchism sought the violent overthrow of all existing orders and the establishment of a stateless, voluntary order. Anarchism appealed most to the urban and rural unemployed in the more backward regions of Eastern and Southern Europe.

More important than anarchism was the appeal of Social Democracy to the working classes in the more industrialized nations of Western and Northern Europe. Grounded in Marxism, Social Democracy was transforming by 1900. Known as "revisionism" in Germany, the emphasis shifted from revolution to evolution. Also, like the Fabian socialists that influenced the Labour Party in Great Britain, the revisionist Social Democrats in Germany looked more and more to a future welfare state as their goal rather than the classless utopia of Marx's dreams. The desire for "gas and water" socialism replaced the ideology of class struggle.

In general, the working class in Europe reacted to changing circumstances less according to national characteristics than to the stage of industrialization reached in a particular area. Where experience was lacking, hostility and friction resulted in radical and often violent protests. Where experience with industrial life went back over two or three generations, a durable, if not always satisfying, relationship between the working class and the industrial order emerged. The industrial system was becoming increasingly acceptable for workers in Great Britain, France, Germany, and Belgium, even if expectations always seemed to race ahead of fulfillment.

Nineteenth-Century Intellectual and Cultural Trends

As noted above, by the late nineteenth century, Western Civilization had a virtual monopoly on specific scientific and technological knowledge that enabled it to exert imperialistic force throughout the world. Unlike the non-Western world, the West unlocked the mysteries of how the universe worked. Beginning with the Scientific Revolution, Europeans began using a new method of inquiry, later known as the scientific method, that resulted in a new understanding of the universe as a machine governed by cause-and-effect natural laws. The universe was not the result of some random chance evolutionary process or the dwelling place of gods, spirits, and demons whose behavior was unpredictable. Nor was it an extension of some divine consciousness.

The Scientific Revolution arose from an understanding of reality that attributed all that exists to the handiwork of a transcendent, eternal, and omnipotent Creator who created all that is out of nothing (*creatio ex nihilo*). This worldview (from the German word *Weltanschauung*) made the eighteenth-century Enlightenment or Age of Reason possible. The intellectuals of the Enlightenment redefined God as an architect, or clockmaker, who having created the universe machine, was no longer involved in its operation. Whatever could not be proven or explained by the application of reason, meaning the scientific method, was ruled either error or irrelevant. Despite its increasing secularization, the Western worldview remained a unified understanding of reality that gave meaning to history and the individual.

With knowledge of how the universe worked, it proved possible to discover more and more of the natural laws and, with that knowledge, create a better world, materially speaking. Thus, Western Civilization experienced an Industrial Revolution. It began in England during the last quarter of the eighteenth century, spread to the European continent after 1815, and by the end of the nineteenth century, made the rise of Western Civilization the central story of World Civilization.

The Industrial Revolution impacted every aspect of human life, not only how people lived but also what they thought, how they understood what it meant to be human, and whether history had any meaning. Industrialization was accompanied by a second scientific revolution in the middle of the nineteenth century that renewed faith in the scientific method as the only reliable means of discovering a true understanding of reality following the romantic revolt of the first half of the century. Romanticism, metaphysics, and religion all lost ground to a growing materialist, secular worldview, the belief that matter is the ultimate reality and everything non-material is merely the product of physical forces.

The secularization of Western Civilization continued at an accelerated pace throughout the nineteenth century. Intellectually, philosophers and theologians, as well as natural and social scientists, had been actively questioning the presuppositions (or axioms) that undergirded Western civilization before the Great War. During the decades before the Great War, a new set of intellectuals brought forth new theories and scientific discoveries that called into question if the individual human being was, after all, a reasoning, rational being in an orderly, meaningful universe. Instead, the individual was adrift in a cold, mysterious universe without coherent answers to the question, "Who am I?" At best, the individual was a random chance "happening" thrown up by an impersonal universe whose ultimate reality was only the molecules of which he or she was composed. The unified worldview that distinguished Western Civilization from all other civilizations, in both its Premodern expression (commonly referred to as the Medieval Synthesis) and its secularized expression (Modernity or the Enlightenment Tradition), was replaced by a fragmented worldview known as Postmodernity or the Enlightenment Tradition in Disarray.

The individual's worldview determines the individual's values and how the individual acts. What is true of the individual is also true for society. "As a man thinketh, so is he" is true for both the individual and the corporate society individuals inhabit. The inner thought world, more so than the external forces and surroundings, determines how the individual acts. Everyone has an inner life of the mind, including the "Butcher, Baker, Candlestick Maker." The influence of worldview on human activity is particularly evident in the works of artists, writers, poets, and musicians, in short, the creators and guardians of culture.

Swan Song

The West's dominant position in the world was based upon several illusions, chief among them the belief that history can somehow be made to stand still. Imperialism is never more than a momentary advantage. It nourishes resentment and envy because the human spirit can never endure humiliation indefinitely. After all, human beings naturally desire to imitate what symbolizes a better life.

The long history of the rise of Western Civilization peaked during the first decade and a half of the twentieth century. Many who lived during that era felt they were living at the dawn of a new age of world peace and progress. Others in Europe and abroad in the colonies sensed they were living on the verge of a history-making change that occurs from time to time in world history. Was it like the fourteenth through sixteenth centuries, a waning of the old or birth of something new? Storm clouds were gathering in the sky above. In the spring and summer of 1914, the storm broke, and Europe and the world were plunged into the most destructive war since the collapse of the Roman Empire in the West.

References

Carr, William. (1979). *A History of Germany, 1815–1945*, 2nd ed. New York: St. Martin's Press.

Hochschild, Adam. (1998). *King Leopold's Ghost: A Story of Greed, Terror, and Heroism in Colonial Africa*. Boston: Houghton.

Pitzer, Andrea. (2017). "Concentration Camps Existed Long before Auschwitz." *Smithsonian Magazine*. https://www.smithsonianmag.com/history/concentration-camps-existed-long-before-Auschwitz-180967049/ (accessed 3 June 2023).

Cyrus L Sulzberger. (1977). *The Fall of the Eagles*. New York: Crown Publisher.

Barbara W Tuchman. (1966). *The Proud Tower: A Portrait of the World Before the War: 1890–1914*. New York: Macmillan.

2

The Great War, 1914–1918

Chronology

1914	Archduke Franz Ferdinand assassinated
	Italy defects from the Triple Alliance
	Fighting begins with the German invasion of Belgium
	First Battle of the Marne and failure of the Schlieffen Plan
	Battles of Tannenberg Forest and Masurian Lakes
	Turkey enters the war on the side of the Central Powers

Twentieth-Century Europe: 1900 to the Present, Fourth Edition.
Michael D. Richards and Paul R. Waibel.

	Western Front established from the English Channel to Switzerland
1915	Beginning of trench warfare along the Western Front
	First use of poison gas at the Second Battle of Ypres
	Italy declares war on Austria-Hungary
	Ill-fated Gallipoli Campaign
1916	Battles of Verdun and the Somme
	Sykes–Picot Agreement
	Battle of Jutland
	Woodrow Wilson re-elected president of the United States
1917	Zimmerman Telegram
	Germany resumes unrestricted submarine warfare
	Russian (February) Revolution
	The United States enters the war against the Central Powers as an Associated Power
	Balfour Declaration
	Russian (October) Revolution
1918	Treaty of Brest-Litovsk; Russia leaves the war
	Major German offensive on the Western Front fails
	Kaiser Wilhelm II abdicates
	Germany asks for an armistice
	War ends on 11 November

On 24 May 1913, Princess Viktoria Luise of Prussia (1892–1980), the only daughter of Kaiser Wilhelm II and Kaiserin Augusta Viktoria, married Prince Ernst August of Hanover. Those who hoped for a "dynastic marriage" expected her to marry Britain's Duke of Windsor, King George V's eldest son. But only a love marriage was suitable for the daughter whom the Kaiser adored. One thousand one hundred guests attended the wedding banquet. More than 250 honored guests were seated around "a quadrangular table, which ran the full length of each side of the banqueting chamber" (Koenig 2020). A correspondent for the *New York Times* reported that the guests attending the banquet "displayed a dazzling medley of resplendent uniforms, glittering jewels, and beautiful gowns" (Koenig 2020). It was the last gathering of the Royal Houses of Europe before the outbreak of the Great War just over a year later.

Otto von Bismarck once prophetically said that someday a general European war would result from some foolish incident in the

Balkans. The war that Bismarck predicted resulted from an event in the Balkans, the assassination of Archduke Franz Ferdinand, heir to the throne of Austria-Hungary, on 28 June 1914. It was known as the "Great War" until the beginning of World War II in 1939, after which it was called World War I. Indeed, some historians suggest that the Great War was only the first round of a truly great war that began in 1914 and did not end until 1945, with a ceasefire between 1918 and 1939.

Some of the same elements that had made Europe master of the world worked in the Great War to destroy it. Industrial productivity and the capacity to mobilize troops and money made possible a horrific carnage few people could have anticipated before 1914. The five years of war and revolution severely damaged the fabric of European life. The contradictions of the prewar period, more or less successfully repressed at the time, emerged to challenge old certainties. It was the end of one era and the beginning of another, darker one.

War or Peace

Historians often look for a casual line of events leading up to a major historical event such as the Great War. It is easy to see, or at least imagine, a series of events, choices, or missteps, that led logically to the event under study, in this case, the Great War. But what appears obvious in hindsight was not so obvious at the time. It is easy to construct a case, supported by relevant documentary evidence, to assign responsibility for the outbreak of war to any one of the major powers—Germany, Austria-Hungary, Russia, France, and Great Britain. Numerous books have been written, and no doubt many more will be written, attempting to explain the outbreak of the Great War in 1914.

Histories of the Great War often cite examples of individuals who, before the outbreak of war, saw some sort of cataclysmic event on the horizon, despite all the optimism about the future that so characterized *la Belle Époque*. There was, however, a common belief among many that the world economy was so interconnected that a major war among the industrial nations was unthinkable. As early as January 1846, Richard Cobden (1804–1865), the English Radical and Liberal politician, manufacturer, and enthusiastic campaigner for free trade, spoke of his belief that the laws of a free-market economy were "drawing men together, thrusting aside the antagonism of race, and creed, and language, and uniting us in the bonds of eternal peace" (Cobden 2021).

A new form of pacifism[1] appeared at the turn of the twentieth century that feared a modern industrial war, not only for the horrors of the battlefield but also for the suffering it would mean for the civilian populations and how it would transform the postwar world. One example was *The Future of War* by Ivan Bloch (1872–1922), a six-volume, four-thousand-page book first published in Russian in 1898 and translated into French, German, and English. Bloch's graphic description of a future war among the European great powers influenced Tsar Nicholas II and led him to sponsor the First Hague Peace Conference. It opened on 18 May 1899, the Tsar's thirty-first birthday. A Second Hague Peace Conference, suggested by US President Theodore Roosevelt, but convened by Tsar Nicholas II, met in June 1907.

Neither of the two peace conferences amounted to anything more than window dressing that hid the fact that the participating nations continued arming and rehearsing for war. While publicly praising Nicholas II, Wilhelm II attributed his cousin's newfound interest in disarmament to Russia's financial exhaustion and Nicholas's "humanitarian nonsense" mixed with "a bit of deviltry" (Sheehan 2008, p. 22). Lord Hugh Gough (1848–1919), British envoy to Germany between 1896 and 1901, informed the German Foreign Office that Britain supported the aims of the First Hague Peace Conference while adding that pronouncements about peace and disarmament would remain just that, pronouncements.

Others, militarists and intellectuals alike, saw in war a cure for what they believed was the sickness of modern society. In an era

[1] The term "pacifism" was coined by Émile Arnaud (1864–1921), a French lawyer and writer, to describe the peace movement he campaigned for. Despite his age, 50 years in 1914, he served in the Great War and was awarded the *Croix de guerre*.

when international relations were filtered through the lens of Social Darwinism, pacifism, or even disarmament, might threaten the very survival of civilization. Alfred Thayer Mahan, for example, interpreted history as an "apocalyptic struggle between Christianity and the forces of evil, whose outcome would ultimately be determined by the power of the sword" (Sheehan 2008, p. 36). If the European great powers were to disarm, civilization itself would vanish. The Prussian Friedrich von Bernhardi (1849–1930), in his popular book, *Germany and the Next War* (1911), argued that the "unqualified desire for peace" had "rendered most civilized nations anemic, and marks a decay of spirit and political courage" (Sheehan 2008, p. 40). "War," wrote Bernhardi, was a biological necessity consistent with "the natural law, upon which all the laws of Nature rest, the law of the struggle for existence" (Von Bernhardi 2021).

The Coming of the Great War

The Vienna Congress restored peace to Europe following the defeat of Napoléon Bonaparte (1769–1821) by establishing a balance of power among the five European great powers—Great Britain, France, Prussia, Austria, and Russia. Prussia's defeat of France in the Franco-Prussian War (1870–1871) and the unification of Germany (1871) that followed destroyed that balance of power and replaced it with the specter of war. A system of defensive alliances, primarily the work of German chancellor Otto von Bismarck, substituted for the balance-of-power principle as the mechanism for maintaining peace in Europe after 1871. As designed by Bismarck, the alliances were meant to isolate France, which Bismarck reasoned was the greatest threat to future peace.

The first and most enduring of Bismarck's alliances was the Dual Alliance between Germany and Austria-Hungary concluded in 1879, which provided that one partner would aid the other if Russia attacked either. The Triple Alliance, completed in 1882 between Germany, Austria-Hungary, and Italy, bound the three to act together if France attacked either Germany or Italy. To allay Russian fears of a hostile Austro-German alliance, Bismarck signed the Reinsurance

Treaty with Russia in 1887. It provided for one partner to assume a policy of benevolent neutrality if the other partner was attacked. Thus, France was left isolated, while Germany was neatly allied with the other great powers on the continent. "The key," Bismarck said, "was always to be in the majority of three in any dispute among the five great European powers." Peace was maintained, that is, until Bismarck's retirement in 1890, when his alliance system began to unravel.

With Bismarck retired, Wilhelm II embarked on a "new course" in foreign policy, which aimed at elevating Germany to world-power status. The new foreign policy initiative, together with Wilhelm II's decision to build a naval fleet that could rival that of Great Britain, was a direct challenge to Britain's position as the world's leading power. Germany's challenge came when Britain's atrocious treatment of the Boers[2] (including women and children) during the Boer War in South Africa (1899–1902) was causing increasing international criticism. A growing feeling of diplomatic isolation and concern over Germany's increased power and threat to British interests led Britain to abandon its traditional foreign policy of "splendid isolation" and seek allies of its own.

In 1902, Britain concluded the Anglo-Japanese Alliance, followed in 1904 and 1907 by two informal "understandings," or "ententes," that resolved outstanding imperial disputes with France and Russia, respectively. Autocratic Russia was already in a formal defensive alliance with democratic France, concluded in December 1894. Russia, one might justly say, had been pushed into the waiting arms of France by Wilhelm's decision in 1890 not to renew the Reinsurance Treaty. When considered together, the new alliances between France, Russia, and Britain comprised what became known as the Triple Entente. By 1907, Europe was divided into two increasingly hostile camps, the Triple Alliance and the Triple Entente.

Just as the continent was polarizing into two hostile camps, the Balkans emerged as the new "hot spot" in Europe. In 1908, Austria-Hungary annexed Bosnia and Herzegovina, which it had been

[2] Boers were descendants of the Dutch settlers from the 17th–19th centuries.

administering since 1878 on behalf of Turkey. Austria's action, supported by Germany, inflamed Serbian nationalism. The Serbs had hoped to create a Great Serbia in the Balkans, and they regarded Bosnia, with its large Serbian population, as a necessary part of such an independent state. Serbian nationalism was encouraged by the Russians, who, following their defeat in the Russo-Japanese War (1904–1905), turned their attention to the Balkans, over which region Turkish power and influence were disintegrating.

As predicted decades before by Otto von Bismarck, the Great War started over an incident in the Balkans, the whole of which, he had contended, was not worth "the healthy bones of a single Pomeranian musketeer." The event that served as the impetus for war was the assassination of Archduke Franz Ferdinand (1863–1914), heir to the throne of Austria-Hungary, by a 19-year-old Serb named Gavrilo Princip (1894–1918) on 28 June 1914. But it was not for the Archduke that the "Guns of August" was unleashed.

If Austria had acted promptly to punish Serbia for its part in the assassination, the rest of the world would no doubt have accepted its decision. But Austria hesitated. Austrian prestige demanded some military action against Serbia, but prudence, perhaps fear, demanded that Germany's backing be secured first. The delay allowed time for Russia to conclude that Russian prestige could not allow Austria to crush Serbia. Similar crises had occurred in the past but were resolved through diplomacy. In the final analysis, what transformed the July crisis into the cause célèbre for the Great War was a breakdown of diplomacy.

On 5 July, Austria obtained German support for whatever action it took against Serbia. Germany believed that the so-called "blank check" was justified, in part, because it feared for its own position in Europe should Austria decline as a power. Germany did, however, expect Austria to act while world opinion was still favorable. But Austria delayed further to win over Count István Tisza (1861–1918), Hungary's prime minister, and then to launch an investigation into Serbia's actual role in the assassination. In the meantime, Russia's position had begun to harden, and it warned Austria that it would not tolerate the humiliation of Serbia.

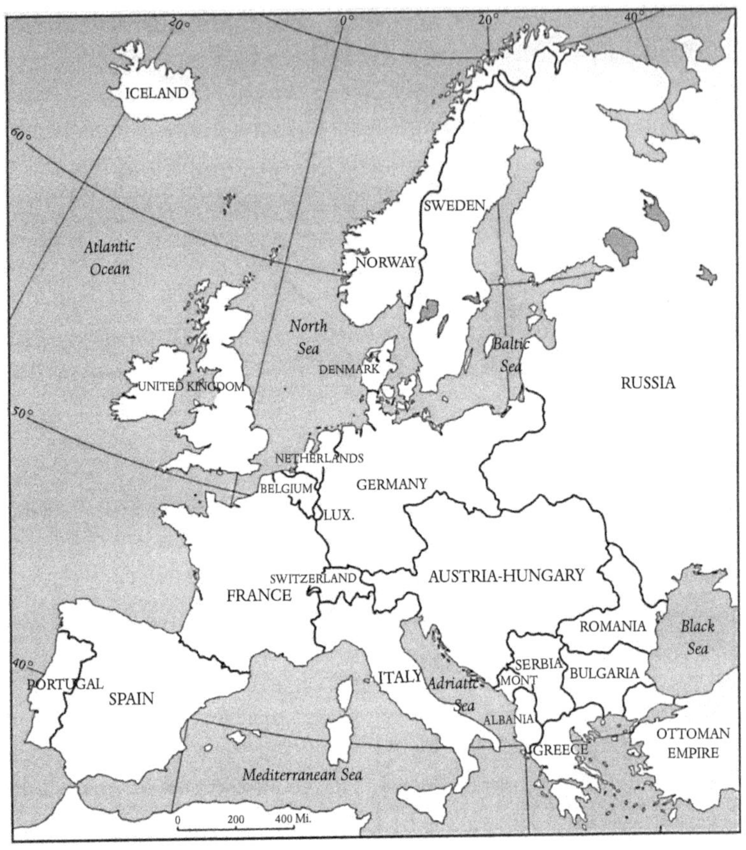

Europe in 1914.

Austria ignored the warning and presented an ultimatum to Serbia on 23 July. Most of the demands called for the Serbian government to suppress all public criticism or other activity that might incite the Serbs against Austria-Hungary. Serbia accepted all but one or two clauses that would have allowed the Austrians to participate in the Serbian investigation of the assassination plot; this, Serbia contended, would infringe on its sovereignty. All the powers, Germany and Austria included, saw Serbia's reply as remarkably conciliatory. Yet, Austria went ahead with mobilization and declared war on 28 July. Although Germany was already beginning to have second thoughts, it did not effectively apply pressure to halt Austrian preparations for war.

Also, on 28 July, the Russians ordered a partial mobilization and then, for technical reasons, on 30 July, ordered full mobilization. Otherwise, Russia had concluded, it would have no chance of influencing Austria. Full mobilization by Russia made it imperative that Germany put the Schlieffen Plan into effect. Since this plan called for Germany to deal with France first, then quickly turn back to the east, each day that the Russians spent mobilizing before the Germans launched their drive to the west further jeopardized the plan's success. Now, it was all a matter of railroad timetables. Germany attacked France, violating Belgian neutrality in the process. Britain came into the war to aid the French and defend the neutrality principle. Of all the great powers, only Italy remained out of the conflict for the time being.

There was no real reason for the outbreak of war in 1914. A great many volumes have been written by historians trying to explain what caused the Great War, who, if anyone, was to blame for it, and why the Schlieffen Plan failed. Regarding the first question, as the German historian Fritz Fischer has alleged, it is true that Germany ambitiously pursued world-power status. As the English historian A. J. P. Taylor has demonstrated, it is also true that the German plan for mobilization was tantamount to a declaration of war since the said mobilization was to be completed outside Germany—inside France and Belgium. When all the arguments and counterarguments have been considered, however, the comment of the British prime minister, David Lloyd George (1863–1945), that the European great powers simply slithered over the brink into a war no one desired remains the best explanation. Diplomacy had failed.

The war the diplomats failed to prevent in July 1914 was not the war the generals were prepared to fight. During that fateful month, they had assured their reluctant monarchs that the conflict would be a brief and glorious little war, not unlike the wars of German unification, in which the rapid deployment of troops on open battlefields had decided the day. The troops, they claimed, would be home for Christmas. However, the military strategies in which the generals of the day were schooled differed little from those employed by their counterparts who waged the Napoleonic wars a hundred years earlier. Tragically, a century of remarkable technological "progress"—one that included the development of railroads, telegraphs, telephones, airplanes, submarines, machine guns, tanks, poison gas, flame throwers, and a great many other wonders of modern civilization—shortly transformed a little conflict in the Balkans into what will be forever remembered as one of the most gruesome wars in history, the Great War, World War I.

The Great War, 1914–1917

The blustery saber-rattling monarchs of those ancient and soon-to-be vanquished empires of Germany, Austria-Hungary, and Russia tried to avert war in the final hours before the first gun sounded. There was a rapid exchange of notes between Wilhelm II and his cousin, Tsar Nicholas II. But neither the Kaiser nor the Tsar was in command of the snowballing events. Events were progressing under their own momentum. If anyone was in control of the direction of those events as the crisis deepened, it was the generals. However, they were captive to concrete plans for mobilization and war, plans with which they felt unable to tinker, even in the minutest detail.

The fateful role played by the war plans was particularly evident in the case of Germany. The Schlieffen Plan presupposed a two-front war with France and Russia. It was a bold plan that called for the rapid movement of German forces through neutral Belgium to the north and west of Paris in a sweeping arc that would encircle and crush the French armies. With France defeated, German forces would be redeployed to the Eastern Front to deal with the Russian troops, which would just then be completing mobilization, according to German calculations. The war would be over within six weeks, and Germany's position as a world power secured.

The Schlieffen Plan was a daring gamble. Although it looked good on paper, several miscalculations and unforeseen exigencies undid its successful execution. Belgium rejected a German demand to allow free passage of its troops across Belgian territory on 3 August. That afternoon, German troops were pouring into Belgium. Although no match for the swiftly advancing Germans, the Belgians put up a brave fight, slowing the German advance and costing the German army time needed for the successful execution of the Schlieffen Plan. On 4 August, Great Britain declared war on Germany for violating Belgium's neutrality guaranteed by the 1839 Treaty of London, to which the German Confederation led by Prussia was a cosignatory.

Belgian resistance was not factored into the Schlieffen Plan. Neither was the speed with which the Russians managed to throw an army into East Prussia on 17 August. To meet the Russian threat and believing the war against France already won, General Helmuth von Moltke (1848–1916) detached two corps from his vital right wing and sent them east. It was a fatal error. With other corps already detached to hold the Belgians at Antwerp, von Moltke's move seriously weakened the German army's right-wing, upon which the Schlieffen Plan depended. On 30 August, with the Schlieffen Plan days behind schedule, Moltke began to have doubts, turning his right flank south while still east of Paris. This maneuver opened the door for the French commander-in-chief, Joseph Joffre (1852–1931), to launch a counterattack against the German left flank along the Marne River. The First Battle of the Marne, 5–9 September, remembered as the "Miracle of the Marne," saved France from a swift defeat by halting the German advance. General von Moltke resigned in disgrace.

Meanwhile, the Germans had managed to halt the Russian advance in the east in the Battles of Tannenberg Forest (30 August) and Masurian Lakes (15 September). General Aleksandr Samsonov (1859–1914), the Russian commander at the Battle of Tannenberg, attempted to redeem his honor by committing suicide, while Field Marshal Paul von Hindenburg (1847–1934) and General Erich Ludendorff (1865–1937), the victors of Tannenberg, emerged as heroes. As the war progressed, the two men became virtual military dictators of Germany.

Cheering crowd in Berlin greets the announcement of mobilization. George Grantham Bain Collection/Library of Congress/Public Domain.

The so-called race to the sea ensued in the wake of the failed Schlieffen Plan in the west. The opposing armies, the French corps joined by the British Expeditionary Force (BEF) and the Belgium army against the German army, tried to outflank each other as they steadily moved north to the English Channel. By 25 December, the soldiers, who went into battle with expectations of being home for Christmas, stood opposite each other in a line of trenches that stretched from the English Channel in the north to Switzerland in the south, a distance of about 400 miles. There followed nearly four years of stalemate. The line of trenches remained virtually unchanged despite the expenditure of millions of casualties in futile attempts to break through the lines and turn the stalemate into a war of motion the generals could understand. This "troglodyte world" of trench warfare would later strain the imaginations of artists, writers, and poets, as they tried to depict it for those who had not experienced the horror of it firsthand.

Trench Warfare

The Great War was like no other war before it, although there were some hints of what this first industrial war might entail. The American Civil War (1861–1865), the Boer War (1899–1902), and the Russo-Japanese War (1904–1905) each foreshadowed in some way what "industrialized warfare" would mean. Even "Queen Victoria's little wars" in the colonial world should have provided some insight. The effectiveness of rapid-firing machine guns at, for example, the Battle of Omdurman in Sudan (1898) demonstrated the obsolescence of massed cavalry or infantry charges in modern warfare. The new reality was that unless there is a decisive victory, in the beginning, an industrial war becomes a war of attrition, in which victory goes to the side that is best able to make use of its human and economic resources.

Siegfried Sassoon (1886–1967), a British infantry officer and war poet, once commented, "when all is said and done the war was mainly a matter of holes and ditches." And in the Great War, these holes and ditches were enormously complicated. The frontline of trenches was not simply a matter of two ditches facing each other. Trenches usually were arranged in three zigzagging, roughly parallel lines. First came the frontline trench, usually about eight feet (2.4 m) deep and four to six feet (1.3–1.8 m) wide with a parapet of earth or sandbags rising another two or three feet (0.6 or 0.9 m) high on the enemy side. Behind the frontline trenches were two support trenches that contained first aid stations and kitchens. There were bunkers that served as command posts, communication centers, or storage for food and weapons. Between the three trenches were various communication trenches through which ammunition, reinforcements, and food were brought to the forward trenches. Running out from the front line into "No Man's Land" (the space between the front lines of the opposing armies) were "saps," shallow ditches leading to forward posts for observation, listening, grenade throwing, and machine-gun placements. "No Man's Land" was an area that averaged perhaps 250 yards (230 m). It was a macabre landscape covered in craters created by artillery shells, row upon row of barbed wire, unexploded ordinance, and bodies and body parts in various stages of decomposition, the remains of failed assaults on the enemy's frontline.

The sights and sounds of trench warfare were enough to change forever those who experienced it. Surviving life in the trenches depended in part on developing a numbness to the surrounding horror. Fritz Kreisler (1875–1962), an Austrian infantryman who survived the war to become a master violinist and composer, described it:

French trench along the Western Front. Bain News Service/The Library of Congress/Public Domain.

> A certain fierceness arises in you, an absolute indifference to anything the world holds except your duty of fighting. You are eating a crust of bread, and a man is shot in the trench next to you. You look calmly at him for a moment, and then go on eating your bread. Why not? There is nothing to be done. In the end you talk of your own death with as little excitement as you would of a luncheon engagement (Eksteins 1989, pp. 152–153).

Many of those who lost the ability to feel human emotion, to feel pity or fear, would be forever there in the trenches, never able to return to the life they knew before the war. The enthusiasm that greeted the call to arms in July–August 1914 died in the trenches. Life in the trenches had to be experienced to be understood. Those who had not experienced it could never understand the veteran whose nights were filled with nightmares and whose days were filled with fear. If the civilians back home could somehow see it, wrote Wilfred Owen (1893–1918), one England's greatest poets, who died one week before the Armistice, then

> My friend, you would not tell with such high zest,
> To children ardent for some desperate glory,
> The old Lie: *Dulce et decorum est*
> *Pro patria mori**.
>
> (Walter 2006, pp. 141–142)

(*"It is sweet and becoming to die for one's country," a quotation from the Roman poet Horace.)

Throughout the Great War, the generals on both sides hoped to break the stalemate on the Western Front and turn the conflict back into a war of motion. The strategy for the great breakthrough was the same on both sides. Large numbers of troops were massed at some spot along the front. Artillery bombarded the enemy trenches unceasingly (for seven days and nights at the Battle of the Somme) to "soften up" the enemy's position. Then, the artillery fell silent, and the command was given for the infantry to "go over the top" and across the No Man's Land. The advancing infantrymen typically were cut down by enemy machine guns before reaching the first line of the enemy's trenches. Perhaps the first line of trenches would be taken, but eventually, the assault failed, and the advancing columns, or what was left of them, fell back to their own trenches to await the enemy's counterattack. Again and again, this approach was repeated, without significantly altering the line of the opposing trenches.

Between assaults, life in the trenches was a constant struggle against boredom, extremes of weather, and the pitiless assault of the vermin that infested the trenches. At Flanders, rains transformed the battlefield into a quagmire of mud into which a fallen soldier could disappear and drown. Winter along the Western Front could be so cold that wine froze in November, and rations became chunks of ice. To such discomforts were added the ever-present battle against vermin attracted by the stench of the trenches and the men and corpses that occupied them.

Some pests, such as flies, fleas, and mosquitoes, were a nuisance that the battle-hardened warrior could get used to, but the lice and the rats were different. Lice laid their eggs in the soldiers' clothing and multiplied with terrifying speed. Nothing helped. Hot baths and washing clothing, when possible, brought only temporary relief. Soldiers on both sides took consolation in the belief that the lice afflicting the enemy were larger.

Rats were everywhere, attracted by the rotting corpses in the trenches. Soldiers reported rats as large as cats or small dogs. The battle against the rats, fought with spades, clubs, or whatever was readily available, was unceasing. For some, "rat hunting" became an obsession, vented during the interludes between assaults. The only relief from the rats and other vermin came from a gas attack, which temporarily cleared the trenches of the vermin. But, like the enemy across No Man's Land, the rats and the lice returned.

The Course of the War: 1915

Though the Schlieffen Plan had failed, the Germans were in a strong position at the beginning of 1915. They had gained control of Belgium and the northern industrialized regions of France. In April, the Germans launched a major offensive against the British at Ypres in Belgium. It is primarily remembered as the Germans' first use of poison gas. Taking advantage of favorable winds, the Germans released the gas from canisters in their own trenches. The offensive failed. The Germans assumed a defensive posture on the Western Front while simultaneously attempting to defeat the Russians on the Eastern Front and rescue their beleaguered ally, Austria-Hungary. Austria's conscripts from among its polyglot empire's minorities were deserting in large numbers. The German offensive forced the Russians to abandon both Galicia and Poland, but failed to trap the Russian armies.

After Italy defected to the Allies in August of 1914, Turkey entered the war on the side of the Central Powers. In an effort to relieve pressure on the Western Front and open a supply route to their ally, Russia, the Allies launched a campaign against Turkey aimed at capturing Constantinople. The campaign, known as the Battle of Gallipoli or Gallipoli Campaign (17 February 1915 to 9 January 1916), was poorly planned and executed and a disaster. If victory eluded the Germans in 1915, so did it elude the Allies.

Direction of Allied war efforts in the West remained in French hands during 1915. General Joffre launched a series of offensives beginning in May that failed. By the end of the year, despite great losses, the Allies had gained nothing. The front remained virtually in the same place where it had lain at the beginning of the year.

Sausage Machine: 1916

The common soldier, we are told by the British novelist and poet Robert Graves (1895–1995), spoke of the front as the "sausage machine" because "it was fed with live men, churned out corpses, and remained firmly screwed in place" (Davenport 2013). A sausage machine was an appropriate image for the major battles fought along the Western Front during 1916. Each side began the year believing that the elusive great breakthrough could be achieved by massing enormous quantities of men and firepower along a limited sector of the front.

The Germans set the example at the Battle of Verdun. The battle opened on 21 February with a German artillery bombardment that rained two million shells down on Verdun and its ring of forts. General Henri-Philippe Pétain (1856–1951) was sent in to take command of the fortress's defense. "They shall not pass," Pétain declared, which became a famous motto. When the bloodletting finally halted almost ten months later, on 16 December, half a million men had perished in the sausage machine.

To relieve pressure on Verdun and end the war, the Allies planned a major, three-pronged offensive for the summer of 1916. The British were to attack along the Somme River. The Italians were to attack Austria along the Isonzo River, and the Russians were to launch a major offensive into both Poland and Galicia.

The Russian offensive opened on 4 June, but after some initial success, the Russian steamroller ran out of steam and stalled without achieving its objectives. The Italians attacked the Austrians on 6 August with their usual results. Despite heavy casualties, they were able to capture only the town of Gorizia. Meanwhile, on 1 July, the British began the bloodiest battle of the war along the Somme.

The site chosen by the British command was heavily fortified by the Germans and of no strategic importance. An impressive arsenal of heavy and light artillery, tanks, and airplanes was assembled along a 23-mile front. The British had a record number of artillery pieces, a total of 1,500, or an average of one for every yard of the front they were responsible for. The British began the battle on 24 June with a seven-day-and-night bombardment of the German trenches. The British guns fired four million rounds on the first day. Sir Douglas Haig (1861–1928), commander of the Allied forces, expected the artillery bombardment to win the battle before the infantry, and possibly even cavalry, would move in to "mop up" whatever resistance remained.

The Allied artillery barrage failed to do its job. It did not, for example, cut the barbed wire as expected. The German machine gun crews simply went underground and waited. When the British and French infantry went "over the top," on 1 July, the Germans emerged from their dugouts and manned the machine guns. The slaughter that ensued was made all the more certain by orders that the advancing infantrymen attack in formation while carrying 66 pounds of equipment each. The result was the highest casualty rate in the history of modern warfare. On the offensive's first day, the British alone suffered 60,000 casualties, including 40 percent of their officer corps. Not one yard had been gained. When the battle ended on 18 November, the British had sacrificed over 400,000 men and the French over 200,000. German casualties stood at about 450,000.

Away from the front, the Austrian Emperor Franz Joseph died on 21 November 1916, after 68 years on the throne. His successor and grandnephew, Karl I, began looking for a way out of the war. Perhaps more important for the future was the reelection of Woodrow Wilson (1856–1924) as president of the still "neutral" United States.

The costliest calendar year of the Great War, 1916, had been a bloodbath during which human lives became a matter of statistics, just like any other material resource. The civilians on the home front, too, were beginning to feel the intensive stress of prolonged industrialized war.

The Home Front

Unless there is a decisive victory early in the war, a modern industrial war will be decided on the home front. In a prolonged war, the advantage lies with the side that is best able to organize its economic and human resources. Otherwise, the heroism of the soldiers at the front is in vain. None of the belligerents was prepared for a long war. By the end of 1915, each government was taking steps to wage "total war." As a result, the role of government in regulating economic life and manipulating public opinion reached heights from which it has never fully descended.

Germany was the first to mobilize its economic resources. As early as 1914, Walther Rathenau (1867–1922), one of the nation's leading industrialists, began organizing each branch of production to allocate raw materials to producers who were the most efficient and involved in work of the highest priority. Rathenau also pushed efforts to develop substitute products and to manufacture some items synthetically. His *Kriegsrohstoffabteilung* (KRA or War Raw Materials Administration) became a model for state organization and regulation of the economy. It was not until the end of 1916, however, that a comprehensive attempt was made to mobilize the human resources of Germany through the Auxiliary Service Law, which placed all males between the ages of 17 and 60 at the disposal of the war effort.

Germany's eastern ally was less successful at organizing the home front. In Austria-Hungary, the competition of the two halves of the empire for food thwarted any attempt to set up a unitary agency such as Germany's KRA or Britain's Ministry of Munitions. As the war deepened, the inherent ethnic conflicts crippled all such efforts at organizing the economy or public opinion. Indeed, urged on by Allied propaganda, the empire's various nationalities and ethnic groups did what they could to undermine the war effort.

If the outlook in Austria-Hungary was grim, it was virtually hopeless in Russia. No belligerent suffered more from a failure of leadership than Russia, which did the least of any of the warring nations to mobilize the home front. The Tsar and his officials greeted with hostility all efforts at cooperation by citizens with the government to bring together resources and solve supply and distribution problems. The government saw these as attempts to bring in reform and revolutionary change through the back door, thereby undermining the autocracy.

The British and French faced fewer problems than the three empires in the east, but both nations still struggled to improvise the means to conduct war on an unprecedented scale. Rumors of a shortage of shells led to a broadening of the Liberal cabinet in Britain into a nonpartisan regime in May 1915. In July of that year, a Ministry of Munitions was created, headed by David Lloyd George. He quickly turned the ministry into the British equivalent of Germany's KRA, controlling the allocation of resources and men and the level of profits from the manufacture of arms. In France, the government (i.e., the military) had extensive authority to commandeer resources in a time of war, a tradition going back to the revolution of 1789. France, like Britain, benefitted from the Royal Navy's blockade of Germany. Both allies could draw upon imperial resources, as well as those of the United States. Germany could not.

Everywhere, the increased role of big government in regulating the economy was one of the most important legacies of the Great War. The United States Congress declared war on Germany on 6 April 1917 and began a massive mobilization of the American economy and its people. A military draft was introduced in 1917, resulting in a military force of almost five million men, including volunteers and draftees. To ensure an adequate food supply for the new army and to help feed the European Allies, President Wilson created the United States Food Administration (USFA) and appointed the future president, Herbert Hoover (1874–1964), United States Food Administrator. Bernard Baruch (1870–1965), a leading financier, was at the head of the newly created War Industries Board charged with aiding private industry to produce for the war effort. Farmers were assured of a fair price for what they produced. Civilians were encouraged to conserve food and resources for the war effort.

In the atmosphere of total war, civilians, no less than soldiers, were a vital resource that had to be mobilized. Each nation introduced conscription to ensure adequate fighting forces and that skilled workers remained in the factories. The war benefitted the working classes. Unemployment virtually vanished, and the increasing importance of the labor force and its loyalty led to an increased acceptance of workers' rights in general and trade unions and collective bargaining in particular.

The demand for soldiers also opened up employment opportunities for women at home. Women stepped in to fill the slots left in the factories by men in training camps and on the front. In Britain alone, approximately 1.5 million women obtained jobs previously not open to them or in which they had only nominal representation. As with labor, the role played by women in the war effort helped to advance women's struggles for equality. It was much harder after the war for society to resist, for example, the demand for women's suffrage.

On the negative side of the ledger, civil liberties suffered as opposition to the war mounted. As enthusiasm for the war among the general populace slackened with so many men and boys away and bombarded by one dreary newspaper headline after another, governments stepped up the level of war propaganda they generated in attempts to shore it up. Atrocity stories about the enemy, often false or exaggerated, helped to transform the war into a moral crusade for justice.

Opposition to the war on moral or other grounds was viewed as treasonous. The Defence of the Realm Act (1914) in England permitted the arrest of dissenters as traitors and censored or suspended the publication of newspapers. In France, civil liberties were suppressed after Georges Clemenceau (1841–1929) became a virtual dictator in November 1917. Newspaper editors were drafted for publishing negative reports on the war or, in at least one case, executed for treason.

The United States, the land of freedom and liberty, was no less vigorous than the European powers in suppressing all signs of opposition to the war and perfecting the use of propaganda to build support for America's entry into the conflict. Scholars, clergymen, and entertainers of every sort were recruited to shape public opinion. The popular evangelist and former baseball player William Ashley "Billy" Sunday (1862–1935) combined salvation with patriotism in his popular sermons. He portrayed the war as a struggle between Heaven and Hell. If Hell was turned upside down, said Billy, "Made in Germany" would be found stamped on the bottom.

Citizens' civil liberties, guaranteed by the US Constitution, were openly and "legally" violated. Private patriotic organizations (vigilantes) worked with the FBI to find draft dodgers, spies, or any person or organized group who opposed America's war effort. The Espionage Act of 1917 and the Sedition Act of 1918 made any criticism of the military, government, or even the American flag a federal offense. Violations were punishable by fines, imprisonment, or even death. The war led to fear and hysteria in all warring nations, often calling into question the very ideals they were fighting—and dying—to guarantee.

The War around the World

The European great powers were imperial powers with colonial possessions around the world, at least in the case of Great Britain, France, and Germany. Hence, the Great War was fought all over the world, not just in Europe. Also, the British and French used native colonial troops in Europe. The fact that the Ottoman Empire was one of the Central Powers and that Russia stretched from Central Europe across Eurasia to the Pacific Ocean also globalized the war.

Except for Gallipoli, the war against the crumbling Ottoman Empire was largely overshadowed by the war in Europe. The Turks wanted to capture the Suez Canal to cut Britain's lifeline to India. The British meant to defend the canal and secure the supply of oil. They mobilized an army of two million, including many troops from India, Australia, and New Zealand. The heavy use of airplanes, trucks, and tanks in the prosecution of the war turned oil into a vital resource.

The war in the Middle East was, at least, a brand of war the generals understood. It was one of motion in which cavalry still played an important role. Colonel T. E. Lawrence (1888–1935), a British army intelligence officer serving in Cairo, Egypt, in 1914, was instrumental in effecting an Arab revolt against the Turks. The Arab irregular forces led by Colonel Lawrence captured the strategically important port of Aqaba on the Gulf of Aqaba in July 1917. A British force under the command of General Edmund Allenby captured Jerusalem in December 1917 and Damascus in October 1918.

To bring the Arabs into the war against Turkey, Sir Henry McMohan (1862–1949), British high commissioner in Egypt, made certain commitments to Sharif Hussein bin Ali of Mecca (1853–1949). In an exchange of correspondence between McMahan and Sharif Hussein (July 1915 to January 1916), McMahan offered or appeared to suggest British support for an independent Arab state that, if the war went their way, would include all of the Arab lands then under Turkish rule. Sharif Hussein understood those lands to include Palestine. However, the British were simultaneously seeking the support of the Jewish people. In a letter dated 2 November 1917 to Lord Walter Rothschild (1868–1937), a leader of the Jewish community in Britain and pro-Zionist, British Foreign Minister

Arthur James Balfour (1848–1930) stated that Britain would use its influence to secure in Palestine a national home for the Jews. The letter was made public and has been referred to ever since as the "Balfour Declaration."

The Balfour Declaration lay at odds with promises made to the Arabs. So, practically speaking, promises were just that, promises. On 19 May 1916, Britain and France reached an agreement known as the Sykes–Picot Agreement, in which the Arab lands belonging to the Ottoman Empire would be divided among the two. Neither the promises made to the Arabs nor the Balfour Declaration were to be implemented in the manner the Arabs or the Jews expected. The European great powers did not envision a postwar world significantly different from the period before the Great War. They did not realize that arousing nationalist feelings among colonial peoples would have fatal consequences for their empires.

The outcome of the war in Africa, however, came as no surprise. Except for German East Africa, the German colonies were taken by British and French military forces, assisted by Portuguese and South African forces. Although of no great significance for the outcome of the war in Europe, the struggle for German East Africa was one of the most interesting of the whole war. In it, Colonel (later General) Paul von Lettow-Vorbeck (1870–1964) fought a guerilla war with a mixed force of German and African (Askari) soldiers. Always vastly outnumbered and forced to depend on captured supplies or what could be found at hand, Lettow-Vorbeck was nonetheless able to carry on the war in German South East Africa from November 1914 until a telegram arrived informing him that the war was over in Europe. He surrendered undefeated to British forces on 25 November 1918, two weeks after the fighting ended on the Western Front in Europe. His remaining army consisted of 155 Germans, 1,168 Askari, and approximately 3,500 porters.

Minor battles were fought elsewhere in the world. When hostilities began in 1914, the Japanese, allied with Britain since 1902, seized German possessions in China and some minor islands in the Pacific. German Samoa surrendered in August 1914 to a small force from New Zealand. German New Guinea surrendered to a small force from Australia after a brief skirmish. Two minor naval battles were fought in 1914, the Battle of Coronel off the coast of Chile in November and the Battle of the Falklands off the coast of Argentina in December. The Germans won the first and lost the second. The only major naval battle of the war, the Battle of Jutland (May 1916), was indecisive. The German Navy sunk more English tonnage than the English did German, but since the German fleet returned to port and never ventured out again, the Battle of Jutland is usually seen as a victory for the British.

The Decision, 1917–1918

When 1917 opened, all of the belligerents were at the point of exhaustion. Yet, the scales were not clearly tipped in anyone's favor. It seemed possible that either side might snatch victory from the jaws of defeat. What eventually assured an Allied victory was the entry of the United States into the war on 6 April 1917 as an "Associated Power" of the Allies. It was almost sure that the United States would eventually enter the war on the Allies' side. Many historical ties between the United States and the Allies encouraged sympathy for the Allied cause among Americans. Most important, however, was the role played by President Woodrow Wilson.

Wilson was a very complex person, but like the German Kaiser and the Russian Tsar, he was a deeply flawed man, woefully unequal to his challenges in foreign affairs, especially when it came to the war in Europe. He possessed very little knowledge and no real understanding of European history or the challenges presented by the war. Equally important were personality flaws that had deep roots in lifelong physical illnesses and psychological traumas. He was a supreme egotist. His vision of himself and his mission, writes historian G. J. Meyer, was "an expression of his egotism, his vision of himself as *the* indispensable man, *the* one voice able to speak for the freedom-loving people not only of the United States but of the world" (Meyer 2017, p. 9).

Wilson narrowly won reelection in 1916 with the slogan, "He kept us out of the war." American public opinion favored the United States to remain neutral, but the United States never behaved as a neutral power. It was the chief financier for the Allies. As the war progressed, the Allies became increasingly dependent upon loans from American banks to pay for food and war material. Wilson encouraged such loans while discouraging loans to Germany (Spykman 1929, p. 156). By April 1917, the Allies were nearing the end of their financial resources. Only by entering the war on the Allies' side could American investors be assured that they would not lose their investments due to a German victory or negotiated peace. The United States would, as Wilson put it in his message to Congress on 2 April, grant the Allies "the most liberal credits, in order that the resources of the United States might so far as possible be added to theirs" (Spykman 1929, p. 156).

Three events in the months of 1917 resulted in shift in American public opinion in favor of the United States entering the war on the side of the Allies. The first was Germany's resumption of unrestricted submarine warfare on 1 February. Second was the so-called Zimmermann telegram made public on 1 March. The third was the outbreak of the revolution in Russia on 8 March.

On 17 January, 1917, British naval intelligence intercepted a telegram from the German foreign minister, Arthur Zimmermann (1864–1940), to the German envoy in Mexico, suggesting a possible alliance between Germany and Mexico. American public opinion, already angered by Germany's decision of 31 January to resume unrestricted submarine warfare, was further aroused by the release of the telegram to the public on 1 March.

The American entry into the war was made more plausible by events unfolding in Russia during early 1917. A revolution broke out in Russia between March 8 and 14 that toppled the autocratic tsarist regime (see Chapter 3). Former deputies of the Duma established a Provisional Government as a first step toward creating a liberal-democratic government. The end of autocracy and the promise of constitutional government in Russia helped move American opinion toward intervention in the war. It was easier for Americans to enter a war "to make the world safe for democracy" if they were fighting alongside a constitutional rather than tsarist Russia. However, neither the Zimmermann Telegram nor the revolution in Russia led President Wilson to seek a declaration of war on Germany. It was the renewal of unrestricted U-Boat attacks followed by the sinking of the American merchant ship *Housatonic* carrying supplies to Britain on 3 February by the German submarine *U-53*. Although the captain of *U-53* allowed all of the merchant ship's crew off into lifeboats and towed them to safety, Americans were outraged by the violation of their nation's "neutrality."

Believing that German crimes against American lives on the high seas were of such a nature that they could only be addressed by the United States entering the war, Wilson asked Congress for a declaration of war. On 6 April, Congress complied with the president's request. With the vast human and material resources of the United States available to the Allies, it appeared only a matter of time before the Central Powers would be defeated.

In a final desperate effort to achieve victory on the Western Front, Germany launched the last major offensive on 21 March. Ludendorff threw everything he had left into the offensive. The Allies were taken by surprise. The Germans made significant gains against the British sector, briefly turning the war back into a war of movement. On 23 March, the Germans began bombarding Paris from 75 miles (120 km) using the so-called Paris Gun (a.k.a., the "Williams Gun"), the largest artillery piece of the Great War. On 30 May, the Germans were within 55 miles of Paris. As in 1914, the French government made preparations to leave the capital. Time, however, was running out for the Germans.

On 18 July, bolstered by nine fresh American infantry divisions, the Allies counterattacked. A surprise British assault on 8 August, assisted by 450 tanks, gained 5 miles in half a day as the German lines began to crack. Ludendorff called it "the black day" of the German army. On 4 September, the Germans retreated to the Siegfried Line, a defensive line from Lens to Rheims. With military defeat imminent, and in an effort to prevent a "revolution from below" as had just occurred in Russia, Ludendorff and Hindenburg informed the Kaiser on 29 September that they needed to reach an armistice immediately.

The news of the impending defeat stunned the Kaiser. After admitting he could not work miracles, he appointed his cousin, the liberal Prince Max von Baden (1867–1929), chancellor. On the following day, the Prince asked President Wilson for an armistice based on Wilson's principles for peace, referred to as "Wilson's Fourteen

Points." The armistice would be preliminary to a peace conference at which the warring nations would negotiate a peace settlement. With sailors at Kiel mutinying, the Kaiser yielded to advice from Hindenburg and abdicated on 9 November. At the request of the British royal family, he was granted exile in the Netherlands. Two days later, at 5 A.M., a German delegation signed the armistice. Under the terms of the agreement, the fighting stopped at 11 A.M. on 11 November 1918. At long last, "all quiet on the Western Front."

References

Bernhardi, Friedrich von. (2021). Wikipedia. Wikimedia Foundation. https://en.wikipedia.org/wiki/Friedrich_von_Bernhardi#cite_note-eb-2 (accessed 29 October 2021).

Cobden, Richard. (2021). "Richard Cobden's 'I Have a Dream' Speech about a World in Which Free Trade Is the Governing Principle (1846)." Online Library of Liberty. Liberty Fund Network. https://oll.libertyfund.org/quote/richard-cobden-s-i-have-a-dream-speech-about-a-world-in-which-free-trade-is-the-governing-principle-1846 (accessed 28 October 2021).

Eksteins, Modris. (1989). *Rites of Spring: The Great War and the Birth of the Modern Age*. New York: Anchor Books.

Koenig, Marlene Eilers. (2020). "The Marriage of Princess Victoria Luise and Prince Ernst August of Hanover." *Royal Musings*. http://royalmusingsblogspotcom.blogspot.com/2020/05/the-marriage-of-victoria-luise-of.html (accessed 27 October 2021).

Meyer, G. J. (2017). *The World Remade: America in World War I*. New York: Bantam.

Davenport, M. J. (2013). *First Over There: The Attack on Cantigny, America's First Battle of World War I*. New York: Thomas Dunn Books, St Martin's Press.

Sheehan, James J. (2008). *Where Have All the Soldiers Gone? The Transformation of Modern Europe*. Boston: Houghton Mifflin Company.

Spykman, Nicholas. (1929). "The United States and the Allied Debts." ZaöRV. https://www.zaoerv.de/01_1929/1_1929_1_a_155_184.pdf (accessed 4 June 2023).

Walter, Matthew George. (2006). *The Penguin Book of First World War Poetry*. London: Penguin Books.

3

Revolution and Peacemaking, 1917–1919

Chronology

1917	Russian (February) Revolution
	Russian (October) Revolution
1918	Woodrow Wilson's "Fourteen Points"
	Treaty of Brest-Litovsk; Russia leaves the war
	Armistice on the Western Front, 11 November
	German Republic proclaimed
	Russian Civil War (1918–1920)

Twentieth-Century Europe: 1900 to the Present, Fourth Edition.
Michael D. Richards and Paul R. Waibel.

1919	Paris Peace Conference
	Weimar Constitution adopted in Germany
	Versailles Peace Treaty with Germany
	League of Nations Covenant signed

The Europe that welcomed the armistice in November 1918 was very different from the Europe that enthusiastically greeted the outbreak of war in August 1914. The "old order" had fallen, but no one was quite sure what the "new order" would be like. At its outset, the Great War was an old-fashioned affair of kings, emperors, and statesmen defending dynastic and or national honor against the aggressor. By 1916, it had become a war for territorial expansion. In 1917, the Russian Revolution and the entry of the United States transformed the Great War into an ideological struggle, a crusade for a new world order. Woodrow Wilson, the president of the United States, and V. I. Lenin (Vladimir Ilyich Ulyanov, 1870–1924), the Bolshevik leader of the new Russia personified two very different visions of the future. Each proposed a new world order entirely different from what Europeans had known before the war. Each vision, in its own way, held out the hope that the Great War might not have been in vain.

Wilson's vision took shape partly in response to Lenin's call for an immediate peace of justice without victors or vanquished. Wilson, who as late as 1916 campaigned for reelection on his record as an isolationist, began to speak of a new democratic international order based upon the abstract "universal principles of right and justice." Before a joint session of Congress in January 1918, he outlined in his "Fourteen Points" the principles on which he believed a just peace settlement had to be negotiated (Table 3.1). They included "open covenants openly arrived at," the principle of national self-determination, and a "general association of nations" to assure the political independence and territorial integrity of each nation. In the ensuing months, as the peace conference unfolded, Wilson's "general association of nations," the League of Nations, became his chief goal, the basis of his new world order.

Wilson and Lenin had much in common. Both were products of Enlightenment thought. Both believed in the innate goodness of man. Hence, they were both humanists, but with a difference.

Table 3.1 Wilson's Fourteen Points

1. No more secret agreements ("open covenants openly arrived at")
2. Free navigation of all seas
3. An end to all economic barriers between countries
4. Countries to reduce weapon numbers
5. All decisions regarding the colonies should be impartial
6. The German army is to be removed from Russia. Russia should be left to develop her own political setup
7. Belgium should be independent like before the war
8. France should be fully liberated and allowed to recover Alsace-Lorraine
9. All Italians are to be allowed to live in Italy. Italy's borders are to be "along clearly recognizable lines of nationality"
10. Self-determination should be allowed for all those living in Austria-Hungary
11. Self-determination and guarantees of independence should be allowed for the Balkan states
12. The Turkish people should be governed by the Turkish Government. Non-Turks in the old Turkish Empire should govern themselves
13. An independent Poland should be created which should have access to the sea
14. A League of Nations should be set up to guarantee the political and territorial independence of all states

(History Learning Site 1918/Woodrow Wilson/Public domain)

Wilson's belief that human beings are by nature good, possessing certain inalienable natural rights, led him to become a liberal Democrat, for whom the loss of American lives to U-Boat attacks was a crime that justified American intervention in the Great War. Lenin's humanism was more abstract. He had great compassion for humanity in general, but, as a Marxist, he viewed individuals as expendable cogs in the wheels of history. And although Lenin defended orthodox Marxism as objective truth, he did not adhere, as Marx did, to historical determinism. Lenin was a voluntarist for whom willpower (the will of the leader) was the decisive factor in determining the flow of history.

Wilson's vision appealed mainly to middle-class liberals, who wished to replace the old world of aristocratic privilege and secret

Lenin led the Bolsheviks to victory and led the government of the new Soviet Union from 1917 to 1924. Bain News Service/The Library of Congress.

diplomacy with a new international order of democratic nation-states cooperating in a League of Nations. The new order was a free and democratic, but not a classless, world order. None of Wilson's Fourteen Points dealt with Lenin's most pressing concern, constructing a new social order. In Lenin's view, the imminent world revolution, for which the Russian Revolution was a catalyst, would sweep away both nation-states and classes to liberate humankind from the corruptive influence of past historical development. Although Lenin's program appealed to millions, millions more feared it. Those who feared his ideas did so because behind them lay the fact of the Russian Revolution and the forces it had unleashed. No one, however, Bolsheviks or bourgeois democrats quite knew what might develop from the events of 1917 in Russia.

Revolution in Russia

The Russian Revolution of 1917 was two revolutions. The first occurred in February, according to the Julian calendar, then in use in Russia and resulted in the creation of a liberal Provisional Government. The Provisional Government was organized by former deputies of the Duma, which the Tsar suspended in September 1915. The second, or Bolshevik Revolution, occurred in October in the Julian calendar.[1] It was carried out by the Bolsheviks, a radical Marxist faction within the Soviet of Workers' and Sailors' Deputies, or Petrograd Soviet. The Petrograd Soviet came into existence on the same day as the Provisional Government. From its beginning, the Petrograd Soviet functioned like a shadow government, issuing its own decrees and countermanding decrees of the Provisional Government.

That there was a revolution in Russia at all was due to the failure of the Tsar's government to deal adequately with the demands of the war. That failure, in turn, was the result of several factors. Russia was the most effectively blockaded of the belligerents. At the same time, it was unable to exploit its vast natural resources due to its general economic backwardness and the Government's unwillingness to organize the economy and society for a total war effort. In short, it was an abdication of authority by the Tsar's Government that led to the creation of the Provisional Government and the Petrograd Soviet.

There were three different coalition governments during the period of the Provisional Government from 18 March to 7 November 1917. The first consisted of middle- and upper-middle-class liberals from the Kadets (Liberal Constitutional Party) and Octobrists (moderate constitutionalists), and Aleksandr Kerensky (1881–1970), a member of a moderate Labor Party, the lone socialist. In May, several Mensheviks (the moderate wing of the Social Democratic Labor Party) and Socialist Revolutionaries (a radical party with a peasant base) joined the coalition. Kerensky became minister of war and began preparation for a new offensive intended to contribute to the allied war effort. After the July Offensive failed, Kerensky took the post of prime minister and formed a second coalition government on 6 August. Kerensky also led the third and final coalition cabinet from 8 October to 7 November, when the Bolsheviks seized power.

1 Most accounts of the Russian Revolution refer to the "February Revolution" and the "October Revolution" even though they actually took place in March and November, respectively, according to the calendar in use in the West.

Why the Provisional Government failed (and why there was a second revolution in October) is one of the great historical questions of 1917. But the reason for the failure of the Provisional Government is not as simple as sometimes believed. While it is true that the Provisional Government forgot the first duty of any government was to govern, there were both ideological and practical reasons why the Provisional Government failed to act decisively. It was a coalition of liberals committed to defending civil liberties. But, none of them felt they had the right to make any far-reaching changes in Russian society until a constitutional assembly had been elected and met to draft a constitution. They believed that the fundamental issues of what kind of Government should replace the monarchy must be decided by a duly elected Constituent Assembly. Until then, the Provisional Government saw itself as "provisional," the transitory caretaker of national sovereignty.

This overly cautious and legalistic approach, more than anything else, crippled and then doomed the Provisional Government. It had claimed authority but was both unwilling and unable to exercise power. Faced with growing economic problems and the pressures of continuing an increasingly unpopular war, it could not provide the firm leadership the Russian masses were desperate for in 1917.

The expectations of the people were a significant challenge faced by the Provisional Government. Tsarism had ended, and "democracy" was now established, or being established, but "democracy" meant something different to each group within Russian society. Given its legalistic interpretation of its provisional status, the Provisional Government was unable to address these expectations. Its failure to respond to the peasants' demand for land with some land reform programs is an example of the Provisional Government's overly cautious approach to governing. Rather than address the needs of the masses, it made the fatal decision to continue the war and even launched a new, major offensive in July.

It was the decision to continue the war that doomed the already floundering Provisional Government. In part, it was a matter of honor. Many in the Provisional Government felt that Russia had to fulfill certain obligations to its allies, but there were other, more selfish, reasons for continuing the war. In May 1917, the Provisional Government continued to pursue the acquisition of Constantinople and the Turkish Straits, two of the major war aims of the Tsarist Government. Despite widespread and very vocal public opposition, the Provisional Government failed to see the necessity of extricating Russia from the war, a hard reality that Lenin forced the Bolsheviks to accept in 1918.

The arrival of Lenin in Petrograd in mid-April 1917 altered the course of the Revolution. Lenin was living in exile in Switzerland when the February Revolution occurred. It was the German military that facilitated Lenin's return to Russia as a "secret weapon" in the war with Russia. As early as 1915, Lenin advocated a revolution in Russia as a prerequisite to peace. He and his fellow Bolsheviks argued for peace at any cost, even the defeat of Russia if necessary. The German High Command decided in April of 1917 to secure Lenin's return to Russia, along with 31 other prominent Bolsheviks. The Germans provided Lenin and his co-conspirators with an estimated 50–60 million marks to fund, what they no doubt hoped would be, the overthrow of the Provisional Government and an end to the war with Russia.

Upon his arrival in Petrograd, Lenin immediately persuaded the Bolsheviks to embrace his interpretation of the Revolution. In what came to be known as the "April Theses," Lenin called for immediate peace, a transfer of governmental authority to the Soviets, and nationalization of land. Lenin argued that the second stage of the Revolution, the "proletarian revolution," was at hand, and it was the task of the Bolsheviks to take the lead. The April Theses were initially rejected by the Bolshevik leadership, although published in *Pravda* (the Bolshevik newspaper) on 7 April as Lenin's interpretation.

The Bolsheviks rapidly increased in number during the spring and early summer of 1917 in an atmosphere of growing anarchy. At the same time, the Provisional Government was losing even the limited power it once had. Aleksandr Kerensky, minister of war after 19 May, attempted to rally the troops for a new offensive. On 1 July, the Russian offensive began against the Austro-Hungarian and German lines in Galicia. After some initial success, the Russian offensive collapsed, and on 19 July, the Germans counterattacked, all but destroying the Russian army as an effective fighting force. Meeting little resistance, the German army pursued the retreating Russians through Galicia and Ukraine. The Russian troops began deserting in large numbers. Lenin correctly observed, "The army voted for peace with its feet."

The failure of the July Offensive was disastrous for the Provisional Government. The cabinet resigned, and a new government was formed with Aleksandr Kerensky as prime minister. Growing chaos caused fear among some liberal and conservative army officers, business people, and political leaders who feared that Russia was drifting toward civil war. This liberal–conservative coalition found a champion in the colorful Cossack general, Lavr Kornilov (1870–1918), Kerensky's new commander-in-chief.

Fearing that his commander-in-chief was plotting a coup, Kerensky dismissed Kornilov on 8 September. Kornilov refused to obey and ordered army units to begin marching on Petrograd. Swift action by the Petrograd Soviet, however, robbed Kornilov of the support of the troops. The soldiers simply deserted as they approached Petrograd. The Kornilov "coup," if indeed it was ever meant to be such, fizzled out. The Provisional Government was saved, but by the action of the Petrograd Soviet, not its own.

What existed in Russia in September 1917 was a kind of organized anarchy. No single organization could speak for all the people. A fermentation process was at work within the armed forces, among the peasantry and the industrial workers, and within various national and ethnic groups. The aspirations of these many different groups could not be adequately expressed in conventional political terms, as Kerensky was trying to do by patiently preparing for the election of a Constituent Assembly. The energies of the masses had been unleashed by the destruction of the traditional authorities. No government could succeed unless it tapped those energies or, at the least, managed to ride their currents.

From his hideout in Finland, where he fled in mid-July when the Provisional Government cracked down on the Bolsheviks, Lenin sought to direct the raw energy of the masses to seize power. He saw the possibility of combining the anarchistic rebelliousness of the masses with the revolutionary efforts of the vanguard of the proletariat, the party. In September, he wrote to the Central Committee of the Bolshevik faction: "the Bolsheviks must seize power at this very moment."

Lenin's proposal met with opposition from some of his closest associates, who argued that the time was not right. The differences were resolved at a secret meeting of the Central Committee attended by Lenin on the night of 23 October. Lenin prevailed, and the Central Committee agreed to prepare for a coup. Since Lenin wished to remain in hiding, the leadership of the coup was given to Leon Trotsky (Lev Davidovich Bronstein, 1879–1940), who was head of the Military Revolutionary Committee of the Petrograd Soviet.

The seizure of power by the Bolsheviks took place on 7 November (25 October) 1917. Actually, "seizure of power" is too glorious a phrase to convey the reality of the confused situation in Petrograd. It would be more accurate to say that once the Provisional Government failed in its attempt to destroy the Bolsheviks and the Military Revolutionary Committee, power was dumped into the lap of the Bolshevik faction. Trotsky's preparations made it appear that power had been seized in the name of the Soviet movement. Not all members of the Second Congress of Soviets, meeting at that time in Petrograd, accepted that notion, but the delegates who remained at the meeting, although a minority, voted to accept a Bolshevik government. For the time being, it was also accepted in Moscow and other important cities. Perhaps more important, it was accepted in most areas at the front. In the provinces, distant from the central authority, in any case, a watchful attitude was adopted. At the same time, centers of resistance sprang up, but the Bolsheviks managed to retain power without great difficulty in the last months of 1917.

The situation became much graver in 1918. The revolutionary Government faced several complex problems. First, it had to contend with the Constituent Assembly, elected in November after the Revolution. The Bolsheviks were badly outnumbered, notably by the Socialist Revolutionaries, who had received strong peasant support. At the initial meeting of the Constituent Assembly in January 1918, delegates began immediately to sharply criticize the

Government. The Government responded by dispersing the assembly at the end of the first day; there was not enough organized support for parliamentary rule to counter this move.

The second problem could not be dealt with so easily. It involved ending the war with Germany. Trotsky led the Russian delegation in negotiations with Germany and Austria beginning in December, but he could not moderate the harsh demands laid down by the German general staff. Lenin, as he had so often in the past, used his powers of persuasion and prestige to persuade the Bolsheviks to accept the German terms, harsh as they were. With great reluctance, Russia signed the Treaty of Brest-Litovsk on 3 March 1918, abandoning Poland, Lithuania, Ukraine, the Baltic provinces, Finland, and Transcaucasia. Russia lost significant portions of its industrial capacity and food-raising capabilities but gained time in which to attend to internal problems without the constant demands of war impinging. It was a substantial but necessary sacrifice. Otherwise, it is difficult to imagine how the Bolshevik government could have survived the three years of civil war that followed.

Civil War in Russia

The Bolsheviks moved quickly to consolidate their control. They moved the capital from Petrograd (St. Petersburg) to Moscow, a more secure location in the interior and farther away from Europe. Leon Trotsky resigned as foreign minister to become war commissar in March 1918. The Red Army, created in January by Trotsky, had become a formidable force, ready to defend the Bolshevik government from those within Russia and possible intervention from Russia's former allies or Japan. Some former Tsarist generals joined the Red Army of their own free will; others served because the Bolsheviks held their family members as hostages. In July 1918, the Bolsheviks expelled the Left Socialist Revolutionaries, a splinter group that had broken off from the Socialist Revolutionaries, from the Government. That same month, the Congress of Soviets adopted the Constitution of the Russian Soviet Federated Socialist Republic.

Meanwhile, the Tsar, along with his wife, children, and their doctor and servants, were imprisoned in the town of Yekaterinburg, on the eastern side of the Ural Mountains, where Europe and Asia meet. All of them were executed on the night of 16/17 July by their captors, who feared they might be liberated by a White[2] Army that was closing in on Yekaterinburg. There remain many questions concerning the fate of the Tsar and his family, but, indeed, the execution of the entire Romanov family served as a sort of notice that there was no turning back. Tsarist Russia was history. It remained for the victor of the civil war, either the Reds or the Whites, to determine the future of Russia. On 2 September, the Bolshevik government proclaimed a "Red Terror" against all those considered counterrevolutionaries.

The Reds enjoyed certain advantages over the Whites. The Reds were unified geographically as well as ideologically. They controlled the most important provinces of the former Russian Empire, which gave them control of the economic resources, including the railroads and internal lines of supply and defense. To ensure that the Red Armies received the necessary supplies and manpower, the Government introduced a set of policies commonly referred to as "War Communism." Factories were nationalized. Throughout the areas controlled by the new Government, what amounted to a military discipline was implemented. Strikes were prohibited. Vital resources, including food, were rationed, and the peasants were forced to fulfill quotas for grain production and other agricultural products.

In contrast, the Whites never ideologically unified or agreed on military strategy. They attacked the Reds from the north, east, and south with armies that never totaled more than a quarter million. They lacked leadership, both military and ideological. Whereas the Reds were able to unify their troops and the civilian population in the areas under their control, the Whites were never able to do so. They lost the struggle for the people's hearts, who came to fear a White victory more than a Red victory. The final battle of the civil

[2] Those who opposed the Bolsheviks (Reds) were collectively referred to as the Whites.

war was fought in Crimea, around the town of Perekop, between 7 and 15 November 1920. The Russian Civil War ended in a victory for the Red Army, but at the expense of an estimated 10 million lives.

It is noteworthy that the Whites lost the civil war despite assistance from imperial Russia's allies during the Great War. Great Britain, France, Japan, and the United States became embroiled in the civil war. Allied involvement was, however, never coordinated and primarily limited to material support for the White Armies. The British and French governments decided on intervention with three goals in mind. The first was to safeguard stockpiles of military supplies provided to the Tsarist Government and stored at Archangel. The second was a desire to use the Czech Legion located along the Trans-Siberian Railroad against the Bolsheviks. Finally, they hoped to revive an Eastern Front against Germany and Austria-Hungary. In July, President Wilson agreed to commit 5,000 American troops to the effort.

Once the Great War ended in November 1918, the Allies faced numerous complicated global issues resulting from their victory. Interest in what was happening in Russia declined rapidly, and those interventionists that remained in Russia began seeking an honorable exit. By the end of October 1922, the last of the foreign troops (Japanese) departed, leaving the Russian people with a deep and lasting distrust of the Western powers. At the same time, fear that communism might spread beyond Russia was growing in Europe and the United States.

Revolution in Germany

The revolution in Germany was, like the Russian Revolution, actually two revolutions or attempted revolutions. Forces on the left attempted a "revolution from below" but were checkmated by forces on the right, who carried out a "revolution from above." The result was the establishment of an "accidental" republic that lacked popular support. The traditional elites of the army, judiciary, bureaucracy, church, wealthy landowners, and industrialists remained entrenched and hostile toward the republic. During the republic's brief existence, the forces of extreme right and left struggled to achieve their respective revolutionary goals until the final victory of the extreme right in January 1933.

Once the Allied armies broke through the Hindenburg Line on 29 September 1918, even General Erich von Ludendorff, commander of Germany's last offensive, had to accept reality. The main challenge facing Ludendorff and the High Command in October 1918, once it became clear that Germany had lost the war, was how to save the old order. Guilt for the defeat had to be spread as broadly as possible without including the military leadership. The solution was to create a broad-based civilian government of center-left parties that would be burdened with the task of asking for an armistice and making the necessary peace. Hence, Prince Max von Baden (1867–1929) was appointed chancellor; ministers became responsible to the *Reichstag*; the Prussian three-class voting system was abolished, and the Kaiser lost much of his control of the armed forces. Germany became a constitutional monarchy but not a republic. All of this was to create a responsible civilian government capable of accepting the burden (or blame) of defeat while at the same time preventing a possible Bolshevik-style revolution from below.

Nevertheless, Germany seemed ripe for a revolution from below in November 1918. On 3 November, the sailors at the Kiel naval base mutinied. It was a spark that ignited revolution across Germany. On 8 November, Kurt Eisner (1867–1919), an Independent Socialist,[3] established a Constituent Workers', Soldiers', and Peasants' Council in Munich and proclaimed the Republic of Bavaria. Revolt also broke out in Berlin, on 8 November. On the following day, Prince Max von Baden announced both the Kaiser's abdication (to which the Kaiser had not yet agreed) and his own resignation as chancellor. As he resigned, he transferred his powers to Friedrich Ebert (1871–1925), leader of the Majority Social Democrats. The transfer of power gave an aura of legitimacy to Ebert's Government, although Prince Max

[3] The Independent Socialists split off from the Majority Socialists (SPD, or Social Democratic Party of Germany) in 1915 to protest the SPD's continued support of the war. In 1917, the Independent Socialists formed the USPD, or Independent Social Democratic Party of Germany. The Spartakusbund and KPD (Communist Party of Germany) evolved out of the USPD.

von Baden had no actual constitutional authority to do so. The "Ebert Cabinet," which called itself the "Council of Peoples' Deputies," derived its authority from the Workers' and Soldiers' Councils of Berlin and the two parties on the left, the SPD and the USPD.

The moderate socialists in the SPD and USPD were willing to accept government responsibility and the burden of making peace because they, as well as the trade union leaders and a majority of the people they represented, feared a revolution from below as much as the traditional elites did. Initially, the socialists intended to help preserve a constitutional monarchy. The abdication of the Kaiser and the proclamation of a republic by Philipp Scheidemann (1865–1939), deputy leader of the SPD, on 9 November, were not a part of the original plan. Once it was a fact, however, Ebert and his supporters felt the immediate need to establish order first and then elect a Constituent Assembly that would draft a constitution, which, in turn, would determine the nature and extent of reform.

Ebert was distraught when he first learned that his deputy had proclaimed a republic. Scheidemann had reacted more or less instinctively to a momentary crisis. He was having lunch, eating a bowl of potato soup at the *Reichstag* on 9 November, when he was informed that Karl Liebknecht (1871–1919), a radical leader of the Spartakusbund, a splinter group from the USPD, was about to proclaim a Soviet Republic from the balcony of the imperial palace. The Spartakusbund originated as a group of radicals who opposed war with Russia. After aligning themselves with the USPD between 1916 and 1918, they renamed themselves the Communist Party of Germany (KPD) in January 1919. Attempting to preempt Liebknecht's announcement, Scheidemann went to the window and made a brief speech to the crowd outside, which he concluded with, "Long live the new! Long live the German Republic!" Hence, Germany became a democratic republic because the alternative, a Soviet Republic, was simply too frightful.

Much ink has been spilled by historians trying to explain why the Social Democrats, a party whose historical roots and party program were Marxist, did not initiate fundamental changes in Germany once they achieved governmental responsibility. The reasons given are varied. One reason is simply that a radical revolution lacked a mass base of support. Also, the radicals in Germany faced strong opposition from the conservative, traditional elites. The army, even if it had been defeated on the battlefront, was still a formidable force in German internal affairs. The bureaucracy continued to function efficiently. And even though the old imperial Government had collapsed, most of the other institutions in Germany were still sound and committed to preventing any real change in German society. Finally, the more radical forces found little sympathy for their demands among the Majority Socialists.

Any chance that the Majority Social Democrats would lead a "real" revolution in Germany was short-circuited by the so-called Ebert–Groener Pact on 9 November and the Stinnes–Legien Agreement on 15 November. In the former, General Wilhelm Groener (1867–1939), Ludendorff's successor offered the Ebert government the support and protection of the army in exchange for Ebert's promise to "suppress Bolshevism," that is, to suppress the soldiers' councils and recognize the authority of the officer corps.

The Stinnes–Legien Agreement was concluded between employers and trade union leaders on 15 November. The employers agreed to recognize the unions as the only legitimate labor representatives, abolish company unions, hire returning soldiers, and implement codetermination in all firms employing at least 50 workers. In return, the trade unions agreed not to push for any changes in the existing property structure of Germany.

Many have argued ever since November of 1918 that the real "stab in the back" occurred when, as a result of the Ebert–Groener Pact and the Stinnes–Legien Agreement, the Majority Social Democrats allegedly were taken captive by the forces on the right. Caught between a revolution from above and a revolution from below, they opted for the former. Whatever the truth, the leftist uprisings during 1919 were swiftly put down by the army and the Freikorps, paramilitary associations of former soldiers. A revolt in Berlin in January 1919, led by the Spartakusbund, also was crushed. Rosa Luxemburg (1871–1919), the most consistent advocate of revolution among the Socialists, and her colleague, Karl Liebknecht (1871–19), were the leaders of the Spartakusbund. They were murdered by members of the Freikorps, to which Ebert had turned to abolish the revolt. Further uprisings in February and March in Berlin, Munich, and other areas, and the brief Soviet Republic proclaimed in Bavaria in April were all likewise suppressed. The German Revolution, unlike the revolution in Russia, stopped halfway.

Elsewhere in Central Europe, defeat in war, the disintegration of old prewar governments, and the powerful example of 1917 in Russia created potential revolutionary situations. In Austria, there were disorders throughout 1919 but no successful revolution. In Hungary, a revolution in October 1918 created a government of socialists and communists, and in March 1919, that Government became a communist dictatorship under Béla Kun (1886–1936). Communist Hungary did not last long, however. Romanian troops invaded in April. At the same time, a counterrevolution began, and by 1 August, Béla Kun fled the country. Miklós Horthy (1868–1957), a former admiral in the Austro-Hungarian Navy, ruled as regent and head of state until 1944.

Despite setbacks, by the end of 1919, the fate of the world revolution was still undetermined. Revolutionaries remained optimistic, but as events played out, much of their optimism was unfounded. Success in Russia was based on two factors, the utter collapse of the old regime and widespread rebellion among the lower classes in the cities and especially in the countryside. Neither factor led to success in Germany, where the empire collapsed, but the institutions and traditional elites undergirding it remained. There was no German equivalent to the Russian peasantry on which the small radical groups could base their activity. In Central Europe, a large peasantry existed. But it was fragmented by ethnic and national differences and kept under control by the great landowners, the aristocracy, and the military who, sometimes with difficulty (as in Hungary), managed to dominate politics after the Great War in every Central European state except Czechoslovakia. The only successful revolution outside Russia in the immediate postwar period occurred in Turkey, where army officers and nationalists rallied in 1919 and 1920 to prevent the victorious Allied Powers from imposing peace terms on their nation.

Revolution, if relatively unsuccessful by 1919, still had an enormous impact on postwar Europe. In the United States and Europe, there was a considerable and often irrational fear of a Bolshevik menace. A good deal of energy and time was spent at the Paris

Peace Conference working out methods by which the Russian Revolution might be quarantined or possibly destroyed. An informal counterrevolutionary movement developed that led to dictatorships, initially in Eastern and Southeastern Europe, then in Italy and the Iberian Peninsula, and finally, Germany.

Peacemaking, 1919

Amid the disorder and turmoil, when the threat of revolution looked a good deal more imposing than it did by the end of 1920, the Paris Peace Conference opened on 18 January 1919. It lasted until 21 January 1920. The victorious powers met not simply to end the Great War but also to reconstruct the world. The number of delegates to the conference included those from small nations that had played no role in the war but seized the opportunity to be on the side of the victors by declaring war on Germany during the final months, e.g., Guatemala, Nicaragua, Costa Rica, Haiti, and Honduras. Most spent their time in Paris attending parties and

President Woodrow Wilson and French President Raymond Poincaré enjoy cheering crowd in Paris. Bain News Service / The Library of Congress.

enjoying the city's various diversions. The actual work of drafting the Versailles Treaty with Germany was the work of the "Big Four" (France, Great Britain, Italy, and the United States), actually the "Big Three," following Italy's noncooperation after being denied the territorial compensation it demanded for its participation in the war. Some individuals showed up claiming to represent countries that did not exist, e.g., Ho Chi Minh (1890–1969), the future leader of the Socialist Republic of Vietnam. Neither the Central Powers nor Russia (now the Soviet Union) was allowed to participate.

There is a natural temptation to compare the Paris Peace Conference with the Vienna Congress (1814–1815) that concluded the Napoleonic Wars. Both came after major Europe-wide conflicts and attempted to set the map of Europe right and draft a peace that would last. However, the Vienna Congress succeeded, whereas the Paris Peace Conference failed. The Paris Peace Settlement provided only a 20-year cease-fire before Europe, and the world, was plunged into a second and even more devastating war. Apart from the brief wars of German unification, there was general peace in Europe for 100 years following the Vienna Congress.

The Europe of 1919 was very different from the Europe of 1814–1815. The diplomats who went to Vienna represented monarchies and were answerable only to their respective monarch. Hence, they enjoyed a freedom of action not allowed the diplomats of 1919. The peacemakers in Paris had to answer to a public who had suffered four long years of industrialized warfare and had been subjected to a constant bombardment of propaganda aimed at demonizing the enemy, not only their governments but their citizens as well. Citizens of the victorious nations expected that the evil enemy should suffer, as they were taught to believe, for causing the most destructive war in Western history. Also, the peacemakers in Paris were meeting when Europe erupted with turmoil and revolution fed by the new "isms" that had emerged during the intervening century.

The Vienna Congress was guided in its decision-making by three guiding principles: balance of power, legitimacy, and compensation. Every decision was weighed against the guiding principles. There was an agreed-upon basis for peace in Vienna that was not present at the Paris Peace Conference. Every decision made in Paris was a compromise among the victors. The treaty with Germany, commonly referred to as the Versailles Treaty because it was signed in the Hall of Mirrors at the Palace of Versailles outside Paris, was to be a victors' peace based on two fallacious assumptions. The first was the belief that Germany alone was to blame for the war. The second was the premise that future peace in Europe and the world required the destruction of Germany as a great power. To further emphasize Germany's position and humiliate the German people, the blockade of Germany was to continue until the final treaty was accepted and signed by Germany.

France, represented by Georges Clemenceau (1841–1929), wanted a treaty that would assure French national security and require Germany to pay for war damages. David Lloyd George, Britain's representative, was compelled by the results of the December 1918 elections to side with Clemenceau and thus supported harsher peace terms than he felt were justified. Lloyd George, a leader of the Liberal Party, had campaigned on the slogan "a country fit for heroes to live in." Given the new economic realities at the war's end, the promise of "a country fit for heroes to live in" required a hard line on reparations from Germany.

Although many reasons can be given as explanations for why the Paris Peace Conference was a failure, two stand out. One was the failure to include Russia (now the Soviet Union) and Germany, especially the latter. Russia was not represented both because the Bolsheviks, if they were the legitimate Government, had little interest in what seemed to them a meaningless farce and also because of the fear of Bolshevism among the delegates of the "civilized" nations gathered at Paris. They feared, as the British historian A. J. P. Taylor has pointed out, that Soviet Russia represented a "genuine element of social change," which threatened to spread. Hence, the need to at least quarantine, or, if possible, snuff out, Bolshevism.

That Germany was not allowed to join the conference was a serious flaw. As the Versailles Treaty took shape, it became clear that it would be a victors' peace. The demand that Germany pay the costs of the war necessitated an admission of guilt by Germany for having started the war, thus the inclusion in the treaty of the infamous Article 231, or "war-guilt clause." To require Germany to accept the burden of reparations, the amount of which the treaty left unspecified, was an injustice. But Germany's acceptance of responsibility for the war was a burden that could only be imposed, as it could never be willingly accepted.

Perhaps an even more critical factor was the role of President Woodrow Wilson, who personally represented the United States. Wilson was a complex person burdened by believing in the Calvinist divine providence and predestination doctrines. Wilson arrived at the conference "as a latter-day Savior from the New World," notes historian A. J. P. Taylor, "convinced of his own intellectual superiority and righteousness" (Taylor 1966, pp. 62, 45). Europeans, in general, cheered Wilson upon his arrival, but many of those who worked with him had a different opinion. In the eyes of the European leaders with whom Wilson had to negotiate, he appeared disconnected from the real world of 1919. The peace conference became a contest between new-world idealism, represented by Woodrow Wilson, and old-world realism, represented by Georges Clemenceau. David Lloyd George found himself attempting to mediate between the two adversaries, or as he put it, do the best he could "considering I was seated between Jesus Christ and Napoleon" (David Lloyd George Biography, n.d.).

The extent to which his unwillingness to make the treaty a bipartisan political issue at home resulted in the US Senate's, and the people's, ultimate rejection of it also has been examined at length. What remains indisputable is Wilson's sincere commitment to a just peace as a basis for building a new world order. He believed that the League of Nations was the essential cornerstone of that new order, but its existence required the postwar cooperation of the victors. To see the League become a reality, Wilson was forced to compromise, often at Germany's expense. He justified these compromises in the sincere belief that whatever defects the treaty contained could be repaired in later years by international cooperation through the League.

The Treaty of Versailles with Germany was presented to the German delegation on 7 May and signed on 28 June, five years to the day after the assassination of the Archduke in Sarajevo. The ceremony took place in the Hall of Mirrors at the Palace of Versailles outside Paris, where on 18 January 1871, the German Empire had been proclaimed. Individual treaties were signed between September 1919 and August 1920 with the other former members of the Central Powers.

Germany was seriously weakened by the terms of the Versailles Treaty, although not fatally so, as the French had initially wanted. It lost some territory in its west: Alsace-Lorraine was returned to France, and a part of Schleswig was ceded to Denmark after a plebiscite. In addition, a few border communities were transferred to Belgium (but restored to Germany in 1926). The coal mines of the Saar were placed under French control for 15 years, after which a plebiscite would determine the national status of the area. The Rhineland remained a part of Germany, despite extensive French efforts, but the area west of the Rhine and a strip 50 km to the east were "demilitarized." Allied troops were to occupy the river's west bank for 15 years. In the east, Germany lost a good deal more territory. A large part of Posen and West and East Prussia were ceded to Poland. Danzig was declared a free city within the Polish customs union. Memel was ceded to the Allies and later taken over by Lithuania. Upper Silesia's fate was to be determined by plebiscite. Germany also lost all of its colonies.

Europe Between the Wars

As a military power, Germany was much reduced in size. It was allowed an army of no more than 100,000 men with limitations on the types of weapons they might have. Its navy was reduced in size and was forbidden to have submarines. Furthermore, Germany was not allowed to have an air force. The Treaty of Versailles was regarded by most Germans as extremely unfair and harsh. They had, of course, forgotten their treaty-making efforts at Brest-Litovsk. The "war guilt clause," reparations, unilateral disarmament, and the loss of territory in Europe and colonies outside Europe all furnished texts for German nationalists in the next decade.

Had the Treaty of Versailles been the only product of the Paris Peace Conference, Europe might have maintained political stability

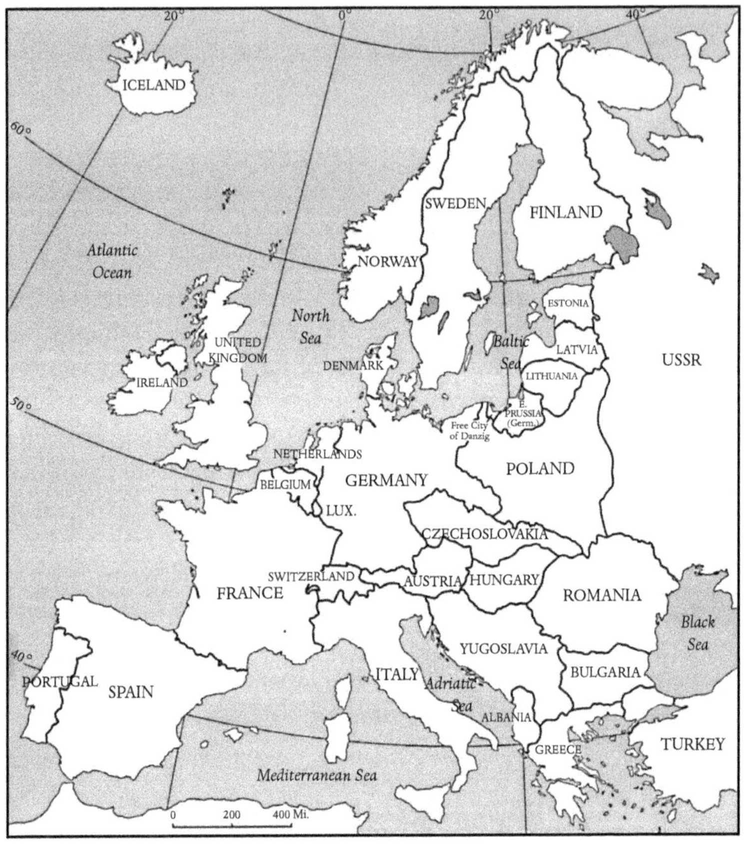

Europe between the wars.

in the 1920s and 1930s. There were, however, four additional treaties and the League of Nations Covenant. The failure of several of these agreements, combined with the limited success of the Treaty of Versailles created an extremely volatile situation in the 1930s. Of the four treaties, two can be disregarded: the Treaty of Sèvres with Turkey never went into effect; the Treaty of Neuilly with Bulgaria had no important repercussions. The other two, the Treaty of St. Germain with Austria and the Treaty of Trianon with Hungary created problems that were never fully resolved between the two world wars. Instead, two new problems were created. First, Austria and Hungary, before the war, were semiautonomous parts of the Habsburg Empire and each dominant in its own sphere. Each became a small, relatively weak state. Austria, in particular, was an anomaly, a landlocked state of over six million, of whom two million lived in Vienna. The state was lopsided in every imaginable way, but especially economically. Unfortunately, Austria was not allowed to join Germany for fear that this would unduly strengthen the latter.

The other problem involved creating a series of new or reconstituted states in Eastern Europe and conflicting claims over territory and population. The idea of national self-determination was extremely difficult to apply in this area with any fairness. Czechoslovakia, for example, included areas in which the majority of the population was German or Polish. These areas had been included for strategic reasons, as was the Sudetenland, with its majority of Germans, or for historical reasons, as was Teschen with its Polish majority. Poland included areas with German majorities. Romania and Yugoslavia had large concentrations of Magyars. Numerous other examples could be cited of the impossibility of a simple, fair division of territory according to the principle of national self-determination.

The irony of the settlement in Eastern Europe was that the frontiers established by the treaties and the quarrels arising from them had torn apart what had been an important economic unit. Factories were now in one state, their sources of raw materials in a second, and their traditional markets in a third. That reality contributed to the weakness and instability of the area. It prevented any possibility that the states of Eastern Europe could serve as a proper counterbalance to either a resurgent Germany or the strengthening Soviet Union.

The League of Nations

The Paris Peace Settlement, as mentioned, failed to provide lasting peace. With the benefit of hindsight, we can see that its failure was partly due to an inability to recognize, or perhaps an unwillingness to accept, the new realities of 1919. By the end of the war, the economic and financial center of the world had shifted from Europe to the United States. Pax Britannica ended with the Great War, but no one, least of all Great Britain wanted to admit it. Neither was the United States ready to assume the new responsibilities being thrust upon it.

Wilson fought hard to have the League of Nations[4] made a part of each of the treaties that together comprised the Paris Peace Settlement. The European Allies saw the League as a means to involve the United States in postwar Europe. To secure French support for the League and to soften France's demands for a harsh and punitive treaty with Germany, Wilson agreed to a defensive alliance with Great Britain and France. But the US Senate refused to ratify the Versailles Treaty without alterations to protect United States sovereignty, changes Wilson refused to accept. Therefore, the United States rejected the treaty and with it both membership in the League of Nations and the defensive alliance.

Blame for America's failure to ratify the treaty or join the League is often laid at the feet of Wilson. There can be no doubt that Wilson, at the time suffering the aftereffects of a major stroke, completely mishandled the whole affair back home. But much of the blame must be assigned to the American public. Many Americans felt that participation in the war in Europe had been a mistake. With the war over, most Americans wanted to return to a policy of isolationism (except when it came to collecting war debts), or as the popular slogan of the time put it, "back to normalcy."

The United States turned its back on Europe, but to say that in so doing, it doomed the peace is too severe. Problems arising from the imperfect treaties might have been minimized or entirely avoided if the League of Nations Covenant had been successfully

[4] The full text of the Treaty of Versailles and the League of Nations Covenant is available as a PDF file online at http://foundingdocs.gov.au/resources/transcripts/cth10_doc_1919.pdf.

implemented. The Covenant contained adequate machinery for maintaining peace in the world. It made provisions for an International Court of Justice, submission of disputes to arbitration or to the Council or Assembly of the League, and even using force to resolve conflicts.

Apart from America's refusal to participate, the League was made ineffective by the absence of both Germany (which did join in 1926) and the Soviet Union (which joined in 1934, shortly after Germany left). There were other pertinent factors as well. In the formative period, Britain and France, each having a different idea of how the League should be run, canceled each other out. Later, in the early 1930s, the League failed some crucial tests (e.g., the Italian invasion of Ethiopia), perhaps because the issues involved were not seen as central to European politics.

Given the ineffectiveness of the League, all that was left to maintain the peace was a return to the old-fashioned principle of the balance of power. But that was not possible so long as Soviet Russia remained ostracized and Germany held down by the Versailles Treaty. One of the neglected realities of the 1920s was that Germany was still potentially the most powerful nation on the continent. All it needed was to get out from under the restrictions of the Versailles Treaty.

Europe and the world faced an uncertain future in the spring of 1919, as Germany, bowing before the inevitable, signed the Versailles Treaty. Europe and its relationship with the world had changed, but much of this was ignored. Scattered groups and individuals recognized the changes. Their voices were sometimes heard in the first troubled years of the 1920s, but they were soon overwhelmed by the majority's refusal to acknowledge the full extent of change in Europe.

The punitive Versailles Treaty and the still-born League of Nations as much as guaranteed that another Great War would follow what the French poet Romain Rolland (1866–1944) in June 1919 called a "Sad Peace! Laughable interlude between the massacres of peoples!" One of the most devastating indictments of the Versailles Treaty was *The Economic Consequences of the Peace* (1919), by John Maynard Keynes (1883–1946), a member of the British delegation and one of the most influential economists of the twentieth century:

> If we aim at the impoverishment of Central Europe, vengeance, I dare say, will not limp. Nothing can then delay for very long the forces of Reaction and the despairing convulsions of Revolution, before which the horrors of the later German war will fade into nothing, and which will destroy, whoever is victor, the civilisation and the progress of our generation. ("John Maynard Keynes on the Necessity of a Generous Peace After World War I" 2015)

Perhaps no one provided a better epitaph for the Versailles Treaty than Woodrow Wilson, himself, nearly a year-and-a-half earlier in his "Peace Without Victory" speech before a joint session of Congress on 22 January 1917.

> Victory would mean peace forced upon the loser, a victor's terms imposed upon the vanquished. It would be accepted in humiliation, under duress, at an intolerable sacrifice, and would leave a sting, a resentment, a bitter memory upon which terms of peace would rest, not permanently, but only as upon quicksand. Only a peace between equals can last. ("First World War" 2008)

The greatest tragedy of Woodrow Wilson's career writes Michael Kazin in *War Against War: The American Fight for Peace, 1914–1918* (Baker 2017), was that by leading the United States into the war and thereby ensuring an Allied victory, he "foreclosed the possibility of a negotiated peace," leading to the "punitive peace" of the Versailles Treaty and all that followed (Baker 2017). Unlike the Vienna Peace of 1815, which was hammered out by both the victors and the defeated, determined to draft a just peace that would last, the Paris Peace of 1919 was a dictated peace that merely provided a twenty-year cease-fire.

Ferdinand Foch (1851–1929), Supreme Commander of the Allied Forces during the Great War, commented on 28 June 1919, the day the Versailles Treaty was signed, "This is not a peace. It is an armistice for 20 years." Twenty years, two months, and three days later, on 1 September 1939, German forces invaded Poland, igniting World War II in Europe.

Intellectual and Cultural Legacy of the Great War

The new view of reality destroyed the foundational premise of classical liberalism and democracy, as well as humanism's belief in the innate goodness and rationalism of humankind. The experiences of the Great War, together with the economic crises and social dislocations that followed, and in part resulted from the war, further deepened anxiety over the future. Those who had experienced the "troglodyte world" of trench warfare might well agree with the view that Western civilization was dying.

The French writer Paul Valéry (1871–1945) expressed the disillusionment and despair felt by the postwar intellectuals. The storm that was the Great War had passed, leaving those who survived restless and uneasy, "as if the [next] storm were about to break" and fearful of the future. The damage done to the mind observed by Valéry and other intellectual guardians of civilization cast a shadow over the future.

Paul Bäumer, the main character in what is perhaps the best-known novel of the Great War, *All Quiet on the Western Front* (1929), while visiting a military hospital, reflects on how the war dehumanized the generation that experienced it. The cumulative knowledge of the past, Bäumer concludes, "must be all lies and of no account when the culture of a thousand years could not prevent this stream of blood being poured out..." (*Modern History Sourcebook* 1997). For those who survived the war in the trenches, the knowledge of life is limited to "despair, death, fear, and fatuous superficiality cast over an abyss of sorrow." What can the future hold for a generation whose calling for the past four years has been killing one's fellow human being?

"The war," wrote Ernst von Salomon, a former Freikorps member, "will never discharge them; they will never return home; they will always carry the trenches in their blood" (Salomon, p. 87). How could the soldier of the Great War ever return to life as a civilian and take up once again the daily routine of a peaceful citizen? The war would end for some, but for some veterans, it would never end. The warrior who returned physically and mentally scarred was forever marching, forever haunted by memories that could never be exorcised.

No one better expressed the postwar mood than the German school teacher and philosopher Oswald Spengler (1880–1936). Spengler's *The Decline of the West* (1918–1922) was the most famous postwar prophecy of impending doom. Spengler viewed Western civilization as a living organism that, like any other living organism, must pass through the stages of life from birth to death. The signs of degeneration were everywhere, said Spengler. Western civilization was on its deathbed, its demise unavoidable.

Spengler's ideas were widely spread, especially in Germany, where they were often discussed and cited. Those on the extreme right exploited them by claiming to construct a new order upon the ruins of a dead civilization. The German philosopher Friedrich Nietzsche (1844–1900) prophesied the rise of supermen (übermenschen) who would create new myths to take the place of God, who the advance of civilization had murdered. In a sense, Hitler can be understood as one such "superman," and the Nazi racial state as one such myth. Likewise, Lenin, Stalin, and the Soviet Union may be understood as fulfillments of Nietzsche's prophecy. Other writers used the theme of apocalypse to emphasize the possibility of restoring European civilization from a new Dark Age.

This approach culminated in two remarkable books that appeared at the end of the 1920s: Sigmund Freud's *Civilization and Its Discontents* (1930) and José Ortega y Gasset's (1883–1955) *The Revolt of the Masses* (1930). Both men emphasized that civilization was an artificial product of human effort, maintained only by work and sacrifice. In line with his research before the Great War, Freud stressed the idea that civilization was based on the repression of natural instincts, so one paid a psychic price for living in a civilized society. From his vantage point at the end of the 1920s, Freud saw the failure to maintain civilization as exacting an even higher cost in the long run: the destruction of all human values.

In *The Revolt of the Masses,* Ortega argued that civilization was being eclipsed by a new age of barbarism. The postwar era was witnessing the emergence of a new "mass mentality," "the commonplace mind," one that knows no standard by which to judge the legitimacy of anything, one that demands conformity and the annihilation of all those who refuse to become just like everyone else. There can be no culture where there are no ruling principles or standards by which to define culture. The average individual claims to have ideas, but in reality, what he claims to be ideas are "nothing more than appetites in words…" Ortega's view of the masses was the foundation upon which the new authoritarian dictatorships are based.

The new Bolshevik order in Russia also benefitted from the despair of the postwar years. There too, a Nietzschean prophecy was apparently being fulfilled. The new socialist individual and the Marxist doctrine of progress toward a future utopia on earth attracted many, especially leftist intellectuals, who sought to escape despair by a leap of faith. Many took the pilgrimage to the Soviet Union during the 1930s. Some, like the American journalist Lincoln Steffens (1866–1936), returned convinced that they had been to the future and that it worked. Others, however, like the British journalist and Fabian socialist Malcolm Muggeridge (1903–1990) and the Lithuanian-born anarchist Emma Goldman (1869–1940), came back thoroughly disillusioned. Muggeridge expressed his disillusionment in a novel, *Winter in Moscow*, published in 1934, and Goldman in a memoir not so subtly titled *My Disillusionment in Russia* (1923). The Soviet Union was not an answer to despair but rather a symptom of postwar demoralization.

The fine arts were powerful ideological weapons in constructing a new culture in Nazi Germany, Fascist Italy, and Marxist–Leninist Russia. Hitler, who in his youth wanted to be accepted as an artist, understood how the arts could be the key to unlocking the conscious and subconscious mind and thus further the inner conversion of the individual. Both the visual and performing arts have the power to transform dry ideology into images and myths that move the individual emotionally. Like one who experiences a religious conversion, the newly born-again believer will follow the one who embodies the "gospel" to which he or she has been converted.

Many intellectuals, artists, and writers of various sorts during the 1930s took one side or the other in the great ideological struggle between fascism and communism. The "Auden Generation," for example, included the poets W. H. Auden (1907–1973) and C. Day Lewis (1904–1972); important continental writers such as André Malraux (1901–1976), Ignazio Silone (1900–1978), Arthur Koestler (1905–1983), and artists such as Max Beckmann (1884–1950) and Max Ernst (1891–1976) lent their talents in one fashion or another to the defense of democracy and the criticism of fascism. The support offered to fascism by intellectuals and artists was less substantial. Scattered examples, such as the playwright Gerhart Hauptmann (1862–1946) in Germany or the novelist Louis-Ferdinand Céline (1894–1961) in France comes to mind. Commitment by artists and Intellectuals usually meant a defense of democracy (and often a defense of the socialist democracy of the Soviet Union) and a condemnation of fascism.

The experiences of the Great War also helped promote the careers of the utopian demagogues of the 1930s and 1940s in other ways. Not only were the new discoveries of science and the latest philosophical theories beyond the comprehension of the masses, but so too was the carnage of the war. The social and economic dislocations resulting from the collapse of the old order drove many people to seek answers. It was easy for the new demagogues to direct the resentment of the masses to an identifiable enemy, be it the Jews, capitalists, communists, or simply the establishment. Somewhere, some personified evil force was to blame for the chaos from which it benefitted.

It was also possible to preach the mass extermination of the enemy race or class. The Great War had cheapened life. It left behind images of mass death previously unknown. If millions of lives could be sacrificed to gain a few yards of churned-up earth, did it not make more sense to sacrifice millions of lives to create a classless or racially pure utopia? The Holocaust of Nazi Germany and the "GULAG" of Soviet Russia were, to some extent, conceivable because of the images left by the Great War.

The new worldview taking form even before the Great War emphasized a fragmented view of reality. Many of the purveyors of culture after the Great War developed a technique of fragmentation to fit that new worldview. Art often became a vehicle for the new worldview.

In art, the transition began with the impressionist painters in the 1870s. In the name of "realism," they rebelled against the practice of portraying the world around them with camera-like realism. The impressionists (e.g., Claude Monet [1840–1926], Pierre Auguste Renoir [1841–1919], Camille Pissarro [1830–1903], Alfred Sisley [1839–1899], and Edgar Degas [1834–1917]) emphasized the play of light as they perceived it. In so doing, they abandoned objective reality (portraying the world around them) for a subjective response to the real world. The impressionists asked what was "real," the object, or the artist's mental "impression" of it.

The impressionists were succeeded by a group known as the postimpressionists. They sought reality in the recesses of the mind. Reality was now the observer's (i.e., individual artist's) mental reflections upon the sensory images coming into the mind as light waves. Among the leading postimpressionists were Paul Cézanne (1839–1906), Vincent Van Gogh (1853–1890), Paul Gauguin (1848–1903), and Georges Seurat (1859–1891). By 1910, postimpressionism yielded to abstract art.

The abstract artists abandoned reality. No longer did the artists see their task as simply painting, in any form, the objective world around them. As with the new physics, there was no fixed reality. Reality was what the artist said it was. A painting was not a portrait or even an impression of reality. Instead, it "created" reality. Also, there could no longer be an objective standard by which to judge good or bad art. Art had become a vehicle for the new fragmented worldview.

The message of most artistic movements of the interwar years was one of anarchy, even nihilism. In responding to the disillusionment of war, the Dadaists rejected all order and reason. Believing that the Great War revealed the absurdity of all of life, the Dadaists embraced nihilism. The life span of Dadaism, the first "anti-art art," was brief. Beginning in the mid-teens, it ended in the mid-twenties, when it yielded the field to surrealism. Influenced by Freudianism, surrealism sought reality in the unconscious beyond the reach of reason. Both Dadaism and surrealism were responses to the apparent chaos of the time, but without any hint of an answer.

In the skilled hands of artists like Otto Dix (1891–1969), George Grosz (1893–1959), Pablo Picasso (1881–1973), Max Beckmann, Käthe Kollwitz (1867–1945), and others, the new fragmented techniques were employed to make paintings powerful statements against the insanity of war and the decadence of postwar society and politics. The message that passed through the artist's brush onto the canvas also passed through the poet's or novelist's pen onto the page and thence into the reader's mind. James Joyce (1882–1941) used the literary technique known as "stream of consciousness" in his novel *Ulysses* (1922) to portray a single day in the lives of middle-class Dubliners. In both the title and the style of *The Waste Land* (1922), T. S. Eliot (1888–1965) used a fragmented form of poetry to convey a fragmented message:

> I sat upon the shore
> Fishing, with the arid plain behind me
> Shall I at least set my lands in order?
> London Bridge is falling down falling down falling down
> *Poi s'ascose nel foco che gli affina*
> *Quando fiam uti chelidon*—O swallow swallow
>
> (Eliot 2022)

Joyce and Eliot were among the avant-garde. Interwar literature aimed at mass consumption consisted primarily of realistic novels and accepted poetic styles. The same was true of music and the new art form, the cinema.

Jazz was a peculiarly American contribution to both popular and high culture between the wars. It first appeared as a distinct form of music in New Orleans around the turn of the century, where it was "composed" and performed without written music by African-American street musicians who had no formal training in music. From New Orleans, it spread to Chicago and Harlem. After the war, the "Jazz Age" was born, as white jazz bands began to appear across America and Europe. Jazz music found a home in Paris, one of the two centers of European culture during the 1920s. There, and later in Berlin, the other locus of cultural life in the 1920s, Josephine Baker (1906–1975), an African American from St. Louis delighted audiences by dancing the Charleston, wearing only a string of bananas around her waist, as she sang jazz favorites. The first talking motion picture was *The Jazz Singer*, starring Al Jolson (1927).

Berlin, where "life was a cabaret," was a Mecca for those from all over Europe seeking a decadent lifestyle that included jazz, nightclubs, drugs, liquor, prostitution, and homosexuality. Berlin was also the center of the motion picture industry before the Nazi ascent to power. In Weimar, Germany, film became a serious art form. Pictures like *The Cabinet of Dr. Caligari* (1920) and *The Golem* (1920) merged technique and message to produce works of expressionist art. Perhaps the best-known and perhaps the most significant film produced in Weimar Germany was *The Blue Angel* (1930), starring Marlene Dietrich (1901–1992). Some critics have seen it as an allegory of the triumph of the new (and decadent) Germany over the old. Through their music and atmosphere, *The Blue Angel* and Bertolt Brecht's (1898–1956) stage play, *The Threepenny Opera*, captured the mood of Weimar Germany's cultural life. The *Threepenny Opera* premiered at the Schiffbauerdamm Theater in Berlin with a musical score influenced by jazz and composed by Kurt Weill (1900–1950).

It was in the 1920s, especially the last half of the decade, that one could begin to speak of a "popular culture" as distinct from "high culture." Of course, the popular culture of postwar Europe had its roots in the last half of the nineteenth century. But it was in the 1920s that it developed into what we know today. Initially the property of the working classes, popular culture had become by the late 1920s largely a matter of entertainment, recreation, fashions, and fads which, for a short time, might bind people from different social backgrounds together and blur the still significant differences that existed.

Whether good or bad, popular culture in the affluent and vital late 1920s developed most of the attributes familiar in today's society. Entertainment became increasingly commercialized and built on changing fashions. New songs, new dance steps, and new movie stars followed one another at an accelerating pace. The growth of spectator sports was only one example of the trend toward passive involvement in culture. In all areas of entertainment, the lowest common denominator was sought in order to attract as wide an audience as possible.

The masses were the passive consumers of culture during the interwar years. The consequences of the new worldview, which preoccupied the scientists and philosophers and found anguished expression in the creative works of the artists and poets, did not immediately affect the masses. It was not until after World War II that the assumptions of the new world view (in the form of, e.g., existentialism) would filter down to the masses through the mass media. Catalyzed again by war and economic dislocations, they would find violent expression during the 1960s and 1970s before giving way in the last quarter of the century to an individual quest for personal peace and affluence, one troubled still by a vague feeling of anxiety.

The end of the Great War did not open the way to a better future. The victorious European Allies did not share Woodrow Wilson's idealistic vision of a new world order. They saw in the war's outcome an opportunity to strengthen their positions in Europe by taking advantage of the defeated Central Powers. Neither Wilson nor the British and French leaders had foreseen the Russian Revolution and how fear of its spread would impact international relations in the future. Imperialism survived the war. The British and French divided the former German colonies and agreed to exploit the former Ottoman Empire's Middle Eastern territories mutually. The League of Nations meant to guarantee a better future, proved wholly ineffective. The end of the war that many hoped was a war to end war proved to be only a cease-fire.

References

Baker, Kevin. (2017). "The War to Stay out of the War against War". *The New York Times* (4 January). https://www.nytimes.com/2017/01/04/books/review/war-against-war-michael-kazin.html (accessed 28 July 2022).

"David Lloyd George Biography." (n.d.). Biography Online. https://www.biographyonline.net/politicians/uk/lloyd-george.html (accessed 20 November 2021).

Eliot, T. S. (2022). "The Waste Land by T. S. Eliot." Poetry Foundation. https://www.poetryfoundation.org/poems/47311/the-waste-land (accessed 30 July 2022).

"First World War: Extract from Woodrow Wilson's Speech to the American Senate on 22 January 1917." (2008). *The Guardian* (14 November). https://www.theguardian.com/world/2008/nov/14/woodrow-wilson-senate-address-1917 (accessed 22 November 2021).

History Learning Site. (1918). "Woodrow Wilson's Fourteen Points." (1918). History Learning Site. http://www.historylearningsite.co.uk/woodrow_wilson1.htm (accessed 31 October 2023).

"John Maynard Keynes on the Necessity of a Generous Peace after World War I." (26 May 2015). Equitable Growth. Washington Center for Equitable Growth. https://equitablegrowth.org/john-maynard-keynes-necessity-generous-peace-world-war/ (accessed 22 November 2021).

Taylor, A. J. P. (1966). *A History of the First World War*. New York: Berkley Publishing Corp.

Part 2

Overview: 1919–1945

Europeans who might have hoped the end of the Great War would lead to a revival of the world of 1914 were deeply disappointed. The reality was Europe after the war was already very different from prewar Europe. The old empires had vanished and in their place were newly proclaimed republics struggling to survive in a hostile environment. Almost everywhere communist parties championed an alternative to both the old order and the new liberal idealism of Woodrow Wilson and his supporters.

In all of the former great powers, there were signs of serious trouble ahead. Great Britain, perhaps the foremost great power in 1914, suffered from the economic impact of the war. France, a so-called victor in the war, was fragmented and politically confused. Germany, a key player in any process of recovery in Europe, was a republic with no republicans. Burdened by the harsh terms of the Versailles Treaty and dependent on anti-republican forces for survival, the Weimar Republic faced what seemed a grim future. Italy, although one of the victors in the war, suffered from injured national pride as well as economic and social problems. In the Soviet Union, a new style of authoritarian government was developing, one that eventually would present a serious challenge

Twentieth-Century Europe: 1900 to the Present, Fourth Edition.
Michael D. Richards and Paul R. Waibel.

to the historic values of Western civilization for the remainder of the century.

Overlaying the political and economic problems was a pervasive disillusionment and intellectual uncertainty that called into question the very foundations of European civilization. A generation that had experienced four years of trench warfare found it difficult to continue to believe in a rational order of the universe. How could the Great War have happened? Was it a failure of diplomacy or a chance event in a universe of random chaos? Novel theories emerged to explain the human predicament, and prophets waited in the wings, as Friedrich Nietzsche had predicted, to offer new myths for the birth of new orders.

Nonetheless, by 1925, there were hopeful signs for the future. The Dawes Plan in 1924 dealt with the reparations issue in such a way as to stimulate economic recovery in Germany and elsewhere in Western Europe. The Locarno Treaties in 1925 seemed to herald an era of rapprochement between Germany and France. Many Europeans began to believe that lasting peace was, after all, possible. All too soon, however, the Great Depression, originating in the United States, ended the new prosperity and optimism.

The Great Depression changed everything. It discredited political and economic liberalism, especially for the middle class which had been a traditional bastion of the liberal order. Liberal governments failed to deal effectively with the high rates of unemployment, creating grave doubts among the working class. They, even more than the middle class, began to look for alternatives to liberalism.

Economic crisis created political crisis in most parts of Europe. The Weimar Republic fell apart in the early 1930s, creating an opening for Adolf Hitler and the Nazi Party to come to power. Hitler, like Joseph Stalin in the Soviet Union, constructed a new authoritarian dictatorship that differed not only from liberalism but also from traditional conservative dictatorships. Where the traditional conservative dictatorship sought merely to maintain the status quo, the new authoritarian dictatorship wanted to bring about a new ideological order.

By the late 1930s, the Depression was overshadowed by the imminent threat of another world war. Efforts to prevent this were scattered and unsuccessful. The League of Nations failed utterly. Britain and France made efforts, but even with the Soviet Union seeming to offer its support, Britain and France accepted empty promises at the Munich Conference in 1938 and allowed Hitler to destroy Czechoslovakia, setting the stage for the beginnings of World War II the following year.

World War II was a global war, involving eventually the United States, Japan, and China among others. It was, in effect, a war of empires, the old empires of Great Britain, France, and the United States, and the challengers, Nazi Germany and Japan. The Soviet Union, while not a traditional empire, created a different kind of empire in the course of the war. The result of the war was the completion of Europe's descent from its dominant position and the emergence of two new great powers, the Soviet Union and the United States.

Barbarism on the one hand and technical brilliance on the other marked World War II. The Manhattan Project, the Anglo-American effort to construct an atomic bomb, reflected both facets. Building the bomb required assembling gifted scientists and coordinating their work. Using the bomb on civilian populations, although probably a factor in the Japanese decision to surrender, horrified large segments of the world population.

The Holocaust, the systematic killing of millions by the Nazis, an attempt at genocide, caused many to wonder if European civilization had not completely lost its bearings. There was no military justification for the Final Solution. If anything, it ran counter to efforts by the Nazis to win the war. What was additionally chilling is that it was carried out in a methodical and businesslike manner. The fact that the Holocaust originated in Germany, seemingly the most civilized of European countries, was particularly disturbing. Was this the result of a *Sonderweg*, a special historical path, or was it something that any nation might be capable of doing?

Other aspects of the war offered hope. Advances made originally for military purposes in such areas as medicine and communications could be transferred to civilian life. During the war, many people began to see the need for social and economic change that would provide a better life for the average person. Finally, there was also a determination to establish an international system to prevent future wars and to coordinate efforts to solve common problems.

At the end of the war, Europe, badly damaged economically and spiritually and politically fragmented, faced a world in which two immensely powerful nations, the Soviet Union and the United States held the keys to the future.

4

Recovery and Prosperity, 1919–1929

Chronology

1919	German National Assembly drafts the Weimar Constitution
1920	"Kapp Putsch" led by Wolfgang Kapp
1921	Russian Civil War ends
	Lenin introduces the New Economic Policy (NEP)

Twentieth-Century Europe: 1900 to the Present, Fourth Edition.
Michael D. Richards and Paul R. Waibel.

1922	Washington Naval Conference
	Rapallo Treaty between Germany and the Soviet Union
	Mussolini's so-called March on Rome
1923	"Beer Hall (Munich) Putsch" led by Adolf Hitler
	Ruhr occupation (June 1923–August 1924) triggers Great Inflation in Germany
1924	Lenin dies; power struggle between Leon Trotsky and Joseph Stalin
	Stalin proclaims the possibility of "Socialism in One Country"
1925	Locarno treaties between Germany, France, and Belgium
1926	General Strike in Great Britain
1928	Kellogg–Briand Pact
1929	Joseph Stalin succeeds Lenin as the leader of the Soviet Union
	Lateran Accord between Italy and the Papacy

The Europe that emerged from the Great War was very different than Europe in its golden age before the war. All of the European powers that entered the war did so believing they were under attack or threat of attack. What might be called "war aims" were formulated only later when the cost of the war had become so great that only victory was acceptable. Those who went to war in 1914 or 1915 no doubt foresaw the war ending like wars in the past. The relative power of the belligerents would change, and territorial adjustments would be made, but Europe's old aristocratic order would continue unchanged. The entry of the United States on the Allies' side and the Bolshevik Revolution in Russia, both in 1917, changed the outcome of the war. The old order was exhausted, and both President Woodrow Wilson and Vladimir Lenin, leader of the Soviet Union, were determined to see a new and more just political and social order replace the old order of privilege.

Both the victors and the defeated European powers were devastated by the war. Their economies were disorganized, and their populations were traumatized. Even the United States, the only country to benefit from its participation in the Great War, could not escape all of its ill effects. What most people desired more than anything else was a return to life as it was before August 1914. It was a longing that found expression in slogans like "back to normalcy" and "a fit country for heroes." They wanted to reconstruct their lives. They wanted to look forward to a better future, one that included peace and security for everyone. Above all else, they desired never again to experience the nightmare of 1914–1918. However, for some veterans and civilians, the nightmare would never end.

The two most striking outcomes of the Great War were, first, the passing of the antique empires of Germany, Russia, Austria-Hungary, and the Ottoman Empire. The second was the new role of the United States of America as a necessary but reluctant participant on the international stage. The economic health of the European nations was subsequently tied to the health of the American economy. Recovery and future prosperity depended upon the domestic and foreign policies of the United States in this new "American century."

Wilson's vision appeared to make gains during the first decade following the war. In 1914, there were 17 monarchies and three republics; in 1919, there were 13 monarchies and 13 republics. Germany, Austria, Hungary, Czechoslovakia, and Turkey were proclaimed republics. In Russia, the autocratic rule of the Tsar was replaced by what Lenin called "democratic centralism," a Soviet republic that soon revealed itself to be even more autocratic than tsarist Russia.

The territorial redistribution in Eastern Europe resulted in the new nations of Finland, Estonia, Latvia, Lithuania, Poland, Czechoslovakia, Yugoslavia, and Albania, and altered borders for Austria, Hungary, Romania, Bulgaria, Greece, and Turkey. The new map of Europe did not, however, reflect the two noble goals of President Wilson: national self-determination and governments that represented the will of the people in assemblies freely elected by the people, with written constitutions that defined the limits and responsibilities of governmental power.

A constitutional and parliamentary government, republican more often than monarchical, was the norm in much of Europe by the mid-1920s. Universal male suffrage was generally accepted. On the continent, socialist parties had to face the question of active participation in government. In Germany, the Social Democratic Party (SPD) formed a significant component of the coalition government, whereas, in France, the Socialists backed away from full participation. Everywhere the centrist parties formed the backbone of the ministries.

Women after the War

Before the war, women could vote only in Finland (1906) and Norway (1913). In 1918, Britain gave the vote to women over 30. In 1928, all women in Britain received the vote. Weimar Germany, Poland, Czechoslovakia, Austria, the Low Countries, and Scandinavia also enfranchised women after the war. Unfortunately, gaining the vote did not in most cases lead to greater participation in politics by women or increased attention to women's issues. And, although women had proved capable of handling jobs traditionally held by men during the war, they mostly went back to those occupations traditionally held by women after the war and to raising families in the postwar period.

Signs of International Cooperation

There were several examples of cooperation in international relations during the 1920s. In 1922, the Washington Naval Conference made progress toward limiting the size of navies among the five postwar great powers. Some 70 ships were scrapped; a 10-year moratorium on the construction of any new battleships was declared; and the five signatories agreed to limit the tonnage of capital ships to a ratio of: 5, Great Britain; 3, United States; 1.75, Japan; 1.75, France; 1.75, Italy. In April 1922, Germany and Soviet Russia signed the Rapallo Treaty, by which they reestablished diplomatic relations, renounced all financial claims against each other, and pledged cooperation. It initiated five years of close collaboration between the two ostracized powers. Also, in 1922, the "Little Entente" of Czechoslovakia, Yugoslavia, and Romania was formed under French auspices to dampen the fears of both France and the East European successor states of a revived Germany.

Perhaps the most promising development was the Locarno treaties concluded in December 1925. In the principal treaty signed by France, Belgium, and Germany and guaranteed by Great Britain and Italy, Germany accepted as final its western borders with France and Belgium as fixed by the Versailles Treaty. The inviolability of the demilitarized Rhineland was also confirmed. The Locarno treaties were the work of German Foreign Minister Gustav Stresemann (1878–1929), French Foreign Minister Aristide Briand, and British Foreign Secretary Austen Chamberlain (1863–1937). All three men were committed to international cooperation based upon the fulfillment of the Versailles Treaty. A new spirit of conciliation swept through Europe in the wake of the Locarno agreements. The fact, however, that Germany specifically refused to accept its eastern borders as permanent should have cast a shadow over the "spirit of Locarno."

Perhaps the best expression of the widespread optimism engendered by the spirit of Locarno was the Kellogg–Briand Pact of 1928, which outlawed war as an instrument of national policy. It was proposed to US Secretary of State Frank B. Kellogg (1856–1937) and Briand and subsequently signed by 64 nations. The Kellogg–Briand Pact had more immediate significance because Germany and the two leading non-League members—the United States and the Soviet Union—signed it. As the following decade was to demonstrate, however, outlawing war and calling for peaceful resolution of international disputes while not providing any means for enforcement was only a pious gesture or, as one US senator put it, an "international kiss." In 1928, spirits were high amidst economic prosperity and international conciliation. No one could see the Great Depression waiting ominously in the wings to shatter the illusion. A closer look inside the European powers during the 1920s reveals disturbing signs of future distress.

Great Britain

On the eve of the Great War, three major problems had threatened to overwhelm the British government: (1) the question of Irish home rule, (2) the vote for women, and (3) a broad-based dissatisfaction among workers. The first two issues were resolved at the war's end, although not to everyone's complete satisfaction. Agreements in 1920 and 1921 resulted in the division of Ireland into Northern Ireland, which remained attached to Great Britain as an autonomous area, and the Irish Free State, which gained Dominion status. It was a far-from-definitive solution that essentially removed the Irish problem from British politics for the first time in over a century. The second issue was resolved when women over 30 were given the vote in 1918.

The third issue was more intractable. Great Britain's problems between the wars were rooted in the economic impact of the Great War. As an island nation with an empire upon which the sun never set, British prosperity and British influence depended upon foreign trade. But Britain's dominant position in world trade was severely shaken by the war. Many reliable trading partners developed their industries, reduced imports, or established new trade relations with other nations (e.g., the United States and Japan). Still, others were too impoverished by the war to continue as major trading partners. An example of the latter was Germany, Britain's leading continental trading partner before 1914. At the same time, the cost of the war had increased the national debt by about 1,000 percent. During the course of the war, Britain had exchanged its creditor position for that of a debtor.

In some crucial ways, Britain had become less competitive industrially. It did not participate to the same extent as Germany in the rapid development of electrical and chemical industries. A large part of its industrial base consisted of the older coal, iron, steel, textiles, and shipbuilding industries. In these labor-intensive industries, Britain had lost the competitive edge. When in 1925, the Exchequer put Britain back on the gold standard, the problem was only exacerbated. British goods became too expensive, resulting in decreased exports. The "invisible exports" (e.g., income from shipping and foreign investments) offset the losses for a while. But the decrease in exports hit those traditional industries that employed large numbers of workers especially hard. The result was chronic unemployment of at least one, often two or more, million persons during the 1920s.

Chronic unemployment led to frequent strikes culminating in the General Strike of 3–12 May 1926. The broader labor conflict began with a strike by the coal miners. The miners' wages had dropped by one-third in the previous seven years. Mine owners suffered from Germany's providing "free" coal to France as reparations, a part of the Dawes Plan (1924) that helped assure reparations would be paid, and the Ruhr occupation ended. Britain's return to the gold standard in 1925 contributed to the mine owners' problems by inhibiting exports and raising interest rates.

In solidarity with the miners, the Trades Union Congress (TUC) called for a general strike, which most of Britain's organized labor heeded. At its peak on 4 May, more than 1.5 million workers were out on strike. The Conservative-led government of Stanley Baldwin (1867–1947) saw the general strike as a threat to the very principles upon which parliamentary government rested, which could lead to anarchy. Leaders of the Labour Party began to fear that the radical elements among the unions threatened to derail the party's growing acceptance in the public's eyes as a legitimate alternative to the Conservative Party. On 11 May, the Chancery Division of the High Court ruled that the General Strike was not protected by the Trade Disputes Act of 1906, thus opening the way for employers to seize the unions' assets. The unions capitulated the following day, ending the strike without achieving their goals.

The dominant theme in British politics during the 1920s was the decline of the Liberal Party and the rise of the Labour Party amidst a generally conservative political mood among voters. Until 1922, the Liberal Party governed with the support of the Conservatives. In the parliamentary elections of 1922, Labour emerged for the first time as "His Majesty's Loyal Opposition." Twice during the 1920s, the Labour Party led a minority government headed by Ramsay MacDonald (1866–1937) and supported by the Liberals. The Labour Party did not attempt anything radical during their first term in office from January to October 1924 or during their second term from May 1929 to August 1931. Instead, by governing very timidly, primarily in line with the policies set by the Conservatives, the Labour Party earned respect among middle-class voters, the key to becoming the standard alternative to the Conservatives. The Labor government's boldest action was establishing diplomatic relations with the Soviet Union.

The Conservatives, with their belief in deflation, strict economy in government spending, and a passive foreign policy, best represented the mood of most British voters during the 1920s.

France

During the 1920s, France was preoccupied with Germany due to economic and security considerations. France had suffered greater proportional losses than any other country in the Great War. Northeast France had been a battlefield for almost four years. Much of the nation's prewar industry was devastated. It borrowed heavily to rebuild the war-ravaged areas. Plagued with inflation, a rising national debt, and an unbalanced budget, the French looked to war reparations from Germany for financial relief.

The hard line toward Germany also seemed necessary because of France's feelings of insecurity. When the United States and Great Britain refused to ratify the defensive alliance with France, the French were left to fend for themselves. Thus, France adopted an uncompromising attitude toward Germany, determined to keep Germany weak and isolated. At the same time, it sought to replace the old prewar Franco-Russian alliance with alliances with the new Eastern European states (e.g., the Little Entente in 1922). It was a dangerously shortsighted policy that could only hope to succeed so long as both Germany and the Soviet Union remained prostrate.

The political situation in France remained confused and unstable during the 1920s. The Socialist Party split in 1920 into the French Communist Party, affiliated with the Communist International (Comintern), and the Socialist Party. In May 1924, the Left Cartel, a coalition of Socialists and Radicals, assumed government control from the National Bloc, a coalition of centrist and rightist parties. The Socialists and Radicals disagreed on how to deal with the troubled economy. Between April 1925 and June 1926, six cabinets came and went as Socialists and Radicals remained deadlocked.

In July 1926, Raymond Poincaré (1860–1934) returned to power at the head of a National Union ministry that governed France until July 1929. With the support of the Radicals and the centrist and rightist parties, Poincaré pursued a conservative economic policy. Poincaré had headed the government between 1922 and 1924 when France (together with Belgium) occupied the Ruhr industrial district of Germany, with disastrous results for the Weimar Republic and France. Between 1926 and 1929, however, Poincaré's conservative policies restored financial stability in France.

In 1928, France went on the international gold standard with the franc worth about one-fifth its prewar value (as opposed to one-tenth at its low point two years before). The devaluation of the franc was a disguised repudiation of much of the national debt, which had been contracted in terms of the prewar franc. It was a brutal blow for many in the middle classes, the value of whose savings and investments were undermined. The determination grew never to allow the franc to be touched again. Devaluation brought financial stability, however, and "normalcy" to France. Mainly because of Poincaré's measures, France was better prepared than most European countries for the worldwide economic difficulties beginning in 1929.

Weimar Germany

In January 1919, while Berlin was in revolution, German voters elected a National Assembly to draft a constitution. Because the delegates to the constitutional convention met in the town of Weimar, the German Republic became known as the Weimar Republic. The National Assembly chose as president Friedrich Ebert, the leader of the SPD and former saddle maker, bartender, journalist, and party bureaucrat. The constitution drafted at Weimar was the very model of a democratic constitution. However, two aspects of the constitution proved fatal for the Republic. Article 48 allowed the president to rule by decree during times of national emergency. Also, the lower house of the *Reichstag* was to be elected by universal suffrage, but according to a system of proportional representation, resulting in a plurality of parties that made it virtually impossible for any one party to achieve a majority. Indeed, during the Republic's life, no party gained a majority.

The survival of the Republic became dependent upon the cooperation of the so-called Weimar parties—the SPD, Catholic

Center Party (Z, or Zentrum), and German Democratic Party (DDP). These parties were ideologically incompatible but willing to collaborate because the alternative was too frightening to contemplate. Significant differences of opinion on both economic and political questions were merely papered over. Most Germans did not prefer the Republic and even associated it with defeat and betrayal. The traditional elites of the army, judiciary, bureaucracy, church, and landed and industrial wealth remained openly hostile. Symptomatic of German feeling toward the Republic was the election in 1925 of Paul von Hindenburg, war hero and supporter of the monarchy, as president, following the death of Ebert.

One way in which the threat from the right saw expression was in the form of attempted coups in 1920 and 1923. On 13 March 1920, Wolfgang Kapp (1858–1922) tried to seize power in Berlin in what became known as the Kapp Putsch (a carefully plotted, sudden attempt to overthrow the government). Kapp was an extreme nationalist who, together with Alfred von Tirpitz (1897–1916), grand admiral and commander of the German navy between 1911 and 1916, founded the Fatherland Party in September 1917 in an effort to revive the "spirit of 1914" and snatch victory from impending defeat in the Great War. The Fatherland Party was dissolved in December 1918. In 1919, Kapp joined General Ludendorff and other extreme nationalists in the National Union. The National Union campaigned for a counterrevolution to overthrow the Weimar Republic and establish a conservative militaristic government. Kapp joined the conservative National People's Party and was elected to the *Reichstag* in 1919. He blamed socialists, communists, and Jews for Germany's defeat.

The attempted coup began on the morning of 12 March, when a group from the *Freikorps*[1] known as the Ehrhardt Brigade occupied Berlin. The army and Freikorps had cooperated when it came to suppressing the Spartacus revolt in January 1919 or any other communist uprising, but they were not quick to defend the Republic from threats from the right. Kapp, supported by Ludendorff, proclaimed himself chancellor. The government left Berlin and

[1] The Freikorps in the post-WWI era were mostly veterans of WWI organized as paramilitary militias and were used against coups the German Communist Party attempted.

called upon the army to suppress the coup. General Hans von Seeckt (1866–1936), chief of staff of the army, declined the government's command. "German soldiers do not fire on German soldiers," he replied.

Kapp and his followers did not have the support of the citizens of Berlin. The bureaucrats did not obey Kapp's orders and kept the official state seal from Kapp, thus leaving him without the authority to withdraw funds from the Reichsbank or conduct any official state business. He did issue a couple of decrees, including one to confiscate supplies of matzo flour needed for the upcoming Jewish holidays. The SPD called for a general strike. For four days, Berlin was at a standstill. Unable to govern, Kapp "resigned" and went to Sweden. The Ehrhardt Brigade marched out of Berlin, but not before firing a volley directly into a crowd of spectators.

The attempt by Adolf Hitler (1889–1945) to seize control of the government in Munich, on 8–9 November 1923, preliminary to a "march on Berlin," also came from the right. The National Socialist German Workers Party (NSDAP or Nazi) was a minor right-wing party based in Bavaria in 1923. Bavaria was governed by a triumvirate led by Gustav von Kahr (1862–1934). There was widespread support for separation from Germany in Bavaria. Kahr organized a meeting of Bavarian nationalists for the evening of 8 November at the Bürgerbräukeller, a large beer hall in Munich. Kahr and his supporters intended for Kahr to make a speech to announce Bavaria's secession from Germany. Bavaria was once again to become an independent state.

When Kahr was only minutes into his speech, Hitler suddenly jumped onto a chair, fired two shots into the ceiling, and announced that he was forming a national government. Armed Nazis took control of the crowd. The following day, Hitler, joined by General Ludendorff, led a march down Ludwigstrasse in the direction of the Feldherrnhalle, a mid-nineteenth-century monument honoring the Bavarian army. Hitler had envisioned the affair as the beginning of a Mussolini-style "march on Berlin," but before long, the group was confronted by a cordon of armed Bavarian police who fired on them. Eighteen individuals, fourteen demonstrators, and four policemen were killed. Hitler fled the scene and was later arrested. Only Ludendorff continued the march, walking unopposed through the police cordon. He, too, was later arrested.

Ludendorff and Hitler were both tried for treason. Ludendorff was acquitted, and Hitler was sentenced to five years of imprisonment, of which he served only nine months. The failure of the Kapp Putsch and Hitler's "Beer Hall Putsch," separatist revolts in the Rhineland, and communist revolts in Saxony and Thuringia indicated a relative lack of strength among extremist groups in 1923. A more significant threat to the stability of the Republic was the hyperinflation caused by the Franco-Belgian occupation of the heartland of German industry, the Ruhr.

War reparations were the main sticking point in Franco-German relations and the foremost issue in German domestic politics in the early 1920s. France believed that Germany could pay enough in reparations to finance the reconstruction of France and other costs related to the war. The Germans doubted this. In January 1923, the French and the Belgians occupied the Ruhr to force Germany to pay. The German government encouraged a program of passive resistance, which it tried to finance by printing more and more money.

Money lost all, or nearly all, its value during the Great Inflation. Bailes of paper currency became "... paper for pulping." Chronicle / Alamy Stock Photo.

The currency quickly lost all value other than the value of the paper for pulping.

In July 1914, one US dollar was worth 4.2 marks. In January 1919, one US dollar would purchase 8.9 marks. When the Ruhr occupation began in January 1923, the figure had risen to 17,972 marks, an unbelievable sum. Still, it was nothing compared to the 4.2 trillion marks that a single US dollar would bring on 15 November 1923 (Table 4.1). Examples of inflation are numerous. One university student recalled ordering a cup of coffee listed on the menu for 5,000 marks. When he finished the first cup, he ordered a second. After drinking the second cup, the price of two cups of coffee had risen to 14,000 marks. Factory workers and teachers were paid daily at 11 A.M., the very hour that the banks closed for the day. A worker described payday at a factory:

> At 11:00 in the morning a siren sounded, and everybody gathered in the factory forecourt, where a five-ton lorry was drawn up loaded brimful with paper money. The chief cashier and his assistants climbed up on top. They read out names and just threw out bundles of notes. As soon as you had caught one you made a dash for the nearest shop and bought just anything that was going (Public Broadcasting System 2013).

The material impact was significant; the psychological shock was even greater. The middle class, whose financial base was wiped out, was the hardest hit. The American author Pearl S. Buck (1892–1973)

Table 4.1 Inflation in Weimar Germany

1914	\$1 = 4.20 marks
1919 (Jul.)	\$1 = 14.00 marks
1921 (Jan.)	\$1 = 64.90 marks
1922 (Jan.)	\$1 = 191.80 marks
1922 (Jul.)	\$1 = 493.20 marks
1923 (Jan.)	\$1 = 17,972.00 marks
1923 (Sept.)	\$1 = 100 million marks
1923 (Oct.)	\$1 = 1 trillion marks
1923 (Nov.)	\$1 = 4.2 trillion marks

was in Germany in 1923. She wrote later of how the German people were dazed, confused, wondering how such a thing could happen. "Yet they had lost their self-assurance," she remembered, "their feeling that they themselves could be the masters of their own lives if only they worked hard enough; and lost, too, were the old values of morals, of ethics, of decency" (Public Broadcasting System 2013). How could such a thing happen? Many began turning to the rightist parties for an explanation and a solution.

Finally, the government was reorganized under the leadership of Gustav Stresemann from the German People's Party (DVP). Stresemann, who served as foreign minister from 1923 until his death in 1929, carried through a policy of "fulfillment" concerning reparations. A new mark, the Rentenmark, was issued at the rate of one new mark for one trillion of the old inflated marks. Soon the mark stabilized at its old prewar value of 4.2 marks to the dollar.[2]

"Fulfillment" was based on the assumption that the surest route to revising the Versailles Treaty was to avoid open confrontation and work with existing possibilities. Positive results were not long in coming. In 1924, the Dawes Plan provided a realistic scale for the payment of reparations and a foreign loan (supplied mainly by American banks) of 800 million gold marks. Together with the end of the Ruhr occupation, these measures enabled the German economy to recover rapidly. By 1928, German industrial production was second only to the United States, and unemployment was reduced to 650,000.

In contrast to its early years of strife and turmoil, the Weimar Republic passed the last half of the decade in relative tranquility. Following his attempted putsch, Hitler spent his time in prison writing his political creed, *Mein Kampf* (1925). After his release, he rebuilt the Nazi Party to make it stronger organizationally and more intensely loyal to him personally. Yet, Hitler could not make much headway in the late 1920s. He was the best-known figure of the extreme right but not a significant politician until he cooperated

[2] The fact that much of the positive diplomacy of the 1920s was the result of the personal relationship between Stresemann and Briand made Stresemann's death all the more tragic.

with the German National People's Party (DNVP) in the 1929 referendum on the Young Plan for the reorganization of reparations. This move brought him into national prominence. The DNVP, based on the hostility of the prominent aristocratic landowners and some industrialists toward the Weimar Republic, seemed a much more substantial threat to the Republic than any group on the extreme right.

Nonetheless, the principal danger to the Republic in the late 1920s lay not without but within. The army had achieved a position of almost complete autonomy. It was even more isolated from the mainstream of life in the Weimar Republic than the imperial army had been before the Great War. The civil service remained composed mainly of technically competent but uncommitted people. Some were actively disloyal to the Republic. Business interests combined and organized to the point where they possessed enormous powers that the government could not begin to control. The 1925 election of Paul von Hindenburg as president, a man unsympathetic to parliamentary control of the government, created another problem for the Republic. A republic with such a president and so many groups antagonistic toward it could hope only to survive if it avoided the necessity of dealing with serious problems.

Italy

Although Italy was on the winning side in the Great War, its military performance was less than impressive. The peace conference awarded Italy much less than it felt entitled to by the Treaty of London (1915) between Italy and the Triple Entente. The secret treaty promised Italy territory along the Aegean Sea that was part of the Austro-Hungarian Empire in exchange for Italy declaring war against Germany and Austria-Hungary. Economic and social problems exacerbated injured national pride. The aftereffects of the war included a massive national debt, rapid inflation, and increasing unemployment. Between 1919 and 1921, angry workers and peasants began occupying factories and land. Italy appeared to some Italians on the verge of a "Bolshevik" Revolution.

The political system offered little hope for the future. The two largest parties, the Socialists and the Catholic *Popolari*, were each deeply divided. In 1921, the Socialist Party split into socialist and communist factions. The *Popolari* remained united in its support of the Catholic Church but divided over economic and social issues. Neither the Socialists nor the *Popolari* could govern alone or imagine governing with the other. The smaller Liberal and Radical parties could not deal with the political and social crisis of 1919–1922, even when they possessed a working majority in the parliament.

Into this confused situation stepped the small Fascist Party, formed in 1921 by Benito Mussolini (1883–1945), a former school teacher and former editor of the Socialist Party's newspaper, *Avanti*. Mussolini was expelled from the Socialist Party in 1914 when he called for Italy's entry into the war on the Allies' side. As the leader of the Fascist Party, he denounced Marxism and liberal democracy while vaguely talking of social and economic reform.

From the beginning, Italian Fascism lacked any coherent doctrine or concrete reform program. Instead, the emphasis was on action. It was a mass movement akin to a religious revival. Like both National Socialism (Nazism) and Marxism–Leninism, it claimed to abolish class distinctions and fuse the masses into an organic whole. Once asked to describe the kind of order he was attempting to establish in Italy, Mussolini coined the term "totalitarianism." However, it must be noted that Mussolini never achieved such total control in Italy. Italian Fascism was a mix of ideas drawn from Friedrich Nietzsche, Georges Sorel, Henri Bergson, and other pre-1914 intellectuals, dynamic and romantic.

Mussolini organized a Fascist Party militia, the Blackshirts, to terrorize peasants, organized labor, socialists, and communists alike. While much of the disorder caused by workers and peasants ended by 1921, the Fascists became the actual source of most of the continuing unrest during 1921. They were perceived by many, though, as saving Italy from Bolshevism.

Matters came to a head in October 1922. Mussolini demanded the formation of a Fascist cabinet. The premier refused and wanted to declare martial law. King Victor Emmanuel III (1869–1947) would not consent to martial law, evidently fearing the power of the Fascists and also believing that the Fascists might govern responsibly if given the opportunity. The premier resigned, and Mussolini was asked to form a government. The Fascists' threatened "March on Rome" turned out to be only a train ride into the capital for Mussolini and some of his colleagues.

During the next few years, Mussolini and the Fascists moved slowly to gain government control. The elections of 1924, held according to the 1923 Acerbo election law, which gave the party with the largest number of votes two-thirds of the seats, provided the Fascists an overwhelming position in the Chamber of Deputies. However, it was not until the murder in 1924 of Giacomo Matteotti (1885–1924), a socialist deputy who had strongly criticized the Fascists, that the party broke decisively with parliamentary constitutional government. Shortly after the murder, most of the non-Fascist minority of the chamber left in the Aventine Secession. They were not allowed to return. The Fascists took control of both houses of parliament.

Mussolini dreamed of creating a corporate state at home and a new Roman Empire in the Mediterranean. According to theory, the corporate state harmonizes capitalism and socialism through a system of corporations (22 in Fascist Italy), each of which had councils of employers and workers. Strikes by workers or lockouts by employers were forbidden. Ideally, labor and management worked together to resolve disputes, set wages, determine working conditions, and set production levels. Although a National Council of Corporations was established to make policy, the corporate state was a fraud. All decision-making remained firmly in the hands of the government, which favored the interests of the industrialists over those of the workers.

Neither Mussolini's domestic nor foreign policy was successful. Eventually, Mussolini's belligerent but largely unsuccessful foreign policy drew Italy into a fatal alliance with Hitler's Germany. The only real success he enjoyed in either area was the Lateran Accord of February 1929, which resolved the "Roman Question" that had plagued Italy since the Kingdom of Italy seized Rome in 1870. According to the agreement, Italy paid financial damages to the Catholic Church, recognized the Vatican City as a sovereign state ruled by the pope, Roman Catholicism as the state religion, church marriages, and approved compulsory instruction in the Catholic faith in the nation's schools. In return, the state received the right to veto the appointment of Italian bishops. Perhaps most importantly, the church agreed to refrain from involvement in politics. With the Lateran Accord, Mussolini effectively neutralized what was potentially the most effective opposition to Fascism. For Pope Pius XI (1857–1939), the Lateran Accord regularized the position of the Catholic Church in Italy and gave Catholicism the kind of independent status required by an international movement. Defenders of the Accord in the 1930s could point to the substantive differences between Fascist Italy and Nazi Germany over racial policy. The introduction of racial laws in Italy in 1938 and Nazi Germany's persecution of its Jewish population in the 1930s led Pius XI to mount challenges before his death in 1939. (See Chapter 5 for more discussion of the Papacy and its relations with Fascist Italy and Nazi Germany.)

The Soviet Union

The Soviet Union[3] was the nation that faced the most difficult tasks in bringing about recovery from the war. Interest among Europeans in its fate was probably more significant than interest in any other nation except Germany. The Allies did intervene in the Russian Civil War (see Chapter 3) but only half-heartedly and without any coordination or clear objectives. Despite the allied intervention supporting the White armies, the Reds were victorious. During the Civil War, the Communist Party under Lenin's leadership consolidated its control through the implementation of what was called "War Communism."

[3] The constitution of 1918 referred to the state as the Russian Soviet Federated Socialist Republic (RSFSR). In 1924, when additional territory was added, a new constitution was drafted which created the Union of Soviet Socialist Republics (USSR). In 1918, the Bolsheviks began to refer to themselves as the Communist Party.

Historians disagree about whether War Communism was a series of emergency measures necessitated by the Civil War or a means by which the political independence of the people was undermined by eliminating their economic freedom. It was an attempt to ignore orthodox Marxism's requirements by destroying the market economy and immediately replacing it with state-controlled socialism. It involved nationalizing all property, beginning with church, monastic, and crown lands and eventually including personal property. All banking and commerce, both internal and external, became a state monopoly. At one point, money was temporarily replaced by an official barter system. Workers' control of industry was ended by decree in 1918, and industry was nationalized over the next two years. At first, agricultural products were requisitioned from the peasants. Then, in November 1918, all land was nationalized. Workers were forbidden to strike, and in 1920, compulsory labor was introduced.

No one disputes that War Communism was disastrous. Without counting deaths caused by the war or including those who emigrated, the population dropped by an estimated 16 million between 1917 and 1922. Industrial production fell below prewar levels; agricultural production to less than half. People fled the cities for the countryside. The two largest cities, Moscow and Petrograd (St. Petersburg), lost more than 58 percent of their prewar population in the two years from 1918 to 1920. Both Lenin and Trotsky later admitted that War Communism failed to achieve its goal. War Communism clashed with reality, concluded Trotsky, and reality won.

By 1921, several serious rebellions in the provinces took place in protest against the harsh policies of War Communism. War Communism was abandoned in 1921 when delegates to the Tenth Party Congress accepted the New Economic Policy (NEP), sponsored by Lenin. The NEP allowed peasants to sell their surplus grain on the open market after paying a tax based on a percentage of the harvest. Retail trade and private enterprise were partially restored, while what Lenin called the "commanding heights" of the economy—banking, large industry, transport, and foreign trade—remained under government control.

The NEP did not come quickly enough to prevent a severe famine in 1921–1922, but it did result in reasonably rapid economic recovery

Joseph Stalin, General Secretary of the Communist Party of the Soviet Union (CPSU). The Library of Congress/Public Domain.

over the next few years. By the mid-1920s, standards of living improved, and illiteracy was reduced. By that time, however, Lenin was dead. His death in 1924 marked the beginning of a struggle for power which by 1929 resulted in the emergence of Joseph Stalin (Iosif Vissarionovich Dzhugashvili [1878–1953]) as the most influential figure in the party and government and the beginning of new experiments with the society and economy of the Soviet Union.

In his "testament," dictated by Lenin in December 1922 following his first stroke, and in a postscript added in early January 1923, Lenin first criticized Stalin and then recommended his removal from the post as General Secretary of the party. For a time, Stalin seemed a relatively obscure figure, without much power, but he had acquired considerable influence through a series of bureaucratic posts.

Lenin's untimely death removed a key leader just at the point where the Soviet Union had to contend with unpromising prospects for revolution elsewhere in Europe. Lenin had already departed from Marxist doctrine by seizing power in a country that was only beginning to industrialize. The policy of War Communism during the Civil War had shown that Lenin could be impetuous and go well beyond the guidelines formulated by Marx and Engels. The NEP, on the other hand, indicated that Lenin could be pragmatic. How he might have handled the emerging power struggle between Trotsky and Stalin is an intriguing question. In the late 1980s, Soviet leaders attempting to reform the Soviet system invoked the spirit of Lenin and regarded Stalinism as a departure from Lenin's guidelines. The unanswerable question is how Lenin would have responded to the opportunities and dilemmas of the late 1920s.

The power struggle within the Soviet leadership between Stalin and Leon Trotsky soon focused on two opposing views regarding the future of the Soviet Union. In 1924, Stalin introduced the idea of "Socialism in One Country." According to this concept, the Soviet Union could create the conditions for socialism, an industrial economy, without the aid of revolutionary states elsewhere in Europe. Socialism in One Country was contrary to Trotsky's theory of "Permanent Revolution," which called for assistance from other centers of revolution. Trotsky was closer to Marxist orthodoxy than Stalin, but Stalin's approach caught the imagination of many Russian Communists. Also of great importance, Stalin used his enormous power as the chief bureaucrat to promote allies. By 1925, Stalin had allied with the party's right wing and greatly weakened Trotsky and his allies.

Stalin completely crushed the "left" opposition consisting of Trotsky, Grigori Zinoviev (1883–1936), and Lev Kamenev (1883–1936) by 1928. He then adopted some of the ideas long associated with the left, ideas concerning economic planning and rapid industrialization based on the control of agriculture. Essentially, Stalin believed that state control of agricultural production was necessary for the rapid industrialization of the Soviet Union. Collectivization of agriculture and industrialization had to be accomplished simultaneously.

At this point, Stalin was extremely powerful but far from all-powerful. His ideas were accepted because they appeared to meet the needs of the Soviet Union as the Communist Party perceived them. Many at the time viewed Stalin as an efficient bureaucrat who could get things done. Stalin was also quite knowledgeable about conditions in the Soviet Union. Assisted by Vyacheslav Molotov (1890–1986), Stalin had detailed information concerning the economy.

Nonetheless, he was drawn to the idea of overcoming obstacles by heroic efforts on the part of Russian workers and peasants.

In its original form, Stalin's first Five-Year Plan was ambitious but not unrealistic. Stalin's arbitrary modifications of the Five-Year Plan and collectivization became not just ambitious but, in many cases, utopian. In 1929 and 1930, Stalin and his colleagues implemented programs that would drastically change the lives of four-fifths of the population—those living in the rural areas—and eventually make the Soviet Union a significant industrial and military power.

The Smaller States

The Eastern European states that emerged from the old Habsburg Empire began the 1920s with constitutional and parliamentary governments. Each was plagued by a lack of experience with parliamentary forms of government, severe economic problems stemming from largely agrarian economies no longer in touch with prewar markets and resources, and problems between ethnic minorities. Except for Czechoslovakia, all turned to authoritarian governments by 1930.

On the whole, the instability of Eastern Europe stemmed from the strength of the older centers of power—the landholding aristocracy, the military, and the dominant ethnic groups—when confronted by some newer forces for democratic forms of government and more modern social and economic arrangements. Exacerbating this was economic problems caused by the breakup of the old economic unit formed by the Habsburg Empire and diplomatic tensions brought on by its location between two rival powers that bordered the region west and east, Germany and the Soviet Union.

The desire to establish national borders that reflected the nationalities proved impossible. The new nations of Eastern Europe contained significant national minorities within their borders that contributed to the failure of representative governments. In Poland, for example, nearly a third, and in some areas, a majority of the Polish population were ethnic minorities. The granting of a corridor, referred to as the Polish Corridor, to the North Sea through Prussia was sure to make Poland's future security precarious. The minorities problem and severe economic problems led to the failure of democracy in Poland and the establishment of an authoritarian dictatorship under Marshal Józef Piłsudski (1867–1935).

Austria became a reluctant democracy in 1920. The Allies refused the widespread desire for union with Germany in the peace settlement. Plagued by economic crises, the Austrian Republic limped on until March 1933, when during a parliamentary crisis, Chancellor Engelbert Dollfuss (1892–1934) dissolved parliament and established a dictatorship modeled on what was referred to as Austrofascism.

The other half of the former Austro-Hungarian Empire, Hungary, separated from Austria following a coup led by Michael Károlyi (1875–1955) and became a republic in November 1918. The republic lasted only until March 1919, when it was overthrown by a Communist putsch led by Béla Kun (1886–1938). The Hungarian Soviet Republic ended on 2 August 1919, following defeat by Romanian forces that intervened to destroy Communism in Hungary and prevent it from spreading. The former Austro-Hungarian admiral Miklós Horthy (1868–1957) was proclaimed Regent of the reestablished Kingdom of Hungary following elections in January 1920. The Kingdom of Hungary was a kingdom without a king. Horthy ruled Hungary dictatorially with the title of Regent until he was ousted in October 1944 by German occupation forces after attempting to make a separate peace with the Soviet Union.

A crazy quilt union of various former Habsburg territories under Serbian leadership called Yugoslavia (Land of South Slavs) appeared in 1918. It was initially called The Kingdom of the Serbs, Croats, and Slovenes. The Kingdom of Serbia included Banat, Bačka, and Baranja (formerly territories of the Kingdom of Hungary), the Kingdom of Montenegro, and Kosovo and Vardar Macedonia. The existence of 20 ethnic minorities and no national language prevented the creation of national identity. The Constitution of 1921 provided for proportional representation, resulting in 45 political parties and 23 governments between 1918 and 1928. On 6 January 1929, Alexander I (1888–1934) proclaimed a royal dictatorship.

In October 1918, a Czechoslovak National Council proclaimed independence from Austria-Hungary and organized a provisional government. The Slovak National Council voted to unite with the

Czechs. A land reform bill was passed to confiscate large landed estates (with compensation to the landowners) and redistribute the land in allotments of 25 acres (10.1 hectares) each to peasant families. A constitution modeled after the French constitution was adopted in February 1920. Blessed with a good industrial base and able to overcome the tensions caused by its ethnic diversity, Czechoslovakia remained a democracy until 1939, when Germany annexed it.

The two Balkan kingdoms of Romania and Bulgaria were on opposite sides in the Great War. Romania chose the Allies, while Bulgaria joined the Central Powers. Romania emerged from the war nearly twice its prewar size. In fact, between the wars, the kingdom was often referred to as România Mare, or "Greater Romania." Its government was a liberal constitutional monarchy from 1918 to 1925, when Carol II, who had renounced the throne in 1925, returned to Romania and established a dictatorship. Its territorial acquisitions merely increased the problem of ethnic minorities that plagued virtually all of the so-called successor states of Eastern Europe.

Bulgaria emerged from the Great War as one of the defeated Central Powers. Bulgaria suffered the consequences of its poor choice when it signed the Treaty of Neuilly in November 1919. It agreed to cede its Aegean coastline to Greece, recognize Yugoslavia, and cede nearly all of its Macedonian territory to Yugoslavia. Also, it ceded Dobruja to Romania and reduced its army to 20,000 men from a wartime high of 1,200,000 in 1917, when its total population was only 4.5 million. In addition to the territorial losses, Bulgaria agreed to pay reparations of £100 million ($445 million). Bulgaria remained during the interwar years an impoverished, predominately agricultural nation plagued by ethnic tensions and a right-wing authoritarian government behind a superficial parliamentary façade.

The Principality of Albania came into existence in 1914. From its founding, it was, and remained, without a foundation on which to construct a unified nation. It ended the Great War occupied by Italian, Serbian, Greek, and French forces. Its population was fragmented by political, religious, and ethnic diversity. Economically it, like much of the Balkans, was agricultural and impoverished. Only Woodrow Wilson's intervention prevented the Paris Peace Conference from effectively partitioning Albania between

Yugoslavia, Greece, and Italy. Governments came and went with great frequency until Ahmet Zogu (1895–1961) established himself as King Zog I. Albania became a constitutional monarchy with a republican constitution. In reality, it was a military dictatorship.

The Bolshevik government in Russia made known the secret agreements between the Allies concerning postwar territorial adjustments, much to the embarrassment of the Allies. The Treaty of Sèvres (1920) with the Ottoman Empire partitioned the Middle East in agreement with the Sykes–Picot Agreement (1916) between Great Britain and France, effectively dividing the Middle East between the two allies. Among the terms of the Treaty of Sèvres (1920) was the internationalization of the Strait of Bosporus and the partition of western Anatolia between Greece, France, and Italy.

The threat to the territorial integrity of Turkey aroused Turkish nationalism led by Mustafa Kemal (c. 1881–1938), later known as Atatürk. Under Mustafa Kemal's leadership, the proposed partition of Turkey was prevented. In 1923, the Sultanate was abolished, and the Republic of Turkey was proclaimed, officially ending the Ottoman Empire. Under Kemal's presidency, which lasted until he died in 1938, Turkey transformed itself into a modern secularized state with a political system and economy able to withstand the effects of the Great Depression. Turkey was the only member of the Central Powers during the Great War that was treated as an equal when negotiating a treaty with the Allies (Treaty of Lausanne).

Greece entered the Great War in 1917 as a deeply divided country. The division was between those who wished to remain neutral, a position favored by the king, and those who wanted to enter the war on the side of the Allies, the position desired by the Prime Minister and his followers. With the end of the war, Greece participated in the attempt to carve up Turkey. The result was the Greco-Turkish War of 1919–1922, which ended with Greece's defeat. The Treaty of Lausanne (1923) included an agreement between Greece and Turkey. Both sides committed atrocities, including the massacre of several hundred thousand Greeks and Turks. Over 1.5 million Christians and almost half a million Muslims were forcibly uprooted and moved to either Turkey or Greece. The sudden influx of so many immigrants forced from Turkish territory only added fuel to the political instability in Greece between the two world wars.

Outside the three major democracies of Britain, France, and Germany, democracy was firmly established in the Low Countries (Belgium, Luxembourg, and the Netherlands), the Scandinavian countries (Denmark, Sweden, Norway, and Finland), and Czechoslovakia. Belgium was severely affected by the Great War but managed a rapid recovery under the popular King Albert I (1875–1934). The most troubling question concerned the country's division between the French-speaking Walloons in the south and the Dutch-speaking Flemish in the north. The Dutch Netherlands escaped the problem of postwar adjustment that most other European nations experienced. Under Queen Wilhelmina (1880–1962), the Netherlands enjoyed considerable prosperity in the 1920s based on their colonial holdings in the Dutch East Indies.

In the Scandinavian countries, the 1920s and 1930s were times when parliamentary governments, universal suffrage, and the welfare state became firmly rooted. Each country instituted various social services, including multiple plans to aid the elderly and provide illness, accident, and unemployment insurance. Another characteristic of the Scandinavian societies was their mixed economies. Some government-run enterprises coexisted with many privately owned businesses and a few others in which government and private capital actively cooperated. Many developments in the Scandinavian countries between the wars foreshadowed general trends after World War II.

Three new states—Estonia, Latvia, and Lithuania—appeared after the Great War on the eastern coast of the Baltic Sea. Each contained a significant German minority, often wealthy landowners with great influence. Each of the new democracies enacted land reform programs that alienated the German population. The Baltic states feared for their future as Germany regained its dominant position under the Nazi regime during the 1930s. Efforts by Soviet Russia to recover their lost territories increased their feelings of insecurity. Threatened by both Germany and the Soviet Union, they tried to improve relations with the Soviet Union while vigorously suppressing communism. By 1939, all three had abandoned democracy in favor of a dictatorship.

Europe and the World Beyond

President Woodrow Wilson hoped that the Versailles Treaty and the League of Nations would be the crowning achievements of his administration. However, for various reasons, including the president's unwillingness to compromise with the Republicans in the Senate, the Senate refused to ratify the treaty on 19 March 1920. The Senate had already voted against joining the League on 17 January 1920. Technically, the United States remained at war with Germany until the Treaty of Berlin in 1921. The mood of the American people that lay behind the nation's return to isolationism was summed up in the slogan "back to normalcy," coined by the Republican Warren G. Harding (1865–1923) during his campaign for the presidency in 1920.

Many Americans felt that it had been a mistake for the United States to enter the Great War. A desire to return to isolationism in foreign affairs was evident in increased tariffs on imports to protect the postwar economic boom. In 1921, Congress passed an emergency immigration act establishing a quota system for new arrivals. Immigration from any one country was limited to 3 percent of the number of people of that nationality living in the United States at the time of the 1910 census. The total number of immigrants allowed entrance fell from just over 800,000 in 1920 to just under 200,000 in 1921–1922.

What is referred to as a spirit of nativism and provincialism characterized the decade. Fear of Bolshevism led to America's first "Red Scare," a grim foreshadowing of the McCarthyism that would appear in the 1950s. Some Americans blamed the Germans for the Spanish flu epidemic of 1918–1919 that claimed around 700,000 lives in the United States.[4] Rumors spread that German agents were sent by the Kaiser to "seed" Boston Harbor with influenza germs. The Ku Klux Klan spread from the south to the North and Northwest, where it was largely anti-Jewish, anti-Catholic, anti-immigrant, and anti-Communist.

4 It is hard to determine how many people died worldwide. Some estimates go as high as 100 million; most estimates are around 50 million. Seventeen million died in India, alone.

After a brief period during which the US economy readjusted to peacetime demand, it entered a boom period that would last until the stock market crash in 1929. The United States emerged from the Great War as the wealthiest nation globally. The financial capital of the world moved to New York City. Wages increased. At the beginning of the century, the average worker earned approximately $675 per year for a 59-hour week. That figure rose to $750 by 1919 and finally to $1,236 on the eve of the Great Depression. Millionaires were made seemingly overnight through speculation in the stock market. The belief that prosperity would continue was expressed by Herbert Hoover (1874–1964) in his acceptance of the Republican nomination for the presidency at the convention in August 1928:

> We in America today are nearer to the final triumph over poverty than ever before in the history of any land. The poor-house is vanishing from among us. We have not yet reached the goal, but given a chance to go forward with the policies of the last eight years, and we shall soon with the help of God be in sight of the day when poverty will be banished from this nation. (Howard 2020)

China and Japan

Although China was declared a republic in 1912, there was no real central government in China during the 1920s. The period between 1916 and at least 1928 is known as the Warlord Era, during which powerful generals turned provinces into their personal domains. Theoretically, the national government was located in Beijing (Peking) until 1926, when it was moved to Nanjing. Nanjing was controlled by Chiang Kai-shek (1887–1975), the de facto leader of a nonfunctioning Republic of China. In reality, Chiang Kai-shek was one of the more powerful warlords and the one who commanded what he called the National Liberation Army. Meanwhile, a militant communist movement under the leadership of Mao Zedong (1893–1976) strengthened during the 1920s. As a result, Chiang Kai-shek gained greater recognition in the West as the leader of China's "legitimate" government.

Japan made territorial gains as a result of the Great War. German rights in Shandong, China, were transferred to Japan. Germany's holdings in the Pacific north of the equator also were transferred to Japan as mandate territories under the League of Nations. During the 1920s, Japan appeared to be a democratic state in which democratic forces balanced the military's influence. During the 1930s, both the army and the navy pursued their own foreign policy objectives without the approval of the civilian government. More and more, Japan fell under the spell of militarism. It could be said that the independent actions of the military leaders drew Japan deeper into conflict with China and ultimately led to war with the United States in 1941.

The late 1920s were a time of economic prosperity and political stability for the United States and large parts of Europe. However, the liberal parliamentary governments of the period in Europe were seldom more than modestly successful. The experiences of Weimar Germany were a good measure of the parliamentary government's lack of strength and popularity. There were also some resounding failures in Eastern and Southern Europe, where authoritarian regimes emerged. Two important tendencies, which became much more influential in the early 1930s, were the decline of the liberal center in politics and, quite closely related, the growth of extremist movements on the margins of parliamentary life.

The prosperity of the later 1920s was already showing signs of faltering before the spectacular crash of the American stock market in 1929. Beneath the glitter lay areas of significant vulnerability. Particularly important was the precarious base for the credit structure in Germany and other areas in Central Europe, dependent as it was on American loans. There were indications, even in 1928, that Europeans might have to face a period of economic readjustment. That readjustment turned out to be more severe than anyone had predicted, involving political and cultural ramifications of great significance. The resources for meeting such a severe crisis were lacking. Europe and much of the world entered a time of trial that would extend for the better part of two decades.

References

Howard, Spencer. (2020). "Kicking off a Presidential Campaign – Herbert Hoover's 1928 Acceptance Speech." National Archives and Records Administration, 11 August 2020. https://hoover.blogs.archives.gov/2020/08/11/kicking-off-a-presidential-campaign-herbert-hoovers-1928-acceptance-speech/ (accessed 5 June 2023).

Public Broadcasting System. (2013). "Commanding Heights: The German Hyperinflation, 1923." https://www.pbs.org/wgbh/commandingheights/shared/minitext/ess_germanhyperinflation.html#:~:text=In%20 1923%2C%20at%20the%20most,surprise%20by%20the%20financial%20 tornado (accessed 6 June 2023).

5

From Depression to War, 1929–1939

Chronology

1928	Soviet Union abandons Lenin's NEP and implements the first Five-Year Plan (1928–1932)
1929	Great Depression begins in the United States
1930	Beginning of presidential dictatorship in Germany
1931	Japan invades Manchuria

Twentieth-Century Europe: 1900 to the Present, Fourth Edition.
Michael D. Richards and Paul R. Waibel.

1933	Second Five-Year Plan in the Soviet Union (1933–1937)
	Hitler appointed as chancellor in Germany
	The German *Reichstag* passes the Enabling Act
1935	Hitler repudiates the disarmament clauses of the Versailles Treaty
1936	John Maynard Keynes publishes *The General Theory of Employment, Interest, and Money*
	Spanish Civil War (1936–1939)
1937	Japan invades China
1938	Third Five-Year Plan begins in the Soviet Union
	Munich Conference
1939	Nazi–Soviet Nonaggression Pact
	Hitler invades Poland
1941	Japanese attack on Pearl Harbor

The world order of 1914 no longer existed after the Paris Peace Conference. Despite the widespread desire to return to the "normalcy" of the period before the outbreak of the Great War in 1914, there was no way back. The map of Europe after the war portrayed a fragmented image of Europe in its golden age. Fragmented, too, was the collective psyche. The trauma of the war and the influenza pandemic of 1918–1919 shattered the prewar confidence in a future world made in the image of Western Civilization. Hidden beneath the prosperity of the Roaring Twenties was an economic crisis that would hasten the destruction of the peace settlement and be remembered as the Great Depression. It would prove to be the death blow to the struggling democracies in Europe and hasten the slide into a second and far more destructive world war.

The Great Depression

The start of the Great Depression is usually associated with "Black Thursday," 29 October 1929, the day that stock prices on the New York Stock Exchange "virtually collapsed," according to the *New York Times*, "swept downward with gigantic losses in the most disastrous trading day in stock market history" (Boardman 1989,

p. 104). Historians like specific dates to mark the beginning and end of historical events, and Black Thursday is convenient for dating the beginning of the Great Depression. The "boom years" of the mid-1920s industrial prosperity hid the fact that the world economy never recovered from the impact of the Great War.

The economic system that evolved in Europe since the birth of modern capitalism during the Age of Discovery (the 1400s–1600s), further defined by the laissez-faire economics of the Industrial Revolution (eighteenth and nineteenth centuries), was shattered. Its underlying financial basis was disrupted, undermining the economic base of the middle class's prosperity. The middle class was the bedrock of laissez-faire economics. The loss of their financial freedom threatened their self-identity and the validity of their moral values. As a result, many began to question if free enterprise economics and its political counterpart, representative government, were outdated, not equal to the new postwar realities. Perhaps the crises of the 1930s required new theories and ideologies accompanied by action.

The American Connection

On Tuesday, 29 October 1929, the bottom fell out of the New York Stock Exchange. On that day, stocks traded lost a total value equal to more than twice the value of all currency in circulation in the United States. Despite a steady rise in the stock market during the last six weeks of the year, the crisis deepened and became international during 1930.

The failure of the New York stock market sent shockwaves through Europe. Even before the New York crash, the European economy was experiencing difficulties. Agriculture had been a troubled sector since at least the mid-1920s. Wartime demand had resulted in vastly increased production of agricultural products in North America, some areas of South America, and Australia. But after the Great War, prices dropped steadily as cheap foreign grain poured into Europe. Canadian or Australian grain could be shipped to Europe cheaper than grain from Eastern European agricultural states to Western Europe. In 1930, the price of wheat was at its lowest level since the Reformation.

There were other danger signs, largely ignored. The Great War had destroyed the monetary foundations of the European economy. The convertibility of the prewar European currencies depended on the gold standard and free trade principles. Both were abandoned due to the economic demands and impact of total war. The war's end left the national governments struggling to regain confidence in the value of their currencies. The monetary problem was complicated by the fact that the European nations were deeply in debt to the United States, debts that had to be paid in dollars or gold. The newly formed state of Poland had four different currencies in use. A single US dollar in 1922 (about £0.745) was worth 83,600 Austrian crowns. At one point, the Greek government introduced a new approach to taxation. All banknotes were called in, each one was cut in half, and one-half was returned to the original owner (Mazower 1999, p. 104). The most dramatic example of hyperinflation was Weimar Germany in November 1923, when $1.00 was worth 4.2 trillion marks.

A hidden weakness in the postwar European economy was its dependence upon American finances. The great prosperity of 1924–1929 was financed by American loans, while the prosperity of America itself was financed by credit. In 1924, the American financier Charles Dawes (1865–1951) chaired a committee that produced the Dawes Plan for the payment of reparations by Germany. Included in the plan were arrangements for an immediate loan of 800 million gold marks. By 1925, American banks had loaned Germany three billion gold marks. More money flowed into Germany between 1924 and 1929 in loans than flowed out as reparations payments. The German economy prospered, and that prosperity bubbled over into the rest of Europe as money flowed in a circle from the United States to Germany in the form of loans, to France and Great Britain in the form of reparations payments, and back to the United States as payment of war debts. If anything disrupted the flow of credit, the whole edifice would collapse. And this is what happened between 1929 and 1932.

American prosperity in the 1920s was based more on speculation in stocks than on producing and consuming goods and services. Stocks were often purchased on "margin" (on credit), with the stocks themselves serving as collateral. Although some working-class people speculated in stocks, most workers did not share in the prosperity. Wages remained low for workers, which, together with the depressed agricultural sector, meant that the purchasing power of the masses could not keep up with production—in short, workers did not earn enough to afford to purchase the products they made. The collapse of the stock market set in motion a vicious cycle. As a result, the financial crisis became an industrial crisis. Bank failures led to the closing of factories and rising rates of unemployment. As unemployment spread, reductions in production and more plant closings followed. Factories cannot produce what the public cannot afford to purchase.

The Great Depression spread from America to Europe. In 1928, Americans were already withdrawing funds from Europe to invest in stocks. As the Depression struck, Americans ceased investing in Europe and began withdrawing funds from European banks in significant quantities. The hardest hit were banks in Germany and Central Europe. The decline in American industrial productivity, the withdrawal of American capital from the world market, and the low prices paid for agricultural products and raw materials combined to reduce production, trade, and the movement of money everywhere.

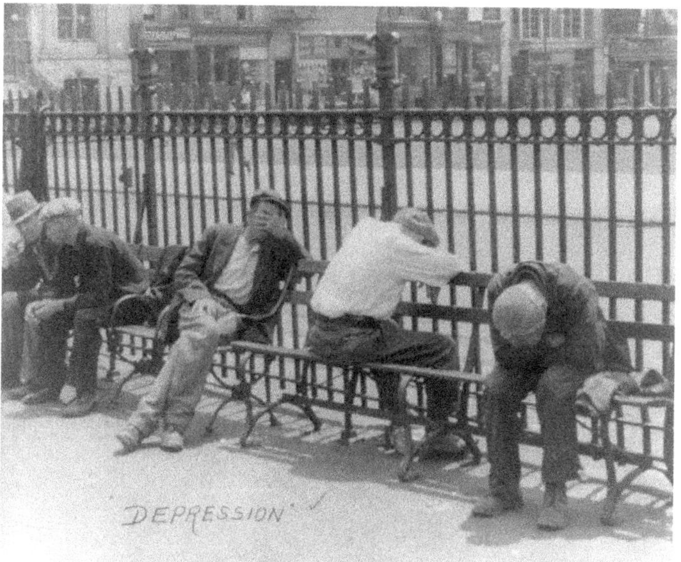

Men in England sit on a bench displaying the sense of despair and hopelessness that became common among the unemployed. Barry, Mark Benedict/The Library of Congress/Public Domain.

The crisis was international, but not much was done at that level to deal with the problem. In 1931, President Herbert Hoover of the United States proposed a moratorium of one year on all intergovernmental debts to recognize the difficulties of transferring sums of money for payment of reparations or war debts. The suspension was accepted by European leaders and regarded as an acknowledgment of the connection between reparations and war debts; the latter would not be paid unless the former was paid. That this was not the American understanding became clear the following year, when Americans refused to include a plan for setting aside reparations in an agreement on war debts. American insistence on payment of war debts prevented resolving the issue by consensus. Germany repudiated reparations in the next few years. In 1933, a third international effort at finding a solution floundered when the United States declined to cooperate. Most other countries had already begun their efforts to find a way out of the crisis.

Responses

The Great Depression, or "World Slump," was made all the more severe by the near-universal commitment to classic (or orthodox) liberal economic theory. According to classic economic theory, the problem was a loss of confidence in the monetary system and the need to become more competitive in the world market. The solution, then, was "deflation," balancing government budgets and reducing the cost of production by, for example, lowering wages. Believing that the economy had to "right" itself, liberal economists, most politicians, and businessmen were prepared to tolerate a high level of general misery. The accepted theory convinced them that any attempt by governments to maintain wages or maintain unemployment benefits by deficit financing would only insulate inefficient sectors of the economy, leading to a worse economic disaster in the future.

What the classic liberals feared was what others, who saw underconsumption as the root problem, believed it necessary to save capitalism by making it work. Unlike the liberals, these advocates of a "middle road" between unbridled capitalism and a command economy saw the necessity of some public management and planning. In addition, they advocated what economists call "deficit spending," that is, the use of public funds raised by borrowing. Unlike the socialists, they were committed to preserving private property. Like the economic policymakers of the post–World War II era, theirs was a program that would allow as much planning as necessary and as much freedom as possible. The leading advocate of this new consumer-based economic theory was the Englishman John Maynard Keynes (1883–1946), who expressed his ideas in *The General Theory of Employment, Interest, and Money* (1936).

Keynes's belief that governments could, in effect, spend their way out of economic slumps found many advocates. In Britain, Sir Oswald Mosley (1896–1980), one of the most talented members of the Labour Party, authored a memorandum in 1930 that called for ending the Great Depression through government intervention and deficit spending. He bolted the party when his ideas were rejected and founded the British Union of Fascists. Perhaps the best application of what has since become known as Keynesian economics was Franklin Roosevelt's New Deal in the United States, lasting roughly from 1933 to 1939. In the end, however, the massive spending for defense during World War II, rather than the New Deal programs, ended the Depression in America. Likewise, the huge expenditures for rearmament after Hitler came to power in 1933 ended the economic slump in Germany.

The Depression in Germany: The Nazis Come to Power

The Great Depression helped make possible the Nazi "seizure of power" in 1933 by discrediting political and economic liberalism, especially for the middle class. It also caused serious doubts among the working class as to the ability (or even desire) of the liberal democratic governments to deal with the unemployment, and its accompanying miseries, caused by the Great Depression. As both deserted the middle, pro-Republic parties for the extremes, the Weimar

Republic, which never really commanded the enthusiastic support of the German people, fell victim to Hitler and the Nazi revival.

On 3 October 1929, Gustav Stresemann died just three weeks before "Black Tuesday" at the New York Stock Exchange. Stresemann was perhaps the only German statesman who could have led a coalition to resist Hitler. During the previous six years, Stresemann led Germany out of the Great Inflation of 1923 through the Dawes Plan and Locarno treaties and accepted the Young Plan (for the reorganization of reparations) just two months before his untimely death. As the Depression began to strike Germany, the Republic was left without a pilot at the helm.

Recession and rising unemployment at the beginning of 1930 led to the fall of the Weimar Republic's last truly parliamentary government, the Grand Coalition (1928–1930), led by Chancellor Hermann Müller (1876–1931), a Social Democrat. As unemployment rose, available funding for unemployment insurance proved inadequate. Müller's proposal to reduce benefits while raising the unemployment insurance rates met with strong opposition from industry and organized labor. The result was the fall of the Müller government and its replacement by a new government headed by Heinrich Brüning (1885–1970) of the Catholic Center Party. Unable to govern through the *Reichstag*, Brüning resorted to rule by presidential decree. Germany became, in effect, a presidential dictatorship.

The economic and political crisis continued to deepen under Brüning. Germans went to the polls in national elections no fewer than four times in 1932. In 1932, the people elected delegates to the *Reichstag* in July and again in November. The results of both elections were similar. The Democratic and the People's Parties, two pro-Republic Weimar Coalition parties, did poorly. From nearly 14 percent of the vote in 1928, they declined to under 3 percent in 1932. The Center Party largely maintained its electorate, but the Social Democrats lost voter support heavily while remaining a significant party. They dropped from nearly 30 percent of the vote in 1928 to just over 20 percent in 1932. The center of the political spectrum had won about 55 percent in 1928 but only around 35 percent in 1932. Yeats's line, "The centre cannot hold," had come true.

The extremes gained at the expense of the middle. On the left, the Communists steadily increased their vote share from about 10 percent in 1928 to nearly 17 percent in 1932. The Nazis became a major political force on the right, rising from under 3 percent of the vote in 1928 to 37.8 percent in July 1932, the largest percentage ever received by a party during the Weimar Republic. With 230 seats, the Nazis were almost twice as large as the second-largest party, the Social Democrats.

The growing strength of the Nazi movement was evident also in the presidential elections of March and April 1932. In March, Hitler came in second behind president Hindenburg in a campaign featuring four candidates from the extreme right to the extreme left. In the runoff election in April, Hitler again came in second. Hindenburg's reelection was credited to his having received the support of the left-of-center voters, who saw him as the only means of preventing Hitler's election.

On 30 May 1932, Hindenburg replaced Brüning as chancellor with Franz von Papen (1879–1969), a conservative Catholic aristocrat best known for political intrigue. Although Hindenburg hoped that Papen could put together a majority in the *Reichstag*, he did not. On 12 September, the *Reichstag*, by a vote of 512 to 42, passed a vote of no confidence in the chancellor. Papen dissolved the *Reichstag* and called for new elections on 6 November. The Nazis lost two million votes, dropping from 37.8 to 33.1 percent of the votes cast. The government crisis continued. Rejecting Papen's suggestion of a military dictatorship, Hindenburg dismissed Papen and replaced him on 2 December with General Kurt von Schleicher (1882–1934). Schleicher's tenure as chancellor lasted only until 28 January, when the 85-year-old and possibly senile President Hindenburg yielded to the advice of Papen and the president's son, Oskar, and offered Adolf Hitler the chancellorship on 30 January 1933.

It is perhaps appropriate to note that the Weimar Republic had been "hollowed out" even before Hitler came to power by those constitutionally responsible for the Republic but very much opposed to it as a political system. Hindenburg was a committed monarchist who assumed the presidency out of a sense of duty to the Kaiser. He saw himself as a caretaker head of state until the exiled Kaiser returned to take his rightful place.

Article 48 of the Weimar Constitution gave the president, the constitutional head of the state, the power to rule by decree during a national emergency. From the chancellorship of Heinrich Brüning to the end of the Republic in 1933, each chancellor (appointed by, and responsible to, the president, not the *Reichstag*) governed through emergency decrees issued by President Hindenburg. Since neither Brüning, Papen, Schleicher, nor Hitler was able to command a majority in the *Reichstag*, the Weimar Republic became a presidential dictatorship after March 1930.

With Papen as vice-chancellor, the old elites thought they could control, even "use," Hitler. They were fatally wrong. On 27 February 1933, the *Reichstag* building was mysteriously set on fire, destroying the central chamber in which the parliament met. Hitler claimed there was sufficient evidence that Communists were responsible and intended that the fire should be a signal for a communist uprising. He convinced President Hindenburg to issue the Decree of the Reich President for the Protection of People and State (*Verordnung des Reichspräsidenten zum Schutz von Volk und Staat*). The decree silenced opposition to the Nazis, especially from Communists and Social Democrats. Civil liberties, including freedom of the press and speech, were suspended. The Communist Party (KPD) was suppressed, and some 4,000 of its members were arrested. Among them were the party chairman, Ernst Thälmann (1886–1944), and party founders, Wilhelm Pieck (1876–1960) and Walter Ulbricht (1893–1973).

On 5 March, against a backdrop of fear and violence, Germans once again went to the polls. Despite efforts to suppress the communist and social-democratic vote, the Nazis failed to win a majority. They received 43.9 percent of the votes cast. With support from the German National Peoples' Party (DNVP), the Nazis could command a majority, but less than the two-thirds needed to legally establish a dictatorship.

The inglorious end of the Weimar Republic came on 23 March, when the *Reichstag* passed the Enabling Act (*Ermächtigungsgesetz*), granting Hitler dictatorial powers for four years. The necessary two-thirds majority for passage was achieved by preventing the Communists and 21 Social Democrats from attending. Also, the

Catholic Center Party voted for the Enabling Act. Only the remainder of the Social Democratic delegates led by Otto Wels (1873–1939) was courageous enough to vote against it. When the final vote was announced, the Nazi delegates rose to their feet and sang the "Horst Wessel Song," the party anthem.

The New Dictatorships

What followed the Nazi seizure of power in Germany, like what followed the Bolshevik Revolution in Russia and, to a lesser degree Mussolini's March on Rome, was the emergence of a new type of authoritarian state peculiar to the twentieth century. These new authoritarian dictatorships[1] were very different from the traditional conservative dictatorships that arose as attempts to salvage something of the old order from the threat of advancing liberalism. In the traditional dictatorship, it was enough to give at least passive support to the regime, such as paying taxes, obeying the laws, serving in the military when called upon, and recognizing society's traditional class structure. The individual willing to do so was allowed considerable personal freedom. Such "garden variety dictatorships" arose during the 1920s and early 1930s in Portugal and the Eastern European "successor states," for example, Poland, Hungary, and Yugoslavia. Their goal was conservative, to maintain the status quo. They did not seek a wholly new ideological order based upon a following whose total being, mind, and body were subject to authoritarian leadership.

Although Mussolini's Fascist regime had many characteristics in common with the Hitler and Stalin regimes, it was more akin to the traditional dictatorship. *Il Duce* ("The leader"), as Mussolini was known, never achieved total power. For example, he did not interfere with the judiciary and remained subject to the Fascist Grand Council, which could and did dismiss Mussolini in July 1943.

[1] We are deliberately avoiding the use of the term "totalitarian." Although the term was originally coined by Mussolini, its usefulness for the 1930s and 1940s was compromised by its employment during the Cold War.

The new authoritarian dictatorships of Hitler and Stalin were very different. They were the very antithesis of classical liberalism. Conceived during the total war effort of the Great War and given birth during the Russian Civil War, they reached maturity in the Nazi Third Reich and Stalinist dictatorship. Like a great religious revival, the new dictators harnessed the masses in idolatrous worship of the state (or party, or leader) and a never-ending violent struggle against enemies, both within and without. The individual as a rational being who possessed certain inalienable natural rights ceased to exist, becoming a mere faceless object at the disposal of the state instead. Individualism was denied as well as the traditional liberal belief in reason, progress, and the essential harmony of human society. Loathing the middle class, the mainstay of classical liberalism, the new authoritarian dictators promised a classless state (never achieved). The masses were recruited for a permanent revolution by employing a large state police apparatus and a carefully crafted program of systemic terror.

The fateful confluence of several trends already discussed above made the success of the new authoritarian dictators in Germany and the Soviet Union possible. These included the weakening of the Enlightenment tradition in European thought. The mainstay of liberalism, the middle class, saw its financial security eroded by taxes, inflation, and various expropriations. Finally, the failure of the liberal democratic governments to deal effectively with the suffering caused by the Great Depression caused the working class, like the middle class, to abandon its faith in political and economic liberalism.

While Nazi Germany and the Soviet Union appeared to be highly similar in broad outline, there were also striking differences that must be discussed. Nazi Germany was based on stark racism. Membership in the *Volksgemeinschaft* (national or racial community) was based on blood lines. Only those people of German descent qualified. People who had come from elsewhere, especially Jews, could not qualify, no matter how long they had lived in Germany or how assimilated they appeared to be. Jews, because it was assumed that they would destroy the Germanic community given the chance, were to be excluded from positions of power and influence, encouraged to leave Germany, and, ultimately, during World War II, to be rounded up and physically eliminated. Another striking difference is that the Nazi program was a major factor in the onset of World War II, a process that brought what had become once again the most militarily powerful and highly industrialized economy to its knees.

By contrast, the Soviet Union, at least in theory, offered a community that all could embrace. There was, of course, both racism and antisemitism in the Soviet Union, but, in theory, only aristocrats and capitalists would be excluded as irredeemable. The Communist International existed, supposedly to extend the blessing of Communism to all the peoples of the world. In reality, of course, the Soviet Union frequently operated as a great power. The final difference between the two great experiments is that the Soviet Union, at enormous cost in human lives and suffering, some of it deliberately inflicted on suspect groups like the kulaks, so-called rich peasants, remade Russia in little over a decade into a great power that was able, with assistance from allies, principally the United States, to withstand the Nazi onslaught in World War II. This is contrasted with the fact that the Nazi dictatorship had at its disposal a highly industrialized economy, a highly educated and sophisticated population, and a powerful military. These assets were largely destroyed in the course of World War II.

The Nazi Dictatorship

Once legally installed in power by presidential appointment and passage of the Enabling Act, Hitler spent the next two years bringing every aspect of life in Germany under control of the Nazi party, a process referred to as the *Gleichschaltung*, or coordination of society. It altered the relationship between the individual and the state and between individuals. All aspects of society and culture were brought under the control of the state, including the individual's thought process. Joseph Goebbels (1897–1945), Hitler's Minister of Propaganda and Public Enlightenment summed it up best at the end of 1933 when he said: "If liberalism took as its starting point the individual and placed the individual man in the center of all things, we have replaced the individual by the nation and the individual man by the community" (Pipes 1981). Germany was to become a *Volksgemeinschaft,* a national or racial community in which traditional social classes would be replaced by a mass of "folk (i.e., racial) comrades." The Nazi dictatorship was a rejection of European history since the Enlightenment.

In 1933, all independent organizations were abolished or absorbed into Nazi-led organizations. Thus, for example, all labor unions were abolished, and workers were required to join the German Labor Front. A Reich Chamber of Culture under Goebbels was established to oversee and coordinate all media production and dissemination aspects. In January 1934, the *Reichsrat*, the upper house representing the state governments and individual state legislatures, was abolished. Germany became a centralized national state for the first time in its history.

At the end of 1933, only two key institutions remained outside the state (i.e., Hitler's control)—the *Reichswehr* (army) and the churches. To secure the support of the military (*Reichswehr*) and remove any opposition within the Nazi Party, Hitler purged the party leadership in the "Night of the Long Knives" (29 June). Ernst Röhm (1887–1934) and several hundred SA (*Sturmabteilung*, or storm troopers) were shot. Röhm, leader of the SA, wanted to see the SA replace the *Reichswehr* as the principal military force. With Röhm's removal and the SA's future role in the Third Reich greatly diminished, the *Reichswehr* no longer feared the SA as a potential rival. Nothing stood in the way of the *Reichswehr* giving its loyalty to Hitler. After Hindenburg's death on 2 August, all members of the *Reichswehr* swore an oath of personal allegiance to Hitler, now *Der Führer* ("The leader").

The "coordination" of the churches proved more difficult. Attempts to establish a National Reich Church under Ludwig Müller (1883–1945) as Reich Bishop were less than successful. Evangelical Christians, including Karl Barth (1886–1968), Dietrich Bonhoeffer (1906–1945), and Martin Niemöller (1892–1984), formed the Confessing Church in opposition to the Reich Church. Many of the Confessing pastors, including Bonhoeffer, subsequently suffered martyrdom at the hands of the state.

Hitler was somewhat more successful in neutralizing the Roman Catholic Church as a center of organized opposition. In what was one of his most spectacular foreign policy successes, Hitler signed the Reich Concordat with the papacy on 20 July 1933. By the terms of the concordat, the Catholic Center Party disbanded, and the Catholic clergy was required to give up all political activity. Henceforth, Catholics who opposed the Nazi state and its policies (e.g., the Holocaust) had to do so as individuals. Although there were courageous individuals among both Catholics and Protestants, the organized institutional churches generally capitulated to and openly supported the Nazi regime and its policies. A partial exception to this is the activities of Pope Pius XI in the late 1930s with his encyclical *Mit brennender Sorge* ("With Deep Anxiety"), 1937. Written in German instead of in Latin, it was smuggled into Germany and read from the pulpits of all German Catholic Churches on Palm Sunday (21 March that year). It criticized in rather general terms what it saw as breaches of the Reich Concordat of 1933. It did not mention by name Hitler, National Socialism, or the Nazi Party. The reaction of the Nazi Party was to increase persecution and obstruction of the Catholic Church but within the confines of the Reich Concordat. Pius XI commissioned in 1938 another encyclical that was to criticize persecution of the Jews and antisemitism more directly, but died before it could be issued. It was quietly shelved by his successor, Pius XII (1876–1958), who preferred a less confrontational approach. Defenders of Pius XII point to his efforts during World War II to aid refugees, prisoners of war, and where possible, Jews. Others criticize him for never speaking out clearly against Nazi policies.

The Stalinist Dictatorship

Old Bolsheviks, members of the Communist Party before the October Revolution in 1917, called the events of the early 1930s "the great change." Western historians have labeled them the "Stalinist revolution." Whatever label one might choose, it was a revolution far more profound than the revolution of 1917. The primary goal of the later revolution was to transform the Soviet Union into a significant industrial power, which in turn would be the basis for a modern military machine capable of securing the Soviet Union from the threat of annihilation by hostile capitalist powers.

The Stalinist dictatorship was constructed between 1928 and 1938. The emphasis was on economic development during the first period from 1928 to 1933. Stalin aimed to make the Soviet Union a major industrial power within ten years through rapid industrialization. Lenin's strategic retreat from socialism (NEP) was abandoned in 1928 in favor of economic planning. The First Five-Year Plan, begun in 1928, aimed at developing heavy industry. The results were impressive, if uneven, backed by a mixture of dedicated enthusiasm and physical and psychological coercion. Capitalism was eliminated, a socialist economy established, and agriculture collectivized.

The brutal process of collectivization of agriculture was meant to destroy the independence of the peasants and provide the food supply necessary for industrialization. The peasants were forced into collective farms and given production quotas to meet. The quotas were often greater than the farmers could produce. When the peasants resisted by burning their crops and farm buildings and slaughtering their livestock, they experienced severe repression. Many died when planning failed to produce expected results. The result was widespread famine in the grain-growing regions of Soviet Russia between 1931 and 1934. At least five million are believed to have died across Soviet Russia. Nearly four million were in Ukraine, where the event was known as the Holodomor (from *moryty holodom,* to kill by starvation). Millions more were sent to labor camps in Siberia and the Arctic regions of the Soviet Union. Some concessions were made to the peasants during the Second Five-Year Plan (1933–1937). A Third Five-Year Plan was launched in 1938. However, it had to be suspended due to the German invasion of the Soviet Union in 1941.

Stalin, the consummate bureaucrat, was well aware of the human costs not only of collectivization but also of rapid industrialization. To a large extent, he seems to have regarded this as the regrettable by-product of the need to create a modern economy in the Soviet Union, which would be indispensable for its survival in a hostile world. While new opportunities opened for many in the new political system and the industrialized economy, it was at a great cost. In addition to the millions who died in the 1930s, millions more lived in inadequate housing, often with inadequate food supplies or basic items such as shoes or soap.

Stalin and many other leading Communists may have believed that only the harshest methods would lead to the desired results. In Stalin's case, he was undoubtedly affected by an event in 1932 that profoundly changed his personal life. This was what appeared to be the suicide of his second wife and mother of two of his children, Nadezhda "Nadya" Alliluyeva. A dedicated party member, she was much younger than Stalin. Before her death, Stalin and his family had a busy social life with visits from members of her family, the family of his first wife, and Georgian friends. After her death, Stalin retreated into a Kremlin apartment. While his children continued to live with him, he spent long hours at work and mainly saw a small group of top officials, frequently at dinners that lasted well into the night. This isolation may help to explain the paranoia that appeared to grip the top echelon of the Communist Party in the 1930s.

At the same time, the basis for the Stalinist state was formed. By 1933, Stalin could not be seriously questioned without also calling into question the right of the Communist Party to rule. Those who challenged Stalin in any fashion had to be eliminated. This Stalin set out to do, beginning in 1934, in a series of actions that made Hitler's "Night of the Long Knives" seem benign by comparison. In the winter of 1934–1935, Stalin began a reign of systematic terror meant to physically eliminate all individuals and groups who might challenge his regime. The murder of Sergei Kirov (1886–1934), leader of the Communist Party in Leningrad, at the end of 1934 appeared to provide a pretext for Stalin's purge of party leaders he perceived to be a threat to his control. A series of show trials were staged in 1936, 1937, and 1938 to convict and execute key party officials (usually close associates of Lenin) on preposterous charges to which the accused confessed following extreme physical and mental torture. Millions were arrested by the secret police (NKVD), often at random to fill quotas, and either executed without trial or sent off to a slow death in the GULAG, the growing network of prisons and labor camps. When the purges ended in 1938, millions of innocent citizens continued to languish in the GULAG, the government and party bureaucracies and the military high commands were decimated, and the population of the Soviet Union lived in fear.

The Road to War in Europe

Virtually all historians agree that World War II in Europe resulted from Hitler's aggressive foreign policy. There can be no doubt that Hitler included war in his plans to create a Greater German Reich that would last a thousand years. However, the war he got was not the limited war in Eastern Europe he desired. Remove Hitler from the equation, and World War II was not inevitable.

From hindsight, it may be concluded that if Hitler were to be removed from power and war avoided, it would have to have happened before 1936. During his first two years in power, the years of the *Gleichschaltung*, Hitler pursued a cautious foreign policy. It was necessary to secure his position at home and begin secret rearmament without alarming Great Britain and France. After 1936, his position in Germany was secure enough and rearmament sufficient enough that only military defeat could oust him from power. But the aversion to war, the understandable commitment to avoid a replay of the Great War, was so strong among the Western democracies (England and France, not to mention the United States) that appeasement seemed the most logical foreign policy. Indeed, it was the policy that best represented the wishes of the populace of Britain and France in the 1930s.

Hitler removed Germany from both the League of Nations and the Geneva Disarmament Conference in October 1933 while giving assurances of his desire for peace and pledging peaceful cooperation with all countries that treated Germany as an equal. In 1934, Hitler signed a nonaggression pact with Poland to isolate France while also appearing to desire peaceful change.

Hitler's first overtly aggressive move came in March 1935, when he repudiated the disarmament clauses of the Versailles Treaty, introduced military conscription, and announced the existence of an air force. Although the League of Nations condemned Hitler's unilateral action, the British and French took no action to enforce the treaty. In fact, Britain signed the Anglo-German Naval Treaty with Germany in June 1935, implicitly legitimatizing Hitler's violation of the Versailles Treaty. Neither did Britain nor France do any more than protest when Hitler remilitarized the Rhineland in March 1936.

Until November 1936, when Hitler and Mussolini formed what Mussolini called the "Rome–Berlin Axis," Hitler was without an ally. In fact, before that time, Fascist Italy stood with Britain and France against Hitler. Mussolini had been alarmed by an attempted coup by Austrian Nazis against the government of Engelbert Dollfuss (1892–1934) of Austria in July 1934. Then, when Hitler announced that Germany would rearm, Mussolini joined Britain and France in the so-called Stresa Front to oppose Hitler. The Stresa Front was the last act of unity involving the three Allies of the Great War. What shattered the Stresa Front and sent Mussolini rushing into the waiting arms of Hitler was Italy's attack on Ethiopia in October 1935.

The attack on Ethiopia was partly an attempt by Italy to avenge its defeat at the Battle of Adowa in 1896. It was also meant to connect Italian Somaliland and Eritrea. In attempting to understand why Mussolini attacked Ethiopia, one must not overlook his megalomaniacal dreams of rebirthing the Roman Empire. No doubt he felt Ethiopia was an easy kill. Ethiopia's air force consisted of a mere 12 outdated fighter planes. The Ethiopian army included tribal warriors armed with spears and shields. Still, they bravely resisted the Italians, who resorted to using mustard and phosgene gas against the Ethiopians.

Both Italy and Ethiopia were members of the League of Nations. Despite that fact and Italy's use of illegal chemical weapons, the League of Nations limited its action to condemning Italy's aggression and imposing minor economic sanctions. It stopped short of placing an embargo on oil to Italy. Only by cutting off Italy's source of the oil it needed to prosecute its invasion could the League have saved Ethiopia. By taking only a weak-willed stand, the League merely offended Mussolini, pushing him into an alliance with Hitler while effectively ending the League's role as an agent for collective security.

Mussolini and Hitler found an opportunity for cooperation when civil war broke out in Spain in July 1936. The Spanish Civil War (1936–1939) was, according to the US ambassador at the time, the "dress rehearsal for World War II" (Bowers 2019). King Alfonso (1886–1941) was deposed, and a republic was proclaimed on 14 April 1931. The government of what is commonly referred to as the Second Spanish Republic introduced measures aimed at modernizing Spain. Some measures proved unpopular, including agrarian reform and granting Home rule to Catalonia. Especially unpopular with the largely devout Roman Catholic population was secularizing education. The latter included banning the Jesuits who operated the finest schools in Spain and seizing all Jesuit property.

In 1935, President Alcalá-Zamora (1877–1949) called for elections to the Spanish parliament (*Cortes*) on 16 February 1936. The outcome was the formation of a Popular Front Government that included the Socialist Party, the Communist Party, and the Republican Union Party. The new government released left-wing political prisoners, introduced agrarian reforms that hurt the landed aristocracy, and banned the Spanish *Falange*, a political movement that condemned socialism, Marxism, republicanism, and capitalism. The *Falange* desired Spain to become a Fascist state similar to Mussolini's Italy.

The civil war began in July 1936 with a revolt of the Spanish military based in North Africa. General Francisco Franco (1892–1975), commander of the Army of Africa, quickly emerged as the leader of the nationalist forces. The civil war was a brutal war with atrocities committed by both sides. The British and French governments followed a "no intervention" policy that banned military intervention. The United States declared neutrality and took measures to prevent Americans from providing arms to either side. Germany, Italy, and the Soviet Union send supplies and, in the case of the first two, military personnel.

The Republic received some aid from the Soviet Union. Volunteers from a number of countries, including Britain, France, and the United States, were recruited by the Communist International (Comintern) to fight with the Republic's forces. Three-thousand American volunteers formed the Abraham Lincoln Brigade that fought for the Republic. The nationalists received aid from Germany, Italy, and

Portugal. Hitler and Mussolini used the Spanish Civil War to refine military tactics, strengthen national pride, and test the resolve of the democratic powers. The civil war officially ended on 1 April 1939, with the nationalists victorious. The outcome was seen as a victory for Hitler and Mussolini and a defeat for the Western democracies.

On 5 November 1937, Hitler met with his generals. He informed them that Germany's need for living space (*Lebensraum*) in the east would necessitate a war not later than 1943–1945. In the meantime, he meant to destroy both Austria and Czechoslovakia to protect Germany's flank. Two weeks later, Hitler met with Lord Halifax (1881–1959), British Foreign Secretary and a leading appeaser. After Hitler spoke of Germany's need to deal with various border disputes and minority problems in Eastern Europe, Lord Halifax informed him that Britain would accept peaceful change in the status quo. Hitler took Halifax's response as a sign that he could proceed.

First on Hitler's agenda was the annexation of Austria, the so-called *Anschluss*. In February 1938, Hitler summoned the Austrian chancellor, Kurt von Schuschnigg (1897–1977), to Berchtesgaden. Hitler demanded concessions, including participation by the Austrian Nazis in the government. When Schuschnigg called for a plebiscite on Austrian independence, he was forced to resign and was replaced by Arthur Seyss-Inquart (1892–1946), an Austrian Nazi. Seyss-Inquart invited the German army to enter Austria. On 13 March, Austria's union with Germany was proclaimed to cheering crowds. Again, the Western democracies protested but did nothing.

Hitler was ready to move against Czechoslovakia, the only one of the "successor states" created by the Paris Peace Conference still a democracy, in 1938. In fact, Czechoslovakia was the only model of democratic government, fair treatment of minorities, and industrial progress in Eastern Europe. Also, both France and the Soviet Union had treaties with Czechoslovakia, committing them to maintain Czechoslovakia's territorial integrity. Britain, however, favored appeasement.

The Czechoslovakian crisis concerned the fate of the German minority along Czechoslovakia's border with Germany, an area known as the Sudetenland. Encouraged by Hitler, the pro-Nazi Sudeten German Party under Konrad Henlein (1898–1945) demanded autonomy for the

Sudetenland. The crisis intensified during the summer of 1938; then, on 12 September, Hitler threatened intervention unless the Sudeten Germans were allowed to decide their own fate. On the following day, Konrad Henlein called for annexation with Germany.

As war appeared increasingly likely, Britain's prime minister, Neville Chamberlain (1869–1940), flew to Berchtesgaden on 15 September and to Bad Godesberg one week later to assess Hitler's demands and find a way to satisfy them without risking a war. When the Czechs refused Hitler's terms and war seemed inevitable, Mussolini proposed a conference in Munich. Britain, France, and Germany were invited, but not Czechoslovakia or the Soviet Union. The Soviet Union urged the Allies to resist Hitler's demands and offered military assistance to Czechoslovakia if war broke out between Czechoslovakia and Germany.

Theodor Kordt (1893–1962), German Ambassador to Britain and member of the German resistance, met with Lord Halifax at 10 Downing Street in London. He urged Britain to take a firm stand against Hitler's demands. Kordt gave assurances that certain German generals would act against the Nazis if Britain did so. Chamberlain's government resisted all such calls for a courageous response to Hitler. Neither Kordt's nor Stalin's offers were considered. The appeasers were committed to peace at any price.

The Munich Conference convened on 29 September. Hitler presented the western Allies with a choice between sacrificing Czechoslovakia or almost certain war. They chose to sacrifice Czechoslovakia. Czechoslovakia, the only democracy in Eastern Europe, had been sold out. Hitler once again triumphed over the Western democracies and his opponents at home, the generals and the resistance who urged the appeasers to reject Hitler's demands. Neville Chamberlain returned home to a cheering crowd, waving a piece of paper with Hitler's signature guaranteeing "peace in our time." The former premier of France, Léon Blum (1872–1950), who opposed the Munich Agreement signed by his successor, Édouard Daladier (1884–1970), was more clear-sighted and spoke of a sense of "cowardly relief" that war had been averted.

Several vital developments followed the Munich Conference. In mid-March 1939, Hitler destroyed what was left of Czechoslovakia.

Bohemia and Moravia were annexed, while Slovakia became a separate satellite of Germany. It was the first time Hitler had taken territory not containing a German population. Even Chamberlain had to acknowledge this act as aggression. When Hitler began making demands on the free city of Danzig and the Polish Corridor, Chamberlain reacted by writing out a guarantee of Polish sovereignty in his own hand. Britain's pledge of military assistance for Poland, if attacked by Germany, was endorsed by France. But Hitler, reckless in the glow of his string of successes, did not take the warning seriously. On 3 April, he ordered his generals to prepare for war with Poland (Table 5.1).

Another by-product of the Munich Conference was a shift in Soviet policy toward Germany. Stalin felt that the West's sellout of Czechoslovakia at Munich was evidence of a capitalist plot to direct Hitler's aggression toward the Soviet Union. Perhaps as a

Table 5.1 Timetable of German Aggression

1935 (16 March)	Hitler repudiates disarmament clauses of the Versailles Treaty, restores conscription, announces the founding of *Luftwaffe* (the air force), and expands the army to over half a million. Two-year compulsory military service is introduced in Germany.
1936 (7 March)	Hitler sends troops into the demilitarized Rhineland.
	The Rome–Berlin Axis is formed. Germany and Italy recognize Franco's government and begin intervention in the Spanish Civil War. Germany and Japan sign Anti-Comintern Pact.
1938 (11 March)	*Anschluss* between Germany and Austria.
	Munich Conference. Germany occupies the Sudetenland.
1939 (15 March)	German troops occupy Bohemia and Moravia; Slovakia becomes German puppet state.
	Germany invades Poland on 1 September. Great Britain and France declare war on Germany two days later.

countermeasure, Stalin began to appease Hitler. The Nazi–Soviet Nonaggression Pact was signed on 23 August 1939. A secret portion of the pact divided Eastern Europe into German and Soviet spheres. The Soviet Union was to receive two of the Baltic States (Latvia and Estonia), Finland, Bessarabia, and eastern Poland.

The Nazi–Soviet Nonaggression Pact left Hitler free for his desired little war in Poland. He expected an easy victory over Poland. He also believed Britain and France would not challenge him. On 1 September, German forces invaded Poland and annexed Danzig. Two days later, on 3 September, Britain and France declared war on Germany. On 17 September, the Soviet Union invaded Poland from the east. By the end of the month, Poland fell and was partitioned between Germany and the Soviet Union, and a British Expeditionary Force of 158,000 men was on its way to France.

The Road to War in the Pacific

What transformed the war with Germany in Europe into a second world war was the emerging conflict with Japan in the Pacific. Since the end of the Great War, indeed even before, there was rivalry between the two new great powers, Japan and the United States.

German forces invade Poland on 1 September 1939, thus beginning World War II in Europe. Poland surrendered on 27 September. The Print Collector/Alamy Stock Photo.

Each country felt its vital interests in the Pacific threatened by the other. For Japan, the conflict increasingly took on the nature of a struggle for expansion and survival of the Japanese empire.

Events around the turn of the twentieth century increased tension between the United States and Japan. The Sino-Japanese War (1894–1895), the Russo-Japanese War (1904–1905), and the Spanish–American War (1898) revealed both nations as imperial powers with a growing conflict of economic interests in China and the Pacific. Japan's defeat of Russia in 1904–1905 removed Russia as a significant player in the Pacific. As a result of the Spanish–American War, the United States acquired Guam and the Philippine Islands. Acquiring the Philippine Islands increased American involvement in China and its determination to secure its share of the lucrative Chinese trade. The Open Door Policy proposed by Secretary of State John Hay (1838–1905) in 1899–1900 was meant to secure American access to China while preserving the fiction of China's territorial integrity and independence.

Great Britain had already reduced its role in the region when it concluded the Anglo-Japanese Alliance in 1902. The rising threat of the German High Seas Fleet compelled Britain to turn policing of the Pacific Ocean over to Japan in order to concentrate its naval forces in the North Sea and the Atlantic Ocean. Japan became the dominant maritime power in the western Pacific. This fact led some in the United States to conclude that Japan had become the primary threat to American interests in the Pacific. The result was America's "War Plan Orange" (1911), a plan for a possible war with Japan that remained valid until 1939.

Japan's seizure of the German territory of Kiaochow in November 1914 and its Twenty-One Demands (January 1915) aimed at gaining a virtual protectorate over China further aroused suspicions among Americans of Japanese imperialism. Meanwhile, developments at the Paris Peace Conference (1919) and the Washington Naval Conference (1921–1922) heightened Japanese suspicions of American motives. At the Paris Peace Conference in 1919, Japan requested that a declaration on racial equality be included in the League of Nations Charter. Woodrow Wilson, fearing that such a declaration would assure the defeat of the Versailles Treaty (which included the League Charter) in the Senate, refused to agree. As a kind of consolation prize, Japan was awarded a lease on the Shantung (Shandong) Peninsula in China, formerly belonging to Germany.

Additional gains during the Great War in the central Pacific of the former German Caroline, Marianna, Marshall, and Palau islands meant that Japan threatened American supply lines through the Pacific Ocean. To meet the threat, the United States prevailed upon Great Britain to end its private alliance with Japan and join with the United States, Japan, and other great powers to limit the size of their navies and define their interests in the Pacific region. Japanese military leaders would later see the agreements reached at the Washington Naval Conference (12 November 1922 to 6 February 1923) as an insult to Japanese national pride and an attempt to artificially limit legitimate Japanese imperial interests. However, the conference did afford international recognition of Japan as a significant power in eastern Asia, if not the major power.

Relations between Japan and the United States remained cordial during the 1920s. Both enjoyed immense prosperity. The United States was Japan's number one trading partner, with 40 percent of its industrial product going to the United States. Another 25 percent went to China. Japan was the only nation other than the United States whose investments exceeded its foreign debt. As with the world's other industrial countries, the Great Depression ended Japan's prosperity and set the two great powers of the Pacific on a collision course.

The effects of the Depression in Japan were made worse by an increase of 25 percent in the American tariff on Japanese goods. Wages fell one-third by 1931, rice prices fell below cost, and silk prices collapsed. One-half of Japan's rural population was living in abject poverty. As conditions worsened, real power within Japan's government passed into the hands of a small clique of military leaders, who saw Japan's salvation in an aggressive foreign policy. Under slogans like a "Greater East Asia Co-prosperity Sphere," Japan set out to establish economic control of China and Southeast Asia and military domination of the whole region. Such aggressive imperialism meant conflict with the Soviet Union and the United States.

In 1931, Japan invaded Manchuria, an act of unprovoked aggression which the League of Nations condemned. The League's condemnation and attempt to impose sanctions provoked the Japanese into withdrawing from the League and renouncing the Washington Naval Conference agreements. The United States condemned Japan's aggression but did not join the sanctions. Manchuria was reconstituted as Manchukuo in 1932, under Japanese "protection," and with Henry P'u-i (1906–1967), the last emperor of China, as its (puppet) regent.

Japanese forces invaded China in July 1937. Once again, the League of Nations condemned Japan's aggression, but the deteriorating situation in Europe prevented effective action and even encouraged Japan's militarist leaders. Japanese and Soviet forces clashed along the border between Siberia, Manchukuo, and Korea, despite a nonaggression treaty between the powers signed in August 1937. Relations with the United States grew more tense when in December 1937, Japanese bombers attacked the American gunboat *Panay* near Nanking, followed by Japan's rejection of the Open Door Policy in November 1938.

The United States pursued a cautious policy toward Japan to avoid war until the summer of 1940. With the steady success of German forces in Europe (see Chapter 6), Japan occupied Indochina in 1940–1941. President Roosevelt responded by freezing Japanese assets in America and imposing an embargo on trade with Japan, including oil. When the Dutch East Indies complied with the oil embargo, Japanese imports of the vital resource dropped by 90 percent. Faced with either withdrawing from Indochina and China, as demanded by the United States, or exhausting its oil reserves within two years, Japan saw a solution in gaining control of the Dutch East Indies. That, however, necessitated first defeating or disabling the American and British fleets in the Pacific. On 7 December 1941, Japanese forces attacked the American Pacific Fleet at Pearl Harbor. The Japanese attacked American and British installations at Wake Island, the Philippines, Guam, Hong Kong, and Malaya on the same day. On 8 December, the United States declared war on Japan. In an act of reckless abandon with few parallels in history, Germany and Italy declared war on the United States on 11 December. The war in

Europe and the war in the Pacific became World War II. This global conflict lasted until September 1945, leaving thinking people in the world wondering what had become of civilization.

References

Boardman, Barrington. (1989). *Flappers, Bootleggers, "Typhoid Mary," & the Bomb: An Anecdotal History of the United States from 1923–1945*. New York: Perennial Library.

Bowers, Claude Gernade. (2019). *My Mission to Spain: Watching the Rehearsal for World War II*. New York: Simon & Schuster.

Mazower, Mark. (1999). *Dark Continent: Europe's Twentieth Century*. New York: Alfred A. Knopf.

Pipes, Richard. (1981). *Modern Europe*. Homewood: Dorsey Press.

6

Armageddon

Europe in World War II, 1939–1945

Twentieth-Century Europe: 1900 to the Present, Fourth Edition.
Michael D. Richards and Paul R. Waibel.

Chronology

1939	Germany invades Poland; the Soviet Union invades Poland
	Great Britain and France declare war on Germany
	Winter War between the Soviet Union and Finland
1940	Germany invades Denmark and Norway
	Germany invades the Netherlands, Belgium, and France
	Battle of Britain
1941	Atlantic Charter
	Germany invades the Soviet Union
	Japan attacks the United States at Pearl Harbor
	United States declares war on Japan
	Germany declares war on the United States
1942	Wannsee Conference
	Battle of Midway
	Battle of Stalingrad
	Allied victory in North Africa
1943	Allied invasion of Sicily and Italy
	Mussolini deposed
	Italy joins the Allies
1944	D-Day invasion of German-occupied Europe by the Allies
	Battle of the Bulge
1945	Yalta Conference
	Germany surrenders
	Potsdam Conference
	Atomic bombs dropped on Hiroshima and Nagasaki
	Japan surrenders

In the spring and summer of 1939, the Soviet Union and Nazi Germany performed a complicated diplomatic dance that eventually led to the Nazi–Soviet Nonaggression Pact. Stalin had given up on the idea of collective security. Instead, he cynically used negotiations with England and France as a means by which to encourage Hitler to agree to a nonaggression pact. Hitler, for his part, was eager to begin the invasion of Poland at the start of September, before the fall rains began, and did not want to take a chance on becoming involved in a two-front war.

Midway through August, the tempo of the dance increased rapidly. Stalin invited Joachim von Ribbentrop (1893–1946), the German foreign minister, to Moscow on 23 August. Negotiations took very little time, after which the participants promptly signed the nonaggression treaty. They attached a secret protocol to the treaty that indicated each country's sphere of interest in Eastern and Central Europe.

In the early morning of 24 August, Stalin hosted a late supper for Ribbentrop, at which he toasted Hitler. Ribbentrop joked that "Stalin will yet join the Anti-Comintern Pact" (an agreement between Germany and Japan in 1936, with Italy joining in 1937, that was directed against the Soviet Union [as quoted in the record of the conversation of Stalin and Ribbentrop in the online Avalon Project 2013]). According to Nikita Khrushchev (1894–1971), then a member of the Politburo, Stalin said a couple of days later that he had tricked Hitler. The treaty would keep them out of the war and allow them to save their strength.

The years of war and diplomacy that began with the invasion of Poland in September 1939 completely changed Europe's position in the world. After World War I, Europe was no longer the focal point of world affairs as it had been before. At the end of World War II in 1945, Europe fell to a position of near impotence before the two great world powers, the Soviet Union and the United States. Furthermore, 1945 marked the beginning of a process by which the European colonial empires were gradually and painfully dismantled. Of course, part of the explanation for this startling reversal of fortune lies in the realities that prevailed in 1939. World War I and the Depression in the 1930s had begun to hollow out European Civilization. World War II finished the process. The world was rapidly changing, and Europe's effortless dominance had effectively ended.

Blitzkrieg

The German invasion of Poland, which began on 1 September 1939, made skillful use of a new offensive strategy pioneered by the *Wehrmacht* (Army) known as *Blitzkrieg* (lightning war). *Blitzkrieg* involved combining mechanized spearheads of troops, motorized artillery, tanks massed in groups, and close tactical support by fighters and dive-bombers, all closely controlled by radio. It was a strategy that emphasized surprise and overwhelming force that usually resulted in a rapid, decisive victory. Easy victories in 1939 and again in 1940 encouraged Hitler's belief that Germany did not need to prepare for a protracted war, a view that proved fatal over the next few years.

In the meantime, however, Germany was encouraged by its military prowess. *Blitzkrieg's* tactics resulted in the rapid defeat of Poland. By 8 September, the German forces were outside Warsaw. Soviet forces invaded Poland from the east on 17 September. Caught between two massive armies, Poland surrendered on 28 September, less than a month after the German offensive began.

A strange interlude known as the "Phony War" (*Sitzkrieg*) occurred during the eight months following the fall of Poland. Technically, a state of war existed between Germany and the two Western democracies of Britain and France, yet no military engagements occurred. Hitler expected Britain and France to accept his offers of peace. While Britain and France did not pursue these offers, they had no clear strategy for responding to Germany's recent conquest.

On 3 November, the Soviet Union demanded several small areas from Finland to enhance the defenses of Leningrad. When the Finns refused, Soviet forces invaded Finland, beginning what came to be called the "Winter War," November 1939–March 1940. The Finns did surprisingly well against their much larger opponent, but the massive resources of the Soviet Union eventually prevailed. Stalin did not annex Finland even though it had once been part of the old Russian empire. Finland ceded to the Soviet Union the territories sought by Stalin and some additional territories to enhance the security of Leningrad. After defeating the Finns, the Soviet Union incorporated the Baltic States of Estonia, Latvia, Lithuania, and Bessarabia and Northern Bukovina from Romania.

Hitler and his generals saw the lackluster performance of the Russian Army in the Winter War as evidence that the Russian Army was not a match for the *Wehrmacht*. Stalin's purge of the Army and Navy between 1936 and 1938, which included three of five marshals,

13 of 15 army commanders, and 50 of 57 army corps commanders, contributed to Hitler's fatal miscalculation of the Red Army's future performance on the Eastern Front.

Germany returned to the offensive in April 1940. Once again, *Blitzkrieg* tactics brought swift results. On 9 April, German forces invaded Denmark and Norway. Denmark surrendered within hours, but with British support, Norway fought until 10 June. The attack on France began on 10 May with German forces moving through Belgium and the Netherlands. German bombers destroyed the center of Rotterdam. Forty thousand civilians died, an early indication the new war would be even more senselessly brutal than the previous one.

The battle for France lasted only 46 days, from 10 May to 25 June. The German *Blitzkrieg* moved quickly across France, cutting off the British Expeditionary Force and thousands of French troops around the port city of Dunkirk. The British turned defeat into a kind of victory by evacuating more than 300,000 troops, of which more than 100,000 were French, Belgian, and Dutch, with the help of an armada of small boats and ships. By mid-June, the French cabinet voted to ask Germany for terms of a ceasefire. The armistice was signed on 22 June in the same railroad car in which the Germans had signed the armistice ending World War I. France was divided into a Nazi-occupied zone in the north, including Paris, and an unoccupied zone in the south, which the French were allowed to govern. The latter became known as Vichy France, after its capital in the resort town of Vichy. The head of state of what the Allies called "Vichy France" was Henri Philippe Pétain, the great hero of the battle of Verdun in World War I.

Volumes have been written attempting to explain the Fall of France. During the interwar period, France's plans for a possible future war with Germany were based strictly on defense, even though it was an Allied offense that eventually broke the stalemate on the Western Front in 1918. Symbolic of France's emphasis on defense was the construction of the Maginot Line, a line of fortresses along France's border with Germany from Switzerland to Belgium, but not to the English Channel. It proved to be a waste of resources. When the German invasion occurred, the Germans merely ignored the Maginot Line by going through the Ardennes's hilly and heavily wooded terrain to the north of the line. The Maginot Line weakened France by encouraging a false sense of security and a defensive mentality that surrendered the advantage to the German invaders. The French were prepared to refight the war of 1914–1918, not a war in which tanks and aircraft would overcome the best-constructed defenses.

The German invasion caught the French by surprise, a surprise compounded by their inability to grasp the techniques of *Blitzkrieg*. One French commander, the then-Colonel Charles de Gaulle (1890–1970), had long advocated tactics, including tanks, that might have made a significant difference if employed in 1940. His colleagues had primarily ignored him, but German officers had paid close attention.

The Fall of France reflected the dislike many French felt for the Third Republic, the lack of a clear-cut national purpose, and the scarcity of leaders of imagination and daring. Nevertheless, while the defeat was "strange," as Marc Bloch (1886–1944), a historian and later hero of the French resistance, believed, it did not result from treason, as some have argued, but rather from lousy judgment and failure of nerve.

By midsummer 1940, only Britain remained to carry on the struggle against Nazi Germany and Fascist Italy. Italy joined the war against France at the last minute when France's defeat was inevitable, but Italy's performance in World War II would prove even less impressive than its performance in World War I. Winston Churchill (1874–1965) became prime minister of the United Kingdom on 10 May, the first day of the German invasion of France. More than any single individual, he became associated with the Allied cause in World War II and generally with its more memorable moments.

If that summer was, as Churchill later put it, Britain's "finest hour," it was also a very dark hour. Before the start of July, Hitler engaged in planning for Operation Sea Lion, an invasion of the British Isles. The Battle of Britain began with a German air raid on 10 July 1940. The German objective was to gain control of the air over the English Channel and southern England as a prelude to an invasion of the British Isles. The boast by Reich Marshal Hermann

Göring (1893–1945), commander of the German *Luftwaffe* (air force), that he could bomb the British into surrender proved mistaken. On 7 September, the Germans made a fatal blunder when they shifted from attacking airfields and communications centers to terror bombings of London and other cities. The shift allowed the RAF (Royal Air Force) time to recover. Hitler called off Operation Sea Lion in late October to prepare for his planned invasion of the Soviet Union. Germany lost the Battle of Britain, and that loss, together with the invasion of the Soviet Union on 22 June 1941 and the declaration of war with the United States on 11 December 1941, may rightly be seen as the beginning of the end of the war for Germany.

Several factors help to explain the British success. Perhaps most important was the nature of the German *Luftwaffe* and how it was commanded. It had been designed more for tactical support of the *Blitzkrieg* than for extended bombing runs. Indeed, the German bombers were slow, and their level of fighter protection was often inadequate. The German fighter planes were limited in range and inferior to the RAF's Hurricanes and Spitfires. Equally important

Boy seated in wreckage of building after a bombing raid of London during World War II. Frissell, Toni/The Library of Congress/Public Domain.

was Radar, which was developed by the British during the 1930s. It gave them a crucial few minutes warning of incoming German aircraft. British fighters could meet the German aircraft over the English Channel rather than over southern England. The critical role radar played in Britain's victory was summed up by Wing Commander Max Aitken (1879–1964): "Radar really won the Battle of Britain. . . . We wasted no petrol, no energy, no time" (Roberts 2011).

Operation Barbarossa

War with the Soviet Union was one of the objectives clearly stated in *Mein Kampf* and alluded to on numerous occasions by Hitler. The German people's eastward expansion had played a role in German history as far back as the High Middle Ages, somewhat similar to "manifest destiny" in American history. Hitler considered European Russia, particularly Ukraine, the area where Germany would find the living space (*Lebensraum*) necessary for its expanding population. In his twisted racial ideology, a "war of annihilation," as he characterized the war with the Soviet Union, was necessary. The educated among the conquered Slavs would be annihilated. The masses would be denied an education beyond the very minimum needed for their role as enslaved people for the Third Reich. In addition, Hitler regarded the defeat of the Soviet Union as crucial for the elimination of what he termed "Jewish Bolshevism."

The invasion of Russia, "Operation Barbarossa," began on 22 June 1941. Looking back on that fateful decision, it seems odd that Hitler would take on a country with such vast resources, a country that, since the Nazi–Soviet Nonaggression Pact (August 1939), was supplying Germany with the natural resources necessary to fight a war. However, practical considerations seemed insignificant at the time and appeared to reinforce ideological objectives. The Soviet Union seemed still disorganized by the purges and the Five-Year Plans. In addition, the Russian Army had performed poorly in the Winter War against Finland. Also, the Nazis knew the Soviet Union would only become stronger as time passed.

Stalin chose not to heed warnings of an impending German invasion from his own and foreign intelligence sources. Richard Sorge (1895–1944), a German Communist working in Japan, actually provided the date of the invasion. Stalin finally decided to send an alert message early on the same day the attack began. It came too late to do any good. The Russian military was caught off guard when three million soldiers poured into Russia along a 2,000-mile (3,219 km) front. Most of the invading forces were German but included some Finns and Romanians. Soldiers from Italy, Croatia, Slovakia, and Hungary joined later.

The Soviet forces suffered heavy casualties. Whole armies collapsed and were cut off. Attempts to retreat and regroup turned into routs. Much of the Russian air force was lost in the first days of the invasion. Stalin fell apart and sank into depression. It was two weeks before he finally spoke on the radio. Within weeks, Leningrad was under siege, German troops were advancing rapidly toward Moscow, and most of the rich croplands and important industrial complexes of Ukraine had been conquered.

Despite the early successes, Operation Barbarossa was doomed to fail. Rejecting advice from his generals, Hitler ordered a three-prong attack, one headed north towards Leningrad, a second headed south towards Stalingrad, and the third towards Moscow. The invasion was initially scheduled for 15 May but postponed until 22 June. Mussolini launched a surprise attack on Greece on 28 October with disastrous results. Hitler had to divert German forces to rescue the Italians and secure Germany's rear during the invasion of Russia. That one-month delay may alone have caused Operation Barbarossa's failure because it meant that the severe Russian winter came to the rescue.

So confident was Hitler that Russia would fall quickly, as France had, that the German forces were not prepared for either winter or a prolonged war. Russian forces retreated before the advancing Germans as they had 129 years earlier (almost to the day) when Napoléon invaded Russia on 24 June 1812. First came the rains, a time the Russians called *rasputitsa* (the time when the roads dissolved into mud), followed by early winter. Temperatures around Moscow dropped to −22°F (−30°C). Fires had to be kept burning under the tanks to prevent the oil from freezing. German women back home were urged to donate their winter coats for the soldiers. It is no exaggeration to say that the German Army froze to death before the gates of Moscow, as had the French earlier.

The German Army was stopped short of victory. All three of the German offensives failed to reach their objectives. Victory over the Germans in what the Russian people called the "Great Patriotic War" was still three-and-a-half years in the future. On 6 December, Russian forces began major counteroffensives on all three fronts. As with Napoléon's Army in 1812, Hitler's Army started the long and bloody retreat westward that would end with the Russian capture of Berlin in May 1945.

Turning the Tide

Both in European and the Pacific theaters, 1942 was the decisive year of World War II. The situation for the Allies during the first half of 1942 was dire. American General George C. Marshall (1880–1959) later commented: "Few realized how close to complete domination of the world was Germany and Japan and how thin the thread of Allied survival had been stretched" (Gruhl 2017). "It is certain," he wrote, "that the refusal of the British and Russian peoples to accept what appeared to be inevitable defeat was the great factor in the salvage of our civilization" (White 2011). Three decisive battles—Battle of Midway (4–7 June) in the Pacific, Second Battle of El Alamein (23 October–11 November) in North Africa, and the Battle of Stalingrad (17 July 1942 to 2 February 1943)—mark the turning point of the war in Europe and the Pacific.

Battle of Midway

Without giving advance notice to Germany, Japan launched a surprise attack on the American fleet stationed at Pearl Harbor, Hawaii, on 7 December 1941. Twenty-one ships and 347 out of 402 aircraft were either destroyed or damaged. Although the Japanese inflicted extensive damage to the fleet at anchor in Pearl Harbor, it fell short of achieving its mission to neutralize the ability of the United States to respond to Japan's plans for the next six months.

Pearl Harbor was not the only objective on 7 and 8 December. Part of the Japanese offensive was aimed at British and other American possessions in the Pacific. The Japanese attacked the American possessions of Guam, the Philippines, Midway, and Wake Island, and the British possessions of Malaya, Singapore, and Hong Kong. Japanese objectives in Hawaii and Midway failed, but their objectives elsewhere in the Pacific were achieved: British Burma, Australia's territories of New Guinea and Papua, nearly all of the Dutch East Indies, and a number of islands. They even occupied Attu and Kiska, two of Alaska's Aleutian Islands (Immerwahr 2022).

Despite the damage inflicted at Pearl Harbor, the Japanese attack left undamaged the submarine base, naval repair yards, the oil depots, and the Old Administration Building, which housed the Navy's signals monitoring and cryptographic unit (Fleet Radio Unit Pacific). Most important, perhaps, was the fact that the three aircraft carriers assigned to the Pacific fleet were out to sea and therefore spared. The aircraft carrier would prove to be the decisive weapon in Pacific theater. The Japanese failure to sink the aircraft carriers eventually cost them the war.

In May 1942, Admiral Isoroku Yamamoto (1884–1943), architect of the attack on Pearl Harbor, hoped to involve the United States Navy in a decisive battle by attacking Midway Island, some 1,100 miles west of Hawaii. American codebreakers, successful in deciphering the Japanese naval code, provided advanced warning of Yamamoto's plans. American Admiral Chester W. Nimitz (1885–1966) ordered all available ships, including the strategic aircraft carrier USS *Yorktown* to Midway.

The Battle of Midway was fought from 4 to 7 June. It was a sea battle between two opposing fleets but unique in that it was fought entirely by aircraft. The big ships with their big guns never saw each other and remained out of range of their guns. Before the battle, the Japanese Navy had six aircraft carriers in the Pacific and the American Navy four, three of which participated. The Americans lost just one, whereas the Japanese lost four of their six. It was a disaster from which the Japanese could not recover. They could not replace the carriers or the aircraft and pilots lost in the battle. The United States, protected by two oceans, became the arsenal to produce the materiel and supply the human resources needed by the Allies. In 1943 World War II became a war of attrition, the sort of war that favored the Allies, just as had been the case in World War I.

Battle of El Alamein

The Italian Tenth Army began an invasion of Egypt on 30 September 1940, with the disastrous outcome that had become customary for the Italians. British and Commonwealth forces launched a counter-offensive on 9 December. After repeated defeats, the Italians surrendered on 7 February 1941. Hitler sent an army to North Africa under the command of General Erwin Rommel (1891–1944), later known as the "Desert Fox." Rommel pushed the British back across Libya into Egypt.

The decisive battle was a duel between two gifted generals, Erwin Rommel and Bernard Montgomery (1887–1976). It took place near El Alamein, a small town on Egypt's Mediterranean coast about 100 miles (161 km) west of Alexandria. Rommel's Africa Korps was pinched between two Allied armies. The Battle of El Alamein ended in an Allied victory. The victory led to the German surrender of North Africa in May 1943 and eliminated the Axis threat to Egypt, the Suez Canal, and oil fields in the Middle East.

Battle of Stalingrad

The turning point of the war in Europe, and some would say of World War II as a whole, was the Battle of Stalingrad, 17 July 1942 to 2 February 1943. Stalingrad, a city in southwest Russia on the western bank of the Volga River, was important to both sides for strategic and symbolic reasons. The capture of Stalingrad would allow the Germans to cut supply lines to Russia and inhibit the Russian Army's ability to deploy troops. Also, because the city was named in honor of Stalin, the Russians were as determined to defend it as the Germans were to capture it.

The German Sixth Army, under the command of General Friedrich W. E. Paulus (1890–1957), began the offensive on 17 July with orders from Hitler to capture the city by 25 August. On 28 July, Stalin ordered the defenders to take "not one step back." By late August, the Germans had penetrated the city. What followed was what the German soldiers called a "Rat War (*Rattenkrieg*)." The fighting was intense, waged block by block, house by house, and even room by room. Marshal Gregory Zhukov (1896–1974) began a massive Soviet counteroffensive on 6 November, including attacking the poorly equipped Romanians who defended the German supply lines and were quickly overrun.

The German Sixth Army was encircled and running out of supplies. Hitler expected Paulus and the remaining soldiers of the Sixth Army to die fighting. He refused permission for Paulus to attempt to fight his way out of Stalingrad. Instead, Hitler promoted him to the rank of field marshal, noting that no German field marshal had ever surrendered. Before surrendering on 2 February 1943, Paulus reportedly told his generals, "I have no intention of shooting myself for this Bohemian corporal" (Ray 2018).

The average lifespan of a soldier in the Battle of Stalingrad in winter temperatures that reached −22°F (−30°C) was only 24 hours. Estimated casualties were 800,000 Axis and 1.1 million Soviet soldiers, plus an estimated 40,000 civilians. Of the roughly 90,000 who surrendered, about one-half died on the march to the Siberian prison camps. Only 5,000 eventually returned to Germany after the war (Shirer 1960, p. 883).

The fact that the war had become a war of attrition like World War I was clear in the Battle of Kursk (5–16 July 1943), the largest tank battle in military history. The Russians had the advantage in numbers. They fielded 1,900,000 troops, 5,000 tanks, and 3,500 aircraft. Opposing them were 780,000 German troops, 3,000 tanks, and 2,000 aircraft (Carson 2018). The Soviet forces suffered much larger losses, but their losses could be replaced. In the remainder of 1943, the Soviet Union began steadily advancing on all fronts. In January 1944, the siege of Leningrad was lifted, and Soviet forces were nearing several key cities in Eastern Europe.

D-Day

The Soviet Union suffered far more than any other nation in the European theater. There is no disputing that from the German invasion of Russia in June 1941 until D-Day on 22 June 1944, the Russian people engaged the German war machine virtually alone. It is no surprise that in 1942 and 1943, Stalin continuously pressed his Allies to open a second, Western front in Europe to ease the enormous burden Soviet forces were shouldering in fighting off the Germans. Understandably, Stalin was suspicious that his western Allies might have ulterior motives in allowing the Soviet Union to carry the burden of the war in Europe.

The United States was preoccupied mainly during that period with the war in the Pacific. For its part, Britain spent most of 1942 dealing with Rommel's Africa Korps in Libya and Egypt. The closest thing to a second front in 1942 was the occupation of French North Africa. It was both a diplomatic and military maneuver in that Vichy France nominally controlled the area. The successful liberation of French North Africa helped General Charles de Gaulle emerge as the undisputed leader of the Free French (*les Forces Françaises Libres*), a military organization created after the French government had signed the armistice with Germany.

Neither the Allied occupation of French North Africa nor the Anglo-American invasion of Sicily (10 July–17 August 1943) and the Italian mainland (10 July 1943) provided relief for the embattled Russians on the Eastern Front. Two weeks after the Allied invasion of the Italian mainland, the Fascist Grand Council (*Gran Consiglio del Fascismo*) met and passed a motion to request that King Victor Emmanuel III (1869–1947) assume his constitutional powers and remove Mussolini from office. The king agreed. He subsequently ordered Mussolini arrested and appointed Marshal Pietro Badoglio (1871–1956) as premier. Badoglio disbanded the Fascist Party and opened negotiations with the Allies, which resulted in Italy switching sides on 3 September 1943. In the meantime, German paratroopers had carried out a daring rescue of Mussolini. The Nazis established the Italian Social Republic with the small town of Salò on Lake Garda as its de facto capital and

Mussolini as head of state. What was, in reality, only a puppet state lasted only from 23 September 1943 until 25 April 1945, just over 19 months.

The Italian campaign was not the long-awaited second front that Stalin was demanding. Only with D-Day, 6 June 1944, did the Soviet Union get the relief on the Eastern Front it wanted. Operation Overlord, the landings on the beaches of Normandy by American, British, and Canadian forces, was as much a feat of logistics as anything else. Simply to amass and coordinate the equipment and men needed for the cross-Channel invasion was a tremendous achievement. Waiting for the right combination of weather and tides, and preventing German intelligence from discerning the nature of preparations constituted additional formidable tasks.

By nightfall of the first day, more than 100,000 troops had come ashore. Many more came ashore in the following days, as did an avalanche of materiel. German resistance was surprisingly effective and delayed the "breakout" from the linked beachheads south and east into central France by approximately a month. Optimism that the war might be concluded by the end of the year was dashed when the Germans counterattacked. Coming out of the Ardennes' forests on 16 December, the Germans created a "bulge" in the allied line. What is remembered as the Battle of the Bulge, the most-costly battle for the United States, lasted until 25 January 1945. Hitler's gamble had failed. He committed his last reserves of men, armor, and aircraft in the West to the battle and lost. Germany was losing the war of attrition on the Western and Eastern Fronts.

Home Fronts

World War II was a modern industrial war like World War I. It was a total war; each nation mobilized all its human and materiel resources for the war effort. When Germany and Japan failed to achieve a decisive victory at the beginning of the war, it became a war of attrition. Victory would go to the side best able to mobilize and use its total resources. The side that could stay in the war the longest was destined to emerge victoriously.

All of the nations at war learned from the example of World War I. Each undertook measures that increased industrial and agricultural output and, where necessary, imposed rationing of resources on their civilian populations. As in previous wars, necessity proved to be the mother of invention. Synthetic rubber and oil, acrylic, nylon, rayon, and various forms of plastics were either invented or perfected. The battlefield's demands speeded the development and expanded the use of sulfa drugs, penicillin, and streptomycin (one of the first antibacterial medications discovered in 1943).

Penicillin was the "wonder drug" of World War II. Producing penicillin in sufficient quantities was a daunting problem. US-made penicillin was first used on a patient in March 1942. In June, there was only enough penicillin to treat ten patients. It was first tested for military use in the spring of 1943, and by autumn, it was being used in combat zones, but only for soldiers with life-threatening infections. Production rose from 231 billion units in 1943 to 7,952 billion units in 1945 (Mailer and Mason 2001). Penicillin was not made available to the public until March 1945 in the United States and June 1946 in the United Kingdom.

The people of Britain (United Kingdom) went to war in September 1939 reluctantly. There was no repeat of the enthusiasm accompanying the war announcement in 1914. That observation was generally accurate for both the Allied and Axis powers. The initial wartime measures, such as blackouts and the beginning of "Operation Pied Piper," the evacuation of children from the coastal areas to the interior, were very unpopular. The fall of France and the evacuation of the British Expeditionary Force from the beaches of Dunkirk in May 1940 shocked the British people.

Until the German invasion of the Soviet Union in 1941, Britain stood alone against the German, Italian, and Japanese war machines. Winston Churchill became prime minister on 10 May 1940 and began rallying the home front for the long struggle he saw ahead. Churchill's famous "Blood, toil, tears and sweat" speech of 13 May united the people in a community of spirit unparalleled in any other of the principal belligerents:

> We shall go on to the end. We shall fight in France, we shall fight on the seas and oceans, we shall fight with growing confidence and growing strength in the air, we shall defend our island, whatever the cost may be. We shall fight on the beaches, we shall fight on the landing grounds, we shall fight in the fields and in the streets, we shall fight in the hills; we shall never surrender. . . . ("We Shall Fight on the Beaches" 2021)

As in World War I, Britain was able to call on its empire's human and materiel resources. On 11 March 1941, the United States Congress passed the Lend-Lease Act that allowed the United States to "lend or lease" to Britain or any nation war supplies deemed "vital to the defense of the United States" (Lend-Lease Act 1941, 2022).

On 29 December 1940, during one of his radio broadcasts popularly referred to as "fireside chats," President Franklin D. Roosevelt (1882–1945) promised aid to the United Kingdom in its war with the Axis Powers. Using a phrase not original with him, but ever since associated with the President, Roosevelt referred to the United States as the "Arsenal of Democracy." Just as in World War I, America's entry into the war in Europe and the Pacific in December 1941 all but guaranteed that the Allies would win the war of attrition.

Protected from invasion by two oceans, American industries located in Detroit, Cleveland, Chicago, New York, Philadelphia, Birmingham, Pittsburgh, and other cities, "manufactured" victory for the Allies. At the end of America's first year at war, the United States produced more war materiel than all the Axis countries combined. In that year alone, American factories produced more planes than Japan did throughout the war. By 1944, the number of armaments produced in the United States was double that of the Axis. American factories accounted for one-half of the total war production during World War II.

The people of the Soviet Union suffered more than any other German-occupied county. Until 1943, Germany controlled large amounts of Russian farmland and significant parts of Russian industry. As the German Army retreated, it destroyed as much as possible. In organizing the home front, the Soviet Union had the advantage of an authoritarian government and a tightly controlled command economy from the beginning. Under the Five-Year Plans of the 1930s, some industries shifted to the east. When the war began, entire plants were dismantled, relocated, and put back into production in a matter of weeks. With its population mobilized and considerable American aid from the Lend-Lease Program, the Soviet Union built up its productive capacity and sustained its war effort.

The Russian people and the people of Britain alike met the challenges of the war and made the necessary sacrifices with the hope that victory would bring a better quality of life for everyone. For the people of the Soviet Union, it was the fulfillment of the Marxist promise of a classless society and improved quality of life for everyone. For the Britons, it was the promise of a modern welfare state with a guarantee of a minimal standard of living for all the king's subjects.

When Germany invaded Poland in September 1939, it was unprepared for a general war in Europe, much less one that would bring in the United States. Hitler met with his generals in 1937 and informed them that Germany must be prepared for a war to obtain *Lebensraum* (living space) no later than 1943–1945.

It can be argued that Germany lost the war in part because it failed to commit to total war until it was too late. Throughout 1941, this kind of commitment seemed unnecessary. Quick victories made it possible to reequip the German military without placing much strain on the civilian economy. Occupied countries had the tops of their economies skimmed off for the German war effort. Additionally, Sweden and Switzerland, neutral during the war, were important factors in the German war effort.

When the Soviet Union did not collapse as expected in 1942, however, it became clear something had to be done to coordinate the economy for military purposes. Hermann Göring (1893–1946), who had been in charge of the Four-Year Plan (1936) before the war, made efforts in this direction, as did army personnel. Fritz Todt (1891–1942), minister of armaments and munitions, began a more successful effort that, after his death in 1942 in an airplane accident, was carried on by Albert Speer (1905–1981). Speer, Hitler's personal architect, demonstrated considerable managerial ability in reorganizing the German economy. Speer tripled the production of munitions and weapons between 1942 and 1944. However, Allied bombing raids and a lack of raw materials and manpower resulted in a steep decline in production in 1945.

Speer's efforts, remarkable as they were, were hampered by parallel efforts by Heinrich Himmler (1900–1945) and the Schutzstaffel (SS). The SS, originally a protective guard for Hitler and other Nazi leaders, evolved to become a virtual state within a state; it possessed its own military units and used vital resources for purposes such as the Holocaust that had little to do with the prosecution of the war. Both Speer and Himmler made use of slave labor. For Speer, it was mainly prisoners of war and forced laborers from occupied countries in Eastern Europe. For Himmler, it was concentration camp inmates working in factories attached to specific concentration camps, primarily Auschwitz (Oświęcim) in Poland.

Once the United States entered the war at the end of 1941, every area of civilian life was committed to supplying the nation's fighting men and women with all they needed. Measures undertaken mirrored those taken in Britain. Factories switched to producing the armaments for the United States and its allies. Women worked in factories and farms to free up men for the armed forces. Victory gardens appeared in yards where grass grew previously. Scout groups collected tin cans and other materials for recycling into weapons. Rations stamps were required for most purchases of food and fuel. Hollywood got into the business of producing propaganda to rally the home front.

One area of concern was what to do about citizens whose nationality background caused some to regard them as security risks. The German American Bund, a pro-Nazi organization that modeled itself after Hitler's SA, was banned in 1941. Fourteen thousand Germans and Italians were rounded up, and 2,000 Japanese were arrested. In February 1942, the Army Western Defense Command chief requested authority to remove all Japanese, including Japanese Americans who were native-born United States citizens, from their homes and farms on the West Coast. Although the Justice Department argued against this move, President Roosevelt signed an executive order on 19 February that permitted the designation of military areas from which certain unspecified people might be excluded. Soon after this, more than 100,000 Japanese were imprisoned in relocation camps staffed with armed guards, where they remained until the United States government in December 1944 declared there was no longer a need for the camps and began to empty them. Canada adopted similar measures in 1942 regarding citizens of Japanese descent, particularly in the west coast province of British Columbia.

Collaboration and Resistance

The Third Reich made little attempt to use the situations they had created to construct a "new order" in Europe. Even those among the occupied nations who wanted to collaborate with Germany were forced to do so under disadvantageous conditions. Some groups, Ukrainian nationalists, for example, who were eager to help in the destruction of the Soviet regime, were treated so badly that they had little choice but to resist the Nazis.

In occupied Europe, it was frequently difficult to avoid a kind of collaboration. For instance, how should a civil servant see his position? What he did was mainly for the welfare of the people in his country, but some of what he did might well aid the German war effort.

Vichy France was in many ways a special case. Pierre Laval (1883–1945), premier during much of the existence of Vichy, argued after the fact that his policies were necessary in order to keep the German occupation at a distance. It was better for Vichy authorities to supervise the recruiting of workers for labor in the German war industry than to turn this task over to the Germans themselves. Similarly, Laval argued it was important for the French police to function as fully as possible, even if this meant cooperating with the Gestapo (*Geheime Staatspolizei* or Secret State Police) in tracking down Jews or in dealing with the resistance.

Not many of those involved in the Vichy government could be accurately labeled as fascists. Most were conservatives who practiced collaboration because it seemed unavoidable and also because it appeared to offer the chance to carry out a "National Revolution."

Between June 1940 and April 1942, members of the Vichy government believed they were working to replace the shopworn values and institutions of the Third Republic with something far better. By 1943, however, Henri-Philippe Pétain, Laval, and the rest of the Vichy government found it possible to do only what the Germans allowed or required them to do. What may have been a sensible policy in the shock of defeat in 1940 had become no longer justifiable through a series of almost imperceptible changes.

Elsewhere in occupied Europe, it was less likely than in Vichy France that one could believe he was working for a national regeneration within the context of the German occupation. The pressure to supply the Nazi occupiers with food, workers for the factories, and Jews for the death camps was too great. Here and there, efforts were made to save the young men from labor service and the Jewish population of the country from exportation. The stories of Anne Frank (1929–1945) and Corrie Ten Boom (1892–1983) and her family in the Netherlands and the heroic efforts of Oskar Schindler (1908–1974), the people of Denmark, and the people of Le Chambon in France are the best-known stories of many individuals who chose to resist evil. Many will never be known.

Moral ambiguity will always accompany accounts of resistance or collaboration. It is a case where one must admit that the victors write the history. Nonetheless, the resistance movements accomplished much of crucial importance. They furnished intelligence, helped downed pilots and escaped prisoners of war, and, in some cases, severely hampered the German war effort. In various other ways, the resistance movements left important legacies. Many members of the resistance movements hoped to find different ways of organizing society, politics, and the economy after the war. For some, this took the form of a "European" approach that would counter the dangers of nationalism. For others, the emphasis was on social justice. Various resistance "charters," such as the Charter of the National Council of Resistance in France, provided guidelines for postwar reconstruction programs.

The resistance movements within Germany were plagued by moral ambiguity. Much has been made of the circles, composed mainly of military officers and aristocrats, which attempted to assassinate Hitler on several occasions. Their actions were dictated more by realizing that Hitler's war was leading Germany to disaster than moral questioning of the "New Order" envisioned by the Nazis. For that reason and others, including the demand for unconditional surrender by the Allies, the German resistance did not receive the cooperation of the Allies in their efforts.

The Holocaust

Nazi Germany was an authoritarian state that aimed to create a population of "born again believers" who surrendered all individual identity and will to the messianic leader, the embodiment of the future utopia. Hitler's "New Order," or Third Reich was a society in which biological racism was to be the organizing principle. Racially pure Aryans would rule over the masses of inferior races (*Untermenschen*), who would be kept as a source of illiterate slave labor or exterminated if deemed a biological threat. The ultimate racial enemy was the Jewish people. Racial-based antisemitism was at the very core of Hitler's worldview.

Antisemitism was not peculiar to Nazism. Its dark shadow reaches back at least to the birth of Christianity. It was based on religious prejudice until the last half of the nineteenth century. Previously, a Jew might hope to escape persecution by converting to Christianity. Under the influence of Social Darwinism and the pseudoscience of eugenics, it became a race-based ideology. The Darwinist struggle for survival of the fittest was replaced by negative eugenics, according to which Jews, whom Nazis considered inferior but also dangerous, were to be physically destroyed.

Before the rise of Nazism, Germany, with 0.75 percent of its population being Jewish by religion, according to the 16 June 1933 census,[1] was considered a desirable place of residence by Jews. A census taken on 17 May 1939 counted 330,539 "racial Jews" within Germany as defined by the Nuremberg Laws of 1935, including Austria and the Sudetenland (Blau 1950, p. 162).

[1] Approximately 505,000 out of a total population of 67 million. There were only 37,000 Jews living in Germany in 1950 (German Jewish Population in 1933 n.d.).

The Nazis used increased antisemitic propaganda, exclusion from more and more professions, restrictions on where Jews could live, prohibition of intermarriage with Germans, and progressively more violence against the Jews to force them to immigrate. Before the outbreak of war in September 1939, the treatment of the Jewish population was meant to encourage them to leave Germany by making life in Germany increasingly more difficult. The SA (*Sturmabteilung*), often called "Brownshirts," launched what was called the "Night of Broken Glass" (*Kristallnacht*) on 9 November 1938 throughout Germany, Austria, and the Sudetenland. It was a night of terror that included beatings, rapes, killings, torching of synagogues, and the breaking of Jewish shop windows. All Jewish retail businesses were transferred to Aryans, and the Jewish community was required to pay a fine of one billion marks for the damage done during the night.

Jews who wished to leave Germany found the doors to Jewish immigrants closed everywhere. United States President Franklin Roosevelt, whose wife Eleanor was sympathetic to the plight of the Jews in Germany, organized an international conference on the Jewish refugee crisis in Evian, France, in July 1938. Representatives from thirty-two nations attended the meeting. Only one country, the Dominican Republic, expressed a willingness to accept refugees. After the Evian conference, Hitler is supposed to have commented, "Nobody wants these criminals" ("America and the Holocaust" 2022).

Nine hundred Jews aboard the luxury liner *MS St Louis* departed for Cuba from Hamburg, Germany, in May 1939. They were refused permission to disembark in Cuba. President Roosevelt favored allowing them to enter the United States, but under pressure from Secretary of State Cordell Hull (1871–1955) and Southern Democrats, he chose not to. The refugees were forced to return to Germany, where they later perished in the Holocaust. Eighty-three percent of Americans in 1939 were opposed to admitting refugees. One poll taken in 1944 indicated that one-quarter of Americans considered Jews a "menace."

The Nazis considered emigration a possible solution to the "The Jewish Problem." Heinrich Himmler (1900–1945), commander of the SS and chief architect of the Holocaust, suggested emigration of Germany's Jewish population "to a colony in Africa or elsewhere" (Mazower 1998, pp. 166–167). Emigration, he noted, was the "best" solution, "if one rejects the Bolshevik method of physical extermination of a people out of *inner conviction as un-German and impossible*" (quoted in Mazower 1998, p. 167, emphasis added).

Operation Barbarossa in June 1941 dramatically altered plans for the treatment of the Jews. According to Hitler's reasoning, the war in Western Europe was to be fought according to warfare's "civilized" rules. The war in Eastern Europe was different. It was a war of annihilation (*Vernichtungskrieg*) against the "Judaeo-Bolshevik" enemy requiring mass murder on a never-before-seen scale. The Nazis suddenly found themselves controlling millions of Jews and tens of millions of Slavs who were considered racially inferior by the Nazis. At the end of 1941, Germany was at war with Britain, France, and the United States. Any plan to relocate the Jews of Europe to Africa or elsewhere was no longer possible.

Special SS units known as *Einsatzgruppen* ("task forces" that acted as mobile killing units) followed the German armies as they advanced through Poland (1939) and Russia (1941). Their assignment was "to identify and arrest political enemies, including Jews, Freemasons, members of the Communist Party, religious leaders, and those suspected of political opposition to the Nazi regime" (Westermann 2020). Thousands of people were forced to dig their own graves and then killed by machine gunfire. An estimated 1.5 million Jews were murdered, including 34,000 at Babi Yar, near Kiev in Ukraine, in September 1941. It was an inefficient method for the genocide of Europe's Jewish population. Also, as Himmler noted in a speech to SS officers in Poland on 4 October 1943, it was difficult for SS soldiers to carry out such mass executions and remain "decent" human beings. Future generations, he told them, will say, "We have carried out this most difficult task for the love of our people. And we have suffered no defect within us, in our soul, in our character" (From a Speech by Himmler n.d.).

The killing was not done only by the SS units. In August 1941, a regular army (*Wehrmacht*) officer reported that *SS Sonderkomando 4a* left behind ninety small children, including infants, after having murdered hundreds of adult Jews in the Ukrainian town of Byelaya

Tserkov. His unit found it "necessary to eliminate the Jewish children, particularly the infants." In his report, he noted that "measures against women and children were taken which in no way differ from atrocities carried out by the enemy" (quoted in Mazower 1998, p.168).

It became obvious in 1941 that a more efficient and orderly means was needed for carrying out Hitler's threat made in a speech before the *Reichstag* on 30 January 1939 that if war broke out it would mean the "destruction of the Jewish race in Europe" (Hitler's Threat n.d.). Fifteen high-ranking Nazi officials met at a villa in Wannsee, a suburb of Berlin on 20 January 1942 with instructions from Hermann Göring "to make all the necessary preparations. . . for the Final Solution (*Endlösung*) of the Jewish problem in the German sphere of influence in Europe" ("The Wannsee Conference" n.d.). Chairman of the conference, Reinhard Heydrich (1904–1942), informed the attendees that 11 million Jews would be included in the program.

The meeting lasted only ninety minutes. The participants worked out the logistical problems and the details of responsibility for the collection, transport, killing, and disposal of the millions of human beings under the control of the SS. After reading the fifteen-page typescript of the minutes of the meeting, Germany's President Frank-Walter Steinmeier (b. 1956) said,

> What we see is a smoothly functioning administrative machine, departments coordinating, templates and procedures which—apart from the content of the meeting—are indistinguishable from those that we still have in ministries and administrations. It is the ordinary, the familiar, that jumps out at us, horrifies us and unsettles us. (Bennhold 2022)

The conference did not initiate the concentration camps. They were already in existence. It did not begin the mass killing of the Jews and other so-called *Untermenschen*. That, too, was already underway. Instead, the Wannsee Conference set up the administrative structure for what would be, Joseph Goebbels wrote in his diary, "The complete elimination of the European Jews" (Bennhold 2022).

In Himmler's opinion, there was a correct, even honorable manner in which the Final Solution should be carried out. The case of *SS-Untersturmführer* Max Täubner serves as an example. Täubner was convicted by the SS and Police Supreme Court in Munich in May 1943 for the unauthorized killing of Jews in Ukraine. It was not killing the Jews that was wrong, but rather allowing "his men to act with such vicious, brutality . . . like a savage horde." The court concluded, "[t]hat the conduct of the accused is unworthy of an honorable and decent German man" (quoted in Mazower 1998, pp. 173–174).

There was a difference between the concentration camps and the extermination camps. The concentration camps, of which there were thousands[2] beginning with Dachau, opened in March 1933, housed individuals of various nationalities (Communists, Social Democrats, trade union leaders, and other individuals) who opposed National Socialism.[3] An inmate's stay might be limited or terminal. Death usually resulted from the terrible conditions in the camps, but in some cases, death resulted from the momentary sadistic act by a kapo,[4] camp policeman, or an SS officer and his police dog.

There were six extermination camps in Poland, Auschwitz, Belzec, Chelmno, Majdanek, Sobibor, and Treblinka. Auschwitz, located near the town of Oświęcim in southern Poland, and the most notorious of the death camps, was a large complex with fifty sub-camps. Some were extermination camps. Others included factories that used inmates as slave laborers. Once inmates arrived, they were separated into those who could work and those who went directly to the gas chambers. The gas chambers could handle

[2] "Between 1933 and 1945, Nazi Germany and its allies established more than 44,000 camps and other incarceration sites (including ghettos)" ("Camp System Maps" n.d.). See this source for maps showing locations.

[3] A comparison with the Soviet Union's system of prisoner camps known as the GULAG is appropriate.

[4] Kapos were prisoners selected by the SS officers to supervise forced labor and other administrative tasks. They were recruited from criminal elements and known for their brutality towards the other inmates. If they did not carry out their duties with the appropriate enthusiasm and results, they were demoted to ordinary prisoner status and became subject to the kapos ("Kapo" 2021).

2,000 individuals at one time. Twelve thousand could be gassed and incinerated daily ("Auschwitz Camp Complex" n.d.).

In recent years, considerable research has been done on the alleged role that American firms played in the Holocaust. Documentation exists for at least 43 corporations, including American corporations, banks, and press agencies that profited from participation in the implementation of the Holocaust. Altogether, 500 firms had ties to Auschwitz. American corporations had significant profitable investments in Germany during the Weimar Republic and the pre-war period of the Third Reich.

Before Germany declared war on the United States on 11 December 1941, American companies continued to defend their business operations in Germany. On 11 December 1941, American bank and company assets in Germany were seized (German Administration of American Companies, 1940–1945, 2022). Before and after the outbreak of war between Germany and the United States, American parent companies "followed a conscious strategy of continuing to do business with the Nazi regime" (Dobbs 1998) through their subsidiary companies in Germany and German-occupied territories. Alfred P. Sloan, chairman of General Motors, defended GM's continuing to do business in Nazi Germany as "highly profitable" and that the "internal politics of Nazi Germany should not be considered the business of the management of General Motors" (Dobbs 1998).

Given the role of modern technology in the twenty-first century, the role played by IBM (International Business Machines), an American corporation headquartered in New York, serves as both an example and a warning of what did and can happen when an amoral pursuit of profit guides a corporation devoted to advancing the frontiers of modern technology. IBM provided the early computer technology and machines that enabled the smooth and efficient operations and documentation of the Holocaust, from selection and transportation to the camps to the final disposal of the victims' bodies.

Edwin Black (1950–), an investigative journalist and historian, has spent much of his professional career researching the extent to which American corporations with subsidiaries in Germany and

German-occupied Europe were complicit in the Holocaust. IBM Germany (Deutsche Hollerith Maschinen Gesellschaft), "with the knowledge of its New York headquarters, enthusiastically custom-designed the complex devices and specialized applications as an official corporate undertaking." (Black 2000). IBM NY (IBM New York) officials remained in contact with IBM Germany "monitoring activities, ensuring that the parent company in New York was not cut out of any of the profits or business opportunities" (Black 2000). When in 1941, laws were passed making illegal direct contact between corporate headquarters in the United States and their subsidiaries in Germany and German-occupied Europe, they continued such through their subsidiaries. IBM, for example, continued direct contact through its office in Switzerland (Black 2000).

Plants belonging to American corporations, including Ford Motor and General Motors, located in the United States were a part of the "arsenal of democracy." At the same time, their plants located in Germany and German-occupied Europe were a part of the "arsenal of fascism." Henry Ford's Ford Motor Company operated a plant at Auschwitz. Albert Speer, Minister of Armaments and War Production in Nazi Germany, said in an interview in 1977 that Hitler "would never have considered invading Poland' without synthetic fuel technology provided by General Motors" (Dobbs 1998).

Henry Ford was one of the most prominent and outspoken anti-Semites in America. He and Hitler greatly admired each other. Ford used his weekly newspaper, *The Dearborn Independent*, to spread anti-semitism. He published the notorious *The Protocols of the Elders of Zion* and authored *The International Jew: The World's Foremost Problem,* which was translated into twelve languages and widely read.

The Germans made efforts to run the killing centers as productive enterprises. They collected anything of value—mounds of human hair, warehouses full of shoes, handbags, and dresses. They removed gold crowns and fillings from the corpses before wheeling them into the crematoria. The gold plucked from the inmates' teeth was sent to Berlin before disappearing in numbered bank accounts in Switzerland or the pockets of collaborators at various levels. The economic irrationality of this enterprise was all too apparent. In the middle of the war, beginning to go badly for Germany, vital resources were diverted to implement the Final Solution. From the perspective

Inmates of Buchenwald, a Nazi concentration camp, in April 1945. The young man seventh from the left in the middle row is Elie Wiesel who would later write *Night*, a memoir of his experience, and become a Nobel Prize laureate. National Archives and Records Administration (ARC no. 535561).

of the Nazis, who shared Hitler's racial beliefs, the elimination of Jews and other so-called undesirables (gypsies, homosexuals, and others) was precisely the point of the war.

The Holocaust produced a number of acute moral dilemmas. For example, if the perpetrators did not share Hitler's racial fantasies, then how did they justify participation? Some, of course, insisted they were only following orders. Many were active participants in the Holocaust because they saw the war in the east as a crusade against communism. It is now recognized that the regular Army played a larger role in the mass deaths outside the camps than was earlier believed to be the case. Some soldiers simply wanted to remain part of their unit, taking the bad with the good.

More frequently than one might wish to think, participation in mass killings hardened people; others found they actually enjoyed it. To the extent that the victim appeared to be weak, different, or alien, it was possible to consider that person less than human and,

Werner von Braun and other members of the group that developed the V-2 rocket during World War II shortly after their surrender to American soldiers in 1945. Von Braun is wearing a cast from injuries suffered in an earlier automobile accident. He later played a crucial role in the development of the United States space program. National Archives and Records Administration (ARC no. 531328).

therefore, easier to kill. Indeed, in the camps, where the system operated in such a way as to degrade people and deprive them of any dignity, it was possible for guards and supervisors to see the prisoners as undeserving of life. Some of the perpetrators and many of the observers were appalled by what they witnessed but generally felt there was little they could do as individuals.

For the inmates of concentration camps and death centers, ethical questions also existed. A few survived by losing every shred of humanity and taking part in crimes against their fellow prisoners. Most survivors, however, depended on solidarity with others. Invariably, there would come a time when even the strongest and most resourceful would find themselves lost without the help of a group. Much has been made of the inmates' passivity, of their failure to do anything to protest. To a large extent, this is unfair. First, the system worked in such a way as to disguise what was happening until it was too late. Second, there were uprisings and protests, even though the odds were impossibly high against success. Perhaps the most serious moral questions came in villages and towns before the arrival of deportation orders. Too many refused to heed the warnings or organize in their defense. By the time people had been placed in a ghetto, it was too late for escape in most cases. The Jewish councils the Nazis created to administer some aspects of ghetto life had to make agonizing decisions about compliance or resistance. Nonetheless, there were Jewish partisan groups and a few spectacular but ultimately futile examples of resistance in the ghettos. The Warsaw Ghetto Uprising in April–May 1943 was only the largest and most famous of these acts of defiance.

Finally, there is the question of the many who knew about the Holocaust but did nothing to stop it. While some courageous people worked to help Jews hide or escape to a neutral country, most tried to avoid involvement in or knowledge of the scheme. By the middle of the war, Allied leaders knew the broad outlines of the Nazi plan to eliminate all European Jews, yet they took no direct action against it, military or otherwise. This reflected, in part, a determination to get on with the war as the surest way to deal with a broad range of problems. In other cases, it reflected a global level of antisemitic prejudice that was much higher than many cared to admit.

For example, in the United States, influential figures in both the State Department and Congress blocked attempts to bring in large numbers of Jewish refugees before and during the war. Two members of Congress, one Democrat and one Republican, sponsored a bill to allow Jewish children to enter the United States despite the official immigration quotas. The bill resulted in significant public attention and debate but never came up for a vote in Congress.

The United States State Department erected numerous barriers to impede Jews and others fleeing Nazi persecution from obtaining entry visas. In a memorandum of 26 June 1940, Under Secretary Breckinridge Long (1881–1958), who supervised the Visa Division, advised on how a strict anti-immigration policy might best be implemented:

> We can delay and effectively stop for a temporary period of indefinite length the number of immigrants into the United States. We could do this by simply advising our consuls, to put every obstacle in the

> way and to require additional evidence and to resort to various administrative devices which would postpone and postpone and postpone the granting of the visas. (Breckinridge Long n.d.)

The Holocaust demonstrated the full range of human behavior. Its scale and the cold-bloodedness with which it was carried out set it apart. Between five and six million Jews were killed, approximately two-thirds of Europe's pre-war Jewish population. Most of those killed came from Poland (3 million) and the Soviet Union (1.5 million). Sizable groups also came from Hungary, Romania, and Germany (Table 6.1). The Holocaust occupies a special place in the history of man's inhumanity to man, but one must not think

Table 6.1 Jewish Victims of the Holocaust

Country	*Pre-Final Solution Population*	*Estimated Deaths*
Poland	3,300,000	3,000,000
USSR	3,103,000	1,480,000
Baltic countries	253,000	228,000
White Russia	375,000	245,000
Ukraine	1,500,000	900,000
Russia (RSFSR)	975,000	107,000
Romania	600,000	300,000
Czechoslovakia	180,000	155,000
Hungary	650,000	450,000
Germany/Austria	210,000	240,000
Netherlands	140,000	105,000
France	350,000	90,000
Yugoslavia	26,000	43,000
Greece	70,000	54,000
Belgium	65,000	40,000
Italy	40,000	8,000
Norway	1,800	9,000
Luxembourg	5,000	1,000
Bulgaria	64,000	14,000
Denmark	8,000	—
Finland	2,000	—
Total	8,861,800	5,933,900

The table is based on Dawidowicz (1975).

that it could not have happened in any other Western nation. "In its violence and racism," writes Mark Mazower, "Nazi imperialism drew more from European precedents in Asia, Africa and—especially—the Americas" (Mazower 1999, p. 180). We should ponder a comment made by Hitler during the war, "When we eat wheat from Canada, we don't think about the despoiled Indians" (Mazower 1999, p. 180).

How could the Holocaust happen in the heart of Western Civilization? Edwin Black offers this explanation:

> In the upside-down world of the Holocaust, dignified professionals were Hitler's advance troops. Police officials disregarded their duty in favor of protecting villains and persecuting victims. Lawyers perverted concepts of justice to create anti-Jewish laws. Doctors defiled the art of medicine to perpetrate ghastly experiments and even choose who was healthy enough to be worked to death—and who could be cost-effectively sent to the gas chamber. Scientists and engineers debased their higher calling to devise the instruments and rationales of destruction. And statisticians used their little known but powerful discipline to identify the victims, project and rationalize the benefits of their destruction, organize their persecution, and even audit the efficiency of genocide (Black 2000).

Corporate leaders chose to take an amoral approach to the horrors in which they indirectly, perhaps, participated in their pursuit of financial gain.

The End of the War

American, British, and Canadian forces landed on the beaches of Normandy in Northern France on 6 June 1944 (D-Day) and began advancing eastward toward Germany. Paris was liberated on 25 August, and by mid-September, the Allies crossed the German frontier. The Germans launched their last major offensive on the Western Front on 16 December in a desperate attempt to split the Allied armies, deny the Allies use of the Belgium port of Antwerp, and possibly negotiate an end to the war on the Western Front.

What is remembered as the Battle of the Bulge lasted until 25 January 1945. The Allied offensive along the Western Front resumed in February.

The Russians began a major offensive on the Eastern Front on 12 January 1945. Advancing as much as thirty-seven miles (60 km) per day, they liberated Warsaw on 17 January 1945 and began the siege of Berlin on 20 April, eight days after President Roosevelt's death. Mussolini and his mistress, Claretta Petacci (1912–1945), were captured by Italian partisans on 27 April and summarily executed the following day. Two days later, Hitler and his mistress Eva Braun (1912–1942) committed suicide following their marriage. The leadership of the Third Reich passed to Admiral Karl Dönitz (1891–1980), who instructed General Alfred Jodl (1890–1946), acting on behalf of the German High Command, to sign the unconditional surrender of all German forces on 7 May 1945 (Table 6.2).

Table 6.2 Deaths in the Europe/North African Theaters in World War II

Country	*Military Deaths*	*Civilian Deaths*	*Total*
Soviet Union	8,660,000	16,900,000	25,560,000
Poland	123,000	6,028,000	6,151,000
Germany	3,500,000	1,600,000	5,100,000
Yugoslavia	305,000	1,200,000	1,505,000
Romania	520,000	300,000	820,000
France	253,000	350,000	603,000
Czechoslovakia	246,000	294,000	540,000
Great Britain	397,000	93,000	490,000
Italy	347,000	93,000	440,000
Hungary	136,000	294,000	430,000
Greece	17,000	325,000	342,000
USA	309,000	9,000	318,000
The Netherlands	8,000	200,000	208,000
Belgium	9,000	76,000	85,000
Finland	80,000	3,000	83,000
Canada	34,000	—	34,000

The war was over in Europe, but there was still a war in the Pacific to be won. After the American victory in the Guadalcanal Campaign (7 August 1942–9 February 1943), it was essentially a matter of island hopping, as the Americans moved northwestwardly through the Pacific toward the Japanese home islands. Many feared that an invasion of the Japanese home islands could result in one million casualties. The Soviet Union declared war on Japan on 8 August 1945 and began an invasion of Manchuria. Perhaps to save American lives and to shut the Russians out of postwar Japan, the United States dropped the first atomic bomb on Hiroshima on 6 August. Three days later, on 9 August, a second atomic bomb was dropped on Nagasaki. On the 14th, the emperor stated the war should end and recorded a radio message to the Japanese people. The message was broadcast the following day. It was the first time most Japanese had heard the emperor speak. The formal surrender ceremony took place on 2 September, on board the USS *Missouri*. World War II, the second Great War in the first half of the twentieth century, was over. A new world order and a new type of warfare called the "Cold War" was already beginning.

It is traditional to date World War II between 1 September 1939, when Germany invaded Poland, and 2 September 1945, when the Japanese signed the Instrument of Surrender aboard the USS *Missouri* in Tokyo Bay, Japan. It is likewise customary to think of World War II as a moral crusade in which the Western democracies defended the historical Western values against the new authoritarian regimes in Germany and Italy and the military dictatorship in Japan. What was at stake was what President Franklin Roosevelt (1882–1945) called the "Four Freedoms," the freedom of speech, the freedom of worship, the freedom from want, and the freedom from fear. But perhaps World War II was both a war of good against evil and a war for empire and began much earlier than 1939.

Richard Overy in *Blood and Ruins: The Last Imperial War, 1931–1945* (2022) suggests that World War II may well be seen as a war for empire. It pitted the incumbent imperialists—British, French, and the United States—who did not want to see the status quo changed, against the insurgent imperialists—Germans, Italians, and Japanese—who wanted a restructuring of the world's spoils that would grant them, as they saw it, a fair share. The head of Britain's Navy got it right when he said, "We have got most of the world already, or the best parts if it, . . . We only want to keep what we have got and prevent others from taking it away from us" (Immerwahr 2022). Despite all its talk of defending the Four Freedoms, the United States only went to war when the Japanese began to seize American imperial holdings in the Pacific.

From a global perspective, World War II did not begin with the German invasion of Poland in 1939, nor did it end with Japan's surrender in 1945. For Ethiopia, it began with the Italian invasion in 1935. For Asia, it may be said to have begun even earlier with the Japanese invasion of Manchuria in September 1931. Also, from a global perspective, it did not end in 1945. What became known as a Cold War can be seen as a contest between two rival empires, the so-called "Free World" led by the United States and the "Evil Empire" of the Soviet Union and its allies. And simultaneously with that contest were efforts by various colonies to end the old colonial empires.

References

"America and the Holocaust." (2022). Facing History and Ourselves. https://www.facinghistory.org/defying-nazis/america-and-holocaust (accessed 18 January 2022).

"Auschwitz Camp Complex." (n.d.). United States Holocaust Memorial Museum. https://encyclopedia.ushmm.org/content/en/article/auschwitz-1 (accessed 20 January 2022).

Bennhold, Katrin. (2022). "80 Years Ago the Nazis Planned the 'Final Solution.' It Took 90 Minutes." *The New York Times* (20 January). https://www.nytimes.com/2022/01/20/world/europe/lake-wannsee-conference-final-solution-holocaust.html (accessed 22 January 2022).

Black, Edwin. (2000). "IBM and the Holocaust: The Strategic Alliance Between Nazi Germany and America's Most Powerful Corporation." *The New York Times*. https://archive.nytimes.com/www.nytimes.com/books/first/b/black-ibm.html (accessed 31 October 2023).

Blau, Bruno. (1950). "The Jewish Population of Germany 1939–1945." *Jewish Social Studies*, volume 12, number 2, pages 161–172. http://www.jstor.org/stable/4464869 (accessed 18 January 2022).

"Breckinridge Long." (n.d.). United States holocaust memorial museum. https://exhibitions.ushmm.org/americans-and-the-holocaust/personal-story/breckinridge-long#:~:text=On%20June%2026%2C%201940%2C%20ten,event%20of%20a%20national%20emergency (accessed 6 June 2023).

"Camp System Maps." (n.d.). United States Holocaust Memorial Museum. https://encyclopedia.ushmm.org/content/en/gallery/camp-system-maps (accessed 20 January 2022).

Carson, James. (2018). "The Battle of Kursk in Numbers." HistoryHit (23 August). https://www.historyhit.com/the-battle-of-kursk-in-numbers/ (accessed 25 February 2019).

Dawidowicz, Lucy B. (1975). *The War Against the Jews, 1933–1945*. New York: Holt, Rinehart and Winston.

Dobbs, Michael. (1998). "Ford and GM Scrutinized for Alleged Nazi Collaboration." *The Washington Post* (30 November). WP Company. https://www.washingtonpost.com/wp-srv/national/daily/nov98/nazicars30.htm#TOP (accessed 20 January 2022).

"German Jewish Population in 1933." (n.d.). United States Holocaust Memorial Museum. https://encyclopedia.ushmm.org/content/en/article/germany-jewish-population-in-1933 (accessed 25 February 2019).

Gruhl, Werner. (2017). *Imperial Japan's World War Two: 1931–1945*. New York: Routledge.

From a Speech by Himmler (n.d.). "Before Senior SS Officers in Poznan, 4 October 1943: Evacuation of the Jews." Shoah Resource Center. https://www.yadvashem.org/odot_pdf/Microsoft%20Word%20-%204029.pdf (accessed 6 June 2023).

"Hitler's Threat." (n.d.). Hitler Threatens the Jews. http://stevenlehrer.com/Hitler_threat.htm (accessed 18 January 2022).

Immerwahr, Daniel. (2022). "A New History of World War II." *The Atlantic* (4 April). Atlantic Media Company. https://www.theatlantic.com/magazine/archive/2022/05/world-war-ii-empire-colonialism/629371/ (accessed 4 August 2022).

"Kapo." Wikipedia. (2021). Wikimedia Foundation, 29 November 2021. https://en.wikipedia.org/wiki/Kapo#Domination_and_terror (accessed 20 January 2022).

"Lend-Lease Act (1941)." (2022). Our Documents – Lend-Lease Act (1941). https://www.ourdocuments.gov/doc.php?flash=false&doc=71 (accessed 11 January 2022).

Mailer, John S. and Barbara Mason. (2001). "Penicillin: Medicine's Wartime Wonder Drug and Its Production at Peoria, Illinois." Illinois Periodicals

Online (IPO). https://www.lib.niu.edu/2001/iht810139.html (accessed 11 January 2022).

Mazower, Mark. (1998). *Dark Continent: Europe's Twentieth Century*. New York: Alfred A. Knopf.

Necrometrics. (2013). "National Death Tolls for the Second World War." http://www.necrometrics.com/ww2stats.htm (accessed 1 November 2023).

Ray, Michael. (2018). "Timeline of the Battle of Stalingrad." *Encyclopedia Britannica*. https://www.britannica.com/list/timeline-of-the-battle-of-stalingrad (accessed 8 January 2022).

Roberts, Andrew. (2011). *The Storm of War: A New History of the Second World War*. New York: HarperCollins Publishers.

Shirer, William Lawrence. (1960). *The Rise and Fall of the Third Reich*. New York: Simon & Schuster.

"The Wannsee Conference." Yad Vashem. The World Holocaust Remembrance Center. https://www.yadvashem.org/holocaust/about/finalsolution-beginning/wannsee-conference.html.

"We Shall Fight on the Beaches." (2021). Wikisource, the free online library. Wikimedia Foundation, Inc. https://en.wikisource.org/wiki/We_shall_fight_on_the_beaches (accessed 1 January 2022).

Westermann, Edward B. (2020). "Einsatzgruppen." *Encyclopedia Britannica*, 12 May 2020. https://www.britannica.com/topic/Einsatzgruppen (accessed on 18 January 2022).

White, Matthew. (2011). Source List and Detailed Death Tolls for the Primary Megadeaths of the Twentieth Century. *Twentieth Century atlas - death tolls*. https://necrometrics.com/20c5m.htm#Second (accessed 4 August 2023).

Part 3

Overview: 1945–1989

Three developments marked the first half of the years from 1945 to 1989. First, soon after the end of World War II, Europe found itself in a so-called Cold War. It also contended with various waves of decolonization, first in Asia and then in Africa. Finally, a divided Europe struggled to recover, economically, socially, and spiritually. In 1967, when the European Economic Community (EEC), the European Coal and Steel Community (ECSC), and the European Atomic Energy Commission came together to form the European Community, Western Europe at least could claim to have recovered and reached a period of prosperity. Eastern Europe, under the iron grip of the Soviet Union, was far less successful.

The Cold War began to take shape in 1945 and 1946. Already at the Potsdam Conference (July–August 1945) there was an atmosphere of suspicion. The main sources of disagreement were European: the new Poland and occupied Germany. The Soviet Union was anxious to secure a Poland that would defer to Soviet strategic interests. It desperately wanted assurance that Germany would not again be able to wage aggressive war.

In 1947, the most crucial year of the Cold War, President Harry Truman of the United States put forth what came to be called the Truman Doctrine: America would help governments in danger either

Twentieth-Century Europe: 1900 to the Present, Fourth Edition.
Michael D. Richards and Paul R. Waibel.

from internal subversion or from external aggression. That same year saw the extension by the United States of the Marshall Plan, a package of economic aid to war-ravaged Europe. Some saw the Marshall Plan as an economic counterpart to the Truman Doctrine. It was, however, meant to be simply an American initiative to help the peoples of Europe restart European economies, both in the west and in the east. In the new atmosphere of Cold War, however, the Soviet Union saw it as an American plot to gain economic advantage.

Several events, among them a communist coup in Czechoslovakia, the Berlin Blockade and Airlift, the formation of the North Atlantic Treaty Organization (NATO), the appearance of West Germany and East Germany, and, finally, the victory of the Chinese Communists over the Chinese Nationalists—convinced Europeans and Americans that the Cold War was a real and ongoing conflict. The American response to the Korean War in 1950 and the decision to aid the French in Indochina made the Cold War global, even though the essential issues remained Soviet concerns in Europe.

Colonial empires in Asia were, generally, quickly dismantled in the decade following World War II. The British left the Indian subcontinent and American granted independence to the Philippines. The Dutch failed in their efforts to retain the Dutch East Indies. France withdrew from Indochina after a bitter war against the Vietnamese communists.

Decolonization in Africa began in the 1950s. It largely took place in an orderly manner. A major exception was Algeria, where a million European residents opposed independence and where the French army, defeated in 1940 and in 1954, sought to redeem itself. The British experienced a difficult situation in Kenya with the Mau Mau Movement. Rhodesia and South Africa, so-called white settler colonies, resisted efforts by the black majority in each country to come to power. Belgium granted the Congo independence without, however, doing much to ensure its success. The Portuguese clung to their colonial holdings until the mid-1970s.

The Soviet Union dominated Eastern Europe in the decades after World War II. After Stalin's death in 1953, there were efforts to meet the needs of the people, but each satellite country experienced a variation of the Soviet mode of industrialization: central planning, emphasis on heavy industry, and collectivization of agriculture. By the end of the 1950s, some began to seek a national path to economic development. Yugoslavia, balanced precariously between East and West, experimented with forms of economic organization, neither completely communist nor capitalist.

In the West, the Marshall Plan played an important role in restarting economies. Countries helped by the plan each followed its own brand of capitalism. France emphasized planning and government-directed investing. The German *Wirtschaftswunder* (economic miracle) was largely a product of collaboration between industry and the banks. The major development in the European economy in this period entailed cooperation and integration, first with the ECSC and then with the EEC.

In the 1960s, a divided Europe was no longer a novelty and Europeans had also discovered the possibility of life without colonial empires. Europeans in the West enjoyed a material abundance that only a few had known earlier. The Cold War had become a threat that people had learned to live with.

1968 was a year of revolution that introduced what turned out to be a period of consolidation and attempts to reform in response to dissatisfaction with political, economic, social, and cultural arrangements in both Western and Eastern Europe. The period also featured efforts to deal with rapidly changing geopolitical, economic, and technological realities.

While in 1968 everything seemed possible, the radicalism of the 1960s actually peaked. In Western Europe, radicalism reached a high tide in the events of 1968 in France. For a brief moment, it seemed students and workers would unite to defeat the government of Charles de Gaulle. Not surprisingly, style and youthful enthusiasm were not enough, and de Gaulle and the Fifth Republic prevailed. In Czechoslovakia, Alexander Dubček attempted to renew communism in a reform movement known as the "Prague Spring." Widespread national support and earnest attempts by the Czechs to mollify other members of the Warsaw Treaty Organization failed to prevent the Soviet Union, backed by East Germany and Poland, from crushing the movement in August. In the United States, the 1960s featured a massive Civil Rights Movement and widespread protests against the Vietnam War. In 1968, the assassination of Martin Luther King, Jr. and presidential hopeful Robert F. Kennedy, race riots in major American cities, and widespread protest against American participation in the Vietnam War on college campuses across the country left the American people badly divided. Nonetheless, the Civil Rights Movement brought about fundamental changes in American society through court decisions and legislation.

Between the revolutionary years of 1968 and 1989, Western Europe experienced a period of economic dislocation and political turmoil. The oil price shocks of the 1970s were problematic, but the economic crisis of this period had deeper roots. By the late 1960s, the postwar boom had played itself out. At the same time, the continued growth of the welfare state had become an economic burden. There was additionally a shift in the economy from an industrial focus to more of a service focus. The economy also was becoming increasingly global.

The flexibility of Western European economies and the advantages of institutions like the European Community helped bring about recovery in the 1980s. Government policy, particularly that developed in Britain under Prime Minister Margaret Thatcher, also helped. Her neoconservative policies of privatization, union busting, and downsizing of government were echoed by President Ronald Regan's approach in the United States and adopted in various ways on the continent. Economic recovery brought with it a clearer division of society into winners and losers as reflected in persistently high rates of unemployment.

In the 1970s, the Cold War featured first a period of détente and then a brief revival of its worst feature. This was primarily due to the Soviet invasion of Afghanistan. President Regan, long a Cold Warrior, took a hardline approach in the Caribbean and Central America but also in the Middle East, activities that created some of the dilemmas of twenty-first century foreign policy in these areas. Under the circumstances, it was nothing short of miraculous that Soviet Premier Mikhail Gorbachev was able by the late 1980s to convince Western leaders that it was possible to work on defusing the more than four-decade-old Cold War.

In the 1970s and 1980, the Eastern European satellites of the Soviet Union were hollowed out economically and led in most cases by gerontocracies. In Poland, a working-class protest that eventually allied with intellectuals produced in Solidarity a movement that survived the imposition of martial law to become by the late 1980s a powerful force for change. In East Germany and in Czechoslovakia, less powerful protest efforts managed to keep alive the idea that the political system required reform.

7

Cold War and Decolonization, 1945–1961

Chronology

1945	Formation of the United Nations
	Yalta Conference
	Potsdam Conference
1946	George F. Kennan's "Long Telegram"
1947	Truman Doctrine launches the era of containment in the Cold War
	Marshall Plan offers economic aid to Europe
	Communists forced out of coalition governments in France and Italy

Twentieth-Century Europe: 1900 to the Present, Fourth Edition.
Michael D. Richards and Paul R. Waibel.

	Formation of the Communist Information Bureau (Cominform)
1948	Communist coup in Czechoslovakia
	Berlin blockade and Berlin airlift (June 1948–May 1949)
	Universal Declaration of Human Rights
1949	Federal Republic of Germany (West Germany) founded
	German Democratic Republic (East Germany) founded
	North Atlantic Treaty Organization (NATO) created
	Soviet Union becomes an atomic power
	People's Republic of China (PRC) founded
1950	Korean War (1950–1953)
1953	Death of Stalin
	Uprising in Germany
1954	French defeat at Dien Bien Phu marks the end of the war in Indochina
	Vietnam divided into two states at Geneva Conference
1955	West Germany becomes a member of NATO
	Creation of the Warsaw Treaty Organization (WTO)
1956	Khrushchev's speech denouncing Stalin at the Twentieth Party Congress of the Communist Party of the Soviet Union
	Worker unrest in Poland
	Hungarian Revolution and Soviet intervention
	Suez Crisis
1957	Soviet Union opens a space race with the launching of *Sputnik*
1961	Construction of the Berlin Wall

On Monday, 16 July 1945, there was a break in the conference at Potsdam and President Harry Truman (1884–1972) decided to look at Berlin. Sitting in the back seat of an open Lincoln with James Byrnes (1882–1972), his secretary of state, and Admiral William Leahy (1875–1959), President Truman was driven past miles of burned-out buildings and rubble. The motorcade went down one of Berlin's best-known streets, Unter den Linden, now stripped of its famous Linden trees, past the Reich Chancellery, the Brandenburg Gate, and the *Reichstag*. That night, he wrote in his diary:

> I thought of Carthage, Baalbek, Jerusalem, Rome, Atlantis, Peking . . . [of] Scipio, Rameses II . . . Sherman, Jenghiz Khan . . . I hope for some sort of peace—but I fear that machines are ahead of morals by some centuries and when morals catch up there'll be no reason for any of it. (McCullough 1992, p. 415)

Churchill also toured Berlin that afternoon. Stalin, who had arrived on his armored train only that day, did not. Of course, neither he nor Churchill needed to see the ruins of Berlin to know the destructiveness of World War II. They had only to look at the great cities of their own countries.

More than 40 million people were killed in the European theater of the war. Civilian deaths were nearly three times the number of military deaths. Millions survived with disabilities of one kind or another. Millions more fled before advancing armies or were forced to migrate after the war. The largest group of the latter were Germans forced to move west from what had been East Prussia.

Material losses were enormous. The estimate, in 1945 dollars, was between \$2 and \$3 trillion (\$31 and \$46.5 trillion in 2022), including damage to farmland, destruction of cattle and other livestock, and the devastation of villages, towns, and cities, bridges, railroads, and highways. Germany and every country involved in the war faced the need to rebuild its economy and repair its social fabric. Some countries suffered more than others, of course. Denmark was, comparatively speaking, unmarked by the war. The Netherlands, by way of contrast, endured many hardships, particularly in the "Hunger Winter" of 1944–1945. The Soviet Union, victorious and powerful, had nevertheless incurred enormous losses. And, of course, it seemed Germany could not possibly recover. There was much pessimism; some believed Europe had been hopelessly weakened.

That assessment gained force not only from the emergence of two enormously powerful countries on either flank of Europe, the United States and the Soviet Union, but also from the grave weakening of the colonial empires. In different manners, in some cases quickly and in others slowly and painfully, the empires collapsed and disappeared (see the discussion of this process later in this chapter).

Finally, the spiritual cost of the war and its aftermath was enormous. Europe had fallen back into a level of barbarism during World War II that contradicted the previous decades of progress or simply erased them. The magnitude of the cruelty largely defied understanding. The "Final Solution" naturally was the premier example of barbarism in the war. Still, other events, such as the firebombing of cities like Hamburg and Dresden in Germany and Tokyo in Japan, also were seen as barbaric acts, even if not on the same scale and done with the stated intention of ending the war as soon as possible.

Additionally, the dropping of the newly developed atomic bomb on Hiroshima and Nagasaki was seen by some as beyond cruel and unnecessary, even if others claimed it was done in the interest of forcing Japan to surrender as quickly as possible. All the claims of cultural or moral superiority Europeans had ever made now seemed hollowed out by the events of the war. A spiritual malaise accompanied military impotence and economic devastation.

Additionally, as historian Keith Lowe notes:

> . . . the war did not simply stop with Hitler's defeat. A conflict on the scale of the Second World War with all the smaller civil disputes that it encompassed, took months, if not years, to come to a halt and the end came at different times in different parts of Europe. (Lowe 2012, p. xiv)

In Poland, for example, Polish Communists, with the aid of the Soviet Army, hunted down members of the Polish Home Army, the leading Polish resistance force in the war. In Greece, a savage civil war broke out. Everywhere, collaborators were punished. In Poland and Czechoslovakia, in particular, ethnic Germans were forced to leave. Ukrainians expelled Poles from Polish territory annexed by the Soviet Union. In a terrible irony, in Eastern Europe, many of the old concentration camps filled up again with political prisoners.

And superimposing itself on anarchy and chaos was the beginnings of a decades-long struggle between the two "superpowers" the war had produced. One was the Soviet Union, with its massive army and devastated economy. The other was the United States, with its hugely productive industry and the atomic bomb. The contest between these two giants in the wake of the war would fundamentally reshape Europe and the rest of the world.

Origins of the Cold War

Some observers take the long view and see the Cold War as first appearing with the Allied intervention in the Russian Civil War following the Russian Revolution in 1917. Others prefer to begin with the issue of the second front and other controversial matters during World War II. In both cases, the Soviet Union and the West had reasons for suspicion and distrust of each other. Still, at the end of the war in Europe in May 1945, both sides seemed to want to believe the wartime alliance could be continued in some fashion. However, within three to four years, a Cold War existed between the two super powers. The issues that fractured the wartime Grand Alliance of Great Britain, the United States, and the Soviet Union were evident at the two end-of-the-war conferences, Yalta (February 1945) and Potsdam (July–August 1945).

At the time of the Yalta Conference in February 1945, the American, British, and French forces had recovered from the Battle of the Bulge, but they had yet to cross the Rhine River. The Soviet Union's forces were approximately 100 miles from Berlin and occupied most of the major capitals of Eastern and Central Europe. The military situation at that time had obvious political implications. Americans continued to resist the idea of using military means to achieve political objectives. Still, a specific context for the discussions had already been established.

Yalta is often viewed as either a failure of American diplomacy or a triumph of Russian duplicity. It should not be seen as either, but rather as an agreement that made sense in the context of the times, yet also one badly flawed by misunderstandings. In part, the agreement was shaped by the desire to involve the Soviet Union in the war in the Pacific. Since the Soviet Union had borne the brunt of Allied efforts in the war in Europe, joining the war in the Pacific represented a considerable concession. The lure was Stalin's desire to capture those parts of the Japanese empire that once belonged to Russia. However, Yalta's primary point of contention concerned Eastern Europe and the Soviet Union's interest in the area. Beginning with the Nazi–Soviet Nonaggression Pact (1939), the Soviet Union had worked consistently to ensure the states along its western borders were sympathetic to its interests and nonthreatening to its security.

Poland's future formed a primary focus of concern. The Soviet Union desired a postwar government in Poland that was at least friendly toward the Soviet Union and willing to accede to its wishes, including incorporation by the Soviet Union of territory that had been disputed by the two states between the two world wars. Poland's future government seemingly did not have to be a communist one, but Stalin believed that the Soviet Union had a natural right to act in its interests and had been encouraged in this belief by Anglo-American practices in Italy, where policies based on American and British institutions and values were put in place. The so-called "percentages deal" in October 1944 between Churchill and Stalin, dividing Central and Southeastern Europe into areas in which the Soviet Union or Britain would have predominant influence, was of limited importance but certainly accorded with the Soviet perspective on postwar arrangements.

The problems associated with Yalta came later when the Soviet view, pragmatic and hard-nosed, began to clash with the American view, also pragmatic but colored by ideals drawn from such documents as the "Atlantic Charter," which had been issued by Roosevelt and Churchill in August 1941. Part of the problem lay in definitions. Phrases such as "free elections" or "democratic governments" might be understood in different ways. From the Soviet point of view, an election was not free or a government democratic if the result was a state hostile to Soviet interests. Americans understood such terms literally, although even they might, as in Italy after the war, make it clear what they wanted the outcome of an election to be.

The final and most important issue at Yalta concerned plans for postwar Germany. Proposals to destroy German industrial capacity were not accepted, but it was agreed that the Soviet Union could extract reparations from current production or dismantle individual industrial enterprises and ship them to the Soviet Union. At the same time, the Soviet Union would send agricultural products from its occupation zone to the western zones. It was further agreed that Germany and the city of Berlin were to be divided into four sectors, each to be run by one of the occupying powers but all to cooperate economically. The fate of Germany was the dominant issue for the Soviet Union, and the failure of the other Allies to fully understand this created much of the basis for the Cold War that followed the end of World War II.

When the Allied leaders met between 16 July and 2 August 1945 at Potsdam, a suburb of Berlin, they intended to continue the alliance. The war's end in the Pacific was now in sight, but estimates of when this would happen ranged between several weeks and months. The leaders of the Allies had changed, but Stalin continued to speak for the Soviet Union. Inexperienced but determined, Harry Truman took the place of Roosevelt, who died on 12 April 1945, shortly after returning from the Yalta Conference in February. Both Winston Churchill and Clement Attlee (1883–1967) came to Potsdam to represent Britain. When the results of Britain's parliamentary elections were announced on 26 July, the Conservatives had suffered a stunning loss at the hands of the Labour Party. Thus, Clement Attlee replaced Churchill as Prime Minister and Britain's representative at Yalta.

Truman took a more aggressive stance at Potsdam than Roosevelt had taken at Yalta and in earlier meetings. Roosevelt was at times as suspicious of British imperialism as of Russian communism. Truman mainly distrusted the Russians. Some scholars hold out the possibility that Truman wanted to use the American monopoly of atomic weapons to force the Russians to make concessions, but there is no hard evidence supporting this view. Truman did practice a blunt, no-nonsense kind of diplomacy, and he may have hoped the announcement of the new and devastatingly powerful "A-bomb" would give him some leverage with Stalin. Atomic blackmail would not have worked in any case, however.

Stalin knew a good deal about the American efforts to build the bomb through reports on the Manhattan Project sent to the Soviet Union by Soviet spies. He wanted the Soviet Union to have similar weapons. Lavrenti Beria (1899–1953), Stalin's chief of the secret police, was already directed by Stalin to set up a crash program to build an atomic bomb. The Soviet Union exploded its first atomic bomb on 29 August 1949, ending America's monopoly on atomic weapons.

By midsummer of 1945, serious differences of opinion regarding postwar Europe had already begun to surface between Stalin and the two democratic Western leaders, Truman and Attlee. The most important disagreements concerned the Polish government's composition and occupied Germany's administration. What ensued stemmed mainly from a series of misunderstandings. Essentially, neither the United States nor Great Britain understood the extent to which the Soviet Union wanted to establish a line of defense that would protect it from attack, whether from a resurgent Germany or the United States.

Stalin saw no reason to tolerate a Polish government unreceptive to his plans for reordering Eastern Europe. Stalin contended that if the Soviet Union were to install in Poland a government it sponsored and largely excluded one backed by Britain, this would be the same as what the United States and Britain were doing in Italy and Greece. This, of course, overlooks the fact that what the West was doing in Italy and Greece had a great deal of support from the populations of the two countries.

Potsdam, together with Yalta, had created a volatile situation but not one necessarily fated to lead to confrontation. All were in agreement that Germany would remain united. In 1945 and 1946, the wartime Allies still assumed that there would be an end of the war peace conference like the Paris Peace Conference in 1919 that ended World War I. Germany's future would be decided at that peace conference. Until then, whatever problems might arise could be resolved in the various forums available.

The main forum for discussion was supposed to be the newly created United Nations, which was formed in meetings in San Francisco from 25 April to 26 June 1945. The United Nations officially began on 24 October of that year. While there was a General Assembly in which all members of the UN were represented, the Security Council, on which both the Soviet Union and the United States had permanent seats, was the most important part of the UN. The Universal Declaration of Human Rights was of particular importance, proclaimed on 10 December 1948. In addition, over the years, a number of specialized agencies were established to deal with specific issues. The UN, however, could not overcome the continuing dominance of great power politics.

In the immediate postwar era, what counted the most were various meetings of the Allies where particular problems could be addressed. For example, there were meetings of the foreign ministers of the Allies. For issues involving Germany, there were meetings of the Allied Control Council, the governing body of the Allied Occupation Zones in Germany and Allied-occupied Austria, located in Berlin (1945–1990).

There was no Cold War as yet in 1946. Churchill, however, gave a speech at little Westminster College in Fulton, Missouri, President Truman's home state, on 5 March 1946, "The Sinews of Peace." In it, he famously stated, "From Stettin in the Baltic to Trieste in the Adriatic, an iron curtain has descended across the Continent" (as quoted in the online Britannia Historical Documents 2013). Developments were taking shape that would rapidly move Europe toward the grimness of the Cold War. The two main problem areas, occupied Germany and the new Poland, had become even more intractable. In occupied Germany, there were signs that a common occupation policy would not be established.

In accordance with agreements made at Yalta regarding reparations, the Soviet Union began a policy of wholesale confiscation of equipment and facilities in its zone and also in the other three zones. But it failed to send the agreed agricultural products from its zone to the western zones. The United States feared this would lead to the economic collapse of Germany and require greatly expanded American aid. The American government could see no point in American taxpayers subsidizing German reparations to the Soviet Union. Truman halted Lend-Lease aid to the Soviet Union in May 1945, two months before the Potsdam Conference. The British and

Americans stopped the Soviet Union from taking any further reparations from their zones in 1946. In January 1947, the British and American zones were united administratively into what became known as Bizonia. The French zone joined in April 1949. The three western zones became the Federal Republic of Germany, or West Germany, on 23 May 1949.

Already in 1945, the Soviet Army installed in Poland the "Lublin Poles" (Polish communists sponsored by the Soviet Union) in power. A few "London Poles" (Poles who had worked with the United States and Britain during the war) had been added later to form a coalition government. In 1946, Polish communists worked diligently to break apart the Peasant Party, potentially the most potent political party in Poland, and gain control of another popular political force, the Polish Socialist Workers' Party. The elections scheduled for January 1947 did not look promising for the democratic forces.

The increasing tension between the United States and the Soviet Union appeared in other areas, such as the Middle East and the Balkans. American diplomatic pressure led the Soviet Union to withdraw troops from the northern part of Iran by early May of 1946, but Soviet pressure on Turkey continued. While the Soviet Union did not appear to be trying to influence the civil war in Greece between Greek communists and Greek monarchists, the Greek communists were aided by Yugoslavia's Marshal Tito. By the end of 1946, the British were experiencing difficulties sustaining the monarchists.

Throughout Western Europe, there was no sign of economic recovery. The communist parties in France and Italy were included in coalition governments. They seemed likely to be the main beneficiaries if the economies could not be restarted. In February 1946, George F. Kennan (1904–2005), an American diplomat stationed in the Soviet Union, sent an 8,000-word telegram, the "Long Telegram," detailing his sense of how Russians viewed their history and the present moment. Kennan believed Russia's historical insecurity, exacerbated by communism's idea of the inevitability of war with capitalism, led Stalin always to seek to improve his country's situation. Stalin, however, did respect strength. Hence, a firm response would force Stalin and the Soviet Union to back down (The National

Security Archive 2013). From this essay came the idea of "containment," that is, of meeting every Soviet move with a countermove and anticipating possible Soviet moves in order to preempt them.

Crisis Years, 1947–1948

In 1947, the Cold War began to take shape. The immediate origins lay in the situations in Turkey and Greece. Turkey was under considerable pressure from the Soviet Union to allow a Soviet military presence near the straits between the Black Sea and the Mediterranean Sea. Greece was still involved in a civil war between Greek communists and monarchists. Early in 1947, Britain informed the United States it could no longer afford to supply aid to the two countries.

The United States was tasked with maintaining Anglo-American interests in the eastern Mediterranean. President Truman, in his remarks to a joint session of Congress in March 1947 asked for an open-ended commitment by the United States to help any government threatened by invasion from without or subversion from within. This became known as the "Truman Doctrine." Although the Soviet Union was not specifically mentioned in his address, his sentiments were widely regarded as an expression of hostility towards the Soviet Union and communism generally. The Truman Doctrine signaled America's intention to prevent the expansion of communism beyond its existing borders. In effect, Truman's address became the opening salvo of the Cold War (Harry S. Truman Library & Museum 2013).

In the months after Truman's speech, Secretary of State George C. Marshall (1880–1959) and others in the State Department concerned themselves with the economic and social problems of Europe. What good was the threat of military action to prevent the spread of communism by the Soviet Union if people in Western Europe voted for communism in free elections? As noted earlier, communist parties were included in coalition governments in both France and Italy. European voters saw a noticeable shift to the left during the immediate postwar years. The citizens living among the ruins of bombed-out cities wanted governments that were not ideologically opposed to government intervention to hasten economic recovery.

In areas where the people felt there was little hope for a brighter future, they voted for the Communists. Perhaps the best way to prevent the spread of communism beyond what Winston Churchill called the "Iron Curtain" was to hasten the economic recovery of war-torn Western Europe. The need was obvious. The labor was available. What was lacking was the funds to rebuild Europe. The solution would come in the form of the Marshall Plan.

George Kennan, by then the head of the new Policy Planning Staff at the State Department, quickly put together a report on the European situation recommending American aid. It would, he thought, be up to the Europeans to draw up the plans. Aid should be offered to all of Europe. Any decision leading to a division of Europe should stem from the Russian response to the American offer rather than the offer itself. In large part, the aid would be directed at German economic recovery, which Kennan saw as "a vital component of the recovery of Europe as a whole."

George C. Marshall had planned to attend the Harvard commencement ceremonies in the spring of 1947, where he was to be awarded an honorary degree and give a speech. It was virtually at the last minute that he decided to use the occasion to launch what became known as the Marshall Plan. Marshall indicated he advocated economic measures to meet economic and social problems in his talk.

> Our policy is directed not against any country or doctrine but against hunger, poverty, desperation and chaos . . . Any government that is willing to assist in the task of recovery will find full cooperation, I am sure, on the part of the United States Government. Any government which maneuvers to block the recovery of other countries cannot expect help from us. (George C. Marshall's speech can be found on the internet in the Internet Modern History Source Book (2013).)

Later the Marshall Plan (or the European Recovery Program as it was formally known) was seen as the economic counterpart to the Truman Doctrine. Marshall saw it as a means of speeding European economic recovery. He saw, of course, the political implications of European social and economic stability. He was also aware of the importance to American business of an economically viable Europe.

Although some did not consider the Marshall Plan an American maneuver in the rapidly emerging Cold War, the Soviet Union saw it that way. It walked out of the conference the British and French had called to discuss the initiative. The Poles and Czechs were pressured to drop their interest in the plan. Stalin saw the plan simply as a means whereby the United States could gain control of the European economies. In particular, he had no intention of revealing the extent to which the war had damaged the Soviet economy.

On 10 December 1953, George C. Marshall, Chief of Staff of the United States Army during World War II and Secretary of State from 1947 to 1949, was awarded the Nobel Peace Prize for his work with the Marshall Plan, the massive postwar program of American aid that helped rebuild Western Europe after the war. To the left is Carl Joachim Hambro, President of the Norwegian Storting. AP/Press Association Images.

By the end of 1947, many of the significant elements of the Cold War had fallen into place. In May, the communist parties in France and Italy were forced out of the coalition governments. In September, the Cominform (Communist Information Bureau), successor to the Comintern (Communist International), was established with headquarters in Belgrade, Yugoslavia. The Cominform was seen in the West as evidence of a monolithic communist movement controlled by Moscow and dedicated to the subversion of democratic governments everywhere. Actually, the main task of the Cominform was to tighten Soviet control over Eastern Europe and, in particular, to gain a more significant measure of control over communist Yugoslavia.

The Two Germanies

During the immediate postwar years, the Allied Powers grew farther apart in the administration of occupied Germany. The status of Germany was the most important issue in relations between the Soviet Union and the other Allied Powers. The Soviet Union wanted to ensure that Germany could not threaten it again in the twentieth century. The United States was more concerned about feeding Germany and the connection between its economic recovery and the recovery of the rest of Europe. Neither side seemed to fully understand the other side's position. Each side had learned different lessons from the peacemaking process after World War I.

As mentioned earlier, the Soviet Union set out first to strip its occupation zone in Germany of raw materials and factories. It also exercised its rights to take reparations in kind from the other zones. The Soviet Union's decision to do so was in line with its concerns about security issues and its own economic recovery. Initially, the French also followed a policy of extracting reparations from their zone. They began to see, however, as the British and Americans already saw that it was not to their advantage to destroy the German economy if this meant that later they would have to send food, goods, and money back to Germany to prevent social unrest and instability.

In the American and the British zones, an effort was made to carry out a program of de-Nazification, demilitarization, and democratization, but the programs were only partially successful. In particular, the process of de-Nazification moved slowly and was not especially effective. Many high-ranking Nazis escaped trial because of the often cumbersome process which attempted to comb through the entire population. Other Nazis escaped trial because they were regarded as useful by the United States for scientific projects or espionage. The Americans and the British also made efforts to find Germans who had administrative experience for positions of leadership and were not tainted by association with the Nazis. One such person was the 77-year-old former lord mayor of Cologne, Konrad Adenauer (1876–1967), who became the first chancellor of West Germany.

Russian occupation practices differed considerably. In 1946, the Soviet Union virtually eliminated political parties in its zone and put intense pressure on the old Social Democratic Party (SPD) to unite with the Communists (KPD) to become the Socialist Unity Party (Sozialistische Einheitspartei Deutschlands or SED). The Soviets also carried out an extensive land reform program and nationalization of industry, policies that were partly based on the idea that the destruction of capitalism would eliminate the basis for fascism since fascism was a product of "monopoly capitalism."

Two distinct Germanies were being created. One was composed of the American and British zones, which formally merged economies in January 1947, and, as mentioned above, became known as "Bizonia." The French did not, at first, accept the invitation to join.

The other was the Soviet zone. In 1948, the three Western powers announced the introduction of currency reforms, a necessary prelude to economic recovery and the functioning of the zones as a single economic unit. The Soviet Union responded by closing down rail, road, and water traffic between Berlin and the West.

On 26 June, the United States and Britain responded to the Soviet blockade by organizing an airlift to supply the city. A proposed plan to break the blockade by sending an armored column down the autobahn to Berlin was ruled out as too confrontational. Although Soviet pilots sometimes harassed incoming transport planes, the Soviet Union did not attempt to counter the airlift by shooting down the supply-laden Allied aircraft.

After the airlift was reorganized by General William H. Tunner (1906–1983), it was successful in supplying the more than two million residents of the allied sectors of Berlin for the 11 months during which the Soviet blockade remained in effect. Even after the Soviets ended the blockade; the airlift continued until 30 September 1949. The airlift supplied Berlin with 2,323,738 tons (2,323,738,000 kg) of food, fuel, and other supplies. The successful response to the Soviet challenge contributed significantly to the growth of West European support for American efforts in the Cold War duel with the Soviet Union. The Berlin blockade, which lasted from 23 June 1948 to 12 May 1949, and the Berlin airlift countering it were the most visible signs of increasing Cold War tension.

In 1949, the division between western Germany, which became known as the Federal Republic of Germany (FRG or West Germany), and eastern Germany, the German Democratic Republic (GDR or East Germany) was officially set. West Germany quickly began to move from the status of a former enemy to that of a potential ally of the Western powers. A divided Germany had not been the intention of any of the Allied Powers at the end of World War II, but in the new context of the Cold War, it suited each of them well enough and, in time, came to be seen as the normal state of affairs.

The Cold War Launched

The postwar world in 1949 presented a new, ominous look. In addition to the quarrel over the status of Germany and its division into two separate states, there was the phenomenon of tightening Soviet control in Eastern Europe. The Czech coup in February 1948 was the most dramatic example of Stalin's intentions in Eastern Europe. Czechoslovakia was the only East European nation liberated by the Soviet military that was not yet under Communist control and subservient to Moscow. It appeared to be firmly on the road to a democratic future. When the Communists failed to achieve power in France and Italy in 1947 and 1948, Stalin decided it was time to bring Czechoslovakia under the control of Communists and Social Democrats willing to accept subservience to Moscow. The coup took place during the last days of February 1948. Any hope that a democratic, freely elected government might be allowed to exist within a sphere of influence dominated by the Soviet Union disappeared.

West Europeans and Americans responded to the events of 1947 and 1948 by forming the North Atlantic Treaty Organization (NATO) in 1949. NATO grew out of an earlier pact, the Brussels Treaty (1948), signed by Britain, France, Belgium, Luxembourg, and the Netherlands. In effect, these West European countries invited the United States to join an alliance that it would naturally dominate. Europeans agreed to encourage the formation of an informal American empire in the interests of collective security. In contrast, the Soviet Union imposed its empire on Eastern Europe in the interests of the national security of the Soviet Union. Three

Rioters in East Berlin throw stones at Red Army tanks in June 1953 to protest the increase in work norms set by the government of the German Democratic Republic. Cracks appeared every decade after the formation of the Soviet bloc, but the Soviet Union held its empire together until 1989. Dpa picture alliance/Alamy Images.

Europe During the Cold War.

developments in Asia also contributed to the shaping of the emerging Cold War world. These were the American occupation of Japan, the victory of the Chinese Communists over the Chinese Nationalists in 1949, and, finally, the Korean War (1950–1953).

The United States exercised complete control over the occupation of Japan. General Douglas MacArthur (1880–1964), commander of the occupation administration, used his authority to reshape Japanese political life, establishing a tradition of parliamentary democracy while allowing Emperor Hirohito (1901–1989) to remain a national symbol. MacArthur had less impact on the contours of economic and social affairs, although he did much to improve the status and rights of women. The Japanese themselves decisively rejected militarism. Although they placed themselves under the American security umbrella and became an important economic component of the Cold War, they did not join, as did West Germany, an Asian equivalent of NATO.

The victory of the Chinese Communist Party under Mao Zedong (1893–1976) and the founding of the People's Republic of China on 1 October 1949 shaped the Cold War in two important ways. The People's Republic of China was an enormous addition to what Americans and other observers now regarded as a monolithic world communist movement. In reality, Chinese national interests often clashed with Russian national interests. That would not surprise anyone familiar with the long history of contacts between the two nations dating back to the seventeenth century. But this perspective seemed to have disappeared in the face of concerns about the newly expanded communist movement. In addition, Mao's ideas and the revolutionary romanticism associated with his past accomplishments heightened a fear that every national liberation movement would end up as a victory for the supposedly monolithic world communist movement.

Of the three developments, the Korean War (1950–1953) had the most significant impact on the development of the Cold War. At the end of World War II, the Soviet Union occupied the northern half of the Korean peninsula and the United States the southern half. In the next few years, each power created a Korean administration that conformed more or less to the occupying power's political and economic systems. In North Korea, Kim II Sung (1912–1994), a Korean communist and nationalist, believed his country could quickly reunite the peninsula. Additionally, he thought an invasion of South Korea would lead to a popular uprising in the south. Finally, the Americans seemingly had written Korea off as an area of strategic interest. In any case, they would not have time to intervene. Such was the scenario Kim II Sung presented to Stalin. Although Stalin was generally quite cautious about support for ventures of this sort, he appeared to believe the plan involved little risk. Kim II Sung then persuaded Mao to lend support as well.

The invasion began on 25 June 1950 when North Korean forces crossed the border with South Korea. The invasion was initially successful, pushing the greatly outnumbered South Korean army down the peninsula. The United Nations Security Council met on 27 June to consider a resolution that authorized member nations to offer military aid to South Korea. The Soviet Union was not present to veto the resolution because it was boycotting the meeting over a dispute regarding the government of Nationalist China on Taiwan occupying China's seat on the Security Council. With the passage of the Security Council's Resolution 83, the United States was able to intervene at the head of an international force under United Nations' sponsorship.

Initially, the intervention did not go well, but by August, UN forces outnumbered the North Korean forces. General MacArthur pushed for an amphibious landing at the port of Inchon near Seoul and far to the north of the UN perimeter around the southern port of Pusan. The Inchon landing was a daring but also risky plan. Despite the risks, the landing on 15 September worked as MacArthur had hoped. The UN forces surprised the North Korean forces, retaking Seoul and trapping nearly half the North Korean army. From there, the UN forces drove the North Korean army out of South Korea and up to the Yalu River, the boundary between North Korea and the People's Republic of China. Alarmed, China did more than lend lip service to its support of the North Koreans. The Chinese People's Volunteers Force (CPVF) crossed into Korea, forcing the American troops into a disastrous retreat out of North Korea.

By the summer of 1951, the war had become a stalemate. Talks between United Nations and Communist representatives to achieve a truce began in July. Fighting continued, however, until 27 July 1953, when an armistice was concluded, ending the conflict. A demilitarized zone separating the two Koreas was established along the 38th parallel, more or less the same as the old prewar border. The Korean War has never officially ended. As of the third decade of the twenty-first century, the 1953 Korean War Armistice Agreement remains in place.

Early in 1950, the US National Security Council, an agency created in 1947 to help manage America's response to the Cold War, issued a report entitled "NSC 68: United States Objectives and Programs for National Security." This position paper recommended that the United States oppose the Soviet Union in virtually any situation that might work to the benefit of the latter.

According to "NSC 68," the Soviet Union was "animated by a new fanatical faith . . . and seeks to impose its absolute authority over the rest of the world" (Federation of American Scientists 1950). The document further recommended significantly increased military spending and foreign aid programs. President Truman initially did not act on the document when he received it in early April. Instead, he requested an economic analysis of the proposal. It is possible that if the Korean War had not begun shortly after NSC 68 was presented, no action would have been taken.

Aid to the French in Indochina (see the discussion below) and intervention in the Korean War contributed significantly to the militarization of American foreign policy. In addition, over the next several years, some American leaders thought not simply of containment, but also of "rollback," a policy that would lead, they hoped, to a weaker Soviet Union and the liberation of some of the areas now under its control. The idea of "rollback," popular among Americans from Eastern Europe, was never an official American aim in the Cold War.

The Soviet Union, meanwhile, saw itself as weak and vulnerable. In the late 1940s, it was desperate to gain security. At the same time, domestic politics within the Soviet Union influenced its foreign policy. Two developments were crucially important. First, Stalin's health was failing. World War II had been extremely stressful. In the postwar years before his death in 1953, Stalin probably suffered from arteriosclerosis, the hardening of his arteries, which reduced the flow of blood to his brain and might account for lapses of judgment, such as in the Korean War, memory loss, and the need for extended vacations.

The second factor was the vicious infighting among Stalin's top lieutenants; he manipulated and controlled these men to some extent but could not completely dominate them.

Initially, Stalin turned on Vyacheslav Molotov, long one of Stalin's most trusted lieutenants, because he had been too soft in his dealings with the allies in postwar Europe. He also took away control of the secret police from Beria, who, as a fellow Georgian had been extraordinarily powerful and assigned him the risky task of developing a Soviet atomic capacity as rapidly as possible. Stalin demoted Beria's ally, Georgy Malenkov (1902–1988), a secretary of the Central Committee and an expert on missiles, leaving as the temporary winner Andrei Zhdanov (1896–1948), "the Pianist" as he was called by Stalin's inner circle. Zhdanov, whose power base was in Leningrad, was placed in charge of cultural matters after the war. He launched what became known as the *Zhdanovshchina*, which set forth the idea of two hostile camps and also called for a thorough Russification of the Soviet Union.

Zhdanov, in even worse health than Stalin, died 31 August 1948. Beria and Malenkov used this opening to attack Zhdanov's associates and again rise to power. Nikita Khrushchev (1894–1971), who was head of Ukraine after the war, and Nikolai Bulganin (1895–1975), minister for the armed forces, were two additional survivors and rounded out the inner circle. Stalin, however, who did not trust Beria, moved toward what might have been a new version of the Great Terror with the addition of a virulent antisemitism in the so-called Doctors' Plot. Only the death of Stalin on 5 March 1953 made it possible to avoid a return of terror on a large scale.

Despite all the maneuvers by Stalin and his inner circle, the Soviet Union responded to the many foreign policy challenges that arose. Believing that the United States might use its monopoly of atomic weapons, the Soviet Union spared no effort to create its nuclear weapons arsenal. Its viselike grip on Eastern Europe was another effort to enhance security. Most importantly, its policies toward the two states of East Germany and West Germany betrayed an obsessive, almost irrational, fear of German potential. At the same time, the Soviet Union viewed the United States as an immensely wealthy, powerful, and hypocritical nation that denied the Soviet Union those items essential to its security while reserving for itself the right to act as it saw fit. Paradoxically, the Soviet Union also feared revolution. Although it gave lip service to national liberation movements in other nations, it offered little real help and, in the case of the Chinese Communists, probably hindered their efforts to come to power. In the last years of Stalin's life, the Soviet Union sponsored purges in Eastern Europe designed to place communists loyal to Moscow solidly in control. It also attempted to destroy the power of Marshal Tito and other Yugoslavian communists who were trying to follow a national (read independent) line of development.

Dismantling the Colonial Empires

The postwar dismantling of the colonial empires took place in two large waves. Most of Asia gained independence in the initial wave of national liberation movements in the first several years after World War II. Nationalist movements, some heavily influenced or even dominated by communists, had existed throughout the colonial world before World War II. In some cases, and India is the best example, these movements had made considerable progress toward achieving self-government, if not independence. In most areas, however, the effects of the war created the conditions that made it possible for the nationalist movements to gain independence.

In those areas where the Japanese had smashed colonial regimes, there was a power vacuum that the nationalist movements were able to exploit in their struggle for independence. One such place was the Dutch East Indies, where Indonesian nationalists under Ahmed Sukarno (1901–1970) declared independence in 1945. Although the Dutch returned after the war and attempted to regain control of the islands by armed force, they lacked the resources necessary for that task. The United States was not only unsympathetic to the Dutch cause but actually put them under considerable pressure to grant the Indonesians independence. In 1949, the Dutch recognized the independence of Indonesia. Of the Dutch empire, originally one of the world's great empires, there now remained only a few fragments. The Dutch had regarded the empire as essential to the nation's economy. They were surprised that the loss of empire had little effect on their ability to recover prewar economic levels and even surpass them.

The Vietnamese, like the Indonesians, took advantage of the destruction of the French colonial government during the war. They did not, however, as the Indonesian nationalists did, work with the Japanese during the war. In August 1945, they declared their independence in words taken from the American Declaration of Independence. Ho Chi Minh (1890–1969), affiliated between the wars with the Comintern, created the Viet Minh, a broad-based nationalist movement heavily influenced by Vietnamese communists. He and the Viet Minh took control of the northern part of the peninsula after the Japanese surrender. The British prevented the Viet

Minh from establishing control in the southern part of the peninsula. Instead, they worked with the French to restore the colonial regime.

The uneasy truce between the north and the south broke down in December 1946 after a French attack. Over the next several years, the Viet Minh defeated French efforts to reestablish control over all of Indochina. At first, they used guerrilla tactics similar to those employed by Mao Zedong in China. Later, they moved to conventional warfare. The French, by the early 1950s, counted on large-scale American aid. The United States, still smarting from the victory of the Chinese Communists in 1949 and needing French support in Europe, assisted the French in their struggle to reestablish colonial rule in Indochina. It was the opposite of America's response to Dutch efforts to reassert their authority in Indonesia. In this case, the Cold War requirements overcame what had been an American reluctance to support the reestablishment of colonialism.

The United States did, however, draw the line at sending American troops to Vietnam. When the French attempted to defeat the Viet Minh at the Battle of Dien Bien Phu in 1954, they were shocked when they suffered a major defeat. The Americans debated various possibilities, including using atomic weapons, but ultimately refused to intervene directly in the conflict. The French were forced to accept the inevitable and exit Vietnam. The peace terms were negotiated at the Geneva Conference in 1954. The Russians and the Chinese pressed the Viet Minh to accept a division of Vietnam at the seventeenth parallel. The northern part of the peninsula remained under the control of the Viet Minh. The south was under a non-communist government. It was agreed that free elections throughout Vietnam would be held in 1956 to determine under what government the Vietnamese people wished to unite. When the time came to hold the election, the South Vietnam government, supported by the United States, refused.

The Vietnamese Communists spent much of the two decades after the Geneva Conference struggling against the military forces of the United States, which had been increasingly drawn into attempts to support South Vietnam (see the discussion of American policy in Vietnam in Chapter 9). Unification came only in 1975 when North Vietnam finally succeeded in uniting Vietnam.

Other attempts at national liberation were less successful. The British were able to withstand a challenge in Malaya primarily by Chinese inhabitants influenced by communism. Malaya, which became independent in 1957, merged with other nations in 1963 to form Malaysia. Singapore, inhabited mainly by Chinese, became the Republic of Singapore in 1965. The United States granted the Philippines complete independence in 1946. The Philippines, under the charismatic leadership of Ramon Magsaysay (1907–1957), instituted land reforms and successfully ended a guerrilla insurrection by 1951.

India was the major exception to the pattern of national liberation movements and the most important of all the Asian nations gaining independence in the first wave of decolonization. The British had reluctantly agreed to Indian independence after the war.

Ho Chi Minh speaking to an audience in Paris following the breakdown of negotiations in 1946. Seated behind him is Admiral Thierry d'Argenlieu, the French governor of Vietnam. Later in 1946, the French attacked Ho's forces and began an eight-year war that ended in the defeat of the French in 1954. Press Association Images/AP Photo.

The major problem concerned whether a separate state should be established for the Muslim population of India. Despite the efforts of Mohandas Gandhi (1869–1948) to keep India intact, the British carved Pakistan out of India and granted the two nations independence in 1947. Gandhi was the inspirational leader of the Indian National Congress in the 1920s and 1930s and was the chief exemplar of a nonviolent approach to political and social change in the twentieth century. Although he was assassinated shortly after India became independent, he had a powerful influence on politics for the remainder of the century, not the least on Martin Luther King, Jr. and other leaders of the American Civil Rights Movement.

The British rather abruptly brought the two states into existence with the passage by the British Parliament of the Indian Independence Bill in July 1947. Although India (predominantly Hindu) and Pakistan (predominantly Muslim) did not have to fight for their independence, many thousands of civilians were killed in the aftermath of the partition, as Muslims fled from newly Hindu-controlled areas and Hindus fled from the newly Muslim-controlled territory. Not long after India and Pakistan gained independence, Ceylon (now Sri Lanka) and Burma (now Myanmar) gained independence as well.

In North Africa and the Middle East, where most of the population was Muslim, two crucial situations took shape in the late 1940s and early 1950s. First, in the British mandate of Palestine, Jewish settlers successfully established Israel as a Jewish state.

Palestine had been partitioned in 1947 by the United Nations into a Jewish state and a Palestinian state. When the British left the area after intense pressure from Jewish forces, neighboring Arab states attempted to destroy Israel in the Arab–Israeli War of 1948–1949. Israel not only defeated the Arab coalition but enlarged its territory. Arab defeat led to military revolts in Egypt, Syria, and Jordan and war and waves of terrorism over the next several decades. British and French influence in the area disappeared; an ill-fated effort to regain influence in the joint attack with Israel on the Suez Canal in 1956 misfired (see the discussion of this event in Chapter 9).

The United States became a significant factor in the area's politics over the next half century with mixed results. On the one hand, it was a major supporter of Israel. On the other, the United States worked with most of the other states in the Middle East, making Iran, in particular into a major power in the area by the 1970s (see subsequent chapters for discussion of American efforts to manage developments in other parts of the Middle East over the next several decades.)

The Soviet Union attempted to play a role in Middle Eastern affairs, but generally without success until the Syrian civil war in the twenty-first century. Israel, heavily influenced by the influx of European Jews and the historical legacy of the Holocaust, became the strongest and most prosperous state in the area, in no small part because of US foreign and military aid.

In North Africa, the French faced a significant challenge in Algeria when the National Liberation Front (FLN) began a revolution in 1954. Although the French had considerable success militarily against the FLN, they steadily lost ground in the court of world opinion. The revolution grew increasingly brutal in the methods used by the two sides. For the French, it was particularly troubling since they could not help but note that they were using many of the same methods the Gestapo had used in World War II against the French Resistance.

Both Tunisia and Morocco gained independence in 1956. A similar move for Algeria was out of the question, first of all, because the one million Europeans, or colons, living in Algeria controlled its economy and government and considered it a part of France. For the French army, holding on to Algeria had become a question of honor, of redeeming itself after humiliating defeats in 1940 by the Germans and in 1954 by the Vietnamese. It was only after the May 1958 coup in Algiers, the capital of Algeria, and a close brush with civil war, which brought Charles de Gaulle to power in 1958, that a way was found to extricate France from Algeria in 1962 (see Chapter 9 for discussion of de Gaulle's efforts to resolve the Algerian crisis).

By the mid-1950s, in what might be seen as the second wave of independence movements, the British and the French began moving to grant their African colonies independence. In 1960, the French granted full independence to their African colonies, which had earlier been given autonomy within the French community of nations. The French dream of assimilation and transforming the inhabitants of colonial areas into people whose culture and heritage were French had not prepared the former colonies well for independence. Only a tiny elite had been able to follow the path opened up by French education. Most of the population of the new nations was simply unprepared for life in the modern world.

The British did somewhat better in training a large group of Africans to take over the task of governing themselves. Several areas of the former colonies, however, contained large numbers of white settlers. In those places, there was resistance to independence and considerable violence. In Kenya, the Mau Mau movement (1952–1956) struggled for independence. Most of its terrorist tactics were directed against Africans who were reluctant to support independence, but white settlers were also killed.

Rhodesia, controlled by white settlers, declared its independence in 1965, but after more than a decade of struggle, Rhodesia became Zimbabwe in 1980 when power was handed over to the black majority. The Union of South Africa left the Commonwealth in 1961 and became the Republic of South Africa, a state characterized by an elaborate system of apartheid or state-mandated segregation. Only after adopting a new constitution in 1993 and holding free elections in 1994 did South Africa leave behind the destructive system—in which the white majority lived vastly better than the black majority it controlled—that had shaped its society and economy for most of the twentieth century.

The Belgians, who had not done much better in managing the Congo after taking it away from the Belgian king in 1908, badly mismanaged the granting of independence. In 1960, with very little advance preparation, the Belgians simply withdrew from the Congo and granted it independence. Independence led to five years of civil war in which the United States, the Soviet Union, and the People's Republic of China intervened at one time or another. Between 1971 and 1997, the nation was known as Zaire and ruled by Mobutu Sese Seko's (1930–1997) brutal, corrupt, and inept regime.

By the mid-1960s, the second wave of independence movements had ended. Only a few white settler regimes and the Portuguese colonies remained in Africa. A handful of colonies in the Western Hemisphere and the Pacific still existed. To all intents and purposes, imperialism in the sense of colonial empires had disappeared from the face of the earth.

Many of the newly independent nations retained ties to their former colonial masters. However, they did not always follow the political traditions of the ex-colonial powers. The United States, especially, and the Soviet Union maneuvered for influence in the new nations but with only limited success. A significant movement of the 1950s and 1960s was nonalignment, an effort by new nations to avoid a unilateral commitment to either major superpower.

Many Europeans who had spent most or all of their lives in the colonies found it challenging to return to their home country after independence. They felt considerable bitterness in many cases. Probably, the Dutch did a better job of making room for people returning from their former colonies. The French, particularly in the complicated case of the colons from Algeria and later migrations from Algeria of non-Europeans, did the worst job. The British fell somewhere in the middle. Europeans as a whole, however, once they had recovered from the trauma of decolonization, found the loss of colonies offset by the freedom from responsibilities the colonies had brought with them. In many cases, they discovered new possibilities. Some countries, the Netherlands again may be the best example, built up a far more prosperous and stable economy than they had ever achieved with colonies.

The emergence of dozens of new nations in the 1950s and 1960s changed the nature of international relations. European countries, like all other industrialized and modern states, had to contend with the claims of the so-called Third World. Political independence was only the first step. The next was to provide, in the form of foreign aid, a fair share of the wealth Europeans had gained over the many years from the operations of the modern world economy. Europeans wrestled with this issue and by and large did far better with the emerging nations than either the United States or the Soviet Union.

References

Britannia Historical Documents. (2013). "The Sinews of Peace." http://www.nationalarchives.gov.uk/education/resources/cold-war-on-file/iron-curtain-speech (accessed 7 June 2023).

Federation of American Scientists. (1950). "NSC 68: United States Objectives and Programs for National Security (14 April, 1950)." https://irp.fas.org/offdocs/nsc-hst/nsc-68.htm (accessed 1 November 2023).

Harry S. Truman Library & Museum. (2013). "Address of the President to Congress, Recommending Assistance to Greece and Turkey, 12 March, 1947." http://www.trumanlibrary.gov/library/research-files/address-president-congress-recommending-assistance-greece-and-turkey (accessed 7 June 2023).

Internet Modern History Source Book. (2013). "Marshall Plan Speech." marshallfoundation.org/the-marshall-plan/speech (accessed 1 November 2023).

Lowe, Keith. (2012). *Savage Continent: Europe in the Aftermath of World War II*. New York: St. Martin's Press.

McCullough, David. (1992). *Truman*. New York: Simon & Schuster.

The National Security Archive. (2013). George Kennan's "Long Telegram." https://nsarchive.gwu.edu/document/21042-long-telegram-original.htm (accessed 1 November 2023). The National Security Archive is an independent non-government research institute and library located at The George Washington University in Washington, DC. It is a basic resource for the study of the Cold War.

8

Out of the Ashes

From Stunde Null *(Zero Hour) to a New Golden Age, 1945–1967*

Twentieth-Century Europe: 1900 to the Present, Fourth Edition.
Michael D. Richards and Paul R. Waibel.

Chronology

1945	Nazi Germany defeated
	Japan surrenders
	Labour party wins elections in Britain
1946	Constitution of French Fourth Republic approved
	Italy becomes a republic
	National Health Service established in Britain
	Beginning of the Indochina War between France and the Viet Minh
1947	British rule in India ends
	Truman Doctrine
	Marshall Plan
	Communists forced out of coalition governments in France and Italy
1948	Communist coup in Czechoslovakia
	Christian Democrats win elections in Italy
1949	Federal Republic of Germany (West Germany) founded
	German Democratic Republic (East Germany) founded
	Dutch rule in East Indies ends
1950	Schuman Plan
1952	European Coal and Steel Community (ECSC) established
1953	Death of Stalin
1954	France defeated at Dien Bien Phu
	Vietnam divided into two states at the Geneva Conference
1956	Khrushchev's speech denouncing Stalin at the Twentieth Party Congress of the Communist Party of the Soviet Union
	Worker unrest in Poland
	Hungarian Revolution and Soviet intervention
	Suez Crisis
1957	European Economic Community (EEC) established by the Treaty of Rome
1958	Charles de Gaulle becomes president of France
	French Fifth Republic established
1959	European Free Trade Association (EFTA) established
1961	Construction of Berlin Wall begins
1962	Cuban Missile Crisis
1963	De Gaulle vetoes British membership in the EEC
	Franco-German Treaty signed

	West German Chancellor Konrad Adenauer retires after 14 years in office
1964	Khrushchev forced to retire—replaced by Brezhnev
1966	Grand coalition of the CDU and SPD in Germany ends 17 years of conservative government
	De Gaulle announces French withdrawal from NATO
1967	Military seizes power in Greece
	EEC, ECSC, and Euratom combine to become the European Community (EC)

In 1950, Laurence Wylie, then a professor of French at Haverford College, took his wife and children to the commune of Roussillon for his sabbatical year. Situated in the southeastern part of France, Roussillon contained only about 800 people. At that time, almost half the population of France lived in similar rural communes (a rural commune is defined as containing fewer than 2,000 people). And, as Wylie later realized, many other French had lived in such communes at one time or another before moving to larger towns or cities. As the 1950s began, many French men and women shared the same values and approach to life as the people Professor Wylie encountered in Roussillon.

In 1950, many farmers planted wheat instead of the fruit trees they knew were better suited to the soil and climate. As one of them put it to Wylie (1974, p. 33): "Plant an apricot orchard so the Russians and Americans can use it as a battlefield? Thanks. Not so dumb." His comments reflected the fear common to many Europeans in the early 1950s that a third world war might well break out.

Eleven years later, Roussillon had changed considerably. Upon revisiting in 1961, Wylie noted he could see fruit orchards in every direction from his vantage point atop a hill overlooking the commune. More than agricultural practices had changed. Roussillon had become a resort town, a fashionable place to live. A construction boom was underway. Television had made its entrance by the late 1950s and with it the idea of buying on the installment plan.

Roussillon, by the early 1960s, was representative of one aspect of the new Europe, a Europe more urban, more affluent, more egalitarian, and more confident than it had been only a decade before. By the early 1960s, with only a few exceptions, it had left colonial empires behind, if not all the legacies of colonialism. There was also a loosening of the two great blocs, the East led by the Soviet Union and the West led by the United States, and indications of détente, a relaxation of tensions between the two great powers. The economy continued to grow, and there seemed to be no end in sight for what was increasingly being called a golden age.

Reconstruction

Certain factors worked together to make the post–World War II reconstruction easier than was initially expected. First, the war damage had sometimes been exaggerated. In addition, in some cases, the wartime demolition had a "positive" side. A factory destroyed in the war became an advantage if the factory was replaced by a more efficient plant. In other situations, the economies of the belligerent nations had expanded during the war and were nearly as large, or even larger, than their prewar versions, even after wartime damages had been taken into account. A largely intact productive capacity that could be modernized where damaged, together with a great shortage of goods of all kinds, created a basis for a rapid recovery. The crucial missing factor was the capital needed to finance economic growth.

The United States provided much of the capital needed for recovery through the Marshall Plan (1947) and other smaller programs. Before the Marshall Plan, America had already made available to postwar Europe nearly $15.5 billion in aid, about $7 billion of that in outright gifts. From 1947 to 1952, the United States provided Europe with about $13 billion in aid under the European Recovery Program. After that, Europe financed recovery largely through the expansion of exports.

The Marshall Plan was based on national plans that the Organization for European Economic Cooperation (OEEC) helped to coordinate. These national plans gave Americans some assurances as to how their money would be spent and encouraged participants to use all resources in the most constructive manner.

In many ways, the Marshall Plan's main contribution was psychological. It demonstrated American faith that European economies could be successfully reconstructed and gave Europeans reason to cooperate with one another in the process. Other factors involved in the recovery included increased trade worldwide and several demographic factors in Europe. First, there was a rising birthrate. Additionally, the influx of refugees and, later, the arrival of large numbers of foreign "guest workers" added to the capacity to produce goods relatively cheaply. Heavy consumer demand, especially in housing and automobiles, was vitally important in maintaining long-term economic growth.

A new kind of capitalism, one characterized by extensive state intervention in national economies through the use of devices such as planning and nationalization, also played an important role in recovery. Governments often used their control of central banks and government investment to determine both the rate of growth of an economy and the direction of that growth. Governments extended their activities beyond areas having to do with welfare—unemployment, retirement, working conditions, public health, and housing—to the workings of the economy itself. In some cases, housing, for instance, welfare and economic expansion went hand in hand. Efforts to make the economy function effectively and equitably followed patterns developed in each of the two world wars. All the factors taken together enabled most Western European countries not simply to recover but also to develop at a rapid rate through the first two decades after World War II.

Reconstruction in the West: British Problems

Three major developments characterized Britain in the first decade after the war. The most basic was the distressingly slow recovery of the economy and Britain's failure to share fully in the rapid economic growth of the 1950s. Britain was initially handicapped by an enormous war debt and by foreign policy crises in areas such as India, Palestine, Greece, and Malaysia. Even after relinquishing responsibilities around the world, however, Britain still faced a severe balance of payments problem. It had become less competitive on the world market because of various factors. The industrial plant was aging, labor was more concerned with benefits than productivity, and management was reluctant to modernize facilities and encourage innovation. The loss of markets and the sell-off of investments to help finance the war increased the difficulty of balancing imports by exports. Despite economic difficulties, Britain resisted the idea of long-term economic planning and restricted governmental interference in the private sector. Nationalization was regarded more like a rescue operation than a tool for restructuring or directing the economy.

The expansion of the welfare state formed the second development. This expansion drew on the famous 1942 report by Sir William Beveridge (1879–1963). The Labour Party erected a comprehensive social security system and a socialized medical care program, beginning with the passage of the National Insurance Act and the National Health Services Act in 1946. Criticism was heavy at the time and continued long after Labour had lost power, but both measures quickly became accepted as integral parts of British life. Even during Labour's long absence from power between 1951 and 1964, there were no serious attempts to dismantle the welfare systems.

Finally, Britain spent most of the postwar period in a somewhat inglorious "retreat from empire." The attempt to reassert its old position in world affairs, the conspiracy with France and Israel to take over the Suez Canal in 1956, failed miserably when the United States and the United Nations forced Britain and its allies to back down.

Labour presided over the initial period of recovery and the development of the welfare state. The party became bogged down, however, by infighting. Badly divided between left and right wings by 1951, it lost power to the Conservatives in that year's elections. Winston Churchill returned to serve as prime minister until his retirement due to ill health in 1955. Anthony Eden (1897–1977) thereafter served as prime minister for a short time before the Suez Canal debacle forced him to resign. He was followed by Harold Macmillan (1894–1986), "Supermac," the ablest of the three Conservative prime ministers of the immediate postwar years. In the 1950s, Britain enjoyed a modest economic recovery and the

Of the three participants in the Yalta Conference in February 1945, only General Secretary Joseph Stalin was active during the period of reconstruction that followed the end of World War II. President Franklin D. Roosevelt died April 12, 1945. Prime Minister Winston Churchill was defeated in elections in July 1945 and only returned for another term as PM in 1951. The Library of Congress/Public domain.

easing of international tensions. By the end of the decade, its economy was prosperous if still vulnerable. Heavily dependent on exports, it nevertheless remained relatively uncompetitive because of the factors discussed above.

Reconstruction in the West: French Success

The general pattern of economic recovery outlined above fits the French experience closely. Wartime destruction and social dislocation demanded strong economic measures. Social and economic programs based on discussions in the resistance movement during World War II and the experiences of the Popular Front in the 1930s also had an impact. While some industries were nationalized, the more important factor was the emphasis placed on economic planning. Jean Monnet (1888–1979), the architect of French economic recovery and later of European economic integration, put together a four-year plan that went into effect in 1948. Initial efforts were designed to channel investments into such essential areas of the economy as coal, electricity, steel, and farm machinery. Later plans were directed toward consumer goods, housing, and farm production.

The idea of a national economy with a large public sector, planned and guided from above, was a radical departure from past French policy. Owners of small businesses and farmers resisted it, but during the 1950s and 1960s, a "silent revolution" took place, making France industrially and technologically competitive with other nations. At the same time, large numbers of people moved into urban areas, and agriculture was thoroughly modernized. In little more than a decade, the French economy changed drastically, despite tenacious rearguard actions.

The French version of the welfare state was not as comprehensive as the British system, but it was a more significant break from the past. Aside from some efforts by the Popular Front in the 1930s, French governments had done virtually nothing in welfare reform before the 1940s and 1950s. The new French system provided not only health, maternity, and old-age benefits but also family allowances paid to families with two or more children. It was meant to give the population benefits in such essential areas as health services, education, and family life, which would, first, improve the quality of people's lives and, second, protect them from the effects of catastrophes such as long-term illness, accidents on the job, or unemployment.

Success in the social and economic spheres made it possible for the French to ignore temporarily the conspicuous political failure of the Fourth Republic. Its initial efforts, after its establishment in 1944 by General Charles de Gaulle, were directed to the writing of a new constitution. While the Communists and Socialists favored a strong legislature (National Assembly), the Popular Republican Movement (MRP) and de Gaulle favored a strong executive. The constitution passed in November 1946 called for neither a strong national assembly nor a strong executive. Instead, it resembled to a large degree the Third Republic.

By the middle of 1947, mounting Cold War tensions forced France to take sides. Shortly after the announcement of the Truman Doctrine, the French Communist Party stopped supporting government efforts to regain Indochina. In April, the Communist Party felt compelled to support a strike in the government-owned Renault automobile plant. The premier won a vote of confidence and then demanded the Communists resign from the coalition.

The end of the coalition government based on three major parties created nearly impossible political conditions. Coalitions had to be constructed from several different parties and could survive only by doing as little as possible. Any controversial effort might destroy the government, resulting in the political "immobilism" that was the hallmark of the Fourth Republic.

Colonial questions caused major dilemmas in the 1950s, leading to frequent cabinet changes. Premier Pierre Mendès-France (1907–1982) was successful in 1954 in ending French involvement in Indochina. Unfortunately for France, however, the simmering Algerian crisis exploded that same year.

By 1958, France was on the verge of civil war over Algeria. In Algiers, the French army and the colons (European settlers in Algeria) seized power. Next, the army and colons seized Corsica and made plans to attack metropolitan France, intending to bring to power a government that would keep Algeria French. Charles de Gaulle, then in self-imposed political exile, appeared the only national figure acceptable to all groups. The French army officers and colons willingly accepted de Gaulle as the one person who could keep the country united and Algeria French. De Gaulle did hope to keep Algeria attached to France, although not necessarily in the same manner as the army and colons wished.

De Gaulle was successful in the next several years both in constructing the type of government he had wanted earlier and in resolving the Algerian crisis. Working quickly in 1958 and 1959, de Gaulle supervised the writing of a new constitution approved by referendum on 23 September 1958 and signed into law on 4 October. Since the new constitution provided for a strong executive, de Gaulle was able to deal successfully with the colonial impasse. His prestige and force of personality allowed him over the next several years to pursue a number of goals. Absolutely vital was bringing the Algerian crisis to a close. Initially, de Gaulle tried to keep Algeria attached to France in some way, but when he saw this would not work, he pushed through Algerian independence. For some in the French military, this was completely unacceptable. Although some officers resorted to revolt and assassination attempts, de Gaulle prevailed. France by the early 1960s enjoyed both a strong, rapidly developing economy and a stable, confident government.

Reconstruction in the West: German *Wirtschaftswunder*

The Federal Republic of Germany was a creation of the Cold War, a version of Germany acceptable to the United States, Britain, and France once it became clear no agreement could be reached on uniting all of Germany. Although an artificial construct, West Germany, as it was commonly referred to, proved to be remarkably successful, both politically and economically, going mostly from strength to strength over the 40 years of its existence. Even today, united Germany is, in the main, an enlarged version of West Germany.

As a product of the Cold War, West Germany almost by definition excluded the left from politics. The Communist Party (KPD) was formally banned in 1956. On the extreme right, the neo-Nazi Socialist Reich Party (SRP) was banned in 1952. The Social Democrats found acceptance only after adopting a new party program (Godesberg Program) in 1959, with which the SPD abandoned Marxist rhetoric and became a party of reform. The mostly conservative resistance in Germany had not been interested in radical social and economic change. Instead, the major emphasis was on the reconstruction of the economy and establishing a political system that would not make West Europeans or Americans nervous.

The founding father, or perhaps grandfather, of West Germany was Konrad Adenauer, leader of the Christian Democratic Union (CDU). Adenauer, who had been lord mayor of Cologne before the

Nazis came to power in Germany, was one of the few German politicians with experience and without the taint of association with the Nazis. He also had good connections with the British and the Americans. Elections in 1949 gave the CDU/CSU[1] and the Free Democratic Party (FDP) a majority. Adenauer became chancellor and remained in that office until 1963, governing in a paternalistic fashion and excluding the *Bundestag* (parliament) whenever possible from discussion of political questions. His style of government, featuring a strong executive and a restricted democracy, has been called "chancellor democracy." It was acceptable in the 1950s, despite its authoritarian overtones, primarily because of Germany's economic success but also because of the nation's delicate situation in international affairs. Adenauer seemed indispensable in the latter area.

Adenauer's lieutenant, Ludwig Erhard (1897–1977), emphasized economic recovery and expansion. Much was left up to the private sector. A combination of good business management, including efforts by industry to channel investments and to control prices; government intervention when necessary; and a long period of labor peace enabled German business to become highly competitive in the world market. An expanding economy eventually led in the 1960s to high wages and a comprehensive welfare system. Some commentators believe Erhard's "socialmarket" approach placed an undue burden on the workers. Others emphasize labor cooperation as an essential factor in the robust economy of the 1950s and 1960s.

Although basically a laissez-faire economy, it always experienced some level of government intervention, a good deal of cooperation within industry, and sizable efforts by the larger banks to direct the workings of the economy. While there were no four-year plans on the French model, a good deal of planning took place in the private sector. To a large extent, however, German business simply needed to do what it had done so well before. The factors that had worked to make it successful earlier—concentration of capital and other resources, economies of scale, reduction of competition—worked

[1] What is commonly referred to as the CDU (Christian Democratic Union) is really a coalition of two Christian Democratic parties, the CDU and the CSU (Christian Social Union), the Bavarian version of the CDU.

again in the postwar period to make it successful. Economic success, in turn, helped make political questions less significant.

One question, however, unification, would not go away. Millions of Germans, displaced from their homes after the war, kept it on the political agenda in the 1950s and the 1960s. Unification, then and for many years later, was out of the question. No other European state, especially not France or the Soviet Union, wanted a reunited Germany. Adenauer understood this and worked to place West Germany in European and Atlantic political and economic structures (e.g., NATO). At the same time, he paid lip service to the desire for unification. As German war refugees were integrated into the new West German society, contributing vital skills and labor, some of the tension surrounding this issue and the even more explosive issue of recovery of lands lost to Poland began to diminish. West Germany by 1961 was divided from East Germany in a very physical way, especially after the construction of the Berlin Wall in August of that year. By then, however, the economy was booming, and many West Germans were beginning to live very well indeed. For these people, politics no longer seemed to matter all that much.

Reconstruction in the West: Other Countries, Other Stories

Immediately after the war, Italy was governed by a coalition of the Christian Democratic Party (DC), the Communists (PCI), and the Socialists. The 1946 referendum on the monarchy resulted in the creation of the Republic of Italy. The coalition broke up the following year because of increasing Cold War tensions and disagreements over plans for social change.

The United States played a significant role in Italian politics in the late 1940s. In the 1948 elections, American officials let it be known that the wrong kind of government from the American point of view would lead to a cutoff in Marshall Plan aid. The Christian Democrats won a working majority and governed over the next decade in coalitions, usually with the Social Democratic Party, a splinter from the old Socialists. The Social Democrats were distinguished primarily by their refusal to cooperate with the Communists.

The coalition government, in which the most influential politician was Alcide De Gasperi (1881–1954) from the DC, worked reasonably well at first and restored Italy to economic and social stability by the late 1940s, largely with the help of the Marshall Plan. In the 1950s, the coalitions grew weaker and less able to take initiatives. A curious political trend developed in which the left gained increasing numbers of votes with each election while at the same time becoming more moderate in its approaches. In particular, the PCI, under the leadership of Palmiro Togliatti (1893–1964), moved toward the center under the influence of moderate trade unionists and in reaction to the Soviet suppression of the Hungarian Revolution in 1956. The Socialists (not to be confused with the Social Democrats) moved away from the Communists and openly sought a coalition with the DC.

By the 1950s, Italy enjoyed a high rate of economic growth, becoming a major supplier in Europe of automobiles, refrigerators, office machinery, and other goods. It was an unusually mixed economy. The government-controlled holding company, the Institute for Industrial Reconstruction and the government energy concern were both administered by private enterprises. Together with FIAT, the giant automobile manufacturer, they contributed concentration of capital, reduction of competition, and economies of scale to economic success. Another major element was formed by sources of cheap labor, particularly in the underdeveloped south. Overall, the south gained little from Italy's reconstruction after the war other than the possibility of employment in the factories and other enterprises in northern Italy.

Each of the smaller countries in Western Europe had unique political and economic situations that, except for Spain, Portugal, and Greece, they had considerable success in overcoming. Finland and Austria resolved the problem of relations with the Soviet Union in differing ways: Finland by keeping its foreign policy in line with Soviet wishes and Austria in the form of a treaty in 1955 that ended occupation but obligated Austria to remain permanently neutral. Sweden and Switzerland, both neutral during World War II achieved standards of living fully comparable with that of the United States by the early 1960s. Both Belgium and the Netherlands faced divisive religious and political problems after the war. In the Netherlands, where an elaborate system guaranteed equity for Protestants and Catholics, rapid economic growth helped to smooth out many of the differences. A rapidly growing and changing economy also helped the Dutch weather the loss of empire.

Reconstruction in the East: The Stalinist Legacy

The Soviet Union had suffered enormously in what it termed "The Great Fatherland War," in which roughly 25 million Russians had died. Great stretches of European Russia had been devastated by Nazi and Soviet scorched-earth policies. Nonetheless, Russians were hopeful a new era was at hand, in which wartime sacrifices would be rewarded. Instead, Soviet citizens were bitterly disappointed by a return to the Stalinist practices of the 1930s. The fourth Five-Year Plan, introduced in 1946, stressed heavy industry and armaments.

By 1950, the Soviet Union had reached prewar levels in industry and agriculture through the utilization of its resources, reparations from some nations, and one-sided economic arrangements with its East European satellites. A major industrial power in terms of basic categories like coal and steel production and closing the gap between itself and the United States in some areas, it nevertheless lacked the technological range of a truly modern industrial society. Much of its production in the 1950s was inferior in quality or outmoded in design. There were serious shortages from the consumer point of view. Agriculture, despite the vigorous efforts of Khrushchev, was inefficient and had not recovered from the effects of collectivization in the 1930s.

By 1952 and early 1953, there were ominous signs that Stalin, aging and in poor health, intended to reinstitute the purges of the 1930s. One major piece of evidence was the "Doctors' Plot," supposedly a plot by several prominent physicians to murder important party and government officials. Any plans that may have existed to restart the purges were cut short by Stalin's death in March 1953 (see Chapter 7 for a detailed discussion of Soviet politics from the end of World War II to Stalin's death).

Many Soviet citizens were despondent, believing they had lost the strong ruler who, if sometimes harsh, had kept them from a worse fate and had made the Soviet Union a powerful and respected state. Collective leadership was emphasized since no one dared to claim the ability to fill Stalin's role. Georgy Malenkov (1902–1988) became premier. The secretariat of the Central Committee, Stalin's old source of power, was reorganized by abolishing the office of general secretary. Khrushchev simply became first among equals on the list of secretaries. Lavrenti Beria, head of the secret police, either made a play for power, or his colleagues feared he would. Arrested in June 1953, he was unceremoniously shot. The NKVD (People's Commissariat for Internal Affairs) was reorganized to curtail its independence and renamed the KGB (Committee for State Security).

Infighting continued, but methods changed. Malenkov, identified with the "new course," which had emphasized the production of consumer goods, resigned his post in 1955. The other leaders saw his ideas as endangering security. The old survivor Vyacheslav Molotov (1890–1986), long Stalin's closest associate, remained a significant figure, but the dominant political force increasingly was Khrushchev.

In 1956, at the Twentieth Party Congress, Khrushchev made a so-called secret speech in which he severely criticized Stalin for his cult of personality, his leadership in World War II, and many of his actions in the 1930s. This was the beginning of a process of de-Stalinization, which had several goals. By blaming Stalin for many past wrongs, Khrushchev and his colleagues deflected a good deal of the criticism of the existing situation. Criticizing Stalin was also a way to improve relations with those communist movements that had resented Stalin's autocratic behavior toward them. Finally, distancing the present government from Stalin made the relaxation of Cold War tensions more likely. In a sense, Khrushchev was only trying to find a way to get around Stalin's legacy.

In 1956, Khrushchev also faced difficult situations with Poland and Hungary. Ironically, the Soviet Union was trying not only to re-establish a good working relationship with Tito and Yugoslavia but also to treat countries in the East Bloc as sovereign states. Thus, the

Warsaw Treaty Organization (WTO, commonly called the Warsaw Pact) came into being in 1955, partly in response to West Germany joining NATO but additionally as a way of establishing proper relationships between the Soviet military and the armed forces of the East European states. In the case of Poland, the Polish leader Władysław Gomułka convinced the Soviets of the loyalty of the Polish Communists and the stability of the political situation in Poland. Hungary, for its part, appeared about to leave the WTO, and the Russians resorted to force to end the Hungarian Revolution. (These events are covered in greater detail later in the chapter.)

Although Stalinism had been heavily criticized, the Stalinists were still a powerful force in Soviet politics. In 1957, they nearly succeeded in deposing Khrushchev. Khrushchev, ever the resourceful politician, took his case to the Central Committee, the members of which mostly owed their careers to him. He also had the backing of the military, in particular, Gregory Zhukov (1896–1974), the great Soviet military leader of World War II. It now became clear Khrushchev was the leading figure in the party, even if not all-powerful.

From 1957 until Khrushchev was successfully deposed in 1964, he tried many schemes to create conditions for a more productive, efficient, and technologically sophisticated economy in the Soviet Union. In some respects, he was remarkably successful. The Soviet Union took an early lead in space exploration with the launching of Sputnik I, the first orbiting satellite, in 1957, and with Yuri Gagarin (1934–1968) as the first man in space (1961) (Table 8.1). On the other

Table 8.1 Major Events in Humanity's Journey into Space

1957	Sputnik I (USSR), first earth-orbiting satellite
1958	First dogs in orbit (USSR)
1959	First monkeys sent into space (USSR)
1961	Yuri A. Gagarin (USSR), first man to orbit earth
1963	Valentina V. Tereshkova (USSR), first woman to orbit earth
1965	Alexei Leonov (USSR), first man to leave spacecraft and float in space

Table 8.1 (Continued)

1966	Luna IX (USSR), first soft landing on moon Gemini VIII (USA), first linkup in space
1968	Apollo VIII (USA), first manned mission to orbit moon and return
1969	Soyuz IV and V (USSR), first experimental space station Apollo XI (USA), first manned landing on moon
1971	Salyut I space station (USSR)
1973	Skylab space station (USA)
1975	Apollo XVIII (USA) and Soyuz XIX (USSR) dock while in earth orbit
1984	First untethered spacewalk (USA)
1986	Mir I (USSR), first space station meant to be permanently manned but closed in 1999 Shuttle Challenger (USA) explodes just after takeoff
1989–1993	Magellan mission to Venus (USA)
1989–2003	Galileo mission to Jupiter (USA)
1990	Hubble space telescope (USA) launched (repaired 1993, 1997, and 1999)
1995	Cooperation between US shuttles and Russian Mir space station begins
1997–1998	Mars Pathfinder mission (USA)
1997	Cassini–Huygens launched—bound for Saturn
2000	First crew in International Space Station
2003	Mars Rover (USA) launched, landed 2004
2005	Huygens probe (USA) landed on Saturn's moon Titan
2008	Discovery of lunar water in the form of ice
2009	Kepler Mission launched—first space telescope designated to search for Earth-like exoplanets
2011	First orbit of Mercury
2012	Nuclear-powered NASA rover lands on Mars to seek out life clues
2015	First flyby of Pluto—last original encounter with one of the nine major planets
2019	First soft landing on the far side of the moon
2020	First orbital spaceflight launched by a private company (SpaceX)
2021	Perseverance, the newest American Mars rover, landed

hand, the Virgin Lands campaign, an effort to put into cultivation vast new areas that were fertile but lacked sufficient rainfall, was initially successful but disastrous over the long run. Similarly, efforts to reorganize the bureaucracies of the Soviet Union were well-meaning but not sufficiently thought out. Ultimately, Khrushchev's downfall came from a streak of adventurism in foreign policy. In particular, the Cuban Missile Crisis between the Soviet Union and the United States in 1962, during which the world ventured to the edge of a nuclear holocaust, prompted his colleagues to bring in someone less erratic. (See "Détente" for a discussion of Khrushchev and the Cuban Missile Crisis.) Ironically, they had to delay deposing him because the Chinese Communists had been extremely critical of him, and at the height of the Sino-Soviet split, the Soviets would not admit the Chinese were right about anything.

Reconstruction in the East: The Seemingly Successful German Democratic Republic

The Soviet Union was ambivalent in its relations with the German Democratic Republic (GDR) or East Germany. For many years, it exploited the GDR economically in order to build up its own economy. Set against this, however, was the need to offset the propaganda value of West Germany and, in particular, West Berlin. Additionally, the Soviet Union feared any kind of German resurgence, even if it seemed to be contained by a divided Germany.

Many Germans had returned to the GDR because they had an idealistic vision of what communism might achieve. From their perspective, capitalist West Germany was little better than Nazi Germany. In the first years after the GDR's founding, it was forced to follow the Soviet economic and political model closely and to join in the witch hunt for national deviationists or Titoists. Trials in the GDR, however, did not result in executions, and on the whole, there was less brutality there than in Czechoslovakia or Romania.

Crucial events for the later evolution of the GDR took place in 1953. It was a classic case of mixed signals. The SED (Socialist Unity, or Government Party), led by Walter Ulbricht (1893–1973), its most influential figure, agreed to follow a Soviet line emphasizing social and economic concessions. Coupled with the concessions, however, were increases in some work norms, which led construction workers in Berlin to begin protesting on 16 June 1953. The following day the protests spread to all the major cities and towns. It was a large-scale protest but probably should not be seen as an uprising. Only toward the end of the day did the Soviets send in tanks to help restore order. The irony of 1953 is that it reinforced Ulbricht's position. Over the next few years, he triumphed over a variety of voices within the SED, closing off any real discussion of goals or policies. The SED became a neo-Stalinist party at precisely the time Khrushchev was launching a campaign of de-Stalinization. For the Soviet Union, however, particularly after 1956, it seemed more important to have a strong figure in charge in the GDR than to advance the cause of political reform.

By the late 1950s, the GDR was suffering from the effects of a massive depopulation process. Hundreds of thousands of people each year were flowing out across the border. Almost all the border was sealed off by the end of the decade, but there remained the problem of Berlin, where thousands of people each day crossed from East to West or vice versa to go to work, to shop, or to visit friends. West Berlin was a hole in the dike threatening to drain the GDR, particularly of young, talented, and well-educated people. Khrushchev attempted to resolve the Berlin issue in the late 1950s on several occasions. He threatened to conclude a treaty with the GDR, leaving it responsible for all of Berlin if the United States, Britain, and France were not willing to renegotiate the status of the city. The East German leaders finally came up with a crude but workable solution to the problem: the Berlin Wall. Construction of the wall, under the supervision of Ulbricht's eventual successor, Erich Honecker (1912–1994), began on 13 August 1961. Well into the fall of that year, Berlin threatened to become a flashpoint with, as for example, when American tanks drove full speed right up to the border to face their Russian counterparts only a few feet away. The crisis passed, however, and East Germans resigned themselves to life behind the wall.

A portion of the Berlin Wall as it had developed by the early 1970s. Note that the wall is actually a series of obstacles, fences, and open spaces, as well as walls. From the collection of Paul Waibel.

Reconstruction in the East: The New Poland

Next to Germany, Poland was the country in Eastern Europe about which the Soviet Union worried most. By 1948, Poland was on its way to becoming a carbon copy of the Soviet Union. People like Władysław Gomułka (1905–1982), who emphasized a national approach to communism, were arrested, imprisoned, and in some cases even executed.

By 1956, Poles believed that the situation within Poland was improving. They felt that Poland could find its own way to a socialist future independent of Soviet guidance. At the end of June, however, riots began in Poznań, protesting the low standard of living of the working class. The Polish United Workers' Party (PUWP), the official name for the Communist Party, split between the Stalinists and those who wanted to improve the lot of the workers. Neither the police nor the army would attempt to stop the riots. The government promised the end of collectivization and reforms for the workers. Gomułka was released from prison and returned to power.

Gomułka and his supporters worked hard to convince the Soviet Union of two things: Poland would remain in the Soviet Bloc, and the PUWP would continue to exercise power. The Soviets agreed, not relishing the prospects of fighting the Poles. Aside from abolishing collectivization and de-emphasizing heavy industry, relatively little changed in Poland. Gomułka and the Poles were able to avoid the fate of the Hungarians who, in October and November of 1956, became involved in a revolution.

Reconstruction in the East: Hungary and Revolution

Hungary became a People's Republic in 1949 and followed the Stalinist path of economic development over the next four years to the point of economic collapse. Four months after Stalin's death, Imre Nagy (1896–1958), seen as a moderate, was appointed premier. His policies mirrored Malenkov's new course and included diversion of resources to light industry and an end to forced collectivization. Malenkov's fall from power in the Soviet Union in 1955 led to his protégé, Nagy, being ousted from the premiership. The following year, however, the Hungarian government ran into trouble. In October 1956, it made a fundamental error in calling in the Soviet Army to deal with Hungarian demonstrators. Throughout Hungary, councils were formed demanding free elections, the withdrawal of Soviet troops, and an end to the security police.

At first, it appeared the Hungarians had won the day. Nagy established a new government on 28 October, and Soviet troops began to leave. On 31 October, Nagy went too far by declaring Hungary's neutrality. After that, Soviet leaders believed they had to crush the revolution by force. The Soviet Union smashed the Nagy government and installed János Kádár (1912–1989) as the new leader. This action had several far-reaching consequences. For one, it played an important role in the Stalinists' attempt to oust Khrushchev in 1957. It complicated efforts by the Soviet Union to establish relations with countries in the East Bloc that provided for autonomy and national sovereignty. Communist movements elsewhere in Europe reassessed Soviet

A crowd of Hungarians gathers around a large statue of Stalin that had been knocked off its base in Budapest, October 1956. The Soviet Union used force to suppress the Hungarian Revolution and regain control over the People's Republic of Hungary. Arpad Hazafi / Associated Press.

Communism and in some cases moved to more independent positions. The West reacted very unfavorably, but involved in the Suez Crisis and in no case wishing to challenge the Soviet Union directly, it could only criticize and find places for the large numbers of former Hungarian freedom fighters that were now refugees.

Throughout the 1950s, the Soviet Union dominated the affairs of East and Central European countries with the exception of Yugoslavia. The Soviet Union not only shaped the political systems but also the social and economic systems. Soviet guidance meant leaving aside the examples of Czechoslovakia and the GDR and emphasizing industrialization and urbanization in what had been countries with large peasant populations and small industrial bases before the war. The pattern was roughly the same in each nation: centralized planning, rapid economic growth, and the development of heavy industry at the expense of the production of consumer goods.

On the Way to a United Europe

The division of Europe into two great blocs was both unexpected and unfortunate in the postwar period. Within each bloc, however, there existed considerable interest in European unity. In the East Bloc, the Soviet Union limited and distorted any expression of interest in unity. It also repressed expressions of nationalism. In the West, the movement toward unity built on ideas and concepts coming from the experience of World War II and followed three parallel paths, two of which reached dead ends by the mid-1950s. The first path involved political union. In May 1948, a Congress of Europe took place. Among the participants were such leading Europeanists as Churchill, De Gasperi, Robert Schuman (1886–1963) of France, and Paul-Henri Spaak (1899–1972) of Belgium. The Congress proposed the political and economic unification of Europe and established the Council of Europe to that end. The power of decision lay in the hands of the foreign ministers of the member states, organized as the Committee of Ministers. But they guarded the sovereignty of their respective nation-states jealously. Political integration was not in the cards.

A second effort at integration concentrated on military matters, specifically the rearmament of West Germany. In 1950, the French proposed to create a European army as a means of circumventing the problem of German rearmament and enhancing the defensive capabilities of Western Europe while the United States was embroiled in the Korean War. Before the European Defense Community (EDC) could be organized, however, events passed it by. Stalin's death, the end of the Korean War, and the easing of Cold War tensions in the mid-1950s all worked to remove some of the more pressing reasons for the EDC. The French themselves had second thoughts about such a drastic turn toward supranationalism. The British finished the plan off by declining to participate. Instead, a German military force was created and made part of NATO in 1955. NATO remained a collection of armies with some provision for an integrated command structure.

The third path toward unity evolved from the cooperation called for under the European Recovery Program (the Marshall Plan) and from earlier efforts at economic collaboration between Belgium, the Netherlands, and Luxembourg. Two Frenchmen, Commissioner of Planning Jean Monnet and Foreign Minister Robert Schuman, proposed pooling coal and steel resources in Europe in what became known as the Schuman Plan. Perhaps the most important aspect of the plan was that it included West Germany. The Germans, for their part, welcomed the opportunity to take part on equal terms in an international organization. According to historian Tony Judt (2005), Adenauer stated, *"Das ist unser Durchbruch"* (this is our breakthrough). The plan went into operation in 1952 with France, West Germany, Italy, and the Benelux countries (Belgium, the Netherlands, and Luxembourg) working together in the European Coal and Steel Community (ECSC).

The ECSC was a great success. Its members pressed on to further economic integration in part because of the obvious potential economic advantage. They were also painfully aware of their vulnerability and weakness as individual states. The failure of the French and British to regain control of the Suez Canal in 1956 only served to underline this. In 1957, the Treaty of Rome established the European Economic Community (EEC) or Common Market. The EEC set out to eliminate customs barriers among its member states and create a common tariff structure for trade with the rest of the world.

Three significant events affected the development of the EEC in the 1960s. First, French President de Gaulle, worried that Britain's entry into the EEC would weaken French dominance of the Common Market, vetoed Britain's application in 1963. Second, the Luxembourg Agreement in 1966 resolved clashes between those who favored the Commission, the executive body of the EEC, and those who wanted the Council of Ministers, which represented the individual states, to retain control of the EEC. It required the Commission to consult individual states before making major proposals and noted that no nation could be overturned in the Council of Ministers if it were a matter of national interest. Finally, the so-called Merger Treaty of 1967 combined the EEC, the ECSC, and Euratom (the European Atomic Energy Community) into a single institution, the European Community (EC). Despite these various developments, however, by the end of the 1960s, the EC had not realized the promise many saw in it at the beginning of the decade.

The British sponsored a seven-nation European Free Trade Association (EFTA), a much looser arrangement than the EEC. In Eastern Europe, the Council for Mutual Economic Assistance (variously referred to as Comecon, CEMA, or CMEA), in existence since 1949, took on a new life. Originally constructed as a counter to the Marshall Plan, but little more than a cover for Soviet exploitation of the Eastern European economies, Comecon became directed more toward mutually advantageous economic relations. In this, it reflected not only the example of the EEC but also the desire for autonomy and national sovereignty, which had been dampened in some ways by the events of 1956 but also paradoxically accelerated by events of that year.

Although the widespread interest in European unity in the postwar period gave way quickly to political realities like the Cold War and concerns for national interests, it did result in some important steps toward unity on social and economic policies. It also produced processes, particularly in the EEC, by which more could be achieved. It was one of the most significant and characteristic developments of the first two decades after the war.

A Consumer Economy in Western Europe

The main characteristic of this period in Western Europe was the extent of prosperity. There was, to be sure, a considerable difference between the more industrialized and affluent north and the less developed south. Even within countries, there was a considerable regional difference. The Italian case offers the best example. The north contained most of the industry and employment opportunities. In the south of Italy, there were millions of urban and rural poor. But overall, Europe was prosperous to an extent never before realized in its history.

One means of measuring the development of a consumer economy is to examine the composition of the workforce. A workforce in which the agricultural sector shrinks while the industrial sector remains largely stable and the service sector grows is considered to be moving toward a modern economy, in postwar terms. Using France, West Germany, and Italy in the 1950s as examples, the industrial and service sectors increased in size, while the agricultural sectors declined. In the 1960s, the agricultural sectors continued to decline, with less than 10 percent of the West German workforce engaged in agriculture and related activities. In that same period, the industrial sector declined slightly in France and grew slightly in West Germany and somewhat more in Italy, while the service sector grew substantially in each state. Each economy was becoming increasingly modern.

As the nature of the economy changed, the workforce gained increased amounts of disposable income, that is, more money to spend on food, clothing, and other goods after paying fixed expenses such as rent and taxes. Per capita, disposable income increased 117 percent in the United States between 1960 and 1973, but this was greatly exceeded by European figures for the same period: France, 258 percent; Germany, 312 percent; and Denmark, 323 percent. Disposable income increased more rapidly in nearly every Western European country than it did in the United States, although only Denmark, Germany, Switzerland, and Sweden were close to (or higher, as was the case in Sweden) the total figure for per capita disposable income in the United States. The rates in France and Belgium, despite large increases, remained substantially below the American figure, while those of Britain and Italy were considerably below.

Old patterns of national affluence also shifted in this period. Britain, the wealthiest country in Europe at the start of the century, continued to lag behind most other Western European nations. The beginnings of this trend went back to the interwar period. The French, and especially the Italians, moved dramatically in the opposite direction, constructing much stronger and more affluent economies than they had enjoyed before World War II.

The range of consumer goods and the increasing levels of consumption in this period provide not only a graphic illustration of how much more disposable income Europeans enjoyed but also of a significant sociocultural shift. Not just refrigerators, washing machines, and televisions, but automobiles and houses came to be items Europeans might aspire to own in the 1960s. The rapid increase in ownership of automobiles is a particularly sensitive indicator of how the economy and people's habits were changing. By 1969, two of every ten people in Britain, Sweden, West Germany, and France owned automobiles. The United States was still considerably ahead with a figure of four in ten, but the gap was closing. Television, a shaper as well as a symbol of a consumer society, provides an even better index of change (Tables 8.2 and 8.3).

Along with the acquisition of goods came considerable changes in lifestyles and attitudes. The American-style supermarket began to spread in the late 1960s, competing with the neighborhood butcher, greengrocer, baker, and retail grocer. The number of people running routes through neighborhoods selling milk, bread, coal, or sundries began to decline. Once- or twice-weekly markets became smaller and less important in some areas and disappeared in others. It would be easy to exaggerate the extent of the changes, yet the trends were clear by the late 1960s. While most Europeans welcomed the new prosperity, some viewed it with horror as a kind of Americanization of European society.

Table 8.2 Automobiles in 1957 and in 1965

	1957	*1965*
France	3,476,000	7,842,000
West Germany	2,456,288	8,103,600
Italy	1,051,004	5,468,981
The Netherlands	375,676	1,272,898
Sweden	796,000	1,793,000

Table 8.3 Televisions in 1957 and in 1965

	1957	*1965*
France	683,000	6,489,000
West Germany	798,586	11,379,000
Italy	367,000	6,044,542
The Netherlands	239,000	2,113,000
Sweden	75,817	2,110,584

Social Change

Social change was perhaps most conspicuous among the farming populations of Western Europe. First, the number of farmers shrank in the 1950s and 1960s, while production both per capita and overall increased. These trends were due to what some have termed an "agricultural revolution." Primarily, it involved greater use of machinery and more attention to scientific techniques in areas such as breeding of livestock, selection of seed, use of fertilizers, and utilization of land. In general, it was connected with market-oriented and capital-intensive rather than labor-intensive farming methods. These changes, together with policies favorable to agriculture in the EEC and elsewhere, led to a decline in the number of marginal, self-sufficient farmers and a growing level of prosperity among those who approached farming as if it were an industry. This approach often robbed farm life of intangible benefits that many prized, such as a feeling of kinship with nature, but it also helped close the gap between urban and rural lifestyles. Improvements in transportation and communication also brought the farmer closer to life in the mainstream. The European peasant, long a distinctive social type, had virtually disappeared for better or worse.

The working classes were also changing, although not as dramatically as farmers. In some countries, a process of "embourgeoisement" was far advanced. This meant that Swedish and German workers, for example, differed less and less from members of the middle classes in terms of housing, clothing, leisure activities, and the like. In other countries, Britain, for example, class distinctions continued to remain strong. Practically everywhere in Western Europe, however, the working class had sufficient income to participate in the consumer economy. Advertising and the mass media together created a lifestyle that most of the population, workers or middle class, desired. A common, mass culture began to take shape.

With some reservations and criticisms, workers in Western Europe accepted industrial capitalism by the 1960s. They were increasingly interested in gaining an equitable share of the national income together with better working conditions, expanded fringe benefits, and an extension of the welfare state.

The generally more cooperative attitude was most fully developed in Sweden and Germany. In Britain, expectations were similar, but relations between workers and employers remained somewhat antagonistic. While in France and Italy labor unions became more reformist in the 1960s, they achieved fewer improvements for workers than labor unions in Britain, Germany, and Sweden. In part, working-class satisfaction with its situation had to do with the role played in the economy by guest workers, laborers brought in from Yugoslavia, Greece, Turkey, Spain, Portugal, and North Africa to take the lowest-paying, least-desirable jobs. These groups, especially important in Germany, Switzerland, and the Netherlands and present in large numbers in Sweden and France provided European economies with greater flexibility. In good times, they were available to work cheaply. In bad times, they could, in theory, be shipped back home. Neither for the indigenous working class nor the other elements of the population was the situation of the guest workers a source of much concern in the 1960s.

By the 1960s, the middle classes could be divided into two large groups. On the one hand, many white-collar employees worked as clerks, technicians, sales personnel, lower-ranking professionals (e.g., teachers and nurses), and supervisory and lower-level managerial personnel. On the other, a relatively small number of higher-ranking professionals (lawyers, doctors, university professors), upper-level bureaucrats and managers, and technocrats made up an upper segment. The upper-middle-class segment in the 1960s still controlled a disproportionate share of wealth, political power, and status in European society. It constituted a new elite, composed of the remnants of the older elites and some segments of the traditional middle classes.

The aristocracy had either disappeared or was regarded as a quaint anachronism. The new elite was essentially still a continuation of the old establishment in Britain and France. Elsewhere, the new elite was more open. Education, especially a specialized or technical education, was increasingly a necessity. Family ties still played a role, if a declining one. Like the older upper class, the new elite could be generally characterized not only by educational attainment and social background but also by an attachment, genuine or not, to high culture and by distinctive patterns in housing and leisure-time activity. The role of the very rich differed from country to country; it was, for example, very important in Germany and Italy but minimal in Sweden. The difference had to do mostly with taxation and other income distribution policies. Class differences remained strong in Europe in the 1960s despite the efforts to democratize life. In fact, most of the social tension in Western Europe in the 1960s concerned the degree to which social and cultural institutions continued to work to the advantage of those already a part of the elites and against able and ambitious people lower down the social hierarchy.

Détente

Détente was the product of two crises. One, the Berlin Crisis, was actually a series of crises culminating in the construction of the Berlin Wall in August 1961. Between the formation of the GDR in 1949 and August 1961, about three million East Germans, approximately 16 percent of the country's population, went through Berlin to leave the country. Many of the emigrants were young and well educated. Although Khrushchev may have been worried primarily about the possibility of the United States providing West Germany with atomic weapons, the East German regime worried about the state's survival if the flow of citizens ("brain drain") to the West were to continue.

The second crisis, the Cuban Missile Crisis in 1962, edged the world very close to a thermonuclear war. A series of confrontations in the late 1950s and early 1960s, including not only the Berlin Crisis and construction of the Berlin Wall (1961), but also the U-2 spy plane incident in 1960 (in which the Soviet Union shot down an American high-altitude spy plane), and the failed summit meeting between Nikita S. Khrushchev and US President John F. Kennedy in 1961, had left the two superpowers edgy.

Khrushchev decided in 1962 to take a chance on installing missiles in Cuba to gain an advantage at little cost. There were several reasons why he pursued this risky policy. One reason, of course, was to back up his guarantee to Fidel Castro to protect Cuba from American threats. A second was probably domestic. A cheap but dramatic victory in the Cold War competition would reinforce his position in the Soviet Union. Various disasters in domestic policy and reservations about the de-Stalinization campaign had eroded Khrushchev's power. Other reasons may have played a part, too. Khrushchev may still have hoped to revise the situation in Berlin. He apparently thought it might be possible to trade the removal of missiles in Cuba for the removal of American missiles in Turkey.

Kennedy, for his part, badly needed a diplomatic success after the Bay of Pigs fiasco in 1961 (the failed attempt by Cuban exiles trained by the US Central Intelligence Agency (CIA) to invade Communist Cuba and overthrow Castro; Kennedy had had to take responsibility for it) and the inability of the United States to stop construction of the Berlin Wall. President Kennedy's decision to set up a naval quarantine of Cuba was probably the best move once the crisis had become a matter of public knowledge. Within the small group that Kennedy assembled at the White House to discuss how to respond to Khrushchev's gambit, there were those who believed an airstrike on the Soviet Union's missile sites offered the best approach. Since representatives of the air force could not guarantee complete success, some members of the committee discussed the need for an invasion of Cuba and removal of Castro and his Soviet advisors.

Both the United States and the Soviet Union saw the seriousness of the situation and acted to defuse it. There was a great deal of behind-the-scenes consultation, particularly on the part of the Americans. A serious dilemma arose when Khrushchev's first letter, an emotional and personal appeal from one veteran of World War II to another (Kennedy), was followed by a second, tougher letter, probably authored by the Politburo and signed by Khrushchev. The dilemma was resolved when Kennedy and his advisors decided to respond to the first letter while simply ignoring the existence of the second letter. Khrushchev agreed to remove the missiles in return for a pledge by the United States that it would not invade Cuba and an agreement, not publicized at the time, that the United States would remove its missiles from Turkey. After the crisis, the two powers moved rapidly toward détente.

A direct telephone line, the "hot line," was installed between the White House in Washington, DC, and the Kremlin in Moscow. In 1963, the Nuclear Test Ban Treaty was initially signed by the United States, the Soviet Union, Great Britain, and later by most other nations. Even when America began to play an active role in the conflict in Vietnam, détente continued. The Soviet Union continued to support the forces of North Vietnam but did what it could to prevent the war from widening. The United States, for its part, supported the forces of South Vietnam while pursuing policies designed to keep the Soviet Union as well as the People's Republic of China (PRC), loosely known as "Communist China," from taking a more active role in the war. The United States was caught in a particularly delicate situation wherein certain measures that might lead to military victory over the North Vietnamese had to be rejected for fear they would inadvertently bring the Soviet Union or the PRC directly into the war.

By 1967, Europe had recovered from World War II and was making significant progress in all areas. Industry had become the major factor in almost every European economy, even in Eastern and Southern Europe. The nature of industry was changing as well, especially in Northwestern Europe, where the emphasis was on the production of consumer goods, the development of new products, and the use of new machines and techniques. Standards of living had surpassed prewar levels. Societies were becoming more homogenous, even in Western Europe, where ideology did not work toward egalitarianism as such. In politics, governments in both East and West became more involved in social and economic issues, resulting in the creation or extension of some form of the welfare state. Greater governmental intervention in economic matters meant not only increased regulation but also government-owned sectors of the economy in most states. Of course, in Eastern Europe, the private sector was almost completely squeezed out.

The changing political spectrum in Western Europe had resulted in the virtual disappearance of the prewar type of liberal or conservative party. Two major developments were the emergence of Christian Democratic parties, which dominated the first two decades of politics in Italy and Germany, and reform-minded, nonrevolutionary

Socialist parties in several states. In many ways, the Christian Democratic parties, attracting members with widely differing interests, replaced the old conservative parties. The Socialists were a partial replacement for the liberals, although far more enthusiastic about government intervention. Politics was less polarized than in the period between the wars. Even the large number of votes given to Communist parties in Italy and France and occasional appearances of right-wing protest movements did not alter the essential moderation of West European politics.

Politics had changed drastically in Eastern Europe, with communist states subservient to Moscow (with the exception of Yugoslavia and, later, both Albania and Romania), taking the place of the mostly authoritarian right-wing governments that had existed in the 1930s. In the West, parliamentary democracies existed in all states but Spain and Portugal, which still had 1930s-style authoritarian governments, and Greece, which had a military dictatorship for a brief period.

Europe writ large had not yet made itself into a third great power. In fact, it was losing rather than gaining ground in world affairs, as its steadily eroding colonial empires demonstrated. But it had managed to find its own way. European civilization had done far more than merely survive. It had undergone something of a renaissance, becoming by the late 1960s both a guide and an example, in terms of social policy and relations with Third World countries, for the United States and the Soviet Union.

References

Judt, Tony. (2005). *Postwar: A History of Europe Since 1945*. New York: The Penguin Press.

Wylie, Laurence. (1974). *Village in the Vaucluse*, 3rd ed. Cambridge, MA: Harvard University Press.

9

Metamorphosis

An Era of Revolutionary Change, 1968–1988

Twentieth-Century Europe: 1900 to the Present, Fourth Edition.
Michael D. Richards and Paul R. Waibel.

Chronology

1968	Events of May in France
	Prague Spring in Czechoslovakia and the Soviet intervention
1969	De Gaulle resigns as president of France
	Willy Brandt forms an SPD–FDP coalition in West Germany
1971	Erich Honecker replaces Walter Ulbricht as party leader in East Germany
1972	Basic treaty between East Germany and West Germany
	Strategic Arms Limitation Treaty (SALT I)
1973	Britain, Ireland, Denmark join the EC
	OPEC creates an oil crisis
1974	Return of democracy in Greece
	Portuguese Revolution
1975	Death of Franco and beginning of the return of democracy in Spain
	Helsinki Accords
	First Group of Seven (G-7) meeting
1976	Worker unrest in Poland
1978	Former Christian Democratic premier of Italy Aldo Moro kidnapped and murdered by the Red Brigades
1979	Conservatives under Margaret Thatcher win in Britain
	Soviet military forces invade Afghanistan
1980	Solidarity (Solidarność) gains recognition in Poland
	Death of Tito
1981	Greece joins the EC
	Martial law declared in Poland; Solidarity outlawed
1982	Britain defeats Argentina in the Falklands War
	Brezhnev dies, replaced by Andropov
1984	Andropov dies, replaced by Chernenko
1985	Chernenko dies; Gorbachev becomes the new leader of the Soviet Union
1986	Spain and Portugal join the EC
	Chernobyl nuclear accident

In the late 1960s, protest and rebellion seemed to be the order of the day in Western Europe and the United States. Yet, despite the drama and color of the period, relatively little changed. In Eastern Europe, the Prague Spring seemed to offer an opportunity to make a communist society actually work, but the Soviet Union smashed that opportunity with the assistance of East Germany and Poland. Eastern Europe and the Soviet Union continued into the 1980s much as they had earlier, with less and less success in maintaining productive economies. Western Europe and the United States weathered a rough 1970s and emerged in the 1980s stronger economically, although not without serious social issues.

Radicalism in Western Europe in the Late 1960s

At the end of the 1960s, most Western European countries seemed virtually besieged by radicals questioning political frameworks, social institutions, economic arrangements, and even cultural assumptions. Radicals accused governments of ruling in an authoritarian style at home and aiding "imperialism" and counterrevolution abroad. They viewed social and economic institutions as consciously contrived to perpetuate political and economic power in the hands of ruling cliques while keeping the masses both ignorant of the true situation through manipulation of the media and satisfied through the production of inexpensive consumer goods.

Many radicals saw themselves as part of a worldwide revolutionary movement answering the call of the Cuban revolutionary Che Guevara (1928–1967) for "One, Two, Three . . . Many Vietnams!" Few identified with the established socialist or communist parties. Some called themselves Maoists or professed to be anarchists. Many had quite limited aims and concentrated on reforming what they saw as an undemocratic, elitist educational system designed to reinforce and perpetuate the inequities of the larger political and socio-economic systems.

The organized radical movements, much smaller than the number of protesters who might appear at a demonstration, were primarily students and young intellectuals. They varied widely in terms of their impact on existing systems. France was affected far more than any other Western European country. Germany and Italy both confronted large-scale movements but escaped major crises. Britain and the Netherlands had important, if not greatly influential, movements.

In Germany, the German Socialist Student Federation (SDS) protested against the established system with great seriousness. The first major protest was directed against the Shah of Iran, Mohammad Reza Pahlavi (1919–1980), during his visit to West Berlin in 1967. The next focus of SDS attacks was the publications empire of Axel Springer (1912–1985), the influential newspaper and magazine publisher widely regarded as a pillar of conservatism or even counterrevolution. After one of the SDS leaders, Rudi Dutschke (1940–1979), was shot and seriously wounded in April 1968, protests against the Springer empire intensified. Events in Germany in the spring of 1968 were highly dramatic, but the government escaped a serious challenge. The SDS lacked circumstances similar to France in May, where de Gaulle's policies were widely criticized, and student demonstrations brutally suppressed. Student radicals in Germany found themselves isolated from a general public largely satisfied with existing political and economic arrangements.

France in May 1968

What happened in France in May 1968 can scarcely be understood unless the influence of Charles de Gaulle in French affairs between May 1958 and May 1968 is taken into account. The structure of the Fifth Republic gave de Gaulle a position of considerable power. In addition to his constitutional powers, and somewhat like Adenauer in West Germany, de Gaulle overstepped the boundaries, taking actions that no politician without his force of personality and moral stature would have been allowed to carry out. While de Gaulle was preoccupied with foreign affairs and contacts with the communist bloc and Third World leaders, domestic problems began to surface. One was the odd contrast between the sophistication of French technology and science and the backwardness of some aspects of life in France, two prime examples being the telephone system and housing. Second, society, if increasingly democratic, was still stratified. The different strata were determined mainly by educational achievement, but the way to an appropriate education was paved with money, family background, and connections. The very bright were co-opted into the system, but the system worked here as in other areas mostly to perpetuate the elites.

The 1965 presidential elections furnished one glaring indication of the level of domestic dissatisfaction. François Mitterrand (1916–1996), leader of the leftist coalition of socialists and communists, forced de Gaulle into a runoff. After prevailing in that contest, de Gaulle continued to govern virtually unchecked, seemingly deaf to the rising clamor of opposition.

The events of May 1968, although based on widespread dissatisfaction and student grievances, began as a spontaneous reaction to a specific event of little significance: the arrest of some students demonstrating against the involvement of the United States in Vietnam. On 22 March, a meeting to protest the arrests took place at the University of Nanterre, one of the new universities in the French system. A radical movement called the 22 March Movement came out of the meeting. On 2 May, "Anti-Imperialist Day," members of the 22 March Movement, finding themselves locked out of Nanterre, went to the Sorbonne, the best-known part of the University of Paris. The following day, the police violated traditions of academic freedom by coming into the Sorbonne and arresting hundreds of students. The arrests marked the beginning of demonstrations and confrontations between students and police in the Latin Quarter of Paris. A climax of sorts came on 10 May, the "Night of the Barricades," when events in the streets were described minute-by-minute on national radio. On 13 May, more than a million people demonstrated in Paris against the government. Although workers seized the Sud Aviation plant on 14 May and began a strike movement that eventually included more than 10 million workers, there were only limited connections between the student protests and the strike movement.

Toward the end of May, the government, which had been almost completely ineffective up to that point, dissolved the National

La Chienlit c'est lui! Support the revolutionary French students. Buy L'Enragé, their satirical journal. Granma Bookstore / The Library of Congress / Public Domain.

Assembly and set a date for elections. De Gaulle, who had been mysteriously out of the country for several hours and had gained the backing of the French military, appealed for "civic action" against a "totalitarian plot." Many French began to worry about the possibility of anarchy or a communist takeover. Even in Paris, where sympathy for the students was widespread, people were tired of the confusion and the disruptions caused by the demonstrations and strikes. There was, meanwhile, no consensus among the student radicals as to specific aims and goals. Workers generally wanted only moderate changes, in particular a substantial pay hike. Almost no one in the general public liked the idea of a genuine revolution.

France, closer to a revolution in 1968 than any other Western European country, was not, actually, all that close. Government inactivity, coupled with some blunders, had resulted in a situation in which the overthrow of the government seemed possible.

Nevertheless, the government still maintained a strong position. It had capable leadership in de Gaulle and, especially, in the premier, Georges Pompidou (1911–1974). In the military and the police, it had an overwhelming monopoly of force. Even the social and economic strains were not as severe as they appeared at first. Despite the drama and color of events, the government could only fail by losing its nerve.

The radicals had little chance. The "system" was the enemy, but there was no agreement on how to define the system or what program to follow to combat or replace it. While people like Daniel Cohn-Bendit (1945–), "Danny the Red" (so named for the color of his hair as much as his politics), a student with dual French and German citizenship studying in France, caught the imagination of many, most radicals distrusted leaders and ideas about strategy. Operating almost exclusively on the level of tactics, the radicals lost once the government took the initiative. Additionally, the radicals did not understand the aspirations of those temporarily allied with them, whether those of the working class or the middle class.

The major results of the radical movement were changes in the education system, principally possibilities for revised curricula, less elitist student bodies, and less authoritarian structures of the university administration. In reaction to the events of May, many turned back to moderate or conservative parties. Parties on the left tried to appear moderate to distance themselves from the radicals. The Communist Party in France, which had done nothing to aid the radicals, found itself simultaneously distrusted by moderates and under heavy fire from the radicals. The year 1968, particularly as it played out in France, was the high point of postwar radicalism in Western Europe. Radicals had gained a hearing, but the sweeping, comprehensive changes they envisioned were unacceptable to most Europeans. Most found life alright as it was and worried more that the economy would cease growing or something else might happen to prevent them from achieving goals they had come to see as realistic possibilities. The contrast with the situation in the United States, where two issues, civil rights and the war in Vietnam, could not be ignored, was striking. (See a discussion of the 1960s in the United States later in this chapter.)

The Prague Spring

Within the Soviet Bloc, there were attempts to make the Soviet model of communism work better than it did in the Soviet Union. In some cases, mild deviations from the model had been allowed. Poland had retreated from collectivized agriculture in the 1950s and enjoyed in the 1960s a much more productive agricultural sector. Hungary, as a means of helping people forget the events of 1956, was allowed to experiment with different economic structures and seek trade ties with Western Europe. East Germany, despite Soviet restrictions on the economy, had made considerable economic progress in the 1960s, partly because people realized after the construction of the Berlin Wall that there was no alternative to life in East Germany.

Czechoslovakia was a major disappointment. It had been an urbanized, industrialized state even before World War II. By the early 1960s, however, the Czech economy had deteriorated badly, and the political system was regarded as repressive and ineffective. Communist leadership, particularly that of Antonín Novotný (1904–1975), first secretary of the Communist Party increasingly came under criticism. Questions about the fairness of the political trials held between 1949 and 1954 kept coming up within the Czech Communist Party. Slovak communists, who believed, as did Slovaks generally, that Slovakia had been neglected, were especially active in pressing for party reform and a change in leaders.

In January 1968, Novotný was replaced as First Secretary of the Communist Party by Alexander Dubček (1921–1992), a Slovak and a leader of the moderate reform impulse. Dubček moved first to liberalize the economy by decentralizing it, increasing the emphasis on consumer goods and investments in Slovakia, and establishing more trade with the West. He also lifted censorship and encouraged cultural and intellectual life. Actually, the Prague Spring, a political reform effort that initially appeared in the Communist Party, owed much to a kind of renaissance in the cinema, theater, and literature starting in 1966. Czech writers and filmmakers, in particular, had drawn the interest of avant-garde circles in Europe by the mid-1960s. By 1968, this renaissance and the impetus for reform within the party had come together in an impressive, seemingly irresistible movement for change.

By late spring, the reform movement began to get out of hand. The growth of clubs and discussion groups threatened the communist monopoly of political power. The government granted freedom of speech and press. In a preview of the Russian experience with *glasnost* or openness in the late 1980s, Czechs began exploring their recent history. Dubček sketched a path to democratic socialism over several years and called for "socialism with a human face." Ludvík Vaculík (1926–2015) published a frank criticism of the Czech Communist Party in late June, *The Two Thousand Words*. Some Czech communists began to have second thoughts about the Prague Spring even as others looked to the Party Congress in September 1968, at which a reform program was to be presented. In contrast to the events of May in France, there were no crowds in the streets or barricades but, instead, sustained and intense discussion.

Meanwhile, the Russians, East Germans, and Poles grew apprehensive about the movement. Essentially, they had to decide whether the Czechs resembled Poland or Hungary in 1956. The Czechs held two meetings in the summer of 1968, the first with the Soviet Union and the second with representatives of most of the member nations of the Warsaw Pact. Finally, the Soviets, Poles, and East Germans invaded Czechoslovakia on 20 August. Paratroopers landed on the tarmac and took over the Prague airport, and long lines of tanks and trucks drove over the border into Czechoslovakia. Czechs tried to block the invasion by such acts as removing road signs. Demonstrations followed, and a few people even set themselves on fire in protest, but no one wanted a repetition of the Hungarian Revolution. Brezhnev tried to justify the action by stating that socialist countries had an obligation to come to the aid of a brother socialist country when it was threatened by "counterrevolutionary forces," the so-called Brezhnev Doctrine.

The Prague Spring was a turning point that was not allowed to turn. It is debatable, of course, that even the Czechs could have taken their Soviet-style political and economic system and transformed it into real democratic socialism. Nonetheless, they were more likely to do so than any other satellite country. Dubček did not have the same vision or capacities as Mikhail Gorbachev would have in the late 1980s, but Czechoslovakia might have been a better country in which to attempt Gorbachev-style reforms (see the discussion of Gorbachev and the Soviet Union later in this chapter).

The Soviet Union removed Dubček and other reformers from power. By the spring of 1969, an orthodox communist regime under Gustáv Husák (1913–1991) controlled the country. Ironically, efforts by the Czech communists to construct what some termed "socialism with a human face" failed partly because of the enthusiasm of many participants in the reform movement. They did not sufficiently take into account the rising anxiety of the leaders of the Soviet Union, East Germany, and Poland. Mainly, however, the leaders of these states feared infection from the Czech reform virus.

Husák, moderate in comparison to the pro-Soviet hardliners, was successful in establishing pragmatic policies in Czechoslovakia in the early 1970s. He was not very successful, however, in causing Czechs and Slovaks to forget the promise of 1968. The most prominent group that continued to keep the spirit of the Prague Spring alive was Charter 77, which produced a document early in 1977 that criticized the government for failing to implement the human rights provisions of documents that it had agreed to previously. The regime punished those involved through various actions, from dismissing people from their jobs to imprisoning them. A leading member of Charter 77 was the Czech playwright Václav Havel (1936–2011), who became president of Czechoslovakia after the Velvet Revolution of 1989.

Ironically, the leadership in both East Germany and Poland changed soon after the Soviet invasion ended the Prague Spring. Walter Ulbricht was replaced by Erich Honecker (1912–1994) and Władysław Gomułka by Edward Gierek (1913–2001) in 1970.

Brezhnev's Russia

In the 1960s and early 1970s, Leonid Brezhnev (1906–1982) ruled the Soviet Union as president and first secretary of the Communist Party in tandem with the premier, Alexei Kosygin (1904–1980). They had to acknowledge, however, the importance of several groups within the Soviet system, the military, the KGB, the governmental bureaucracy, and, of course, the Communist Party. Brezhnev and Kosygin wrestled with basically the same kinds of problems that had plagued Khrushchev, an unresponsive and overly centralized economy, unproductive agriculture, and elements in Russian society that enjoyed privileged positions.

Brezhnev, Kosygin, and other members of the Communist Party's Politburo (Executive Committee) steered a course in the 1960s between the arbitrary terror of Stalin and the adventurism of Khrushchev. Although they experimented briefly with ideas calling for a socialist market approach, that is, some attention paid to questions of supply and demand and the profitability of enterprises, their policies were largely conventional and followed two major paths. One emphasized highly concentrated efforts to succeed at particular tasks, the so-called music school approach, most of which had a military payoff. A good example would be the Soviet space effort, which was not intended to race the United States to the moon but aimed at a different goal: creating a space station. The second approach emphasized increasing the number of various components in an industry: more capital, a larger number of workers, a greater supply of energy, and so forth. The first approach achieved some amazing successes but at a high cost. The second worked well as long as larger numbers of workers, or greater amounts of capital could make a tangible difference in a particular industry. What doomed the second approach by the 1960s were, first, the rapid increases in productivity outside the Soviet Bloc and, second, the rapid changes in technology, which quickly began to alter the very definition of a modern economy.

By the early 1960s, the position of the Soviet consumer had begun to improve, with refrigerators and television sets now being items people might finally be able to afford to purchase. The improvements over earlier periods in Soviet history were heartening, but to those able to make comparisons with the consumer economies of Western Europe or the United States, the contrast was startling. Soviet consumer goods tended to be scarce, expensive, and of poor quality. Housing in the cities was difficult to find even 20 years after the war; most of what was available was cramped and poorly constructed. Long lines to purchase almost anything were customary. One estimate is that Soviet women spent as much as two hours a day waiting in lines.

Some had it better. The "new class" of party officials, high-level bureaucrats, military personnel, technocrats, scientists, ballet and movie stars, world-class athletes, and some literary and intellectual luminaries had not merely higher incomes, which was not that much of an advantage, but a range of privileges unavailable to the ordinary citizen. These included a dacha (a cottage or even a rather large house in the countryside) for use on weekends or vacations, special stores with a wider selection than ordinary stores, special clinics for medical treatment without crowds and long waits, official cars for private use, and an "old boy" network that opened up educational and career opportunities to the sons and daughters of the prominent.

Growth rates began to fall in the 1950s and 1960s. By the early 1970s, the Soviet economy was scarcely growing at all. Agriculture remained a major problem despite a sizable investment by the state in the early 1970s. To some, the answer seemed to lie in technology transfers from the West. Certainly, part of the motivation for détente was the idea that if the Soviet Union played by the "rules," it could expect to receive help from Western Europe, the United States, and Japan in bridging technological gaps and overcoming obstacles to rapid economic growth.

In addition to economic problems, the Soviet Union faced growing problems with dissidents, some of whom emerged in response to the neo-Stalinism that characterized the Soviet Union by the end of the 1960s. Neither the Stalin cult of personality nor the practice of arbitrary terror still existed, but Brezhnev became increasingly the center of Soviet politics. Yuri Andropov (1914–1984), head of the KGB, worked out sophisticated methods utilizing the criminal justice system and mental health facilities to deal with anyone considered troublesome by the regime. A major dissident was Aleksandr Solzhenitsyn (1918–2008), whose short novel *One Day in the Life of Ivan Denisovich* was a revelation to many Russians in the early 1960s. The "one day" of the novel took Ivan Denisovich, a Zek or political prisoner, through his experiences in a labor camp in the GULAG, the Soviet prison system. Solzhenitsyn drew on personal experiences and revealed to many Russians who might have only heard rumors about the GULAG, what a brutal institution it was. Other than *One Day in the Life of Ivan Denisovich* and a few short stories, Solzhenitsyn was not allowed to publish in the 1960s. He was also not permitted to accept the Nobel Prize for literature in 1970. Finally, he was deported from the Soviet Union in 1974.

Andrei Sakharov (1921–1989), an eminent Russian physicist and father of the Russian H-bomb was even more important because of his work with the Committee for Human Rights, an unofficial non-governmental organization (NGO) that monitored human rights violations in the Soviet Union. Dissidents were generally restricted to samizdat (literally "self-publishing"—hand- or typewritten manuscripts circulated illegally) or to occasional interviews with western journalists as ways to spread their views. Critics of the Soviet system found themselves relatively isolated and unimportant in Soviet politics, despite the attention paid to them by the West. More important and treated even more harshly were representatives of the nationalist movements in Lithuania, Ukraine, and elsewhere. Also, some groups were suspect because of their religious beliefs. Among these were Russian Baptists and Jehovah's Witnesses. Finally, Soviet Jews were often harassed, and efforts by them to emigrate were generally not well received.

Willy Brandt and Ostpolitik

If the Prague Spring may be seen as a turning point not allowed to turn, the Ostpolitik (Eastern policy) instituted by Willy Brandt in the early 1970s created a small but important bridge between East and West that both could accept with some degree of comfort. Brandt had been the Social Democratic mayor of West Berlin at the height of the Berlin Crisis at the end of the 1950s. In the 1960s, he led the Social Democratic Party (SPD) into a grand coalition with the Christian Democratic Union (CDU). In 1969, in a coalition with the Free Democrats (FDP), the SPD became the governing party.

The Ostpolitik, part of the larger détente between East and West, established a dialogue between West Germany and East Germany. In 1970, Brandt negotiated treaties with Poland and the Soviet Union, and then in 1972, an agreement that led to East Germany and West Germany according each other diplomatic recognition. In particular, West Germany recognized the Polish–German borders as they then existed. A related agreement in 1971 (The Quadripartite Agreement of 3 September 1971) among the four powers that had occupied Germany after the war protected the rights of those powers in Berlin and also West Germany's particular interest in the city. All of the agreements taken together stabilized the status of both West Germany and East Germany and eliminated a major cause of the Cold War, that is, the failure to reach a postwar settlement that would prevent the possibility of German militarism reviving.

Brandt, who was awarded the Nobel Peace Prize for the Ostpolitik and what it had led to enjoyed less success in terms of progress toward social reform in Germany or European unification. Ironically, given Brandt's success with the Ostpolitik, he felt compelled to resign in 1974 after it came to light that a trusted adviser had all along been an East German mole.

The 1960s in the United States

World War II, with the emphasis on liberating peoples from National Socialism and Japanese militarism, made maintaining racial segregation in the United States difficult to justify. Nevertheless, it was successfully defended for more than a decade after the end of the war. In the late 1940s and early 1950s, African Americans and their white supporters undertook brave but largely ineffective efforts to challenge racial segregation. In the mid-1950s, however, two events began a direct, if also slow, challenge to segregation.

The first was the Supreme Court decision in the case of *Brown v. the Board of Education of Topeka* (Kansas) in 1954. Segregation in public schools was based on the doctrine of "separate but equal." Chief Justice Earl Warren (1891–1974), declared that "Separate educational facilities are inherently unequal" (as quoted in Patterson 1966).

The second event was the Montgomery, Alabama, bus boycott in 1955 and 1956 and the emergence of Martin Luther King, Jr. (1929–1968) as a charismatic national leader of the Civil Rights Movement.

Desegregation of schools proceeded slowly, and King's Southern Christian Leadership Conference (SCLC) seemed to lose momentum at the end of the 1950s. The Civil Rights Movement was re-energized by the nonviolent, "civil-disobedience" tactics of sit-ins beginning with the sit-in at the lunch counter of a Woolworth department store in Greensboro, North Carolina, on the afternoon of 1 February 1960. More such sit-ins in other parts of the country led later that year to the formation of the Student Nonviolent Coordinating Committee (SNCC).

In 1961, the federal government began to be drawn into desegregation issues when another activist civil rights organization, CORE (Congress of Racial Equality), sent volunteer riders on interstate buses through the South to desegregate bus terminals. The question quickly became how the administration of President John F. Kennedy would respond to the Civil Rights Movement.

A turning point came in Birmingham, Alabama, in 1963. Reverend Fred Shuttlesworth (1922–2011), a courageous local civil rights leader, aided King in his latest protest, in which he encouraged the black citizens of the city to boycott downtown stores during the Easter shopping season. (African American protest could not hurt local politicians because blacks were largely disenfranchised through "Jim Crow" voting regulations, but local merchants would feel the sting of the boycott.) Inadvertent assistance came from Eugene "Bull" Connor (1897–1973), the public safety commissioner of Birmingham. Connor turned fire hoses on the peaceful demonstrators and let his police officers menace them with police dogs. This made for disturbing images that appeared in newspapers and on television news programs. Events in Birmingham galvanized the Kennedy administration into preparing a civil rights bill.

Some months afterward, on 28 August 1963, the Civil Rights Movement reached a high point in the March on Washington, DC, and King's famous "I Have a Dream" speech at the culmination of the march. Although King's speech was widely admired, the legislation the Kennedy administration had prepared probably would not have been passed by Congress. Instead, Kennedy's assassination on 22 November 1963, created a situation in which his successor, Lyndon Baines Johnson (1908–1973), one of the most skilled legislators of the twentieth century, was able to push through the Civil Rights Act of 1964 and the Voting Rights Act of 1965. These two landmark pieces of legislation did much to change American assumptions related to race relations.

The Vietnam War

Shortly before he was assassinated in 1968, Martin Luther King, Jr. had begun to speak out against the Vietnam War. Other Americans, too, began to have reservations about the American involvement. America had supported the French efforts in the 1950s to defeat the Viet Minh in part because of the important role France could play in the developing Cold War. After the French departed Vietnam in 1954, leaving Vietnam divided between North and South Vietnam, the United States stepped in to support the ostensibly "democratic" government of the Republic of South Vietnam in its conflict with the communist government of the Democratic Republic of Vietnam under its charismatic leader, Ho Chi Minh.

During the Eisenhower and Kennedy administrations, support for South Vietnam had consisted of the sending American military "advisers" and military supplies. It is impossible to know what Kennedy would have done in the rapidly changing situation had he been elected to a second term, but there were some signs he was considering ending American involvement.

President Johnson, who succeeded President Kennedy, was elected to a full term in 1964. He pursued the war in Vietnam with the so-called "domino theory" in mind. According to this idea, if South Vietnam fell to a communist rival, then other Southeast Asian nations were sure to follow suit. Reading what he thought were the lessons of history, Johnson said, "I am not going to lose Vietnam. I am not going to be the President who saw Southeast Asia go the way China went."

The issue reached a peak of sorts in 1968 in the aftermath of the Tet Offensive, an unsuccessful effort by North Vietnamese military forces and their Viet Cong allies in the south to challenge the United States and South Vietnam in the cities. Although militarily a defeat, the Tet Offensive was a propaganda coup in that it had caught the combined US–South Vietnamese forces by surprise and rendered hollow all the pronouncements US brass had made about light at the end of the tunnel. In the war of "search and destroy," a war of attrition, the North Vietnamese and their allies were far from beaten.

The "credibility gap" seemed impossible to close. The so-called wise men, foreign policy experts from past administrations, advised President Johnson that Vietnam was a sinkhole with no end in sight. On 31 March 1968, he ended a speech on Vietnam by indicating that he would not seek nor accept the nomination of his party for president in the upcoming elections of 1970. It was left to Johnson's successor as president, Richard Nixon (1913–1994), and his national security advisor and later secretary of state, Henry Kissinger (1923–), to come to terms with the Vietnamese, North and South, in 1973.

Where the Civil Rights Movement had undoubtedly changed the United States for the better, the Vietnam War and the fierce protest against it had weakened the United States both domestically and in terms of foreign policy. President Johnson's domestic agenda, known as his Great Society legislation, particularly the passage of the Medicare and Medicaid bills in 1965, did accomplish much good, but involvement in the Vietnam War was an important distraction. Also, the cost of the war and the divisiveness it caused was a severe burden on the economy and the social fabric of the nation. The Vietnam War itself resulted in a hesitant approach to foreign policy questions in the 1970s, as leaders were reluctant to risk another significant commitment of men and equipment.

The Price of Oil

The oil price shock of 1973 acted as a catalyst to set off a decade of economic problems that explains much of the pessimism and lack of political will marking the 1970s and early 1980s. The Yom Kippur

War of 1973 between Israel and several Arab states (Egypt, Syria, Jordan, Iraq) provided the context for the first oil price shock. OPEC (Organization of the Petroleum Exporting Countries), founded in 1960, lacked influence until the Arab-nation members of the organization persuaded the other member nations to impose an oil embargo on states that supported Israel in the 1973 war. Soon after the embargo announcement, oil prices worldwide increased to four times the previous level, and the evening news began to fill with images of long lines at gas stations and deserted highways, both in Western Europe and in the United States.

Even before the oil price shock of 1973, Western Europe had experienced some problems with inflation. The oil crunch simply made it worse. It was a prime example of one in a series of structural problems European economies faced. The end of the long postwar boom was perhaps the main contributing factor. Reconstruction was largely complete in the west, and people had bought their fill of houses, automobiles, and durable goods like refrigerators. Consumption could not continue to expand indefinitely, especially after the increase in prices of all kinds of manufactured items caused by the jump in the price of energy.

The Welfare State

Leo Tolstoy's opening lines in *Anna Karenina* might be applied to European welfare states in the 1970s: "All happy families are like one another; each unhappy family is unhappy in its own way." Welfare states by the late 1970s were all unhappy families.

In most countries in Western Europe, the growth of the welfare state had reached a point at which it was straining national economies. As the economy slowed down, unemployment, which had been very low in the 1960s, began to rise. Western Europe was caught in a paradox: inflation led to high prices and increases in interest rates. A recession resulted in large-scale unemployment. "Stagflation" was the term used by some to describe the situation of an economic downturn combined with spiking inflation. Finally, Europe and other parts of the urbanized, industrialized world experienced a technological revolution in the 1970s and 1980s, resulting in an economy radically different from the postwar industrial economy based on heavy industry.

After World War II, there was consensus in most European countries about the need to ensure the basic necessities of life (food, clothing, shelter, education, and health care) and to guard against catastrophes such as unemployment, injury, and illness. There was particular concern about mothers, infants, children, and the retired. While the aims of most nations were similar, the means to accomplish them diverged considerably.

The British system has become synonymous with the welfare state, but that is inaccurate. The welfare systems developed differently. Unlike the United Kingdom, not every European country developed a National Health Service or a social security system operated entirely by the state. Still, most Western European countries offered their citizens free or virtually free health care and family allowances. Workers' income was covered in case of injury or other disability and in case of unemployment. Some provisions were made for the construction of low-cost or public housing. Education, which by the 1970s had become far more widely available even at the university level, was either free or provided for nominal fees.

A major difference among the various systems concerned who paid for services. In Britain and the Scandinavian countries, the state, that is, taxpayers paid most of the costs. In West Germany, employers and employees covered 80 percent of the costs. Employers were responsible for about two-thirds of the costs in France and Italy.

By the 1980s, the welfare state not only existed to ensure an adequate foundation for people's lives and to guard against unexpected disasters but also to provide a range of amenities that included parks, libraries, cultural facilities, and subsidies for artists and writers. Additionally, each generation growing up in the system considered what had been offered to them all their lives as an entitlement and expected the system to be further improved.

A final factor causing many to conclude that the welfare state had to be revised might be included under the term "permissive society." Many critics of the welfare state regarded it as having robbed large groups of people of initiative and self-reliance. Others unfairly blamed the welfare state for new attitudes toward sex and drug use and for problems such as increasing rates of juvenile delinquency. The apparent rise in taxes was more a product of life in a highly industrialized and urbanized society than the existence of the welfare state as such, but whatever the real deficiencies of the welfare state, it became in the 1980s a major target for a new breed of conservative politicians determined to meet head-on modern society's social and economic ills in Western Europe.

Terrorism

Adding to the complicated mix of social and economic issues confronting Europe in the 1970s, at that point, a new and alarming phenomenon emerged and had the effect of making the situation appear a good deal worse than it was. Not only did the terrorists themselves seem to be an affront to constitutional systems, but governments in the response to the challenges terrorist attacks presented on occasion did more damage to civil and human rights than had the terrorists.

Terrorism on the left was largely an outgrowth of the failures and frustrations of the 1960s. When revolution had not occurred at the end of that decade, some radicals turned to terrorism: bombing, kidnapping, and murder. The best known of these groups were the Brigade Rosa (the Red Brigades) in Italy and the RAF (the Rote Armee Fraktion or Red Army Faction) in West Germany. They were aided by the existence of what some fearfully saw as a terrorist international on the order of the old Communist International. The reality was less dramatic than this but still lethal. Centers of terrorist activity existed in the Near East, where the main players were the Palestinian Liberation Organization (PLO), backed by enormous amounts of petrodollars from sympathetic OPEC members. To this mix could be added the activities of the KGB and other East Bloc intelligence services and the existence of independent nationalist movements like the Irish Republican Army (IRA) in Northern Ireland and the Basque separatists in Spain. The latter appeared about the same time as the Red Brigades and the RAF but for different reasons. On the periphery were terrorists and revolutionaries from Japan and Latin America. While these groups aided one another in securing weapons, locating sites for training, and other matters, they seldom worked together on operations. Each group had its own agenda and cooperated with other terrorists only when this served its purposes. The idea of a terrorist conspiracy coordinated by Moscow was simply another variation on Cold War themes.

So far as the Red Brigades and the RAF were concerned, the late 1970s marked the end of any possibility that they would play a major role in national politics. By this time, the RAF had largely moved away from the ideals that had once characterized it to nihilism and criminality. The Red Brigades had also moved in the same direction. In 1978, however, it carried out its most spectacular operation when it kidnapped and later murdered a former premier of Italy, Aldo Moro (1916–1978). The national reaction against this senseless killing was the beginning of the group's downfall; nevertheless, it took the Italian police another five years to destroy the organization. Sporadic right-wing terrorism, particularly in Italy, continued in the 1980s, and disquieting instances of antisemitism also appeared. Most of the terrorism of the 1980s, however, was state terrorism sponsored by countries like Libya and Iran. In most cases, this form of terrorism was directed against dissidents from those countries; Western Europe merely furnished the location of the action.

Overall, Western Europe weathered the outbreak of terrorism in a good fashion. While there was much discussion of antiterrorist legislation in West Germany, particularly a 1977 law requiring a political litmus test for civil servants that reminded many of the Nazi *Berufsverbot* (prohibition against entering a profession) used against Jews and others in the 1930s, both West Germany and Italy came through difficult times with the two constitutional systems intact.

Recovery

In the 1980s, politics seemed to offer a solution to economic and social problems. Certain issues, the welfare state, in particular, seemed to need rethinking. For many conservatives, it seemed that a government willing to divest itself of government-owned operations and reduce controls and regulations could help create a climate favorable to business. US President Ronald Reagan (1911–2004) became the person most closely identified with this political position through his uncanny ability to project an image that matched what large numbers of Americans believed they wanted. It was the British Prime Minister Margaret Thatcher (1925–2013), however, who most successfully translated this approach into national policy.

Thatcherism

Margaret Thatcher, probably the most influential woman in Europe in the last half of the century, inside or outside of politics, served as British prime minister between 1979 and 1990, transforming the Conservative Party and Great Britain in the process. As a young woman, she studied at Oxford and worked as a research chemist. After her marriage in 1951, she studied law and, in 1959, entered the House of Commons. Thatcher rose rapidly in the ranks of the Conservative Party and, in 1975, at the age of 50, became its leader. Four years later, she led the party to victory in the elections of 1979.

British Prime Minister Margaret Thatcher with President Jimmy Carter at the White House, Washington, DC. Trikosko, Marion S./The Library of Congress/ Public Domain.

Over the next 11 years, "Maggie" Thatcher became very popular with the public but much disliked by her political opponents. She quickly came to be seen as the "Iron Lady," tough, decisive, strong-willed, and no-nonsense. Her main contribution to British recovery came in the area of economic policy. That policy had three main components: "privatization," reduction of inflation, and weakening of trade union power. The "privatization" of nationalized industries and national utilities received a great deal of press, but it is difficult to say whether it contributed much to overall economic recovery. Probably more important were the largely successful efforts to reduce the power of the trade unions. Trade unions in Britain had contributed to the lack of competitiveness of the economy through a series of regulations regarding work and seniority that made it difficult for companies to reorganize production for greater efficiency. The new political climate favoring business and trade and the greatly weakened trade unions allowed many British firms to take maximum advantage of opportunities to secure profits. The reduction of inflation, which stood at nearly 22 percent in 1979 but had fallen dramatically to 3.7 percent in 1983, created favorable conditions for investment and economic growth. The Thatcher government was also blessed by the discovery of oil deposits in the North Sea.

For many British, the 1980s was a period of new prosperity. In most respects, the economy was stronger than it had been since the early years of the century. One major downside, however, was the rate of unemployment. At 6.1 percent in 1980, it rose to 11.6 percent in 1985 and then returned in 1989 to about the same level it had been in 1980, 5.3 percent. However, some sections of the country, particularly in the north, did not share in the general prosperity. Generally, the Thatcher years had created a class of big winners, a large group of people who were doing somewhat better or at least okay, and "everyone else," people who were doing very badly with little prospects of improvement.

Part of Margaret Thatcher's popularity early in her tenure as prime minister and vital to her reelection in 1983 was Britain's successful defense of the Falkland Islands, an archipelago of islands near the coast of Argentina, from invasion by the Argentines.

The Argentine regime that launched the minor engagement that became known as the Falklands War (1982) had few friends. Many observers focused on what was, in retrospect, Britain's last imperial hurrah. The spectacle of Britain successfully conducting a long-distance war against Argentina caught the imagination of many Europeans and North Americans. South Americans and Third World countries, not surprisingly, tended to disapprove of British efforts to defend a new world territory of little value to them.

Finally, in the realm of international relations, Thatcher could count on friends in high places. In addition to President Reagan, her ideological twin, she enjoyed good relations with prominent European leaders such as Helmut Kohl and François Mitterrand. She also became, despite her reflexive anti-Communism, an early champion of Mikhail Gorbachev, whom she recognized as "someone she could do business with." All in all, Margaret Thatcher put her stamp on the last quarter of the twentieth century in a way no European leader other than Gorbachev could match.

France

François Mitterrand served as president from 1981 to 1995. He spent much of the 1960s and 1970s rebuilding and strengthening the Socialist Party. When he and the Socialist Party came to power in 1981, he set in motion an ambitious wave of nationalization involving nine industrial groups including steel, aerospace, armaments, electronics, banking, and insurance. In an era when governments and businesses increasingly strived to become both leaner and meaner, Mitterrand was something of an anachronism. Within two years, the government quietly abandoned the socialist policies. Thereafter, a more conventional approach, paying more than mere lip service to Thatcher's ideas, came to the fore.

After the 1986 elections, Mitterrand remained president of France but had to share power with Jacques Chirac (1932–2019), a Gaullist, as prime minister. Chirac reflected the new rightist majority in the National Assembly. Mitterrand returned in 1988 to win one more term as president.

Over the 1980s, the power and appeal of the French Communist Party declined considerably. It gained only 9.7 percent of the vote in 1986, in contrast to the past when it regularly won 20–25 percent of the vote. A less powerful Communist Party on his flank allowed Mitterrand to moderate his positions to some extent, even if he and Chirac could not reach full agreement on domestic policies.

To some extent, the decline of the Communist Party was reflected in the growth of Jean-Marie Le Pen's (1928–) Front National in the 1980s. The Front National was a political movement based largely on hatred and fear. It was racist, chauvinistic, and well to the right in terms of French politics. It was possibly more dangerous than neo-Nazi movements in Germany or Austria, but people did not automatically connect it with Hitler and the Nazis.

Le Pen, an astute and charismatic political leader, knew how to play on the fears of ordinary French men and women. And persistently high rates of unemployment in the 1980s helped to convince many that Le Pen's perspective was worth taking seriously.

By the end of the 1980s, which saw the celebration of the bicentennial of the French Revolution, the French were doing well, despite the ongoing political controversy and nagging unemployment. For the majority, the standard of living had greatly improved since the 1960s. France also was characterized at the time by a greater degree of egalitarianism, especially regarding equality of opportunity as reflected in such areas as education and health care.

West Germany

Helmut Schmidt (1918–2015) was a worthy successor to Willy Brandt and governed West Germany well in the 1970s and early 1980s. He successfully weathered the challenges of the Red Army Faction (RAF) and the economic downturns. He was unable, however, to maintain the previous coalition with the Free Democrats after the 1982 elections. Helmut Kohl (1930–2017) replaced him as chancellor and based his government on a new coalition between the Christian Democrats and the Free Democrats.

Kohl liked to say that his generation was fortunate in that it had not had to participate in World War II or the Holocaust and therefore was not burdened with the guilt felt by the generations that had. Critics quickly pointed out, however, that his generation, having grown up in the Nazi era, had undoubtedly absorbed much of the Nazi outlook and therefore had as much to overcome as earlier generations. From time to time, Kohl made particular comments that have marked him as something of an opportunist, eager to put the Nazi past behind him for good. Nevertheless, he managed to remain chancellor for quite some time, from 1982 until 1998.

In the 1980s, the Kohl government was successful in leading West Germany to a strong recovery, in part because of the policies it introduced and also because of policies Schmidt had set in motion. Additionally, West Germany's powerful central bank, the Bundesbank (Federal Bank) and German business leaders made important contributions. The Kohl government largely followed policies West German governments had been following since the 1950s and 1960s. The major exception was an effort to stop the growth of the welfare state. Businesses were also encouraged to slow the growth of wage-and-benefits packages to prevent labor costs from pricing German exports out of the market. By the end of the 1980s, inflation had disappeared (6 percent in 1981 but −1 percent in 1986) and exports had shown strong growth. The major disappointment for West Germany was the continuing high unemployment figures, especially in a country that had long enjoyed full employment.

The major political development of the 1980s was the growing appeal of the Greens, an outgrowth of the Extraparliamentary Opposition (APO) of the late 1960s. Formed as a party in the 1970s, the Greens were interested primarily in environmentalism but diverse in outlook. Many in the movement disliked the idea of becoming a political party and participating in institutions like the *Bundestag*. Green members of the *Bundestag* introduced new styles of dress and behavior, but they also learned in the course of the 1980s how work was accomplished in that body and in many cases became quite proficient at advancing the Green agenda. In the 1987 elections, the Greens elected 47 members to the *Bundestag*. The

Christian Democrats lost ground but continued to govern in a coalition with the Free Democrats. The Social Democrats remained polarized between a radical left wing and a moderate center. They were also hampered by the lack of an effective standard bearer. Despite the opposition's weaknesses and the relative success of the Kohl government, Kohl's political prospects at the end of the 1980s were not particularly good. As it turned out, however, he stood on the eve of his finest hour.

Other States

In the 1970s and the 1980s, the Italian Communist Party (PCI) provided a major political story. Under the leadership of Enrico Berlinguer (1922–1984), the secretary-general of the PCI from 1972 to 1984, the party undertook a "historic compromise" in 1979 when it explicitly accepted the rules of the parliamentary system. It fared well in the elections in 1976, gaining 34percent of the vote, and became part of an informal coalition between 1977 and 1979. In addition, the PCI controlled most of the major cities and 7 of the 16 regions, which meant it was often the leading political force on a local or regional basis. In the 1980s, even though the party continued to move rapidly away from Stalinism and even Leninism, its vote totals dipped.

In the 1980s, Italians enjoyed a decade of progress. The Christian Democrats continued to dominate national political life but had to concede in the mid-1980s the position of premier to Bettino Craxi (1934–1999), the leader of the Socialist Party. Craxi's government, which lasted from 1983 to 1986, was actually one of the more effective governments in Italian political history. Craxi hoped to emulate the French Socialists, but he was not able to duplicate Mitterrand's successes.

For Portugal and Spain, the events of the 1970s spelled release from decades of dictatorship and the beginning of efforts to catch up with other Western European countries. Portugal began to change after the death in 1970 of António Salazar (1889–1970), dictator since 1932. Marcello Caetano (1906–1980) followed Salazar as prime minister in 1968. Caetano and the remnants of the dictatorship were overthrown by revolution in 1974. Army personnel, radicalized by the long and frustrating struggle to retain the empire, carried out the revolution and established the Supreme Revolutionary Council, which ruled in 1974 and 1975. In 1975, military personnel close to the Portuguese Communist Party attempted a coup, which was unsuccessful. The following year, a new constitution was promulgated. In the late 1970s and the 1980s, the major figure in Portuguese politics was Mário Soares (1924–2017), a reformist socialist. Soares became president in 1986, the same year Portugal joined the European Community.

Spain's dictator, General Francisco Franco (b. 1892), died in 1975. Franco made arrangements for the restoration of the monarchy, with Juan Carlos (1938–), the heir apparent, succeeding to the throne. Despite serious problems with the ETA (the Basque separatists) and an attempted coup in 1981, which Juan Carlos I played a major role in thwarting, Spain enjoyed in the late 1970s and the 1980s both a successful transition to democratic politics and impressive economic growth. Spain entered the NATO alliance in 1982 and the European Community in 1986. The major political figure in Spain in the 1980s and 1990s was Felipe González (1942–), who led the Socialist Workers Party to victory in the 1982 elections. He was 40 at the time. Gonzales served as prime minister from 1982 to 1996.

The East Bloc in Decline: The Soviet Union

If Western Europe experienced something of a roller coaster ride in the 1970s and 1980s, it was all downhill for Eastern Europe (1989) and the Soviet Union (1991). The Soviet Union maintained strict control in Eastern Europe in the 1970s. The Soviet Union was itself a paradox, a world power finally, but also failing visibly in terms of the most vital indices of national well-being: infant mortality rates, life expectancy (especially for males), the incidence of alcoholism, and accident and suicide rates. By the late 1970s, the Soviet Union seemed to have embarked on a kind of Cold War adventurism in Afghanistan, the Horn of Africa, and other trouble spots as a way of denying its economic problems and the disintegration of its social fabric. Leonid Brezhnev, old and ill, had become little more than a parody of a Soviet leader. Trotted out for important state occasions, he had to be helped on and off the podium and often lost his place in speeches.

After Brezhnev's death in 1982, Yuri Andropov, who had played a dark role in Soviet politics as the mastermind of the KGB through the 1970s and early 1980s, appeared ready to make sweeping changes in the Soviet Union. Andropov, as First Secretary of the Communist Party from 1982 to 1984, was presented to the credulous West as a jazz-loving, Scotch-drinking, spy-novel-reading liberal. He never had much opportunity to demonstrate what he intended to do. His principal contribution to the 1980s was his sponsorship of Mikhail Gorbachev (1931–2022). Gorbachev had to wait his turn, however, until after the mercifully brief reign of Konstantin Chernenko (1911–1985) as First Secretary in 1984 and 1985. Chernenko was rewarded for his utter loyalty to Brezhnev and will probably be best remembered as an example of the tendency of a decaying system to push to the top those totally incompetent figures who will finally destroy it.

Gorbachev replaced Chernenko in 1985. Unlike Andropov, he was truly a different sort of Soviet official. A graduate of Moscow University in law, he had come up rapidly through the system, becoming a member of the Politburo in 1980 at the age of 49 and in 1985 Secretary-General of the Communist Party. Although Gorbachev was a communist, he saw the need for far-reaching changes in the Soviet system and believed that Leninism provided an adequate basis for those changes. There is some similarity in what Gorbachev attempted to do in the Soviet Union and what was attempted during the Prague Spring in 1968. One major difference is the extent to which the Soviet bureaucracy was deeply entrenched and determined to protect its prerogatives. What might have succeeded in Czechoslovakia, had not the Soviet Union intervened, was not very likely to succeed in the Soviet Union itself, even given the passage of time and the growing awareness that the system was failing.

Gorbachev advanced several important general propositions: *glasnost* or transparency, *perestroika* or reformation, and new thinking. *Glasnost* was perhaps the easiest of the new approaches to institute.

Censorship was gradually abandoned, and people were encouraged to present the past as accurately as possible in magazines, films, plays, and books. *Perestroika* was the most difficult to put into practice and ultimately Gorbachev's undoing. Economic reform, particularly encouraging modest levels of private enterprise, was hampered by bureaucratic obstructionism, which Gorbachev sought to counter through political reform. Political reform, however, brought into question the primacy of the Communist Party.

New thinking was Gorbachev's most successful initiative, perhaps because it was directed mostly at the West and offered a way out of the Cold War impasse. Although President Reagan was initially suspicious, he began to see possibilities in Gorbachev's proposals. In fact, at the summit meeting between the Soviet Union and the United States at Reykjavík, Iceland, in 1986, Reagan had to be restrained by his advisors from responding too enthusiastically to Gorbachev's overtures. The following year, the Intermediate-Range Nuclear Forces (INF) Treaty was signed, eliminating from the arsenals of both superpowers all ground-based intermediate-range nuclear missiles. Enormously popular in the West ("Gorby Mania" was an extraordinary phenomenon both in Eastern and in Western Europe), Gorbachev experienced increasing difficulty in the Soviet Union in maneuvering between Communist Party hardliners and proponents of radical change.

Solidarity in Poland

The contribution of Poland's Solidarity (Solidarność) movement to the unraveling of the Cold War can hardly be exaggerated. It grew out of the politics of the 1970s. First, in 1970, strikes protesting increases in food prices led to the replacement of Władysław Gomułka by Edward Gierek (1913–2001). Gierek pushed a policy of economic growth based on foreign loans. By 1976, however, it was apparent that unfortunate choices had been made in pursuit of economic growth (e.g., the construction of giant steelworks when demand for steel products was declining). Again, attempts to increase food prices led to strikes.

In the next few years, two developments helped change the terms of confrontation between workers and the government. In one development, an organized intellectual opposition, KOR (Committee for the Defense of the Workers), made contact with workers' groups. Jacek Kuroń (1934–2004), the leader of KOR, was a product of student movements in the 1960s. KOR had, however, been isolated from the workers. Worker protests in the early 1970s suffered from their isolation from students and intellectuals. Coming together in 1980 made a substantial difference in the possibility of resisting government pressure.

In the other development, the Catholic Church in Poland gained enormously in prestige from the election of a Pole, Cardinal Karol Wojtyła (1920–2005), as Pope John Paul II in 1978. The following year, Pope John Paul II made a triumphant tour of Poland and was welcomed by millions of the faithful.

In 1980, the government tried to raise food prices for the third time in a decade. The strikes this time had a center in the Lenin Shipyards in Gdańsk and a leader in Lech Wałęsa (1943–), an electrician at the shipyards and a participant in the events of 1976. In the negotiations between the workers and the government, the workers pressed for and won the right to organize an independent trade union movement, Solidarity. It began to take on a life of its own in 1981, becoming an enormously large and powerful trade union movement. Although there was no place for Solidarity in the communist system, it began to exercise a kind of de facto power, challenging the authority of the Polish Communist Party (technically the Polish United Workers' Party or PUWP). The upshot of this was the appointment of General Wojciech Jaruzelski (1923–2014) as prime minister and the proclamation of martial law. Wałęsa and other Solidarity leaders were imprisoned and Solidarity was outlawed.

Wałęsa, who won the Nobel Peace Prize in 1983, was eventually released from prison. He was able to maintain Solidarity's existence as an organization throughout the 1980s, first as an underground organization and later as an organization unofficially tolerated by the government. As problems mounted for the Polish government and PUWP, the power and influence of Solidarity began to increase. Finally, in 1989, talks between Solidarity and the government started, leading to events that formed one of the most important triggers of the revolutions of 1989.

Erich Honecker's East Germany

East Germany in the 1970s and 1980s seemed to be a success story. There was, first, the connection to West Germany that Brandt's Ostpolitik had developed. For Honecker, it was a double-edged sword. On the positive side stood the prestige involved in formal recognition by West Germany. In addition, entry fees paid by people entering East Germany, West German subsidies of various kinds, and access to the European Community produced income. The negative side was the public's increased contact with the realities of life in West Germany. Greater awareness of the contrast between life in East Germany and life in West Germany became difficult to avoid, given the widespread availability of West German TV programs. Honecker tried to offset Western influences through efforts to encourage East Germans to distance themselves from West Germany and to take pride in East Germany.

There was something of the atmosphere of bread and circuses in East Germany during the 1970s and 1980s. While it was drab and gray compared to the West, it offered its citizens the highest standard of living in the Eastern Bloc. In effect, this was Honecker's agreement with East Germans. Work hard, and you will be rewarded with better housing, good food and clothing, refrigerators, televisions, and the Trabi (the Trabant, the primary East German automobile). As bonuses, the East German regime offered an active cultural life and good health care and educational opportunities. Finally, the government sponsored an amazingly successful sports program modeled on but surpassing that of the Soviet system.

Behind the bribes was an extensive system of surveillance and repression administered by the Ministry of State Security or the Stasi. The Stasi consisted of a sizable bureaucracy that carried out activities both abroad (principally in West Germany) and at home. It was assisted by thousands of people who either volunteered to help or were seduced or coerced into doing so. In some cases, husbands spied on wives and friends informed on friends. Even some pastors became agents of the Stasi. The amount of data gathered was staggering, miles of files. An argument could be made that the Stasi, by the late 1980s, could no longer see the forest for the trees. In any case, it failed to present the East German Politburo with a realistic picture of the country at the very point when one was desperately needed.

A realistic picture would have emphasized an economy rapidly becoming uncompetitive, starved for investment capital, and dependent on technologies that were causing enormous ecological damage. The system had never provided the kind of life it had promised. While small protest groups existed precariously under the umbrella of the Lutheran Church, thousands of other East Germans had decided it was time to leave. Thousands more were ready to jump at any realistic chance of escaping, should it present itself. It is no small irony that East German leaders directed almost all of their attention to the upcoming fortieth anniversary of the state's founding and failed to see how badly those foundations had eroded.

Eastern and Western Europe changed significantly during the 1970s and 1980s. Western Europe weathered difficult times in the 1970s and early 1980s, but at the end of the 1980s, it seemed more economically and politically mature. Though Europe still looked to the United States for leadership, it was increasingly willing to forge its own path. Particularly in the case of the European Community, Western Europe appeared poised to break new ground. Eastern Europe, although it could not know it, stood in 1989 on the brink of fundamental changes.

Reference

Patterson, James T. (1966). *Grand Expectations: The United States, 1945–1974*. New York; Oxford: Oxford University Press.

Part 4

Overview: 1989–Present

The revolutions of 1989 led to a new era that featured initially what appeared to be a New World Order. The Soviet Empire in Eastern Europe was replaced by newly independent countries working to establish democratic governments and capitalist economies. The Soviet Union itself collapsed in 1991 when Mikhail Gorbachev's attempts at *perestroika* (restructuring) met the immovable object of a powerful and conservative bureaucratic establishment. It was replaced by more than 20 republics, of which the Russian Republic was the most powerful.

It seemed to some observers that the Cold War had ended and democracy and capitalism had triumphed. It was apparently the end of history as Francis Fukuyama (1952–) famously noted in his book, *The End of History and the Last Man* (1992). The extraordinary coalition put together by President George H. W. Bush to liberate Kuwait from Saddam Hussein's Iraq appeared to be a physical manifestation of that New World Order.

The 1990s, however, turned out to be a rather messy decade with some successes and a couple of spectacular failures. The disintegration of Yugoslavia, while not entirely unexpected, was an enormous tragedy. To a large extent, it was caused by the political ambitions of one man, Slobodan Milošević, who used the existing nationalistic

Twentieth-Century Europe: 1900 to the Present, Fourth Edition.
Michael D. Richards and Paul R. Waibel.

passions and ethnic rivalries. The result was a series of war and civil wars, ethnic cleansings, and interventions by NATO forces.

The other failure, less destructive but more central to the future of Europe, was the failure of the Russian Republic to find its way. Under Boris Yeltsin, Russia came increasingly under the power of the oligarchs. Using their connections with the government and the security apparatus, they took advantage of the new economic circumstances to amass enormous wealth and political power.

Efforts by the newly independent states in Eastern Europe to establish new political and economic systems eventually if painfully achieved a measure of success. By the end of the decade, several had joined NATO and early in the twenty-first century some became members of the European Union (EU). East Germany was fortunate in some respects in that it was able to join West Germany and use the latter's resources to make the transition to a capitalist economy and to repair the considerable environmental damages caused by East German economic practices. The newly united Germany, of course, became the most powerful factor in European affairs.

Finally, the 1990s witnessed the development of a new source of terrorism, one that claimed to be based on Islam. In addition to the ongoing struggle between Palestinians and Israel and American attempts to neutralize Iran, a major factor was the Soviet intervention in Afghanistan in the 1980s and, after the Soviet Union retreated, the takeover of Afghanistan by the Taliban. In the 1990s, Osama bin Laden and Al-Qaeda established a base in Afghanistan and ran operations from there that attacked American embassies in Africa, the USS *Cole* in a port in Yemen, and the World Trade Center and the Pentagon in 2001.

The first decade of the new century continued to witness terrorist attacks even though the United States and its NATO allies conquered Afghanistan and drove Bin Laden into exile. Most of the terrorists were inspired by Al-Qaeda but usually not directed nor actually aided by the organization. The American invasion of Iraq only created another unstable situation in the Middle East.

The European Union was formed from the European Community in 1993 and in 1999 introduced the Euro, the common currency of most of the members of the EU. In 2004, it added 10 new members.

NATO also grew in this period, adding three new members in 1999 and seven in 2004.

The collapse of the American mortgage system and the system of securities based on it led to a recession in the United States and considerable economic difficulties in Europe. The European banking system was closely connected to the American financial system and dependent on American sources of credit.

Russia in this period went back to war with Chechen Republic, defeating it in an especially brutal campaign. It also intervened military in a conflict between Georgia and one of its districts, South Ossetia. It carved out about 20 percent of Georgia territory as autonomous areas under Russian tutelage. Vladimir Putin served two terms as president, spent a third term as prime minister, then returned as president.

Early in the 2010s, EU countries that used the Euro, faced in some cases a sovereign debt crisis, a situation where government debt was so high compared to the annual gross domestic product that the government could not get credit on favorable terms. The EU followed a piecemeal approach of advancing loans and requiring draconian austerity programs that did little to help those nations with high debt loads. Greece, in particular, struggled to find a way out of the debt crisis.

In the meantime, two events in northern Africa and the Middle East, the Arab Spring and the rise of the Islamic State in Iraq and Syria (ISIS) led to millions of people being displaced or attempting to flee to Europe. In 2015, Angela Merkel, the chancellor of Germany since 2005 and her counterpart in Austria opened their countries to refugees in response to efforts by other European countries to keep refugees out. Merkel was the outstanding European leader in the first two decades of the twenty-first century.

Ukraine, which in 2004 in had undergone the so-called Orange Revolution, was not able to follow with effective reform. Viktor Yanukovych, who had been defeated in 2004 after the Orange Revolution, won the 2010 election presidential election. In 2014, he decided to align Ukraine with Russia despite popular expectations that Ukraine would apply to be part of the EU. The protests that followed drove him into exile in Russia. Russia took advantage of the situation to annex Crimea and to support separatists in the Donbas. Attempts were made to defuse the situation, but despite various agreements Russia retained control of Crimea and increased its support of the separatists. In February 2021, it invaded Ukraine. The initial campaign failed and Ukraine mounted a response that set Russia back.

Three other developments stood out in the 2010s. One was Brexit, the decision based on a referendum in 2016 in which the British by a narrow margin decided to leave the EU. The British government spent the next four years attempting to negotiate an exit. This was finally accomplished by Boris Johnson, who had become prime minister after Theresa May had failed to get three versions of an agreement accepted. Another was the election of Emmanuel Macron in 2017 as president of France. Macron, who had spent relatively little time in politics before the election, had great ambitions both for reform in France and for a change in Europe's relationship with the rest of the world. He was re-elected in 2022, but will face an uphill battle to realize his ambitions domestically or internationally. The third development was the return to power in 2010 by Viktor Orbán (1963–) and Fidesz in Hungary. Over the decade, Orbán and his supporters perfected methods for staying in power through control of the courts and media and a sophisticated approach to rigging the outcome of ostensibly free elections. He won re-election in 2022 even though a broad coalition had been organized to oppose him.

The appearance of Covid-19 late in 2019 in China changed almost everything in 2020 and 2021. It caused enormous economic and psychological harm in addition to killing millions of people around the world. The rapid development of effective vaccines was a great accomplishment, but, so far, the supply has been adequate only for the wealthier nations.

The EU has responded to the economic problems of Covid-19 in a far more cohesive way than its response to the Euro Zone crisis. National Recovery and Resilience Plans are being put together as part of a large program entitled Next Generation (NGEU), which runs from 2021 to 2026.

The centennial issue of *Foreign Affairs* (September/October 2022) has the title "The Age of Uncertainty." In many ways, this reflects

Europe's situation politically, economically, and culturally. Not only philosophers but also culture, whether high or popular, has struggled to make sense of the events of the past several decades, particularly now after a global pandemic and the naked aggression of Russia in Ukraine with its specter of possible escalation to nuclear war. Artists, musicians, poets, and writers have frequently displayed a growing sense of alienation, despair, and fragmentation that characterizes European civilization in transition.

Europe exists in a globalized world in which it is no longer dominant but remains vitally important. It is crucial to understand in some detail key areas of that world. One good place to start is a reckoning with Europe in the twentieth and twenty-first centuries.

10

Post–World War II Intellectual and Culture Trends

Chronology

1940s–1950s	Heyday of existentialist writers, e.g., Albert Camus and Jean-Paul Sartre
c. 1945–1950s	New York School of abstract expressionist art promoted by Peggy Guggenheim's Art of This Century gallery
1949	George Orwell's *1984*

Twentieth-Century Europe: 1900 to the Present, Fourth Edition.
Michael D. Richards and Paul R. Waibel.

1950s	"Pop Art" emerges in England as a reaction to abstract expressionism
1952	John Cage, leading figure in "music of chance," performs *4'33"*
1950s–1960s	Theater of the Absurd popularizes existential philosophy
1954–1963	"Golden Decade" of "rock 'n' roll"
1955	Claude Lévi-Strauss's *Tristes Tropiques* marks the appearance of structuralism
1964	The Beatles appear on the Ed Sullivan Show, launching the "English invasion" of American popular music
1970s	Minimalism displaces Pop Art as the current fad
1973	"Aloha from Hawaii" with Elvis Presley is beamed live around the world on television
1980s	Deconstructionism, or post-culturalism, flourishes
1982	Maya Ling Lin's *Vietnam Veterans' War Memorial* opens
1990s	"Postmodernism" becomes a popular description for the contemporary view of the universe as random chaos
2005	Christo and Jeanne-Claude de Guillebon's *The Gates* exhibited in New York City's Central Park
2012	Harvard University begins offering select courses free

Postwar Intellectual Trends

The damage done to the psyche by World War II was far greater than the ruin of the physical landscape. Faith in reason, the innate goodness of human beings, and the inherent value of the individual, like the belief in universal truths, values, or principles upon which to construct a humane world, all fell victim to apparent reality.

The disintegration of the Enlightenment tradition, which had begun before the Great War, now appeared complete.

An increasingly fragmented worldview during the interwar years influenced the period's art, music, and literature. As the fragmentation of worldview continued in the West and even increased, the message and technique of cultural expression changed during the second half of the twentieth century. The changing views about truth and reality found expression in the works produced by the purveyors of both elite and pop culture. By the end of the twentieth century, there was no longer any accepted standard by which to judge works of art, literature, or music. Terms such as "good," "bad," "beautiful," or "ugly" were meaningless when anything, no matter how outlandish, could qualify as art. The absence of such standards was itself an expression of the new consensus on the nature of man and the universe and whether that consensus itself had any meaning or relevance.

Existentialism

Existentialism is not easily defined, for there is no systematic dogma to which all its leading exponents adhere. The roots of existentialism reach back into the nineteenth century with the writings of Søren Kierkegaard (1813–1855), Fyodor Dostoevsky (1821–1881), and Friedrich Nietzsche (1844–1900). In general, existentialists asserted that the individual must affirm and give meaning to their existence by struggling against the absurdity of a universe that is silent and indifferent to the individual's existence. By choosing to act, the individual gives meaning to their existence.

Postwar existentialism was born in the French resistance to German occupation during World War II. Albert Camus (1913–1960), French-born and reared in French-ruled Algeria, was the premier example of the existentialist writers who came out of the French resistance. Camus confronted the individual's predicament in a world without God that was silent and indifferent to the individual's existence. Before his death in an automobile accident in 1960, Camus's ideas received broad exposure in three novels—*The*

Many individuals at the end of the twentieth century felt as though they were adrift alone in a world where the future was filled with uncertainty and the present haunted by symbols of the past. Photo courtesy of Elizabeth Waibel, private collection.

Stranger (1942), *The Plague* (1947), and *The Fall* (1956)—and two philosophical works, *The Myth of Sisyphus* (1942) and *The Rebel* (1951).

Perhaps the best-known and most controversial of the postwar French existentialists was Jean-Paul Sartre (1905–1980). Sartre's ideas were popularized primarily through works written during the war. Again, as with Camus, it was through a series of novels, especially *Nausea* (1938) and *The Age of Reason* (1945), and plays, such as *The Flies* (1943) and *No Exit* (1944), rather than serious philosophical studies, like *Being and Nothingness* (1943), that Sartre's ideas achieved renown and influence.

Structuralism

Few individuals during the 1960s would have been able to define existentialism. Even fewer were aware that existentialism was filtering down to them through the medium of popular culture and shaping their understanding of reality. Meanwhile, the intellectual trendsetters were moving on to structuralism, hoping to restore some order to the increasing fragmentation.

The existentialists focused on the individual and the individual's need to find meaning. They assumed a universal structure, a kind of hidden harmony or universal code, exists independent of human beings and determines human behavior. The universal code could be found in the human mind, that is, in universal thought processes that are unconscious but determine consciousness. Since these thought processes are universal, the same for the uneducated native and the sophisticated university professor or corporate executive, there is an alleged unity to humanity that transcends all cultural, racial, and class distinctions. It even transcends history. The autonomous individual, who controlled his or her environment and was the master of his or her fate, gave way to the individual as a social creature controlled by his or her environment.[1]

The structuralists failed to uncover the hidden universal structures that were thought to control the human mind and hence all that human beings produced. By the late 1970s, structuralism passed out of fashion and yielded the field to deconstruction.

Deconstruction

Deconstruction was an open denial of the whole Western intellectual tradition with its emphasis on the individual, the individual's ability to reason, and through reason to arrive at a true understanding of reality, which in turn implied the capacity to make meaningful moral judgments, resulting in a reasoned reformation of society.

[1] Structuralism and its successor, deconstruction, were ideally suited for "a world integrated by identification and manipulation of the universal genetic code, computer programs, communications satellites, and multinational corporations, and the absence of major wars. ... A world fragmented culturally and aesthetically, a world of sub-cultures, small-group choices [made] on aesthetic principles and idiosyncratic, nostalgic recapitulations of the past, but one in which a comprehensive, integrating cultural theory is lacking" (Cantor 1997).

Deconstruction had a definite tendency toward nihilism. Deconstructionists held that there was no one hidden meaning to be arrived at as a result of decoding a literary text, for example. There are an infinite number of possible meanings, as many as there are "decoders." Whether what the deconstructionist said of a text had any meaning was questionable, for deconstruction itself could be deconstructed. The author's intent is no help either, for there is no implicit relationship between the author's mind and the words of the text. The deconstructionist critic may interpret a literary text any way he or she wishes, having deduced that interpretation, not necessarily from what the author wrote down, but from what the author left out, what Jacques Lacan (1901–1981) calls the "holes in the discourse."

Deconstructionists believe that agreement on a meaningful history was only possible during the nineteenth century when there was cultural unity among the literate classes of Europe. Historians of different cultural backgrounds would naturally interpret history differently. How, for example, might the history of the nineteenth century appear if written by a middle-class European or an African immigrant? This "discovery" leads to the logical conclusion that one cannot justify requiring today's students to study the history of Western Civilization. For the ever-increasing numbers of those whose cultural heritage is mainly non-European and non-Western, European history is only the story of deeds done by "dead white males," told by their descendants who seek authority through perpetuating their memory.

Postmodernism

Of the isms that have enjoyed a vogue during the latter part of the twentieth century, none is more difficult to define than "postmodernism." The term is old, having been used historically to characterize various trends in the arts. By the end of the century, it took on the characteristics of, as one critic put it, "a trendy buzzword rapidly reaching its sell-by date" (Ward 1997). At the turn of the twenty-first century, postmodernism and postmodernity were commonly used to refer to the third and most recent period in a tripartite division of Western intellectual history into premodernity (the Medieval Synthesis), modernity (the Enlightenment tradition), and postmodernity (the Enlightenment tradition in disarray).

When postmodernism is applied to the areas of thought and history, it is synonymous with posthumanism. It is a fundamental break from the Enlightenment tradition (modernity) and humanism at its core. Whereas the Enlightenment tradition (some would go back to the Renaissance) emphasized the individual, reason, order, and meaning, postmodernism rejects all of the fundamental assumptions of Enlightenment thought as no longer tenable. Thus, postmodernism includes structuralism and deconstruction, or poststructuralism.

Postmodernism is best understood when contrasted with premodernity and modernity as a term commonly used to refer to a contemporary view of reality. During premodernity, roughly the period from the High Middle Ages to the Enlightenment (c. 1000–c. 1700), the reality was an orderly universe with meaning and purpose for both the individual and history. The individual was understood to be capable of understanding oneself and the universe because the individual was a special creation created in the image of the creator, that is, God. The experts were the theologians and philosophers who interpreted God's revelation in Scripture and nature.

According to modernity, roughly the period from the Enlightenment to the mid-twentieth century (c. 1700–c. 1950), reality was an orderly universe of cause-and-effect natural law, but in a closed system. God, the creator, was now a great architect or watchmaker. God created the universe machine but was not involved in its operation. However, his continued existence as creator kept at bay the troubling questions of why anything exists and whether or not there was any meaning for the individual or history. The experts were the scientists who could discover, interpret, and exploit natural law. Thus, humankind had faith in progress and was optimistic about the future.

In postmodernity, the reality is a universe of random chaos without meaning for the individual or history. There is no creator, no God, either as the God of biblical revelation or the great architect of

Deism. There is only the illusion of order. The ultimate reality is impersonal matter. There are no experts to interpret reality, for reality is what anyone says it is at any given moment. Any attempt at a metanarrative (a "big story" that explains the meaning of all that is, e.g., the Bible) to define reality is only the flawed expression of a particular subculture. Another way of looking at the contrast is to understand premodernity as the house that God built, modernity as the house that man built, and postmodernity as the house that never got built.

Culture

War is never kind to the physical manifestations of humanity's cultural achievements. History is impoverished by the loss of cultural monuments due to wars. What wonders of human creativity have disappeared in the flames of warfare? Barbarian hordes put fire and sword to classical civilization in Western Europe, and the Vikings did the same to the early centers of Western Christendom, often leaving behind only written memories. When the dust of World War II had settled, and rebuilding began, cultural monuments were not neglected. Reconstruction of the great opera houses and concert halls was sometimes given priority over providing housing for the many homeless refugees. And such reconstruction was made as close to the original as possible. Postwar Europeans seemed to recognize that houses of culture were, like the cathedrals, reservoirs of the national spirit.

As with the philosophers, postwar culture, whether high or popular, struggled to make sense of recent events. The artists, musicians, poets, and writers displayed in their creative output the growing sense of alienation and despair and the fragmentation that characterized European civilization in transition. It was a continuation of trends already present at the beginning of the century, with perhaps a new reality. Whether in the fine arts or popular culture, influences from the United States tended to dominate. In the fine arts, this was due in part to the prewar flight of creative individuals before the tidal wave of Nazi and communist oppression. The economic dominance of the United States and the presence of American military forces in Western Europe assured that European popular culture would mimic American trends.

Art

The dominant artistic style after the war was what became known as abstract expressionism. Its roots lay in the surrealism of the interwar era. Like the surrealists, the abstract expressionists looked to the psychoanalytic theories of Sigmund Freud and Carl Jung (1875–1961). Believing that faith in reason and rationalism had guided European culture and politics into the horrors of two world wars, they sought a truth beyond reason in the realm of the unconscious. Perhaps what was most characteristic of this artistic style, or concept, was the individualism of the artists associated with it. To understand and appreciate it, one would need to study the output of each artist.

Such a task is beyond this attempt to identify and describe trends in postwar culture. Hence, we note that abstract expressionism was characterized by a lack of recognizable content and an emphasis on gesture and or color. The artist intended to communicate a reality they felt by utilizing the unconscious rather than the conscious will.

Abstract expressionism is often referred to as the "New York School" in that in the postwar period the art scene shifted from Paris to New York. Of course, many of its practitioners were European expatriates and formerly leading figures in surrealism in Europe. Among these were the Spaniard Salvador Dalí (1904–1989), the Dutchman Piet Mondrian (1872–1944), the German artists Josef Albers (1888–1976), Max Ernst (1891–1976), Hans Hofmann (1880–1966), and George Grosz (1893–1959). Max Ernst's third wife (for three years) was an influential art collector and patron, Peggy Guggenheim (1898–1979). Ms. Guggenheim exhibited the works of European expatriates, as well as new artists whom she "discovered" in her Art of This Century gallery in New York City. Among the latter was Jackson Pollock (1912–1956), arguably the best-known abstract expressionist. Pollock might produce a work of art by merely walking around on a canvas stretched out on the floor while dripping paint from cans.

It was perhaps inevitable that some artists would react against the abstract expressionists' emphasis on non-representationalism. That reaction came in the mid-1950s with a return to representation. This artistic movement became known as "Pop Art." For these artists, art should depict the real postwar world, one obsessed with commercialism and mass culture. Influenced by Dadaism, the Pop artists looked to everyday objects and images of mass production for their subject matter—soup cans, comic strips, advertisements of consumer goods, and photographs of the movie and rock stars. Although the Pop Art movement originated in England, America was again the primary home of this movement that was in vogue during the 1960s and early 1970s. Among the leading Pop artists were Jasper Johns (1930–), Robert Rauschenberg (1925–2008), Roy Lichtenstein (1923–1997), and Andy Warhol (1930–1987), "The Prince of Pop."

When one thinks of Pop Art, Andy Warhol immediately comes to mind. He burst onto the Pop Art scene in 1962 with an exhibition of paintings that depicted Campbell's soup cans and Brillo soap boxes. The difference between abstract expressionism with its nonrepresentation and Pop Art's return to representation was noted by Warhol: "Pop artists did images that anybody walking down Broadway could recognize in a split second—comics, picnic tables, men's trousers, celebrities, shower curtains, refrigerators, Coke bottles—all the great modern things that the Abstract Expressionists tried so hard not to notice" (Danto 2010). Unlike the abstract expressionists who were tuned into the problems of alienation and anxiety inherent in the postwar world as expressed by the existentialists and other philosophers, the Pop artists both celebrated and condemned the middle-class values of the consumer culture of the prosperous 1960s.

By the late 1960s and into the 1970s, minimalism displaced Pop Art as the current fad. The minimalists tried to avoid all emotional content or personal meaning. Minimalist painters produced geometric patterns of color, as, for example, in Ellsworth Kelly's (1923–2015) *Red, Orange, White, Green, Blue* (1968), a succession of color stripes on canvas.

Likewise, minimalist sculptors emphasized simple, symmetrical sculptures. The *Vietnam Veterans' Memorial* (1982), designed by Maya Ying Lin (1959–), and consisting of two polished black granite walls with the names of the 58,000 Americans who died in the Vietnam War is perhaps the best representation of minimalist sculpture.

In the 1980s and 1990s, artistic expression went in various directions, characterized by eclecticism. Some artists probed the limits of abstraction, while others chose a style known as the "new realism," reproducing objects with near photographic exactness.

Eclecticism, a kind of "premeditated chaos," is one of the major characteristics of postmodern culture, which borrows at random from the past but only to revive the past in fragments without any unifying continuity with the past or link to the future.

Europe at the beginning of the twenty-first century is no longer the center of the world, replaced as it is by a faceless, soulless internationalism. In the postmodern "Global Village," there is no accepted historic community or tradition to validate knowledge or artistic experience. Multiculturalism does not allow for a common historical tradition upon which an aesthetic standard can be established. Therefore, the definition of what is good art or bad art disappears. Is graffiti sprayed on a wall or the side of a railroad car art or anti-art? When does dabbling on canvas or the wall of a public restroom become art?

Divorced from any historical continuity, postmodern art is transient and dependent upon the viewer interacting with it. Postmodern art, lacking any content or meaning, has often become more spectacular in order to hold the viewer's attention. The Bulgarian-born Christo Javacheff (1935–2020) invented "empaquetage," a technique by which he wrapped anything capable of being covered—for example, the Pont Neuf, the Art Museum in Bern, trees along the Champs-Élysées in Paris, or the *Reichstag* building in Berlin.

Christo and his wife Jeanne-Claude de Guillebon (1935–2009) exhibited *The Gates*, 7,500 saffron-colored fabric panels hanging on 16-foot high frames along 23 miles of New York's Central Park walkways, in January 2005. As to its message, said Jeanne-Claude, there is none: "It's only a work of art." Roland Baladi (1910–1980) proposed transforming the Arc de Triomphe in Paris into a giant snow globe. He planned to enclose it in a plastic dome with artificial snow blowing around inside the dome. It was a piece of conceptual art that, fortunately, remained a concept.

What is called "performance art" of the 1990s was a postmodern version of post–World War I Dadaism. The performance artists meant to be outlandish, to shock, or even to offend the viewer. Some of their art was merely amusing, as, for example, Janine Antoni's (1964–) *Loving Care* (1993), in which she used "her hair as a paintbrush to 'mop' a gallery floor with Clairol's Loving Care black hair dye" (Perry, Baker, and Hollinger 2005) or Yves Klein's (1928–1962) use of "living paintbrushes." While an audience listened to a chamber orchestra play a single note for 20 minutes, Klein, dressed in a tuxedo, directed several naked women covered in blue paint (patented as "International Klein Blue") to smear their bodies on a canvas stretched out on the floor of the Galerie Internationale d'Art Contemporain in Paris. Artist Spencer Tunick (1967–) assembled more than 5,000 nude men and women on 1 March 2010, in front of the Sydney [Australia] Opera House for what he titled "*Mardi Gras: The Base*."

Not all postmodern art was amusing. Some artists used religious or patriotic symbols or objects in ways many considered offensive or blasphemous. Displays of Robert Mapplethorpe's (1946–1989) photographs of homoerotic and sadomasochistic subject matter were so controversial that some museums were forced to close their exhibits. Such provocative art brought forth a public outcry from conservatives for an end to the use of public funding to purchase or support the arts.

Literature, Drama, the Cinema, and Music

Postwar writers also tried to find meaning in a world that appeared increasingly without meaning. One of the themes, or issues, that they explored in light of the changing assumptions about truth and reality was the quest for social justice, a continuation of the preoccupation of such interwar writers as Bertolt Brecht and the American John Steinbeck (1902–1968). Although both of them continued to write after World War II, they did their best work during the interwar period. Another theme, especially during the Cold War era was an indictment of the new authoritarianism (totalitarianism, in Cold War terminology) of the Soviet Union. Some of the more effective of these writers were among those who had embraced Marxism (socialism, communism) during the early years of the Soviet experiment and now tried to come to grips with their disillusionment.

Among these were the Italian Ignazio Silone, the Hungarian Arthur Koestler, and, perhaps best known, the Englishman George Orwell (1903–1950). George Orwell's two most memorable works were written right after the war's end and just before his premature death in 1950. *Animal Farm* (1945) and *1984* (1949) are the best-known and most widely read indictments of the Soviet Union and totalitarianism. Yet, both end in despair, for although Orwell was deeply committed to the defense of human dignity and freedom, it is "Napoleon" and "Big Brother" who triumph over "Boxer" and Winston Smith. Clearly, Orwell saw those "eternal" values of Western civilization in grave danger of being extinguished.

During the 1960s and 1970s, criticism of the communist regime in the Soviet Union was expressed most effectively in the historical and autobiographical novels of the Russian author Aleksandr Solzhenitsyn (1918–2008). In a series of novels beginning with *One Day in the Life of Ivan Denisovich* (1962) that won him the Nobel Prize in 1970 and expulsion from the Soviet Union in 1974, Solzhenitsyn charged that the atrocities committed under Stalin were not his responsibility alone but must also be attributed to Lenin. After the collapse of the Soviet Union in 1991, Solzhenitsyn returned to Russia in 1994 and became a harsh critic of the "new" Russia. In an address given at Harvard University in 1978 ("A World Split Apart"), and again in an address given when he received the Templeton Prize in 1983 ("Men Have Forgotten God"), Solzhenitsyn criticized the West in general for having lost the will to defend the values that had once made Western civilization the envy of the world.

In postwar Germany, the two Nobel laureates Heinrich Böll (1917–1985) and Günter Grass (1927–2015) explored the damage done to the values of European civilization by the war and the failure of the postwar generation to come to grips with its past or to resist the temptation to allow West Germany's economic prosperity to numb the nation's collective conscience. Böll was a prolific writer of novels, short stories, and nonfiction. The best known of his books are *Adam Where Art Thou?* (1959), *Billiards at Half-Past Nine* (1959), *The Clown* (1968), and *Group Portrait with Lady* (1971).

Günter Grass, like Böll, wanted postwar Germans living amidst economic prosperity to remember that they once embraced the darkness of National Socialism. In three novels known as the *Danzig Trilogy*—*The Tin Drum* (1959), *Cat and Mouse* (1961), and *Dog Years* (1963)—Grass tried to understand the attraction that Nazism once held and the power of West Germany's postwar economic miracle to aid in suppressing and forgetting the past. The *Tin Drum* is a particularly disturbing novel that was made into an equally disturbing motion picture.

The struggle to understand postwar Germany lies at the heart of novels written by the East German writer Christa Wolf (1929–2011). She chose to remain in East Germany because she felt the Nazi past was more thoroughly repudiated there than in West Germany. Initially, Wolf saw hope for the future in socialism. At one point, she even served as an informant for the East German secret police, the Stasi. By the mid-1950s, Wolf was becoming increasingly disillusioned with the socialist experiment as the repression of artistic freedom increased. Still, she remained in the GDR until the unification of the two Germanies in 1989, a development she opposed. Her unique contribution was the ability to critique postwar Germany from both perspectives.

Like Christa Wolf, the Czechoslovakian writer Milan Kundera (1929–2023) hoped for a better future in a Communist-controlled postwar Czechoslovakia. He joined the Communist Party in 1948, was expelled from the party in 1950, readmitted in 1956, and expelled a second time in 1970. In 1975, Kundera left Czechoslovakia for France and became a French citizen in 1981. Kundera always insisted that he was not a dissident writer but rather a novelist. His novels are not overtly anti-Communist, but many find in them a critique of the increasing repression of freedom under postwar communism.

Art and literature were means by which philosophical issues and changing world views were communicated to a mass audience. We have noted above how existentialism was communicated more through the novels of Camus and Sartre than through their nonfiction. The theater, the cinema, and music were also powerful means by which serious philosophical statements reached a wider audience. An example from the theater is what was known as the Theater of the Absurd.

The Theater of the Absurd took its name from Albert Camus's description of the human predicament as essentially "absurd." The message of these dramatists who enjoyed a vogue during the 1950s and 1960s was that of existentialism. They portray the individual as inhabiting a meaningless universe in which they feel increasingly alone, isolated, bewildered, threatened, and even terrified by an all-pervasive sense of angst, yet desperately hoping against all hope to find in oneself some meaning. Among those associated with the Theater of the Absurd were Eugène Ionesco (1912–1994), Fernando Arrabal (1932–), Arthur Adamov (1908–1970), and Samuel Beckett (1906–1989).

Samuel Beckett's *Waiting for Godot* (1952) is the best-known example of the Theater of the Absurd. The play portrays two tramps who spend their days waiting for the coming of one Godot, a mysterious individual who may not even exist. Is he like Nietzsche's god, only a belief but one whose hoped-for appearance nevertheless gives the two otherwise hopeless tramps a reason to go on living? *Waiting for Godot* remains one of the most often performed plays of the postwar theater. Perhaps this is so because it, like a few others, communicates so well the dilemma of humanity adrift in a postmodern universe.

The European cinema, unlike the American film industry driven by the demands of a mass market, also served as a medium through which the search for meaning in an alienated world could be shared with a broader audience. European filmmakers like Ingmar Bergman (1918–2007), Alain Resnais (1922–2014), Michelangelo

Antonioni (1912–2007), Federico Fellini (1920–1993), and Luis Buñuel (1900–1983) powerfully explored the complexities of life in a postwar, postmodern world. Bergman's films are said to be filled with "Nordic angst and gloom" (Winders 2001). The central characters in Bergman's films are individuals "who wonder whether they are in this world for some reason. They feel alienated from others, meaningless entities walking around on the earth for a few years and then vanishing into the endless night" (Janaro and Altshuler 2003).

During an interview in which he discussed the making of *The Silence* (1963), Bergman said that he had reached the conclusion that God is dead and, therefore, the universe is silent. Classical music after 1945 developed mainly in two directions. One school, sometimes called the "structuralists," emphasized greater complexity in their compositions. The second school, more in tune with the philosophical assumptions of postmodernism, sought to compose music involving a technique employing random chance. French composer Pierre Boulez (1925–2016) exemplifies the former, and the American John Cage (1935–1992) the latter.

Boulez's compositions are characterized by their extremely complex structure that gives the composer total control over every element of the music. Building upon the serialism and 12-tone technique pioneered by Arnold Schoenberg (1874–1951), Boulez aimed at creating a musical structure, the effect of which is "to eliminate any sense of traditional melody, harmony, or counterpoint along with the emotions they evoke" (Cunningham and Reich 2009). This effort to remove the human element from music led to compositions of "electronic music," beginning in the 1950s.

In electronic music, sounds are arranged, or "ordered," by a computer and then played on an electronic oscillator rather than traditional musical instruments. The invention of the synthesizer in 1955 by engineers at RCA greatly simplified the composition (or production) of electronic music. Karlheinz Stockhausen (1928–2007), a major composer of electronic music, chose to combine electronic music with traditional orchestras in, for example, his composition *Mixtur* (1965). The structuralists, whether following the example of Boulez's complex serialization or the more "programmed" innovations of electronic music, remained faithful to the most basic premise of Western music, that is, composers create their music according to rules that enable them to communicate with their listeners. This was not true of the second school, which turned to creating musical compositions according to random chance.

The so-called music of chance may be illustrated by the career of John Cage (1912–1992). Cage was inspired by the artist Marcel Duchamp (1887–1968), known for his "ready-mades" and Zen Buddhism, especially the *I Ching*, or *Book of Changes*. Like Duchamp, Cage believed that art and music exist all around us. It does not necessarily originate in the artist's mind. Cage used "ready-made sounds" by simply recording the random noises in the surrounding environment. His best-known piece is one titled *4'33"* (1952). The pianist approaches the piano, sits down, and, without ever touching the keys, turns the pages of a nonexistent score at random intervals. The actual music of *4'33"* is the random noises produced by the audience. Cage believed that music should reflect the random chaos of the universe that we inhabit.

Popular Culture

Not surprisingly, American tastes and America's spirit of commercialism were major forces shaping popular culture after World War II. The fear expressed already in the 1920s by novelist Wyndham Lewis (1886–1957), that European culture would become "decivilized" by its "Americanization" as the world became smaller appears to have become a reality at the end of the twentieth century. The reasons for American cultural "imperialism" are varied and perhaps not unexpected.

Post–World War II American popular culture offered a very seductive model when compared to the war-scarred landscape of postwar Europe. The mystique of America as a land of prosperity, opportunity, and an exciting, fast-paced lifestyle grew in influence during the 1950s. American consumerism was associated in the minds of the European masses with prosperity, youth, popularity, glamor, and the latest fashions. Increasingly, Europe's youth took their cue from what they saw in America's movies and television programs or heard in its popular music. The combination of American troops stationed in Europe after 1945, and broadcasts of popular music on the American Armed Forces Radio Network, resulted in little real difference between the American hit parade and those of European nations.

The extent to which postwar European society was shaped in response to the influence of American consumerism would be difficult to overstate. It was particularly true following the collapse of communism in Eastern Europe. As the former Soviet Union became a graphic example of the failure of communism, it no longer served as a model for Europeans wanting to build a new future. America, throughout the twentieth century the flagship of capitalism and, after 1989–1991, the apparent victor in the century-long struggle between capitalism and communism, became the model (for better or worse) for Europe's future. By the end of the twentieth century, the symbols of America's commercial dominance could be seen everywhere. The "golden arches" of McDonald's fast-food restaurants and other logos of American franchises, like Starbucks Coffee, dotted the European landscape and threatened to overwhelm national tastes, much as the franchising of America itself largely destroyed regional tastes. More tourists reportedly visited the Disney theme park built outside Paris in 1992 than visited the traditional monuments of France's cultural and historical heritage.

Rock music and the popular cinema were the two main vehicles for the Americanization of European (even world) culture. As with jazz, that other American musical import that swept across Europe between the two world wars, "rock 'n' roll" had roots in the African-American subculture. It was a blend of various popular American music genres, including rhythm and blues, jazz, gospel, country and Western, and folk music. However, it was two white performers, Bill Haley (1925–1981) and Elvis Presley (1935–1977), who made "rock 'n' roll" the music of the new international youth culture during its "Golden Decade" (1954–1963).

Performing Arts mural by Randy Spicer featuring jazz immortal Louis Armstrong, Eureka, California. Highsmith, Carol M/The Library of Congress/Public Domain.

Europe's youth were attracted to American "rock 'n' roll" music just as Western Europe began to enjoy a measure of economic prosperity. A measure of economic independence allowed European youth to break free of traditional class restraints and indulge their taste for American popular music. What they found in "rock 'n' roll" were a spirit of revolt and overt sexuality. England's "rockers" donned black leather jackets and rode motorcycles in imitation of their new American idols like Elvis Presley (1935–1977), the "King," and movie star Marlon Brando (1924–2004).

In 1964, leadership in popular music passed temporarily to the English groups, epitomized by The Beatles, who emerged from the working-class bars of Liverpool, England, to chart a new course for popular music. The success of their song "I Want to Hold Your Hand" (1964), the most popular rock hit since Elvis' "All Shook Up" (1957), launched them into superstardom. In February 1964, they premiered on the Ed Sullivan Show, a kind of rite of passage for any popular entertainer, individual or group, who aspired to stardom in America. Fans around the world held a vigil in December 1964 when drummer Ringo Starr (1940–) underwent a tonsillectomy. The appearance of their album *Sgt. Pepper's Lonely Hearts Club Band* in 1967, the cover of which was believed to contain hidden messages about the alleged death of band member Paul McCartney (1942–), raised the group to enduring cult status. In 1985, Queen Elizabeth II bestowed upon each member of The Beatles the honor of MBE, Member of the British Empire.

The rock groups that followed The Beatles openly lived the rebellious and promiscuous lifestyle they sang about. An example was the Rolling Stones, a rock group that debuted in February 1963 at the Crawdaddy in Richmond, England. Whereas The Beatles' public image was that of clean-cut musicians in mohair jackets with ties and neatly groomed hair, The Rolling Stones were antisocial outlaws in appearance and behavior. They sang lyrics so explicit that they were sometimes banned from playing on the radio. They openly smoked marijuana, abused drugs, hosted wild parties that included nudity, and even were alleged to practice Satanism. The Rolling Stones quickly achieved cult status in the world of rock music and, despite the questionable quality of their music when compared to that of The Beatles, were still touring and performing before large crowds in 2013.[2] Rock music spoke to, or one might say, expressed the soul of post–World War II's youth. The themes found in the lyrics of rock music were the themes of the postwar generation—feelings of isolation, hunger for love, and sexual liberation. By expressing those universal themes, rock music had a broad appeal that helped to restore a sense of community for a generation of youth who acutely felt the increasing fragmentation of the postmodern world. Although there were "native" European clones of American and British rock stars, rock culture bore a definite "made in America" stamp.

The evolution of popular music reflected three cultural trends—the changing standards of public morality, the ever-increasing role of commercial hype, and a cross-fertilization of cultural influences from around the world that were absorbed into what was becoming, by the dawn of the new millennium, popular music that reflected a global culture.

[2] Paul McCartney (1942–) of The Beatles, Joan Baez (1941–), Bob Dylan (1941–), and Judy Collins (1939–) were among the "great ones" of the classic age of folk and rock music, who were still touring and performing before live audiences in the twenty-first century.

When Elvis Presley made his first television appearance in 1956, his gyrating pelvis was considered so risqué that viewers were allowed to see him only from the waist up. During the 1960s, The Beatles dared use only suggestive language about the emerging drug culture and relaxed sexual norms. By the mid-1970s, British "punk rock" performers like the Sex Pistols were openly and deliberately offensive, even vulgar, in both their performance style and the lyrics of their songs. The 1970s also saw the birth of rap music among urban African-American teenagers. Rap, a kind of chanted poetry that satirizes racism, black culture, and other rappers, generally spoke openly and graphically of life in the urban ghetto, of drug use, and sexual promiscuity as if it were a competitive sport.

The Sex Pistols exemplified the commercialization of popular culture. They were "manufactured" by their promoters as a product to be marketed for a profit. This vulgar commercialization was increasingly characteristic of popular music. Styles of music, like different styles of jeans, were created and marketed with an attentive eye on what might sell. The names of groups or individual artists passed in and out of style, like the logos on jean pockets.

Technological advances made possible the cross-fertilization and international marketing of different musical styles. Musical styles from around the world were imported and synthesized. Indian sitar music was popularized by Ravi Shankar (1920–2012). Reggae, a blending of electric bass and guitars with organ, piano, and drums that originated among the poor of Jamaica, introduced a Caribbean influence into popular music. The appearance of music videos and live transcontinental television broadcasts (e.g., Aloha From Hawaii with Elvis in 1973 and the famous Live Aid show in 1985) demonstrated that rock had become the world's choice in popular music and the chief medium of popular culture.

The cinema, like rock music, did much to create a shared popular culture. European directors, often enjoying government subsidies, continued to dominate the motion picture genre commonly referred to as the "art film." These were "gourmet" films intended for a very small but discriminating audience. Popular cinema, like popular music, was dominated by American-made action films, comedies, and sentimental romances, heavy on entertainment but making very little demand on the viewer's intellect. As the growing popularity of television lured more and more people away from movie houses, Hollywood turned during the 1950s to blockbuster epics like *The Ten Commandments* (1956), *Around the World in 80 Days* (1956), and *Ben-Hur* (1957).

American dominance of the silver screen continued during the last quarter of the twentieth century and into the twenty-first century.[3] American filmmakers like Francis Ford Coppola (1939–), *The Godfather* (1972), and George Lucas (1944–), *Star Wars* (1972), made lavish blockbuster adventure films that enjoyed international popularity. No filmmaker of the late twentieth or early twenty-first centuries could trump Steven Spielberg (1946–) in box office receipts or artistic achievement. Spielberg produced films such as *Raiders of the Lost Ark* (1981) and *E.T. The Extra-Terrestrial* (1982) that warmed the heart and reduced moviegoers to tears, as well as serious films such as *The Color Purple* (1985), *Schindler's List* (1993), and *Lincoln* (2012) that raised the social consciousness of his audience.

The rapid spread of television from the 1950s on and the development of new technology such as videotapes (VHS), digital video disks (DVDs), and cable and satellite television networks assisted the creation of universal pop culture. Since American commercialism was the primary driving force behind the new technology, the culture that it nurtured reflected that of middle-class American youth. American films and television programs were now available to unlimited audiences, and American entertainment stars became international stars. Lucille Ball (1911–1989); Bill Cosby (1937–); Peter Falk (1927–2011), the bungling, lovable detective; and many others were as familiar to Europeans as Mickey Mouse.

Videotapes, video disks, and compact disks (CDs) were but a small part of a revolution in technology that both shrunk the world and, at the same time greatly increased its complexity. According to the US National Aeronautics and Space Administration (NASA), there

[3] Hollywood did not have total control of the world market in actions films. Britain's "James Bond, 007" film series based upon the best-selling fiction of Ian Fleming (1909–1964) achieved international success comparable to any American-produced film series.

were approximately 3,000 artificial man-made satellites orbiting the earth at the beginning of 2022. The launch of Telstar 1 in 1962 made live television broadcasts possible between the United States and Europe. The Public Broadcasting System (PBS) began transmitting programs by satellite in 1978. Home satellite reception became possible in 1980, and by the mid-1990s, more than six million American homes had satellite dishes in their backyards or on the roofs of their homes. A Global Position Satellite (GPS) system was established in 1994. Before the end of the first decade of the twenty-first century, GPS navigation systems were a built-in, in some cases standard, feature of many new automobiles.

Technology made it possible for an individual virtually anywhere in the world to communicate live and visually with anyone anywhere. Instant access to the contents of libraries, art museums, and an ever-growing number of databases was possible with a small device that could be held in the palm of one's hand. In 2012, Harvard University began to offer many of its lecture courses online, accessible to the public. One hundred thousand individuals registered for the initial course offerings. Soon other major universities, including Stanford, Yale, and Princeton, and smaller colleges like Hillsdale College followed Harvard's example. For anyone with access to the new communications technology, any great work of art, rare book, or recorded music or voice was instantly available.

We began this chapter with the postwar intellectuals searching for meaning amidst the physical ruins of European civilization at the end of World War II. Those intellectuals, who pondered the meaning of history and life, concluded that human beings were adrift, alone in a cold and meaningless universe. At the end of the century and the beginning of the new millennium, there were signs that the masses did not agree with that conclusion. There is evidence in popular culture that people did not accept the conclusion that a human being is only a cosmic cipher in a cold, dark universe. The resistance to the gloom and doom of the intellectuals could be seen in the phenomenal popularity, in both book publishing and the cinema, of two mega myths—the *Lord of the Rings* trilogy by J. R. R. Tolkien (1892–1973) and the seven-volume Harry Potter series by J. K. Rowling (1965–). Both Tolkien and Rowling are British authors.[4]

Both the Lord of the Rings and the Harry Potter series are adventure stories centered on a cosmic duel between good and evil. Upon the outcome of each struggle, both of which affirm the ultimate triumph of good, hangs the future of the universe. Tolkien, an Oxford professor of medieval literature, conceived his story and worked on it during the interwar years. He was a member of the Inklings, a group of writers associated with C. S. Lewis (1898–1963), a professor of medieval and Renaissance literature at Oxford University. J. K. Rowling, who published her first Harry Potter novel in 1997, has acknowledged that she was influenced by her reading of Tolkien and Lewis. Both series have broken all sales records in the publishing industry worldwide. Both have been made into motion pictures that likewise have established new records for attendance. Clearly, though the intellectual dream spinners may be adrift in a fog, the average man or woman living under the influence of European civilization is living in a world of hope, a world in which the future is brighter than the past.

References

Cantor, Norman. (1997). *The American Century: Varieties of Culture in Modern Times*. New York: Harper Collins, pp. 434–435.

Lawrence S. Cunningham and John J. Reich. (2009). *Culture and Values. Vol. 2: A Survey of the Humanities*, 7th ed. Independence: Cengage Learning.

Arthur C Danto. (2010). *Andy Warhol*. New Haven, CT: Yale University Press.

Janaro, Richard and Thelma Altshuler. (2003). *The Art of Being Human*. New York: Pearson.

Perry, Marvin, Wayne Baker, and Pamela Pfeiffer Hollinger. (2005). *The Humanities in the Western Tradition: Ideas and Aesthetics. Vol. 2: Renaissance to Present*. Independence: Cengage Learning.

Ward, Glenn. (1997). *Teach Yourself Postmodernism*. Chicago: McGraw-Hill Trade.

James A Winders. (2001). *European Culture Since 1848: From Modern to Postmodern and Beyond*. New York: Palgrave.

[4] *Left Behind* (1995), a science fiction series based loosely on the *Book of Revelation* in the *New Testament* may be cited as another example. Definitely a distinctively American product, and lacking any literary merit, it has been a phenomenal best-selling series internationally.

11

Prelude to the Twenty-First Century

Europe and the World, 1989–2000

Chronology

1989	First free elections in Poland in the postwar period; massive gains by Solidarity
	Fall of the Berlin Wall
	End of the communist regimes in East Germany, Czechoslovakia, Bulgaria, and Romania
1990	Unification of Germany; Helmut Kohl reelected chancellor in the first free all-German elections since 1932

Twentieth-Century Europe: 1900 to the Present, Fourth Edition.
Michael D. Richards and Paul R. Waibel.

1991	John Major replaces Margaret Thatcher as leader of the British Conservative Party and Prime Minister
	First Gulf War
	Dissolution of the Warsaw Treaty Organization
	Attempted coup in the Soviet Union; Gorbachev resigns as president
	The Soviet Union is dissolved at the end of the year
	Slovenia and Croatia leave the Yugoslav Federation beginning its disintegration
1992	Maastricht Treaty sets the process by which the European Community (EC) will become the European Union (EU)
1993	EC becomes the EU
	Czechoslovakia's "Velvet Divorce" results in the formation of the Czech Republic and the Republic of Slovakia
1995	Austria, Finland, and Sweden join the EU
	Dayton (Ohio) Agreement establishes a loosely federated Bosnia, ending the civil war in Bosnia (1992–1995)
1997	British Labour Party under Tony Blair wins the election
1998	Helmut Kohl defeated by Gerhard Schröder; Germany governed by a Social-Democratic/Green coalition
1999	NATO admits Poland, Hungary, and the Czech Republic
	War in Kosovo
2000	George W. Bush becomes president of the United States in an election decided by the US Supreme Court
	Vladimir Putin elected president of the Russian Republic

In the fall of 1989, the Monday evening prayer services held at the Nikolai Kirche (the St. Nicholas Church) in Leipzig, East Germany, became political events. Even more astonishing, in a system in which religion was carefully monitored, the crowds that filled the square next to the church after every service grew from one service to the next. The occasion was used to exchange information that would ordinarily never see the light of day. On 2 October, more than 10,000 protestors marched past the train station, then alongside the Stasi (secret police) headquarters (!) to the town hall, the kind of demonstration that had not been seen since the Berlin uprising in 1953.

On 7 October, Mikhail Gorbachev, head of state of the Soviet Union, appeared in East Berlin to participate in the celebration of the fortieth anniversary of the founding of the GDR. He warned Erich Honecker that "life punishes those who delay." That same weekend rumors spread around Leipzig that any attempt to use the next Monday evening prayer services for political purposes would be met by a show of force. Hospitals were warned they should be prepared to treat injured people. The police presence around the city was beefed up. Local government officials, communist party leadership, and prominent members of the community, including Kurt Masur (1927–2015), the leader of the world famous Gewandhaus Orchestra, issued an appeal. Assurances were exchanged that neither side would offer provocation to the other.

On 9 October, Leipzigers thronged the Nikolai Kirche and other churches in Leipzig for an expanded Monday evening prayer service. Afterwards, thousands of demonstrators marched around the inner city proclaiming *Wir sind das Volk!* (We are the people!) and *Wir bleiben hier!* (We're staying here!). It was a remarkable display of courage in that citizens of Leipzig were well aware of how the Chinese Communist Party had dealt with demonstrations in Tianamen Square the previous June. The march was peaceful and the government did not attempt to break it up. This may well have been a turning point, a point at which the East German government lost the initiative.

The Revolutions of 1989

Two centuries after the beginning of the French Revolution, a wave of revolutions swept through the communist states of Eastern and Central Europe. Many factors contributed to these decisive events. One significant factor was contributed by Gorbachev, who became

Secretary-General of the Communist Party of the Soviet Union in 1985. His policies of *glasnost* and *perestroika* created an attractive model that many in Eastern Europe hoped to emulate. Furthermore, Gorbachev began to hint that the Brezhnev Doctrine, which called for socialist countries to aid a brother socialist country threatened by "counterrevolutionary forces," would no longer be in force. By 1989, Gorbachev was plainly telling communist leaders of the satellite nations they were on their own.

A perhaps even more important factor in the events of 1989 was the re-emergence of the trade union movement Solidarity as a major influence in Polish politics. In the partially free elections the summer of 1989, Solidarity won all of the 161 seats in the *Sejm* (the lower house) it was allowed to contest (the Polish Communist Party had tried to arrange the election so that it would secure a majority of the seats). In addition, Solidarity won all but one of the Senate seats. The election results surprised both the Communist Party and Solidarity. Solidarity negotiated with the smaller parties that had once been controlled by the Communist Party and the result was a new coalition government with Tadeusz Mazowiecki (1927–2013), a Solidarity activist, as premier. The following year, Lech Wałęsa was elected president.

As the Polish Communist Party was losing its grip on Poland, its Hungarian counterpart faced problems of its own. In the summer of 1989, Hungarians began for the first time since 1956 to discuss the Hungarian Revolution of 1956 openly. In a moving ceremony, Hungarians reburied several of the martyrs of that event.

Hungary also contributed to events in the GDR. In the spring of 1989, Hungary removed the barbed-wire fence between it and Austria, symbolizing a new relationship with Western Europe. East Germans were quick to take advantage of the newly lax border control and cross the border into Austria. Once in Austria, they could travel, courtesy of the West German government, to West Germany and a new life. East Germans also crowded into West German embassies in Prague and Warsaw. Eventually, special sealed trains took these East Germans back through East Germany to the West. This was another instance of the East German government responding to events rather than initiating them.

In Czechoslovakia, demonstrators in Prague filled Wenceslas Square in November. Initially, police attempted to break up the demonstrations, but, within a few days, the crowds swelled to overwhelming numbers. The Czech government, like the East German government, seemed always at least one step behind events, very much on the defensive. The center of political gravity moved to the Magic Lantern Theater, where the playwright Václav Havel (1936–2011) and colleagues associated with Charter 77 (a group of activists dedicated to monitoring abuses of human rights as defined by the constitution of Czechoslovakia) worked to give direction to the movement against the government. By December, the old government had resigned and a new government headed by Václav Havel had formed. Alexander Dubček, heroic figure from the "Prague Spring" of 1968, emerged from long years of internal exile in his native Slovakia to lend his presence to what became known as the "Velvet Revolution."

Prague on the eve of free elections in June 1990. Only a few months earlier, the "Velvet Revolution" had swept the communist government from power. Behind the statue of Tomáš Masaryk, the founder of Czechoslovakia, is the headquarters of Civic Forum, the party that won the election. From the collection of Michael Richards.

The revolutionary wave also swept away the communist government of Bulgaria without violence. In Romania, however, Nicolae Ceaușescu (1918–1989), who had ruled in a harsh and increasingly arbitrary manner since the 1960s, attempted to hold on to power by the use of force. Revolutionary forces arrested Ceaușescu and his wife, who had also been a malign political influence. The couple was put on trial, quickly found guilty, and promptly shot. Pictures of the dead couple flashed around the world in television reports.

In a few short months, the unthinkable had taken place. The Iron Curtain had been ripped down and was no more. Instead, a series of new governments eagerly began to experiment with the transition to a market economy and a democratic political system. In the euphoria of early 1990, some thought the transition was a matter of a few hundred days. Instead, years of trial and error lay ahead.

German Reunification

The Fall of the Berlin Wall on 9 November 1989, symbolized for many the end of the Cold War. Pictures of happy East Berliners streaming past guards at the Wall and into West Berlin where they were greeted by ecstatic West Berliners with champagne, flowers, and bananas lit up tv screens around the world. Within a year the German Democratic Republic was no more. At the end of 1991, the Soviet Union dissolved, replaced by 15 independent republics. The Cold War over, statesmen supposedly were putting a New World Order in place. This, of course, was not quite what happened.

Of all the developments launched by the revolutions of 1989, the reunification of Germany was the most consequential for Europe. The GDR, for all its problems, could have remained independent as a new type of social democracy. Many within the old Socialist Unity Party (SED), which quickly renamed itself the Party of Democratic Socialism (*Partei des Demokratischen Sozialismus* or PDS) wanted to remain independent and to reform the political and economic system of the GDR. Many activists in the new citizens movements such as New Forum or Democracy Awakening also hoped to reform the old systems. By December, however, a majority of those who had participated in demonstrations in Leipzig, Dresden, and East Berlin, and other cities and towns in the GDR were beginning to think about the possibility of reunification of Germany. For some it seemed to offer a quick way to achieve a western standard of living. For others, it appeared to be the possibility to bring the two parts of Germany back together again after 45 years of separation.

To his credit, Helmut Kohl (1930–2017), then chancellor of the West German government, understood early on that there was a possibility to achieve reunification in the very near future. Early in 1990, he decided on the political gamble of supporting a process of reunification. There was at first very little support from his west European colleagues and Gorbachev and the Soviet Union were big question marks. Very important in the success of Kohl's initiative was the support of President George H. W. Bush (1924–2018).

In part, Kohl was worried that the continued influx of East German refugees into West Germany would work a hardship on the West German economy. Despite his vision and bold action, he and other supporters of reunification underestimated the difficulty of restructuring the East German economy and raising living standards to West German levels. He also underestimated the difficulties involved in integrating an East German population that had lived under a communist dictatorship for some 45 years.

The first free elections in the GDR, March 1990, were for the *Volkskammer* (the People's Chamber, the parliament of the GDR). The main issue was reunification. West German politicians campaigned for their East German counterparts. The Christian Democrats (CDU) formed a coalition with several smaller parties and strongly backed the idea of reunification. They won a stunning victory over the Social Democrats, who had been lukewarm toward reunification. The new government under Lothar de Maizière (1940–) began negotiations for the introduction of the deutsche mark into East Germany in July. A crucial factor in the unification process was a successful meeting between Kohl and Gorbachev. Germany agreed to pay the Soviet Union a large sum of money to cover the expense of withdrawing troops from East Germany and resettling them in the Soviet Union.

Negotiations between East and West Germans that summer led to unification in October (3 October—*Tag der Deutschen Einheit*—German Unity Day). In the first free elections in all of Germany since November 1932, Kohl and the coalition of Christian Democrats and Free Democrats (FDP) easily beat the Social Democrats. In the east, only a few delegates from the PDS were elected. Some Germans complained that the GDR had been "annexed" (a reference to the *Anschluss* or annexation of Austria in 1938 by Nazi Germany). Unification had been accomplished in less than a year from the beginning of the German Revolution of 1989. Germany began to pour billions of marks annually into the east to bring the infrastructure up to West German standards and also to undo the environmental damage done by the old regime.

The unification of Germany led also to full sovereignty. Alongside negotiations between East Germany and West Germany, there were the "2 + 4" talks involving the two Germanies and the four ex-allies from World War II, the Soviet Union, Britain, France, and the United States. The latter negotiations resulted in a treaty that formally put an end to any remaining rights held by the four powers in Germany.

The whole process changed Europe in profoundly important ways. In some respects, European history after 1990 has been an attempt to deal with the various ramifications of German unification. The unified Germany was larger and far stronger economically than any other European state. A Franco-German partnership in Europe now depended not on the relatively equal weight of the two countries but more on Germany's conscious efforts to maintain it. More than ever, it seemed important to Europeanize Germany.

The most important efforts of Kohl's fourth and fifth terms (he was re-elected in 1994) concerned the reconstruction of what had been the German Democratic Republic. In part, this involved both deindustrialization, the removal of outmoded industrial facilities, and the repair of the environment. East German efforts to develop a major industrial economy had resulted in extensive environmental damage, including pollution from burning sulfur-laden brown coal and the dumping of toxic waste products. Despite the transfer of nearly $2 trillion over two decades, however, projects meant to provide East Germans with a lifestyle comparable to that enjoyed by West Germans have been only partially successful.

The Federal Commissioner for the Stasi Archives, popularly known as the Gauck-Behörde (Gauck Agency), became one of the most important efforts to come to terms with the past of the former GDR. Because the Stasi were such a pervasive influence in the GDR, it seemed important to preserve their files and guard against their misuse. Under the first commissioner, Joachim Gauck (1940–), the archives were established. Anyone with a Stasi file was allowed to see it. Care was taken not to allow the files to be used for political purposes.

This aspect of reconciliation with the disappearance of the GDR has been relatively successful. For those who were 40 and older in 1989, however, the changes have been difficult in many cases. To many it seemed they had spent their entire careers working for something now viewed as worthless. Especially for those who had retired or were about to retire, the newly reunited Germany was a bitter pill. Even among those who had not liked the old regime, there was a certain *Ostalgie* (nostalgia) for the eastern way of life. Many valued, for example, the social guarantees, the slower pace of life, and the idea that people need their neighbors and could expect their help in difficult times.

The Soviet Union Disappears

In something like a magician's trick, the reappearance of a united Germany for the first time since 1945 was followed not long afterward by the disappearance of the Soviet Union. The events of 1989 and 1990 already seemed to underline the decline of the Soviet Union as a world power. President George H. W. Bush's "New World Order," as it took form in the crusade against Iraq in the first Gulf War in 1991, appeared to offer the Soviet Union at best the role of junior partner. By then, it was clear that Gorbachev was not able to make *perestroika* work in the economy. The economy seemed somehow stuck between incompatible economic systems, communism and capitalism. Gorbachev's economic experiments only served to make a faltering economy even less productive.

Gorbachev turned to political maneuvering, seemingly moving back to the right in 1990. In the meantime, Boris Yeltsin (1931–2007), emerged as a rising political star. Elected president of the Russian Republic, he cleverly moved to enhance the power of the republics of the Soviet Union and to decrease the power of the Soviet government and the communist party. By the summer of 1991, he and his fellow presidents of the republics of the Soviet Union had agreed to a treaty creating a federal system that gave the republics a good deal more authority. Gorbachev, for his part, had swung back to the left and seemed ready in August to agree to the treaty.

Before the treaty could be signed, members of Gorbachev's own government staged a coup. They placed Gorbachev, on vacation in the Crimea, under house arrest. Yeltsin, as president of the Russian Republic, climbed on a tank in front of the Russian White House (which housed the parliament) in Moscow and bravely defied the coup. The coup leaders lacked direction and nerve and backed down while the military refused to move against Yeltsin and his supporters. CNN (the Cable News Network) covered the drama. After the coup had ended, an ABC News interview with Gorbachev and Yeltsin made it clear to observers that Yeltsin now had the political momentum.

Gorbachev beholds a shattered hammer and sickle. Valtman, Edmund S./The Library of Congress/Public Domain.

By the end of the year, the Soviet Union was no more. Estonia, Latvia, and Lithuania went their own way. The remaining republics grouped together in the Commonwealth of Independent States, the most powerful and largest of which was the Russian Republic. Other important republics were Belarus, Ukraine, Georgia, and Kazakhstan.

In most respects, the Russian Republic took over the role the Soviet Union had played. It remained an atomic power while other parts of the former Soviet Union gave up atomic weapons. It also replaced the Soviet Union as a permanent member of the United Nations Security Council and continued to negotiate with the United States on disarmament. For a time, it was a member of the G-8 (Group of Eight). It came to regard the eastward expansion of NATO as hostile moves. It sought to maintain leverage over other states that contained sizeable Russian populations such as Belarus, Kazakhstan, Ukraine, and Georgia.

Yeltsin, an astute and energetic politician, had always been a heavy drinker. After the attempted coup, he continued to drink heavily but began also to suffer ill health. As Russian problems mounted in the 1990s, he became less and less able to deal effectively with those problems. The major problem was how to establish a market economy where everything, production quotas, prices, development strategies and so forth, was decided by the state. The existence of an enormous defense sector, accounting for about 25 percent of Russia's gross output, could not be sustained. Its existence also complicated the transition from an emphasis on defense products to consumer goods. A second, related, problem was the existence of so-called "mono-industrial regions," areas in which a particular part of the economy was concentrated. Additionally, welfare functions were usually attached to industries rather than local governments. These factors helped to bring on a depression in the mid-1990s. Where estimates of those in poverty stood at 1.5 percent of the population in the latter years of the Soviet era, by 1993, estimates of those in poverty ranged from one-third to one-half of the population. Life expectancy for males fell drastically from 64 in 1990 to 57 in 1994.

The first Chechen War (a former republic of the Soviet Union, now part of the Russian Republic) began in 1994. Chechnya resisted successfully for nearly a year. Russia managed to take the capital city of Grozny in 1995. In 1997, a peace treaty was signed. The war featured many atrocities, particularly on the part of the Russian forces.

Despite the many problems Russia faced, Yeltsin was able to win the elections of 1996. His most serious competition came from the leader of the communist party, Gennady Zyuganov (1944–), who forced Yeltsin into a runoff election. Vladimir Zhirinovsky (1946–2022) a nationalist and anti-Semite, gained serious support from the extreme right. Yeltsin emphasized that only he could prevent a return to a totalitarian system. While some observers believed that holding elections and running a parliamentary system was an important step forward, others pointed to the corruption of the system and the arbitrary use of power. It was far from clear that democracy had taken root.

Russia was characterized by a kind of robber baron capitalism in the 1990s. It was most successful in Moscow and a few other major Russian cities. The oligarchs, an informal group of enormously rich men, among them Boris Berezovsky (1946–2013) perhaps the best known, had been instrumental in Yeltsin's victory in 1996. These were insiders, former communist party and secret police officials who managed to grab valuable state holdings for pennies on the dollar. In many cases, they worked with the large, well-organized Russian mafia, which operated abroad (in New York City, for example) as well as in Russia. Russia, heavily dependent on the sale of petroleum, natural gas, and other commodities, was hard hit by the recession of 1998. That year, despite a large emergency loan from the International Monetary Fund (IMF), Russia defaulted on its international debt and its currency (the ruble) collapsed.

On the last day of 1999, Yeltsin resigned as president and picked Vladimir Putin (1952–) to replace him as temporary president pending elections in 2000. Putin was for many years an operative working for the KGB in the GDR. He resigned in 1991 and began working in the St. Petersburg administration where there were rumors that he continued to work both with members of the successor organization to the KGB, the Federal Security Service (FSB), and organized crime. In 1996, he moved to Moscow, where he held various positions, including head of the FSB and secretary of Yeltsin's Security Council. There is little doubt that Yeltsin and his family saw Putin as a safe replacement who would, above all, protect the family from reprisal. Additionally, he must have been seen as safe by both the oligarchs and organized crime.

The Disintegration of Yugoslavia

The disappearance of the Soviet Union was perhaps unavoidable, given the distance between communist theory and practice on the one hand and economic and political reality on the other by the 1980s. By contrast, the disintegration of Yugoslavia was largely the work of two political leaders willing to put their own power above the welfare of the people. To be fair, Yugoslavia as a political enterprise owed a great deal to the efforts of Marshall Tito and his death in 1980 probably doomed the delicate, complicated governmental system to some kind of fundamental change.

Nonetheless, two political leaders bear responsibility for the collapse of the country. The better known of the two and the first to fan the fires of ethnic hatred was Slobodan Milošević (1941–2006), the leader of Serbia. The other was Franjo Tudjman (1922–1999), president of Croatia, someone not generally held responsible for his part in the Yugoslav tragedy.

By 1990, Milošević, in order to maintain power in Serbia and also to move toward turning Yugoslavia into a greater Serbia, began to play the nationalism card, playing on Serbian fears of other ethnic groups. He began with Kosovo, an autonomous province of Serbia with an Albanian majority and also with Vojvodina, another autonomous province of Serbia, this with a large Hungarian population. Croatia and also Slovenia met these challenges to the federal structure of Yugoslavia with their own versions of emotional appeals to ethnic separatism.

In June 1991, Slovenia and Croatia declared independence. Serbia's response was to use the Yugoslav army against the two new republics. Slovenia, favored in its geographical location and in its homogenous population, defended itself and avoided civil war. Croatia went to war with Serbia. For many Serbs, this brought back memories of World War II and the activities of Croatian fascists in the Ustasha.

Bosnia's declaration of independence the following year complicated matters even more. It had once been a model of the possibility of a harmonious existence of Serbs, Croats, and Muslims. The population spoke the same language, Serbo-Croatian, although Serbs used the Cyrillic alphabet to write it while Croatians used the Roman alphabet. They differed as well in terms of religion, Serbs belonging to the Orthodox faith, Croats to the Catholic religion, and Bosnian Muslims to Islam. Up to 1992, nonetheless, there had been a good deal of intermarriage and mixed neighborhoods were common.

The Serbian siege of Sarajevo, the site of a Winter Olympics a few years before, became the centerpiece of the Yugoslav tragedy. "Ethnic cleansing," a euphemism that covered anything from forcibly driving a particular group away from a territory to systematic rape of women and killing of men and boys, became a new, disgraceful entry into the political lexicon of twentieth-century history.

The European Community (EC) was unsuccessful in efforts to negotiate a settlement. A United Nations peacekeeping force failed. In 1994, Serbia began to distance itself from the Bosnian Serbs due to the effects of economic sanctions against it. NATO air strikes also began to take effect. Finally, combatants reluctantly agreed to the Dayton (Ohio) Agreement calling for a loosely federated Bosnia. American and other NATO troops arrived soon after to enforce the agreement.

The last act of the Yugoslav tragedy came in Kosovo, where some years before it had begun. After Serbia had worked to ensure Serbian control of every aspect of life in the province, a Kosovar (Albanian) resistance movement appeared. Although Kosovo declared independence in 1991, it was only after the Dayton Agreement seemed to give Milošević a free hand in Kosovo that fighting broke out between the Kosovo Liberation Army (KLA) and Serbian forces. In 1998, Milošević stepped up the level of military action, destroying homes and villages. It appeared that Kosovars would be driven out of Kosovo in a gigantic act of ethnic cleansing. Negotiations were unsuccessful. NATO began a bombing campaign on 24 March 1999.

For some time, it was a stalemate. Serbian troops in Kosovo could only be dislodged by ground troops, which NATO was reluctant to introduce. On the other hand, air strikes continued despite Russian efforts to stop them. In the end, Milošević agreed to withdraw troops from Kosovo in return for an end to bombing and also agreed to the introduction of a NATO peacekeeping force.

Milošević himself became a casualty of the war in Kosovo. In September 1999, he failed to gain reelection as president. When he tried to falsify the results of the election, his former allies deserted him. Nearly two years later, 29 June 2001, the Serbian government handed him over to the International Criminal Tribunal in The Hague to be tried for war crimes and crimes against humanity. Five years later, he died in prison, apparently of a heart attack.

Transition in the Rest of Eastern Europe

While the Fall of the Berlin Wall in November 1989 was the most dramatic event in the breakup of the Soviet empire, Poland, as noted above, took many of the early decisive steps in 1989. It continued to take many of the early first steps in the transition in the early 1990s from Soviet satellite to an independent country that featured capitalism and democracy. In particular, it was the poster child for the idea of "shock therapy" as the best way to move from an old-style command economy to a market economy. No longer would production quotas and prices be set at the top. Instead, the market would determine what was made and for how much it could be sold.

Although Poland benefitted from loans from the International Monetary Fund (IMF) and assistance from the European Economic Community, the transition was painful. Unemployment soared as outmoded industries were quickly shown to be uncompetitive. Inflation compounded the difficulties large segments of the population experienced. The worst was over by 1992. Debate continued, not surprisingly, over whether "shock therapy" had been the best approach. Most Poles were better off than they had been under communism, but a majority believed that little had changed or they were less well off. In the elections of 1993, the reformed Communists, now renamed Social Democrats, returned to power.

In Czechoslovakia, the transition to capitalism and democracy was complicated by the efforts of some in Slovakia to move to independence. Economic reforms damaged Slovakia more than the Czech territory. Civic Forum split into two factions. One, the Civic Democratic Party (CDP) argued for rapid economic transition. The other, Civic Movement (CM), cautioned against the detrimental impact of such a policy. At the same time, Vladimír Mečiar (1942–), the Prime Minister of Slovakia, formed the Movement for a Democratic Slovakia (MDS) and began a campaign to make Slovakia independent. Legislative elections in June 1992 resulted in the MDS as the dominant political force in Slovakia and the CDP as the dominant political force in the Czech territory. On 25 November 1992, legislation was adopted by the Federal Assembly that provided for the establishment of a Czech Republic and a Slovak Republic (later simply Slovakia) as of midnight 31 December. This became known as the "Velvet Divorce," the somewhat ironic denouement to the "Velvet Revolution."

The Czech Republic, now separate from Slovakia, was well positioned to make a transition to capitalism. It did not have a large foreign debt and it had already begun to move slowly toward a free market economy before the November 1989 revolution. Its president, Václav Havel, although unsuccessful in preventing the "Velvet Divorce," quickly emerged as a major voice in European politics. Originally a playwright with an international reputation (his best-known play is *The Garden Party*), Havel became a political figure of some importance and a widely admired intellectual force. He was instrumental in the disbanding of the Warsaw Pact (WTO) and also encouraged the enlargement of NATO toward the east. Perhaps his most famous essay is "The Power of the Powerless," 1978.

Hungary, since the defeat of the 1956 Revolution, had gone through several periods of reform and reconsolidation of communist party control. In 1989, a reformist majority changed the name of the party to Socialist. About the same time the name of the country was changed to Republic of Hungary, "People's" no longer part of the official title. The following year elections involved more than

20 parties and groups. The Hungarian Democratic Forum (HDF) gained 165 of the 386 seats. The Independent Smallholders' Party (ISP) gained 43 and the Christian Democratic People's Party (CDPP) gained 21 and joined the HDF in a coalition government. Outside the government was the liberal Alliance of Free Democrats (ADF) with 92 seats. The communists split into two groups, only one of which, the Hungarian Socialist Party (HSP) won enough votes to enter the National Assembly with 33 seats.

The new government moved quickly to a free market system with the same spike in inflation and unemployment as elsewhere. The economic transition was complicated by efforts to revisit the 1956 Revolution, both to de-criminalize actions by revolutionaries and to hold responsible those who used political power and Soviet backing to defeat the Revolution.

Another issue of importance involved state control over the media. Many began to see the government as drifting to an extreme right position. The HDF coalition began to lose support to the HSP, which in the elections in 1994 formed a new government with the ADF. It was a stunning reversal of fortunes, similar to what had taken place in Poland. The HSP coalition continued the transition to a free market system but with more attention to the social consequences of that transition.

Romania had long been an outlier in the Soviet bloc. By 1989, Ceaușescu's megalomania, his massive social change policies both for rural areas and for the cities, and especially his draconian population policy, which made contraception unavailable and penalized women who had not given birth by age 25, created misery and unrest. Ceaușescu attempted to follow the Chinese prescription of massive repression, but elements in the party and the military decided that the time had come to end his rule. There were violent confrontations between the military and the Securiate (secret police), resulting in the death of many members of the Securiate. As noted above, Ceaușescu and his wife were tried, found guilty, and quickly executed.

The Council of National Salvation scheduled elections for May 1990. In these elections, the National Salvation Front (NSF) gained

80 percent of the vote. The Council of National Salvation continued to dominate Romanian politics. It was widely believed that the Council was made up mainly of former members of the Romanian Communist Party and had been put together to enable the old elite to continue in power. In 1991, matters came to a head with violent clashes between miners and security forces. The government resigned and a coalition government approved a new constitution which called for a multi-party system, a free-market economy, and guarantee of human rights. Elections in September 1992 resulted in the renamed NSF, now the Democratic National Salvation Front (DNSF), emerging as the largest party in the Assembly of Deputies. Ion Iliescu (1930–) of the DNSF was re-elected president.

Romania at this point still had far to go to repair the damage done under Ceaușescu and the Communist Party. One poignant indication of the enormity of the task was the condition of orphanages. Many people, forced to continue unwanted pregnancies, had given up their children to orphanages, which became completely overwhelmed and lacked sufficient staff and resources to care for the children. This immense human tragedy only began to slowly be remedied in the 1990s, often with outside aid.

Changing of the Guard in Western Europe

Reunification of Germany, as important an achievement as it was, was not enough for Helmut Kohl to prevail in the elections of 1998. By this point, Germany was experiencing slow economic growth, higher unemployment, and some dissatisfaction with the cost of revamping the economy and society of eastern Germany. A new coalition, the so-called "Red-Green" coalition came into power. The SPD with 298 seats in the *Bundestag* and the Greens with 47 formed a new government with Gerhard Schröder (1944–) of the SPD as Chancellor and Joschka Fischer (1948–) of the Greens as Foreign Minister. Kohl, who had become involved in a party financing scandal, was replaced as chair of the CDU by Angela Merkel (1954–) in 2000.

The turnover in German politics was actually the last in a series of political shifts within the major western European states. Earlier, in the 1993 legislative elections, the Socialist experiments featuring various efforts to contend with the French economy ended with what was nearly the end of the Socialist party. The Mitterrand Era itself ended in 1995 with the victory of Jacques Chirac (1932–2019), former mayor of Paris and leader of conservative right. Chirac called for parliamentary elections in 1997, a year early, in hopes of strengthening his parliamentary majority. Victory by the left led to a coalition of Socialists, Communists, and Greens, that governed in cohabitation with Chirac until the presidential elections in 2002.

In Britain, John Major (1943–), who had succeeded Margaret Thatcher, won the 1992 election despite many who predicted he would not. His government, however, was not successful. The British economy struggled with recession and Major contended with Euroscepticism on the part of many Conservatives. He was defeated in 1997 by Tony Blair (1953–), who had become the leader of the Labour Party in 1994. Blair, young and charismatic, looked to simultaneously embrace market forces and social justice. After 18 years of Conservative government, he offered a pro-European, modern, progressive viewpoint. Inspired in many ways by President Bill Clinton (1946–) of the United States, Blair himself became a kind of model for other European leaders.

The political transition in Italy was the most extensive of all. Italy was by the 1990s contending with a very high level of debt—some 120 percent of GDP, which required almost 40 percent of tax revenue just to pay the interest on debt. In 1992, just before the general election, "Tangentopoli" ("bribery city" or "bribesville"), an enormous corruption scandal, rocked Italian politics (Kershaw 2018, p. 435). Many prominent politicians, including the Socialist Bettino Craxi (1934–2000) and the Christian Democrat Giulio Andreotti (1919–2013), were placed on trial. Craxi was sentenced to prison but went into exile in Tunisia where he had an estate and protection from the government of Zine El Abidine Ben Ali (1936–2019), a personal friend. Andreotti, one of the most influential and prominent Italian politicians of the postwar era was initially sentenced to prison but eventually acquitted on appeal.

The election of 1994 completely transformed Italian politics. The Christian Democrats, dominant in Italian politics for 45 years after World War II, split into three smaller parties. The Socialist Party suffered major losses. The big winner was Forza Italia, formed in 1993 by Silvio Berlusconi (1936–2023), a media tycoon. Berlusconi and Forza Italia promised a new beginning. Berlusconi stressed his position as a political outsider and made a populist appeal that gained him a large and enduring following. His initial efforts as Prime Minister were not successful and he resigned after nine months rather than face a vote of no confidence. He would return in the new century, however, as a major figure in Italian politics and as a forerunner of numerous European politicians who favored right-wing populist politics.

The European Union in the 1990s

Before the revolutions of 1989, many observers of the European scene had predicted the 1990s would be the decade of the European Community (EC). The 1985 report of the Delors commission (Jacques Delors, (1925–), a leading official in the EC, president in 1990), called for the removal of all physical, technical, and fiscal barriers to the free movement of capital, goods, and people. This would create a single European market. The Single European Act (SEA-1989) legislated the necessary steps for implementing the report. By the time SEA went into effect, 1 January 1993, German unification and other changes in Eastern and Central Europe placed the European Union (EU-the new title for the EC) in somewhat of a quandary. Should it deepen, that is, become more fully integrated by pursuing a common fiscal policy and even a common foreign policy or should it widen by taking in not only some of the old European Free Trade Association (EFTA) states but also some of the new democracies in eastern and central Europe?

Typically, the EU has tried to do both. Meeting in Maastricht, the Netherlands, in December 1991, what then was still the EC put together a treaty, Treaty on Economic and Monetary Union or "Maastricht Treaty" that called for further radical changes, among them a single European currency and a common foreign policy. The idea of a common foreign policy floundered on the inability of the EC to meet the Yugoslav crisis effectively. The idea of a single European currency, the Euro, took off. It was meant in part to integrate Germany even more tightly into the European framework. Those states wishing to join the monetary union had to meet a number of fiscal criteria, among them low inflation, budget deficits no more than 3 percent of Gross Domestic Product (GDP), and a debt less than 60 percent of GDP. Progress toward these and other goals slowed in 1992–1993 as a result of an economic slowdown. To a large extent, the slowdown reflected soaring interest rates caused by Germany borrowing heavily to fund the reconstruction of the former East Germany. Europe began to pull out of the recession in 1994 and in December 1995 the Euro was created. In 1998, 11 of the then 15 members (Austria, Sweden, and Finland had joined in 1995) met the criteria for monetary union. Denmark, Sweden, and Britain had opted out and Greece failed to meet the criteria. In June 1998, the European Central Bank began operation. In 1999, the EU began using the Euro in business transactions and finally, on 1 January 2002, the Euro became the sole currency of 12 EU states (Greece having qualified for membership in 2001). Most of the widening would come in the first decade of the new century.

United States Foreign Policy and Europe in the 1990s

As discussed above, the United States played important roles in European affairs in the aftermath of the revolutions of 1989. President George H. W. Bush was instrumental in bringing about the reunification of Germany. The United States also closely monitored the events that followed the disintegration of the Soviet Union and attempted in various ways to assist a transition to a market economy and a democratic political system, for the most part with little success. Additionally, with NATO, the United States made various efforts to intervene in the civil war in Yugoslavia, particularly in the case of Bosnia and Herzegovina and, later, that of Kosovo.

The most consequential action of the United States, which seemed in the 1990s to have become a single major power in the world, involved the apparently brilliantly successful campaign in 1991 against Saddam Hussein (1937–2006) and Iraq to liberate the small oil-rich state of Kuwait.

After Iraq easily conquered and annexed Kuwait, the United Nations condemned Iraqi actions. Margaret Thatcher played an important role in moving George H. W. Bush to the idea of using military force to deal with the annexation of Kuwait by Iraq. The United States furnished most of the military forces, but the British fielded a sizable contingent and there were French troops as well. The Italians sent several planes. Germany and Japan contributed funding. Other European members of the coalition included the Netherlands, Sweden, Spain, Belgium, Poland, Norway, Czechoslovakia, Greece, Denmark, and Hungary. Neither the Soviet Union nor the People's Republic of China raised objections.

While the liberation of Kuwait seemed to be a successful coordination of political and military power and a potential beginning for a new world order, there were underlying problems that would surface in the next decade. One was the continuing suspicion that Saddam Hussein possessed or was developing Weapons of Mass Destruction (WMD), particularly chemical but possibly also nuclear. In addition, in conjunction with the campaign against Iraq, American troops were stationed in Saudi Arabia as part of an effort to protect that country from the possibility of invasion by Iraq. This appeared to many followers of Islam as an affront in that Saudi Arabia was the location of the two holiest sites of Islam, Mecca and Medina. At the time, however, neither of these problems seemed to have much importance for European interests or even for American interests.

One problem that concerned many Europeans and others around the world was what might happen in the transition from 31 December 1999 to 1 January 2000 with computers. As the new century dawned would computers continue to function? While computers recognized 98 as 1998, what would they do with 00, interpret it as 1900? If computers failed, there was the potential for widespread chaos on and following 1 January 2000. In Europe, the European Commission, the executive of the EU, reported that efforts to solve the Y2K (Year 2000) problem were insufficient in many EU countries. Similar warnings came out in the United States and other countries. For that reason, on New Year's Eve 1999, people anticipating a new year, a new century, and a new millennium were perhaps a bit more anxious than usual.

Reference

Kershaw, Ian. (2018). *The Global Age: Europe 1950–2017*. New York: Viking.

12

Terrorism, Economic Turmoil, Pandemic, Invasion, 2000 to the Present

Twentieth-Century Europe: 1900 to the Present, Fourth Edition.
Michael D. Richards and Paul R. Waibel.

Chronology

2001	Al-Qaeda attacks the World Trade Center in New York and the Pentagon in Washington, DC, with hijacked commercial airliners
	The United States, its NATO allies, and Afghan warlords defeat the Taliban in Afghanistan but fail to capture Osama bin Laden
2003	The United States invades Iraq
	Rose Revolution in Georgia
2004	Commuter train bombing in Madrid
	Orange Revolution in Ukraine
	Bulgaria, Estonia, Latvia, Lithuania, Romania, Slovakia, and Slovenia join NATO
2005	Suicide bombings on three trains in the Underground and a double-decker bus in London
	Grand Coalition of Christian Democrats/Christian Social Union and Social Democrats formed with Angela Merkel as chancellor
	Law and Justice Party (PiS) wins both the parliamentary and the presidential elections in Poland
2008	War between the Russian Republic and Georgia
2009	Treaty of Lisbon (EU) goes into effect
2010	Smolensk air disaster in which the Polish President Lech Kaczyński and other prominent government and military officials die
	Viktor Orbán and Fidesz score an overwhelming victory in the Hungarian elections
2011	Arab Spring popular uprisings in Tunisia, Egypt, Libya, Syria
2012	François Hollande elected president of France
2014	Declaration of an Islamic Caliphate by the Islamic State of Iraq and Syria (ISIS) or Daesh
	Protests in Kiev, Ukraine, lead to the president fleeing the country
	Russia occupies Crimea and aids Ukrainian rebels in the Donbas region of Ukraine
2015	SYRIZA wins the election in Greece

	Joint Comprehensive Plan of Action (JCPOA) limits Iran's nuclear activities
	Terrorist attacks in Paris
2016	Referendum on leaving the EU held in Britain; Leave wins
	Theresa May replaces David Cameron as Prime Minister
	Terrorist attacks in France, Belgium, and Germany
2017	Terrorist attacks in Britain
	Defeat of ISIS by the Syrian Democratic Forces (SDF)
	Emmanuel Macron elected president of France
2019	Boris Johnson replaces Theresa May as Prime Minister
2020	First cases of Covid-19 in northern Italy
	Britain leaves the EU
2021	Social Democrats form a coalition government with the Green Party and the Free Democrats in Germany
2022	Russia invades Ukraine
	Fidesz wins election against the United for Hungary coalition
	Emmanuel Macron re-elected president of France but loses his majority in the National Assembly
	Boris Johnson replaced as Prime Minister by Liz Truss who in turn is replaced after only a month by Rishi Sunak
	Right-wing alliance led by Brothers of Italy wins the Italian elections and Giorgia Meloni becomes Prime Minister

Angela Merkel, chancellor of Germany from 2005 to 2021. Frederic Legrand – COMEO / Shutterstock.com.

The weather along the Eastern Seaboard of the United States on 11 September 2001, a Tuesday, was unusual. The term used by meteorologists was a "severe clear," cloudless skies that were strikingly blue (Graff 2019, p. 9). Four flights were hijacked that morning, two leaving Boston's Logan Airport for Los Angeles, another leaving Reagan National Airport for Los Angeles, and fourth leaving Newark International Airport for San Francisco. One of the flights from Boston crashed into the North Tower of the World Trade Center; the other crashed into the South Tower. Each was loaded with thousands of gallons of aviation fuel that started massive fires. The flight leaving Reagan National Airport hit the Pentagon. Passengers on the flight from Newark had heard that airlines were hitting buildings and organized an attack on the hijackers of their plane. In the struggle that followed, the hijacker piloting the plane lost control and the plane crashed into a field near Shanksville, Pennsylvania. Nearly three thousand people died that day. That evening, President George W. Bush (1946–) addressed a stunned nation and noted that "We will make no distinction between the terrorists who committed these acts and those who harbor them." (Graff 2019, p. 374)

It was quickly determined that Osama bin Laden (1955–2011) and Al-Qaeda (The Base) were responsible for the attacks. Bin Laden, member of a wealthy Saudi Arabian family, had been involved in the struggle of the *Mujahideen* against the Soviet Union in Afghanistan (1979–1989). Concerned in the 1990s about perceived threats to Islam, he had formed Al-Qaeda and staged a series of attacks on American embassies in Africa in 1998 and on the USS *Cole* in Yemen's Aden Harbor in 2000. Bin Laden saw the United States as the main obstacle preventing *jihadis* from toppling autocratic regimes in Muslim states in the Near East. He believed the 9/11 attack would "destroy the myth of American invincibility" (Lahoud 2021, p. 12).

When the Taliban government in Afghanistan refused to surrender Bin Laden and his associates, the United States invaded Afghanistan in a campaign to destroy Al-Qaeda and remove the Taliban from power. The United States was assisted by Afghan groups already fighting the Taliban and also by NATO. Article 5 of the NATO treaty, which stated that an attack on one member would be considered an attack on all members and result in a collective response, was invoked for the first time. The Taliban were quickly defeated but Osama bin Laden escaped capture.

The United States and NATO remained in Afghanistan until finally withdrawing in 2021. Although it and its NATO allies tried to introduce political democracy and social, economic, and cultural change to Afghanistan, the Taliban not only survived but began to regain control in various parts of the country. In part, the United States was distracted by its involvement in the invasion of Iraq. Additionally, Afghanistan was plagued by an enormous amount of corruption. Many Afghans wanted to create a democratic political system and capitalist economy. They also, particularly women, appreciated the new opportunities for education. But many were indifferent or actively hostile to change. Negotiations during the administration of President Donald J. Trump (1946–) with the Taliban to set terms for the withdrawal of NATO and American troops were supposed to be followed by negotiations between the Taliban and the Afghan government, but this did not happen. Instead in 2021, the Taliban overwhelmed the Afghan national government and regained control of the country.

In part, Afghanistan was neglected at a crucial point due to a somewhat quixotic decision to invade Iraq in 2003. Some within the American government advocated a nation-building approach to the Middle East. There is also the possibility that the CIA (Central Intelligence Agency), having failed to prevent the 9/11 terrorist attack, did not want a second intelligence failure and pushed for invasion because there was a possibility that Iraq possessed weapons of mass destruction (WMDs). In any case, Secretary of State Colin Powell (1937–2021), one of the most respected members of the Bush Administration, was persuaded that there was evidence of Iraq's possession of WMDs. His speech to the United Nations laying out this evidence convinced many that an invasion was necessary.

The invasion of Iraq began on 20 March 2003. It was primarily an American venture with some support from the United Kingdom. The Iraqi forces were quickly defeated and President Saddam Hussein (1937–2006) was captured. He was tried for crimes against humanity by the Interim Iraqi Government, convicted, sentenced to death, and executed on 30 December 2006.

No evidence of WMDs was ever found and it became clear that Saddam Hussein had not been involved in the terrorist attacks on 9/11. In the meantime, the Coalition Provisional Authority issued two fateful orders: all Baath Party members (the ruling party under Saddam Hussein) were barred from holding political office, and the Iraqi Army was disbanded. Civil war soon followed.

By 2006, the United States faced both organized opposition to its control of the country and civil war between Sunni and Shiite factions. That year the Bush administration began "the Surge," the introduction of a large number of American troops in order to regain control of the country and end sectarian violence. This resulted in some progress in preparing Iraq to regain sovereignty. In 2010, the United States made an agreement with the newly elected Iraqi government to end the occupation. In 2011, the first chapter of the war on terror ended when a small US force raided Bin Laden's compound in Pakistan and killed him. He was buried at sea.

European Politics in the First Decade of the New Century

Two major trends in European politics appeared during the new century's first decade. One was a noticeable shift to the right. Communism was no longer an important political perspective. Even in a country such as the People's Republic of China, the political, economic, and social systems bore little resemblance to the classical Soviet model. Social Democracy also struggled to maintain a significant role in politics. A second major trend was the rise of prominence of a number of new political figures. Almost all the major figures in the events of 1989 and the 1990s were gone, the last was Václav Havel, whose second term as president of the Czech Republic ended 2 February 2003.

The brightest new star in European politics early in the new century was Tony Blair, leader of the Labour Party and Prime Minister in the United Kingdom from 1997 to 2007. His centrist policies were referred to as the "New Labour" and involved moving away from Labour's traditional emphasis on Social Democracy to a kind of liberal economics. Some characterized it as "Thatcherism with a human face" (Kershaw 2018, p. 470), a reference to the policies of Margaret Thatcher, Prime Minister between 1979 and 1990.

Important steps during the time Blair was Prime Minister included the Good Friday Agreement of April 1998, which resolved the long-standing crisis between Republicans and Unionists in Northern Ireland. Blair was able to build on the earlier work of John Major, his predecessor as Prime Minister. Also important was the transfer of significant governmental power in 1998 to Scotland and Wales. Blair, however, could not escape criticism for his support of the United States in Iraq and terrorist attacks in London in July 2005 called attention to the dangers created by the American campaign in Iraq. Under pressure to resign from within the Labour Party, Blair finally did so in July 2007.

In Germany, Gerhard Schröder (1944–) ended Helmut Kohl's long run of electoral success in 1998 and formed a coalition of Social Democrats and Greens. Although his policies were somewhat controversial, they have been given credit for Germany's relatively strong showing after the economic recession in 2008. Initially,

Vladimir Putin, President of the Russian Republic since 2000 with the exception of one term when he was prime minister. Sovfoto / Universal Images Group / Shutterstock.

Schröder supported the United States after 9/11. German troops fought alongside American troops in Afghanistan – the first German soldiers used in combat operations since World War II. He did not support the American invasion of Iraq in 2003. After serving as chancellor, Schröder worked in various capacities for Russian-owned energy companies. He took a generally pro-Russian line in foreign policy issues and was strongly criticized for not breaking with Putin and Russia after the Russian invasion of Ukraine in 2022.

The German elections of 2005 led to a Grand Coalition of the Christian Democratic Union/Christian Social Union (CDU/CSU) and the Social Democratic Party. Angela Merkel prevailed in the contest for the position of chancellor. In the 2009 elections, the CDU/CSU gained enough votes to form a coalition with the Free Democratic Party (FDP).

Merkel over the next few years developed into Europe's most prominent political figure. Although born in West Germany, she moved with her family to East Germany. She earned a doctorate in quantum chemistry in 1986 and worked as a research scientist until 1989. Elected to the *Bundestag* in 1989, she rose through the ranks of the CDU, becoming General Secretary in 1998. Often compared to Margaret Thatcher, who also was a chemist, she established a reputation for making tough decisions and is regarded by many as the most consequential European political figure of the early twenty-first century.

The 2002 presidential election in France did not turn out as expected. The incumbent president, Jacques Chirac, and the prime minister, Lionel Jospin (1937–), had been governing as members of opposing parties rather than as part of a coalition. Jospin was eliminated in the first round, leaving Chirac to face Jean-Marie Le Pen, the far-right National Front leader. Le Pen had been gaining attention through his nationalist and antisemitic views. Chirac won the second round easily, but this was an indication that right-wing politics were emerging as a significant factor in European politics.

In 2005 the center-right Law and Justice (PiS) won both the parliamentary elections and the presidency in Poland. The new president, Lech Kaczyński (1949–2010) and his twin brother, Jarosław Kaczyński (1949–) were founders of Law and Justice. In 2010, Poland was shocked by the Smolensk air disaster in which the airplane carrying the president and other political and military officials crashed on the approach to the airport in a dense fog. The airplane was on its way to a commemoration of the 70th anniversary of the Katyn massacre (1940). The Soviet Union's NKVD (secret police) had executed more than twenty thousand Polish officers and members of the intelligentsia early in World War II. An investigation of the crash determined that it was pilot error compounded by the president and others insisting the pilot try to land despite the fog.

Hungary joined NATO in 1999 and, despite problems with government deficits, was able to join the EU in 2004. During much of this period, the prime minister was Viktor Orbán (1963–). Orbán was the founder of Fidesz, originally a center-right, pro-European party. Over the years, it moved toward right-wing nationalistic populism. In 2002, Fidesz lost to the Hungarian Socialist Party (MSzP). The Socialist Party had difficulty controlling the government deficit, which led to austerity measures to meet the EU's economic criteria. In the elections in 2010, Orbán and Fidesz scored an overwhelming victory.

Color Revolutions

The initial color revolution[1] was the Rose Revolution in Georgia. In 2003, it resulted in Eduard Shevardnadze (1928–2014), who had been foreign minister under Gorbachev in the Soviet Union, being replaced by Mikheil Saakashvili (1967–). Saakashvili had a law degree from Columbia University and embraced free-market reform. While some changes were made, corruption continued to be a problem. Attempts in 2008 to bring South Ossetiya more firmly under the control of the Georgian government led to the Georgian military shelling the district's capital. Russia, which had been encouraging South Ossetiya to govern itself without reference to Georgia, invaded Georgia and easily overwhelmed its military. Russia also

1 "Color revolution" is a term applied to a number of popular movements in the twenty-first century. While there is some question as to which movements to include, the Rose Revolution in Georgia, the Orange Revolution in Ukraine, and the Tulip Revolution in Kyrgyzstan are generally accepted as the most important.

took over another, larger district, Abkhaziya, and recognized it and South Ossetiya as sovereign states. Altogether, Georgia lost a fifth of its territory and most of its Black Sea coastline.

The next color revolution was far more consequential. In the presidential elections of 2004 in Ukraine, the Prime Minister, Viktor Yanukovych (1950–), strongly supported by Russian President Vladimir Putin (1952–), seemingly won the runoff against Viktor Yushchenko (1950–). Yushchenko had survived an apparent assassination attempt in 2004 when he ingested the dioxin TCDD, a contaminant in Agent Orange used by the United States in the Vietnam War. Although the attack disfigured him, he survived. Yushchenko's supporters, clad in orange, staged mass protests against the results of the initial election and the first runoff. In December, the Supreme Court ordered a second runoff, which Yushchenko won.

Yushchenko's presidency was politically chaotic as Ukraine tried simultaneously to maintain good relations with Russia and join the European Union. One of the main issues in Yushchenko's term as president was the hostile relationship between him and Yulia Tymoshenko (1960–). He appointed her Prime Minister but later fired her after corruption claims emerged. When he failed to support Tymoshenko in the 2010 elections, Yanukovych won the runoff.

Putin's Russia

In 1999, Boris Yeltsin, in bad health and having barely survived a move to impeach him, nominated Putin for prime minister. Although Putin was head of the FSB (Federal Security Service, successor to the KGB), he was not seen as a major player in the politics of the Russian Republic. In the 1990s, Putin had benefitted initially from his connection to Anatoly Sobchak (1937–2000), the mayor of St. Petersburg. After Sobchak lost the election in 1996, Putin moved to Moscow, where he began working with Yeltsin, who in 1998 appointed him head of the FSB. Putin had developed ways of making himself indispensable to powerful politicians. Among the traits that enabled him to advance his career was patience, an ability to analyze situations, and plan accordingly, and a willingness to use whatever methods a situation might require. Rumors persisted that he had connections with organized crime in Russia.

At the end of 1999, Yeltsin resigned as president. His retirement package included immunity from prosecution for acts as head of state. He named Putin as acting president and supported him in the presidential election of 2000.

In the meantime, Russia faced the threat of war with Chechnya once more. The Russian army invaded and conquered Chechnya in a particularly brutal campaign that included the almost complete destruction of its capital, Grozny. In the 2000 presidential election, Putin did little campaigning, citing a need to respond to national problems. He gained 53 percent of the vote.

Over his first two terms as president, he used his position to set a national agenda, stressing the need to make Russia a great power once again. Fortunately for him, the Russian economic situation improved considerably as the country was able to take advantage of rising oil prices over most of the decade.

Putin did not establish a dictatorship as such but rather a carefully managed system in which those who bought into the system could maintain or gain wealth and power. Putin moved early on to gain control of the media in Russia, particularly television. He made it clear that the Russian oligarchs could continue to enjoy their great wealth so long as they did not try to exercise independent political power. Putin also cultivated an image of machismo combined with concern for the welfare of his fellow Russians.

An important issue for Putin was the expansion of NATO. Poland and the Czech Republic joined NATO in 1999 in addition to Hungary as noted above. This was after debate within NATO and Russian opposition. A second expansion involved Bulgaria, Estonia, Latvia, Lithuania, Romania, Slovakia, and Slovenia in 2004. Albania and Croatia joined in 2009.

The European Union

Although the possibility of Islamic terrorism continued to haunt Europe in the decade, Europeans not only participated in important domestic political movements, but also paid much attention to the continued economic integration of the continent and to the possibility of extending the benefits of capitalism to former members of the Soviet bloc. In 2004, the EU took in 10 new members: Cyprus, the Czech Republic, Estonia, Hungary, Latvia, Lithuania, Malta, Poland, Slovakia, and Slovenia. Bulgaria and Romania joined in 2007. Croatia joined in 2013. Although a member of NATO, Turkey remained in limbo during this period.

In 2004, the European Union presented a constitution that, had it been approved, would have resulted in a more centralized federal system. The proposed constitution failed, however, to gain the

Table 12.1 European Community/European Union

1957	The Treaty of Rome created the European Economic Community (EEC), signed by the original six member nations: Belgium, Federal Republic of Germany, France, Italy, Luxembourg, and the Netherlands
1967	EEC merged with the European Coal and Steel Community (1951) and EURATOM (1957) to become the European Community (EC)
1973	Denmark, Republic of Ireland, and United Kingdom joined the EC
1981	Greece joined
1986	Portugal and Spain joined. Single European Act passed
1992	The Treaty on the European Union (Maastricht Treaty) called for movement toward economic and monetary union and intergovernmental cooperation in some areas
1993	EU formally in existence
1995	Austria, Finland, and Sweden joined the EU
1999	Euro introduced for business transactions
2002	Euro became the sole currency of 12 of the 15 members of the EU (Denmark, Sweden, and the United Kingdom opted out of the monetary union)
2004	Ten new members joined: Cyprus, the Czech Republic, Estonia, Hungary, Latvia, Lithuania, Malta, Poland, Slovakia, and Slovenia
2007	Bulgaria and Romania join the EU
2009	Treaty of Lisbon goes into effect
2010	Problems with the Greek economy lead to a crisis of the Euro
2013	Croatia joined the EU

unanimous support required for it to take effect. Although there were clear benefits to be had in a more unified organization, these were weighed against fears of losing national sovereignty. A new Treaty of Lisbon replaced the old draft treaty in 2007. The Treaty of Lisbon kept much of the old treaty but adjusted the political structure to address concerns about national sovereignty. In 2009, all the EU states ratified the Treaty of Lisbon, and it went into effect. By that time, however, the Greek debt crisis was threatening to destroy the Eurozone and all that had been done to integrate the European economy (Table 12.1).

Economic Globalization

The European Union was taking shape within a global economy that developed rapidly in the first decade of the twenty-first century. Much attention was focused on the rise of the Chinese Communist economy. This began after the death of Mao Zedong in 1976 and the rise to supreme power of Deng Xiaoping (1904–1997). Under Deng, China instituted a series of market-based reforms while the Chinese Communist Party (CCP) retained a monopoly of political power. Although Deng and the CCP used the military to crack down on protests in Tiananmen Square in 1989, the economic and social reforms continued through the 1990s. Communist China joined the World Trade Organization (WTO) in 1999 and by 2010 was a major economic player. It enjoyed a substantial trade surplus and used it to purchase United States Treasury bonds, making many American economists somewhat nervous.

What was overlooked in this period was the amount of capital flowing back and forth between the United States and Europe. It dwarfed the amount flowing back and forth between the United States, Asia, and the Pacific rim. "The central axis of world finance was not Asian-American but Euro-American." (Tooze 2018, p. 79; see also the diagram on p. 78.) This reality would have enormous consequences for the outcome of the global economic collapse of 2008.

The Global Economic Collapse of 2008

The global economy had already experienced severe challenges in the late 1990s and the early part of the new century's first decade. However, these challenges paled compared to the economic collapse of 2008, one caused by fundamental flaws in the American mortgage system and securities based on mortgages. Simply put, it became clear by 2007 and 2008 that a large number of mortgages issued by American banks, both big and small, should never have been offered in the first place. With little or no down payment required, the loans were provided to people who simply lacked the income to pay their mortgage payments once the dramatically higher interest rates replaced the initially low interest rates on so-called ARMs (adjustable-rate mortgages). Large American banks and investment houses bundled these unsound mortgages with other, sounder mortgages and then offered them as the basis of securities they marketed and sold as highly secure financial products, thus further complicating the problem. The fact that financial rating firms generally failed to rate the new products accurately presented an additional problem.

As the housing market in the United States slowed, and investors found it increasingly difficult to "flip" houses, that is, sell them to other investors for a profit shortly after purchasing them, the number of foreclosures began to climb, then to spike. The United States housing bubble burst. Companies and individuals who held large quantities of securities based on bad mortgages began to lose large sums of money. Early in 2008, one major investment house collapsed. Another was sold at a great loss. Finally, the American government made the unprecedented decision to bail out several large banks and other financial institutions.

How to deal with the economic collapse was not simply an American question. Given the extent of integration in the Atlantic financial economy, the economic collapse of 2008 was not merely an American problem but one faced also by most European economies. To a large extent, the American approach, the Troubled Assets Relief Program (TARP), became a means of injecting capital into failing banks. On 13 October 2008, nine major American banks were required to take an injection of capital from the government in return for a Federal Deposit Insurance Corporation (FDIC) guarantee. In effect, the American government was buying shares in the banks.

The European approach was largely piecemeal. From the start, Germany resisted the American approach to the financial crisis. Although the French finance minister Christine Lagarde (1956–) suggested joint measures and French President Nicolas Sarkozy (1955–) invited the leaders of Germany, Italy, and the United Kingdom to meet with him in October, nothing came of it. The United Kingdom faced with the collapse of two major banks, moved on its own to deal with the crisis by offering guarantees and a recapitalization plan. The stronger banks opted out of the government offers, but the crisis was nonetheless averted. Other countries took similar paths, but there was no concerted effort. Each county put together its own program of guarantees and recapitalization schemes. The EU did not attempt to construct a standard program.

One little known aspect of the economic collapse of 2008 came from the European banks need for US dollar funding. The Federal Reserve's policy of Quantitative Easing, the buying of mortgage-backed securities, involved both American and foreign banks. Of the latter, a very large number were European banks. As one commentator observed, "What the Fed was struggling to contain in 2008 were not two separate American and European crises but one gigantic storm in the dollar-based North Atlantic financial system." (Tooze 2018, pp. 217–218).

At the end of the first decade of the twenty-first century, Europe found itself not only in an economic storm that had an American center and North Atlantic connections but also home-grown economic and political weaknesses that would prove difficult to master.

The European Union and the Sovereign Debt Crisis

The sovereign debt crisis of the Eurozone, those countries that adopted the Euro as the official currency, was largely a product of governmental mismanagement in an economic environment shaped by the introduction of the Euro in the EU. The difficulty in dealing with the crisis was that although Eurozone countries had economies that differed greatly in terms of size and structure, they used a common currency. When the public debt level of several countries grew well beyond the guidelines of 60 percent of gross domestic product (GDP), those countries were limited in how they could respond by the use of a common currency. They could not devalue their currency to make their exports cheaper and more attractive. At the same time, the EU lacked an institutional structure that could respond to the economic problems of an individual country. Nor, given its cumbersome bureaucracy, could it respond rapidly. In addition, individual countries such as Germany or the Netherlands hesitated to take measures which might mean their citizens would have to contribute funds to deal with problems in other countries. The countries experiencing the most difficulty by 2010, the so-called PIGS (Portugal, Italy, Greece, and Spain), represented a small percentage of the GDP of the Eurozone, but, even so, their problems threatened the financial stability of the entire Eurozone.

Greece and the Sovereign Debt Crisis

Greece experienced the most painful of all the processes of near-default by a government followed by austerity programs connected to loans meant to provide time for the economy to recover, then an even more draconian austerity program and a new set of loans. To some extent, Greece had created the problem with a bloated government and a pension system that allowed many Greeks to retire early. Tax avoidance and benefit fraud were also rampant.

Successive elections brought governments that were further and further to the left. In 2012, the election resulted in a coalition government led by the conservative New Democracy (ND). SYRIZA, a center-left, left party led by Alexis Tsipras (1974–) and PASOK, the social-democratic party, were also involved. Austerity measures were introduced in 2013 and the government appeared to be making progress, but the elections in 2015 brought SYRIZA to power. Tsipras had campaigned to reject a third bailout. Although a referendum in July 2015 resulted in voters turning it down, Tsipras reversed his previous position and reluctantly accepted the third bailout. In August, he resigned and called a snap election. That election gave him and SYRIZA a vote of confidence and the opportunity to form a new coalition government.

In August 2018, Greece officially stated that Greece had regained its sovereignty and would now determine its own destiny. That ended the austerity programs and bail-out loans. The next year SYRIZA was defeated in the 2019 legislative elections and replaced by New Democracy. The Sovereign Debt Crisis was replaced by the Covid-19 crisis and, for Greece, the ongoing influx of immigrants from Syria and other locations.

Politics Elsewhere in Europe

Italy introduced an austerity program in 2011 that was not successful. A so-called "technocratic" government under Mario Monti (1943–), a financial expert, introduced additional spending cuts and tax increases that led to mass protests. Elections in 2013 produced a coalition government and a new protest party led by Beppe Grillo (1948–), a comedian-turned activist. His Five Star Movement gained a quarter of the vote. Silvio Berlusconi's party gained nearly a third of the seats in the two chambers of the parliament. Berlusconi, however, came to the end of his political career with a conviction of tax fraud in 2013. Because of his age, 75 at the time, he did not go to prison but was barred from public office.

In 2014, Matteo Renzi (1975–), the New Democratic Party leader, formed a left–right coalition and announced plans for major economic and political reform. In November 2016, his reform package was rejected and he resigned. Over the next few years, successive governments were unable to avoid recession, austerity programs, and loan packages. In 2021, Mario Draghi (1947–), an economist and the widely respected president of the European Central Bank from 2011 to 2019, formed a national unity government to deal with the Covid-19 crisis. Although very popular in Italy, he was unable to overcome Italy's fractious politics and resigned as prime minister in 2022.

Elections in Italy in 2022 resulted in the victory of a right-wing alliance featuring the Brothers of Italy (FdI) led by Giorgia Meloni (1977–). The victory of the alliance demonstrated the importance of electoral coalitions in Italian politics. The center-left Democratic Party (PD) rejected links to some of the major parties on the left. Meloni was named to lead the new coalition government. She will need to satisfy her constituents while avoiding problems with the European Union. Italy will need to continue to secure pandemic recovery funds from the EU. She has consulted with the former prime minister, Mario Draghi, and seems inclined to follow his lead. Some are concerned that the Brothers of Italy is descended from a postwar neo-fascist group, but many believe this will have little impact on Meloni's tenure as prime minister.

The French economy struggled after the 2008 economic meltdown with rising unemployment and public debt, trade deficits, and low growth. However, it escaped the severe economic downturns experienced by the PIGS and, along with Germany, played a key role in attempting to deal with the sovereign debt crisis. In the 2012 presidential election, Nicholas Sarkozy (1955–) was defeated after a single term. The new president was François Hollande (1954–). Although there was some optimism initially that Hollande and the Socialists would be able to revive the French economy, none of his measures helped, not even a move toward a more business-friendly approach. In 2016, he announced he would not stand for re-election. His approval rating in that year was 4 percent, a record low.

The presidential election of 2017 featured two unusual candidates. One was Marine Le Pen (1968–), leader of the National Rally (formerly known as the National Front). Her father, Jean-Marie Le Pen, had founded the National Front and had a neo-fascist orientation and a reputation for antisemitism. Marine Le Pen succeeded in softening the image of the National Rally by expelling members accused of racism or antisemitism. She remained, however, an opponent of NATO and American influence. She also opposed globalization and regarded multiculturism as a failure. In particular, she was concerned about the influence of Islam in France.

The other candidate, Emmanuel Macron (1977–), was if anything even more unusual. He had served as Minister of the Economy,

Industry, and Digital Affairs under Hollande. After resigning from the cabinet in 2016, he had founded La Republique En March!. This was a left-center party, neither Gaullist nor Socialist.

In the second round of voting, Macron won with 66.1 percent of the vote. A month later, his party gained a majority in the National Assembly. At age 39, he became the youngest president in French history.

Opposition to Macron's labor law and taxation reforms culminated in 2018 in the so-called yellow vest movement. This began as a protest against a proposed fuel tax but later included protests against austerity measures, globalization, neo-liberalism, and immigration. Trade unions and other groups also organized protests throughout his first term in office.

The French presidential elections in April 2022 resulted in a second round with Macron once again facing Marine Le Pen. He won election with 58.5 percent of the votes to Le Pen's 41.5 percent. He was, however, not able to maintain the majority he had enjoyed in the National Assembly. Macron is often seen as remote and a president of the elites even though the average voter's economic situation improved under him. He also played a largely effective role in combatting the economic effects of Covid-19, both for businesses and for households.

Also consequential were the German elections on 26 September 2021. The Social Democrats won 206 seats and took the lead in forming a coalition with the Green Party and the Free Democrats, the so-called "stoplight coalition" after the colors of the coalition partners. Olaf Scholz (1958–), a Social Democrat who had served as Vice Chancellor and Federal Minister of Finance under Angela Merkel, became Chancellor. The opposition Christian Democrats had their worst election results ever. Some attributed this to a belief that no one could take the place of Merkel. In addition, several leading Christian Democrats were involved in corruption scandals. The Greens had their best results and the Free Democrats their second-best showing.

Scholz was tested early by the Russian invasion of Ukraine. He has performed better than many had expected, unhesitatingly halting the approval of Nord Stream 2, a set of offshore natural gas pipelines running under the Baltic Sea from Russia to Germany. He also reversed Germany's military and foreign policies by shipping weapons to Ukraine and increasing Germany's defense budget. While generally supportive of Ukraine, he has drawn criticism for being slow to send weapons to Ukraine and also criticized for measures meant to help Germans escape some of the worst aspects of energy shortages in the winter of 2023. Some European countries wondered whether Germany was doing all it could to share the burden of energy shortages.

The Hungarian parliamentary elections on 3 April 2022 drew a great deal of attention. It seemed possible that Viktor Orbán, the leader of Fidesz (Hungarian Civil Alliance) and Hungary's prime minister since 2010 might lose to the election to the United for Hungary opposition coalition. Instead, Fidesz won handily. Orbán is probably the best example of the new autocrat, one who remakes the electoral system to his advantage and uses the media and the courts to reinforce his power. Instead of terror and a police state, Orbán appeals to a kind of populist nationalism. His administration can also be seen as a kind of kleptocracy, a system in which friends and supporters of Orbán and Fidesz are favored in the distribution of governmental expenditures. Similar systems exist in Poland, Belarus, the Russian Republic, and Kazakhstan.

The Arab Spring and ISIS

At the same time European states were attempting to deal with the economic meltdown of 2008 and the sovereign debt crisis of the Euro Zone, events in the Near East and northern Africa raised hopes and created crises that caused much of Europe and the United States to undertake emergency actions.

The "Arab Spring" in 2011 featured popular uprisings that challenged authoritarian rule. It began in Tunisia, but the movement quickly spread to Egypt, Syria, and Libya. The gatherings in Tahir Square (Liberation Square) in Cairo, Egypt, were the best-known episodes. They resulted in the toppling of President Hosni Mubarak (1928–2020) and subsequently the election of Mohamed Morsi

(1951–2019) as president. In 2013, however, Morsi was removed as president and replaced by General Abdul Fatah al-Sisi (1954–), who established a military dictatorship.

Far more consequential than events in Tunisia or Egypt was the course of the Arab Spring in Syria. In that country, huge protests took place against the rule of President Bashar Hafez al-Assad (1965–). Assad had succeeded his father as head of state in 2000. The Protests led to a brutal crackdown and a civil war that internally displaced millions of Syrians and caused millions more to migrate to other countries.

In Libya, Muammar Muhammad Abu Minyar al-Gaddafi (c. 1942–2011) tried to stop protests against the government. In March, the United Nations Security Council declared a no-fly zone to protect civilians in the rebel-held area. France, which had a long history of countering Libyan influence in Western Africa, was particularly keen to intervene in 2011. The result was the death of Gaddafi and the descent of Libya into chaos.

As noted, events in Syria led to millions of Syrians fleeing to other countries, particularly Jordan and Turkey. For many, the goal was to reach Europe. Libya, after the death of Gaddafi, became a country that offered people from other parts of Africa another possibility of reaching Europe. The expansion of the Islamic State of Iraq and Syria (ISIS) or Daesh added to the flow of migrants.

By 2015, the movement of migrants through Turkey and Libya, principally to Greece and Italy, had become a humanitarian disaster and a crisis for European governments. More than 3,600 migrants drowned in 2015 attempting to reach Italy or Greece. As hundreds of thousands of migrants moved north, hoping to reach Germany or Sweden, countries along the way attempted to block them. Hungary constructed a high fence along its border with Serbia and blocked its border with Croatia. This was exactly the opposite of its reaction in 1989 to East Germans attempting to flee their country by crossing the Hungarian border into Austria. In a remarkable and also controversial gesture, Angela Merkel, the German chancellor, and Werner Faymann (1960–), chancellor of Austria, announced they would accept refugees in their countries. Merkel was criticized by other government leaders and some in Germany for her unilateral initiative.

Not surprisingly, as difficulties in resettling thousands of refugees became apparent, the initial enthusiasm of many cooled. An incident in Cologne on New Year's Eve in which some young men, some of them refugees from Syria, Iran, and Afghanistan, molested women, helped to create a growing hostility on the right toward refugees. The EU attempted to establish a quota system for the distribution of refugees, but Hungary, Poland, Slovakia, and the Czech Republic refused to cooperate. Eventually, the EU made a deal with Recep Tayyip Erdoğan (1954–), the president of Turkey, under which Turkey would accept migrants sent back by the EU and do everything possible to block sea or land routes to Europe. In return, Turkey would receive three billion Euros, and steps would be taken to grant Turkey eventual membership in the EU. Another three billion Euros were to be provided at the end of 2018.

Many of the refugees attempting to reach Europe were fleeing ISIS, which by 2014 had conquered large areas in Iraq and Syria and had announced the founding of a caliphate. ISIS, led by Abu Bakr al-Baghdadi (1971–2019) established an especially brutal regime featuring beheadings and other even more horrific means of execution. The United States backed the Syrian Democratic Force (SDF), largely composed of Kurds from Syria and Turkey, in a campaign against ISIS that captured Raqqa, the capital of the caliphate, in 2019. Baghdadi was hunted down later that year and committed suicide rather than be captured. Unfortunately for the SDF, the administration of President Donald Trump (1946–), withdrew American forces, leaving the SDF exposed to Turkish military that had in the meantime entered Syria.

There was little coordination between ISIS and Muslim terrorists living in Europe. While some had taken part in the caliphate, most were home-grown, radicalized by their European experiences. Nonetheless, the justification for acts of terrorism was the requirement that "believers" struggle against the "godless," i.e., non-Muslim.

Many of the worst attacks occurred in France. This is due in part to lasting scars from the Algerian Rebellion, but it was also due to the refusal of France to try a multicultural approach. One was supposed to adhere to the secularized values of the French Republic. One particular instance was a 2011 ban on women covering their faces in public. Of importance, too, living conditions in the *banlieues* (suburbs) of Paris and other big cities and the racism of many French created resentment.

The initial act of terrorism took place 7 January 2015, when two Al-Qaeda gunmen, children of Algerian immigrant parents, killed twelve staff members of the satirical magazine *Charlie Hebdo*. On the evening of 13 November 2015, coordinated attacks killed 140 and injured hundreds more in cafes and restaurants and at a rock concert. The following year, on Bastille Day, a truck mowed down a crowd walking in Nice, killing 86 and injuring more than 400.

Brussels, Belgium, suffered attacks on 22 March 2016 at the airport and an Underground Station that left 32 dead and 340 injured. At a Christmas market in 2016 in Berlin, 12 people were killed in an attack. In Britain, on 22 March 2017, a car attack killed five people and injured 50 more. On 22 May 2017, a suicide bomber killed 22 people and injured 59 others at the end of a pop concert in Manchester.

To some extent, the wave of attacks between 2015 and 2017 reflected the immense publicity given to the caliphate. However, in the internet age, people could be radicalized without ever having direct contact with terrorists.

Two important consequences of the migrant crisis and the threat of terrorism can be seen in the intensified security measures and diminished civil liberties. An additional consequence was an increase in the influence of the extreme right in politics. The already existing tendency to see western civilization as under siege and in danger of being replaced by Islam and Sharia law gained new life. (Kershaw 2018, pp. 521–522).

Brexit

The 2008 economic meltdown brought the long run of the United Kingdom's Labour Party, in office since 1997, to an end. Labour was blamed for the banking failure and the recession. The general election on 6 May 2010 resulted in defeat and the Labor Prime Minister Gordon Brown (1951–) was replaced by the Conservative David Cameron (1966–). Although his government reduced the budget deficit, government debt continued to rise and reached 87.5 percent of GDP in 2015.

Because Britain was not part of the Eurozone, it could undertake monetary easing. Nonetheless, austerity meant cuts in funding. Even more to the point, the bottom 20 percent of British incomes were far below levels for similar groups in the Netherlands, France, and Germany. The number of homeless increased sharply, as did the use of food banks. The search for scapegoats focused on immigrants and the EU. Many turned toward the United Kingdom Independent Party (UKIP), a nationalistic, anti-globalization party similar to parties in other parts of Europe. As Euroscepticism increased, one crucial issue became reducing immigration from the EU.

David Cameron promised to hold a referendum on Great Britain's membership in the EU if the Conservatives formed a majority government after the election of 2015. After victory in 2015, Cameron thought a referendum was necessary but that he would be able to persuade voters to remain in the EU. The idea was to weaken the Europhobic UKIP. He believed a renegotiation of Great Britain's terms of membership would carry the day. While three-quarters of the House of Commons wanted to remain, Cameron allowed members of his cabinet to support "Leave." Particularly important was the role played by Boris Johnson (1964–), the former mayor of London, who helped move opinion toward "Leave." Some Conservatives emphasized the importance of sovereignty. "Take Back Control" became a powerful argument for leaving. Those who wanted to remain emphasized the negative economic impact of leaving but did little to play up the benefits of remaining.

The results announced on 24 June 2016 were as follows: 51.9 leave and 48.1 remain. Scotland and Northern Ireland voted "remain" and Wales and England voted "leave." Theresa May (1956–), formerly Home Secretary and responsible for immigration, replaced David Cameron as Prime Minister. On 29 March 2017, she formally notified Donald Tusk (1957–), President of the European Council, of Great Britain's intention to leave the EU.

A snap general election the following month produced a minority government of the Conservatives and the Democratic Unionist Party of Northern Ireland. Prime Minister May presented three versions of a draft withdrawal agreement and Parliament rejected all three. In July 2019, she resigned and was replaced by Boris Johnson. After failing to win parliamentary support for a revised Brexit withdrawal agreement, he called a snap election for December 2019. The Conservative Party won 43.6 percent of the vote.

The formal withdrawal of the Great Britain from the EU took place on 31 January 2020. Unfortunately, efforts to deal with the terms of the withdrawal coincided almost exactly with the need to respond to the Covid-19 pandemic which, in turn, was followed by the Russian invasion of Ukraine.

A problematic part of the withdrawal agreement is the "Northern Ireland Protocol." It was intended to avoid a hard land-based customs border between North Ireland and the Republic of Ireland by creating a customs border crossing the Irish Sea that separates the islands of Ireland and Great Britain. The Good Friday Agreement of 1998 had created a special status for border crossings between Ireland and Northern Ireland. They were meant to be largely invisible and no longer a tangible reminder of the thirty-year conflict between Unionists (supportive of a union with the Great Britain) and Republicans (supportive of a United Ireland), which was commonly known as "the Troubles." The Protocol permits goods to move to and from Northern Ireland with either Ireland or Great Britain. Goods moving between Great Britain and Northern Ireland may be subject to duties if they are "at risk" of being eventually sold in the Republic of Ireland, that is, entering the EU's single market. Unionists oppose the Protocol, seeing it as erecting a new border between Northern Ireland and Great Britain. Supposedly this would tilt the future of Northern Ireland to unification with Dublin and Brussels. Republicans welcome closer ties with Ireland, and the cross-community parties, such as the Greens, support the Protocol because they are less focused on the history of the Troubles and more interested in the economic and environmental issues indirectly tied to border issues. There is concern that the issue of the Protocol might eventually lead to the end of the Brexit agreement with the EU or the demise of the Good Friday Agreement, or both, along with the relative peace that Northern Ireland currently enjoys. Early in 2023 Prime Minister Rishi Sunak negotiated what is known as the

"Windsor Framework," modifications of the Northern Ireland Protocol that would decrease the amount of customs checks and paperwork for goods coming across the Irish Sea to Northern Ireland. In theory, it should allow Northern Ireland access to both EU and British markets with relatively few problems.

The British government intended to replace membership in the EU with new trade deals, but progress has been slow in the context of the pandemic and the Russian invasion of Ukraine. Boris Johnson delivered Brexit and managed to survive one vote of no confidence. In July 2022, however, he resigned as leader of the Conservative Party. In the fall, he was replaced as Prime Minister by Liz Truss (1975–). Her initial moves to cut taxes while increasing government spending were widely criticized. After only about a month, she resigned and was replaced by Rishi Sunak (1980–). Sunak's parents were of Indian descent and had migrated to Great Britain from Africa in the 1960s.

Ukraine and Russia

Ukraine's Orange Revolution did not result in the changes supporters had hoped it would. Viktor Yushchenko failed to change Ukraine's politics and economics in any meaningful way. The result was that in 2010, Viktor Yanukovych regained the presidency. In his presidency, corruption grew worse. The oligarchs dominated the economy and politics. Yanukovych, in effect, became just one more oligarch. In 2013, he moved away from the idea of membership in the EU to proposed membership in the Eurasian Customs Union that included Russia, Belarus, and Kazakhstan. This met with widespread protest centered in the Maidan (Independence Square) in Kyiv.[2] On 21 February, 2014, a new provisional government was established. Yanukovych fled by helicopter to Russia.

Putin moved quickly to annex Crimea. It had formally only been a part of Ukraine since 1954. Russians were a majority of the population,

[2] In the following pages, Ukrainian spellings are used. Thus, Kyiv for Kiev, Odesa for Odessa.

and the Russian Black Sea Fleet was anchored there. A request was sent to Russia for protection of Russian citizens in Crimea and in a referendum on 16 March 2014, voters overwhelmingly approved the idea of asking to join Russia. On 18 March, Putin announced the incorporation of Crimea within the Russian Federation.

Sanctions were imposed, including the removal of Russia from the G-8 group. In fact, however, Europe and the United States did little. Russia had clearly violated the Budapest Memorandum on Security Assurances of 1994, in which Ukraine, Belarus, and Kazakhstan gave up nuclear weapons in return for security assurances provided by the Russian Federation, the United Kingdom, and the United States. The unthinkable alternative seemed to be to start a nuclear war.

In the meantime, violent confrontations broke out in eastern and southern Ukraine, where a large percentage of the population was Russian. Some wanted to take the region into Russia. Russia, for its part, supplied weapons and other equipment and sent some paramilitary forces to aid the struggle. Attempts to resolve the conflict had little success. The second Minsk agreement, February 2015, resulted in a ceasefire that somewhat improved the situation. In some ways, Putin's efforts to intimidate Ukraine backfired. Even in eastern and southern Ukraine, a large majority opposed Russian intervention. Intervention actually produced a strengthened Ukrainian nationalism and identification with the West.

On 12 July 2021, Putin published a long polemic, "On the Historical Unity of Russians and Ukrainians." The essay sought to demonstrate that Russians, Ukrainians, and Belarusians are all descended from Kyivan Rus and are bound together by historical experience, culture, and a common religion. The essay also asserted the Ukrainian population was being forced by corrupt elites to take part in an anti-Russian project that worked against Ukrainians best interests. The elites supposedly were drug addicts and neo-Nazis engaged in a genocide of Russians in Ukraine.

In the winter of 2022, Putin assembled large numbers of troops along Russia's border with Ukraine, supposedly for training purposes. Another large contingent came into Belarus supposedly to train with Belarusian troops.

The map provides information on a number of 21st century changes in European geography. The one exception is Kaliningrad, which was a post–World War II change. Merkel. Frederic Legrand – COMEO/Shutterstock.com.

Before 2022, Putin might have been seen as an opportunist, intervening in disputes in Moldova and Georgia and taking advantage of the protest movement in Ukraine to annex territory and support the two breakaway republics in eastern Ukraine. He had also curtailed free speech and opposition organizations in Russia and was widely believed to be conducting a campaign of assassination of political opponents both in Russia and elsewhere in Europe. In addition, Russian agencies under his control were involved in cyber-crime efforts.

The Russian invasion of Ukraine, called by Putin a "special military operation," began 24 February 2022. It was a full-scale invasion meant to take Kyiv quickly, conquer Odesa, and link Crimea with the breakaway republics. Ukrainian resistance was fierce and largely successful. The Russian military's performance was subpar despite efforts after the Russo-Georgian war to reform and strengthen it. Ukraine made good use of equipment supplied by the United States and other NATO countries.

In April 2022, Russian forces broke off the siege of Kyiv and regrouped to the east. After they left the small towns around Kyiv, the Ukrainian military found what it believed to be evidence of war crimes, including torture, rape, and execution of civilians.

The Ukrainian president, Volodymyr Zelenskyy (1978–), played a major role in rallying Ukrainians and provided effective leadership, appearing virtually before various government groups such as the

Volodymyr Zelenskyy. Ukraine Presidents Office / Alamy Stock Photo.

United States House and Senate to appeal for support. Putin, for his part, raised the specter of a third world war and nuclear holocaust.

Why Putin would turn from opportunism to outright aggression is not an easy question to answer. Certainly, he felt Russia's return to its proper role as a great power was long overdue. Observing the United States' failure to manage withdrawal from Afghanistan successfully might have convinced him the United States would not respond effectively or have the support of NATO. Unfortunately, Putin lacks what Nikita Khrushchev had: the ability to recognize that nothing could be worth the risk of nuclear war. Khrushchev, of course, had participated in World War II and had seen what war could do.

One aspect of the Russian invasion is the massive displacement of Ukrainians and a huge flow of refugees to neighboring countries. Some four million left in the first month of the war, about half crossing over into Poland. Poland has responded generously to the sudden influx of hundreds of thousands of Ukrainians. Efforts to welcome Ukrainian refugees were in great contrast to the attempts in 2015 by many EU countries to block the entry of Syrian refugees.

Possibly, the Russian invasion will be similar to its campaign in Afghanistan in the 1980s, extremely costly. This will likely not result in regime change, however. Putin, the oligarchs, the security apparatus, and the military have effectively neutered almost all opposition.

The war is clearly a disaster for Ukraine. Were the war to end in the near future, the numbers of dead and wounded, the millions of refugees, and the destruction of buildings and infrastructure would create a situation that would take huge amounts of money and time to overcome. This will require a major response from the EU, the United States, and other countries.

Europe and the Trump Administration

During the Obama administration, Europeans had been involved with American foreign policy primarily through NATO's collaboration with American efforts in Afghanistan. These efforts had morphed into a campaign to bring Afghanistan into the twenty-first century. Also, of great importance was the effort by the United States, France, Britain, Germany, Russia, and China to reach agreement with Iran to limit Iran's nuclear activities. This agreement, formally known as the Joint Comprehensive Plan of Action (JCPOA), was reached in 2015. Europeans were also interested in US efforts in Syria and Iraq to end ISIS and its caliphate. Finally, Europe and the United States were among the most important signatories of the Paris Climate Accords of 2015.

Almost every American foreign policy initiative changed during the Trump Administration. President Donald Trump appeared not to value NATO or the long involvement of the United States in European affairs. His main complaint was that most NATO countries were freeloaders, not paying their fair share of NATO expenses. He quickly ended American involvement in the Iran nuclear deal (JCPOA) and withdrew the United States from the Paris Climate Accords. He followed up efforts to defeat ISIS, but as soon as Raqqa, the capital of the caliphate, was conquered and ISIS defeated, the Trump administration withdrew American troops to Syrian oil fields the US controlled and left the SDF, which consisted largely of Kurds, to deal with Turkish troops in Syria as best they could.

President Trump wanted to limit American commitment in world affairs, particularly if it meant sending American soldiers into combat. His foreign policy also seemed aimed at avoiding statements about human rights or critical remarks about authoritarian rulers. In particular, President Trump accepted Vladimir Putin's denial that Russia had meddled in the 2016 American presidential race. To his credit, he did try to persuade North Korea's leader, Kim Jong-un, to enter into meaningful negotiations. The net result, unfortunately, was strained relations with South Korea and two meaningless photo opportunity summits.

In the case of Afghanistan, President Trump negotiated with the Taliban on the question of the withdrawal of American troops. While the negotiations continued, the Taliban refrained from campaigns against Americans. The intention was that once the American withdrawal was set, the Taliban and the Afghan government would negotiate some sort of power-sharing arrangement. Unfortunately, this did not happen. Trump was defeated in 2020 in his attempt to secure a second term. President Joseph Biden (1942–) attempted to follow through with the agreement with the Taliban despite indications that the Afghan government would not be able to withstand a Taliban offensive. The American withdrawal was a disaster even though some 7,000 troops were sent back to try to manage the evacuation once the Afghan government had fallen. Thousands of Afghans who had worked with the United States and NATO and wanted to leave Afghanistan were unable to leave because of a Trump administration policy of slow-walking visa applications that called to mind State Department efforts in the 1930s to make applications by European Jews to enter the United States as complicated as possible.

A crucial area for the Trump administration was trade with Communist China. President Trump focused mostly on the balance of trade, which did favor the Chinese. His tactic of choice was tariff wars, which did not deal effectively with the major questions of American–Chinese economic relations. These had to do principally with Chinese industrial espionage and one-sided business arrangements for American businesses in China.

In general, President Trump showed little interest in European questions. He appeared to prefer authoritarian leaders. He also showed great interest in Israel. Late in his administration, largely through the efforts of his son-in-law, Jared Kushner (1981–), the Abraham Accords were signed between Israel and the United Arab Emirates, Bahrain, Sudan, and Morocco.

The Covid-19 Pandemic

To date, there is no definitive answer as to the origins of the Covid-19 pandemic given the refusal of Communist China (PRC) to provide information on what happened with SARS-CoV-2 in Wuhan, Hubei Province, in late 2019. Hubei Province officials attempted to cover up the outbreak and even after PRC officials became aware of the coverup, they failed to alert the World Health Organization and other governments. The PRC locked down Wuhan but did not stop travel from other parts of the PRC to the rest of the world.

Covid-19 first appeared in large numbers in Europe in northern Italy, mainly in Lombardy, toward the end of February 2020. The city of Bergamo became the center of a flood of cases. Authorities were slow to recognize what was happening. The hospital in Bergamo was quickly overwhelmed and had to reorganize extensively to deal with the large number of those infected with Covid-19. At one point, the military had to be called in to help transport corpses to crematoria.

Reactions to the pandemic varied widely from country to county. Austria's response was among the best in Europe. On 25 February 2020, the first two confirmed cases were noted. By 10 March, restrictions were in place and gradually led to a lockdown. Lockdowns were eased and then reinstated in 2020 and 2021.

Sweden's approach was unique in that there were efforts to protect the most vulnerable in the population but no lockdowns. This was supposed to lead to "herd immunity," in which a majority of the healthiest elements of the population would be infected but hopefully not die. Eventually, the virus would run out of hosts and die out naturally.

Boris Johnson's administration initially favored a "herd immunity" approach in the United Kingdom, but by mid-March 2020 had instituted various restrictions. Johnson was criticized for an uneven response to the crisis. In one regard, however, the United Kingdom excelled by rapidly developing one of the first effective vaccines.

In the United States, President Trump appointed Vice-President Mike Pence (1959–) to head the White House Coronavirus Task Force but quickly made himself the central figure in the effort to deal with the pandemic. He agreed to an initial shutdown, but his concern for potential harm to the economy led to an erratic approach. He also found it difficult to work with some state governors. The United States was able, however, to rapidly develop effective vaccines.

The economic impact of the pandemic was enormous. Countries offered generous unemployment benefits and developed programs designed to help people pay rent and other expenses.

An unexpected reaction to the vaccination campaigns was widespread vaccine hesitancy or the outright refusal to be vaccinated.

In part, it was a reaction to the many restrictions over the more than two years of the pandemic. It was also connected to fear among some that the various restrictions were part of a plot by elites to condition people to obey rules. These elites, who controlled industry, the media, and government were supposedly carrying out what some termed the Great Reset. This was supposed to create a docile population accustomed to following orders. This conspiracy theory is somewhat similar to the idea of the Great Replacement, the idea that letting large numbers of migrants and refugees into Europe would eventually result in a Europe dominated by Muslims.

What the Future May Bring

The United States cannot expect to continue to dominate world affairs, but it will remain an essential player. The American public would prefer that the United States not become involved again in another long-running conflict like Vietnam or Afghanistan. So far, the United States has successfully coordinated NATO's response to the Russian invasion of Ukraine. There is recognition that eventually the PRC will try to annex Taiwan and ongoing discussion of how that might be prevented.

The growth in power, both economically and militarily, of the PRC may well determine the course of the rest of the century. So far, Xi Jinping (1953–) has displayed patience. On the other hand, his treatment of Hong Kong and especially the Uyghurs demonstrate that he can be quite ruthless. There are good reasons for him to play a long game. He has been provided a third term as head of the PRC and this may become, in effect, a lifetime appointment. Nonetheless, growth is slowing in the PRC's economy and demographic trends produced by the "one child" policy are worrisome.

The issue of climate change may get lost in all the drama of the 2020s. Ironically, the Covid-19 pandemic has made clear that global cooperation is indispensable in dealing with natural phenomena. While there is controversy regarding the reality of climate change, it is regrettable that people are so easily distracted and seemingly unable to determine what might be prudent responses to this problem.

Finally, Europe in this century is very different from the Europe that existed at the beginning of the last century, but it still has an important role to play in world affairs. Olaf Scholz, the Chancellor of Germany, writes in *Foreign Affairs* about the global *Zeitenwende*, by which he means that Europe and the world are moving from one epoch to another. He contends that Germany, especially, because of its experience after World War II as a divided nation but also the rest of Europe can and must help defend a rules-based international order in place of a world divided into competing blocs (Scholz 2023).

References

Graff, Garret M. (2019). *The Only Plane in the Sky: An Oral History of 9/11*. New York: Avid Reader Press.

Kershaw, Ian. (2018). *The Global Age: Europe 1950–2017*. New York: Viking.

Lahoud, Nelly. (2021). "Bin Laden's Catastrophic Success." *Foreign Affairs*, volume 100, number 5.

Scholz, Olaf. (2023). "The Global *Zeitenwende*: How to Avoid a New Cold War in a Multipolar Era." *Foreign Affairs*, volume 102, number 1.

Tooze, Adam. (2018). *Crashed: How a Decade of Financial Crises Changed the World*. New York: Penguin.

Appendix

Abbreviations and Acronyms

THE TWENTIETH CENTURY and this current century have produced a bewildering array of abbreviations and acronyms for the many political parties, committees, organizations, and institutions that have appeared over the years. No one can hope to remember all the relevant short forms used in European history in this period. The two alphabetical lists should help, however, in quickly determining what a set of initials stands for or how the name of a particular institution is commonly abbreviated. In some cases, the initials will not correspond to the English version of the name. This is because the initials are taken from the name as it appears in the language of the country. For example, the German National Socialist Workers' Party is abbreviated NSDAP, which stands for *N*ational*s*ozialistische *D*eutsche *A*rbeiter*p*artei.

Adjustable Rate Mortgages (USA)	ARMs
Alliance of Free Democrats (Hungary)	ADF
Belgium, Netherlands, Luxembourg	BENELUX
British Union of Fascists	BUF
Brothers of Italy	FdI
Cable News Network	CNN
Central Intelligence Agency	CIA (United States)
Chinese Communist Party	CCP

Twentieth-Century Europe: 1900 to the Present, Fourth Edition.
Michael D. Richards and Paul R. Waibel.

Christian Democratic Party (Italy)	DC
Christian Democratic People's Party (Hungary)	CDPP
Christian Democratic Union (West Germany; Germany)	CDU
Civic Democratic Party (Czechoslovakia)	CDP
Civic Movement (Czechoslovakia)	CM
Committee for the Defense of the Workers (Poland)	KOR
Commonwealth of Independent States (Former USSR)	CIS
Communist Information Bureau	COMINFORM
Communist International (Third International)	COMINTERN
Communist Party (Germany)	KPD
Communist Party (Italy)	PCI
Communist Party (Soviet Union)	CPSU
Conference on Security and Cooperation in Europe (See also the Organization for Security and Cooperation in Europe)	CSCE
Council for Mutual Economic Assistance	COMECON
Democratic National Salvation Front (Hungary)	DNSF
East Germany (German Democratic Republic)	GDR
Eurasian Economic Union	EEU
European Coal and Steel Community	ECSC
European Community (See also European Economic Community; European Union)	EC
European Defense Community	EDC
European Economic Community (See also European Community; European Union)	EEC
European Free Trade Association	EFTA
European Monetary System	EMS
European Recovery Program (Marshall Plan)	ERP
Federal Deposit Insurance Corporation (USA)	FDIC
Federal Republic of Germany (West Germany)	FRG
Federal Security Service	FSB (successor to the KGB)
Geheime Staatspolizei (Secret Police in Nazi Germany)	GESTAPO
German Democratic Republic (East Germany)	GDR
German National Socialist Workers' Party (Nazis)	NSDAP
German Social Democratic Party	SPD

Gross Domestic Product	GDP
Group of Seven (leading industrial democracies)	G-7
Group of Eight (G-7 plus the Russian Republic)	G-8
Hungarian Democratic Forum	HDF
Hungarian Socialist Party	HSP
Independent Smallholders Party (Hungary)	ISP
Independent Social Democratic Party of Germany	USPD
International Monetary Fund	IMF
Islamic State of Iraq and Syria	ISIS
Joint Comprehensive Plan of Action	JCPOA (Iran nuclear deal)
Kosovo Liberation Army	KLA
Kriegsrohstoffabteilung (War Raw Materials Administration)	KRA
Law and Justice	PIS (Poland)
League of Communists of Yugoslavia	LCY
Main Administration of Corrective Labor Camps (USSR)	GULAG
Member of the British Empire	MBE
Movement for a Democratic Slovakia	MDS
National Aeronautics and Space Agency (USA)	NASA
National Salvation Front (Hungary)	NSF
New Democracy (Greece)	ND
New Economic Policy	NEP
North Atlantic Treaty Organization	NATO
Organization for Economic Cooperation and Development	OECD
Organization for Security and Cooperation in Europe	OSCE
Organization of European Economic Cooperation	OEEC
Party of Democratic Socialism (formerly the Socialist Unity Party)	PDS
People's Republic of China	PRC
Polish Socialist Workers' Party	RPPS
Popular Republican Movement (France)	MRP
Portugal, Italy, Greece, and Spain	PIGS (Euro Zone Crisis)

Public Broadcasting System (USA)	PBS
Royal Air Force (United Kingdom)	RAF
Russian Secret Police (1992–present)	FSB
Russian Social Democratic Labor Party (Bolsheviks; Mensheviks)	RSDLP
Schutzstaffel (Protective detachment—SS Nazi Organization)	SS
Secret Police (East Germany)	STASI
Single European Act	SEA
Socialist German Student Federation	SDS
Socialist Party (France)	SFIO
Socialist Revolutionaries (Russia)	SR
Socialist Unity Party (East Germany)	SED
Soviet Secret Police (1935–1953)	NKVD
Soviet Secret Police (1953–1992)	KGB
State Defense Committee (Soviet Union)	GKO
Strategic Arms Limitations Talks / Treaty	SALT
Strategic Defense Initiative ("Star Wars")	SDI
Sturmabteilung (Stormtroopers—Nazi Organization)	SA
Syrian Democratic Forces	SDF
Trades Union Council (United Kingdom)	TUC
Troubled Assets Relief Program	TARP (United States)
United Kingdom Independence Party	UKIP
Warsaw Treaty Organization	WTO
Weapons of Mass Destruction	WMD
West Germany (Federal Republic of Germany)	FRG
World Trade Organization	WTO
Year 2000	Y2K

ADF	Alliance of Free Democrats (Hungary)
ARMs	Adjustable Rate Mortgages (USA)
BENELUX	Belgium, Netherlands, Luxembourg
BUF	British Union of Fascists
CCP	Chinese Communist Party
CDP	Civic Democratic Party (Czechoslovakia)
CDPP	Christian Democratic People's Party (Hungary)

CDU	Christian Democratic Union (West Germany; Germany)
CIA	Central Intelligence Agency (United States)
CIS	Commonwealth of Independent States (Former USSR)
CM	Civic Movement (Czechoslovakia)
CNN	Cable News Network
COMECON	Council for Mutual Economic Assistance
COMINFORM	Communist Information Bureau
COMINTERN	Communist International (Third International)
CDPP	Christian Democratic People's Party
CPSU	Communist Party (Soviet Union)
CSCE	Conference on Security and Cooperation in Europe (See also the Organization for Security and Cooperation in Europe)
DC	Christian Democratic Party (Italy)
DNSF	Democratic National Salvation Front (Hungary)
EC	European Community (See also European Economic Community; European Union)
ECSC	European Coal and Steel Community
EDC	European Defense Community
EEC	European Economic Community (See also European Community; European Union)
EEU	Eurasian Economic Union
EFTA	European Free Trade Association
EMS	European Monetary System
ERP	European Recovery Program (Marshall Plan)
FdI	Brothers of Italy
FDIC	Federal Deposit Insurance Corporation (USA)
FRG	Federal Republic of Germany (West Germany)
FSB	Federal Security Service (successor to the KGB)
G-7	Group of Seven (leading industrial democracies)
G-8	G-7 plus the Russian Republic
GDP	Gross Domestic Product
GDR	German Democratic Republic (East Germany)
GESTAPO	*Geheime Staatspolizei* (Secret Police in Nazi Germany)
GKO	State Defense Committee (Soviet Union)

GULAG	Main Administration of Corrective Labor Camps (USSR)
HDF	Hungarian Democratic Forum
HSP	Hungarian Socialist Party
IMF	International Monetary Fund
ISIS	Islamic State of Iraq and Syria
ISP	Independent Smallholders Party
JCPOA	Joint Comprehensive Plan of Action (Iran nuclear deal)
KGB	Soviet Secret Police (1953–1992)
KLA	Kosovo Liberation Army
KOR	Committee for the Defense of the Workers (Poland)
KRA	*Kriegsrohstoffabteilung* (War Raw Materials Administration)
LCY	League of Communists of Yugoslavia
MBE	Member of the British Empire
MDS	Movement for a Democratic Slovakia (Czechoslovakia)
MRP	Popular Republican Movement (France)
NASA	National Aeronautics and Space Administration
NATO	North Atlantic Treaty Organization
ND	New Democracy (Greece)
NEP	New Economic Policy
NKVD	Soviet Secret Police (1935–1953)
NSDAP	German National Socialist Workers' Party (Nazis)
NSF	National Salvation Front (Hungary)
OECD	Organization for Economic Cooperation and Development
OEEC	Organization of European Economic Cooperation
OSCE	Organization for Security and Cooperation in Europe
PBS	Public Broadcasting System (USA)
PCI	Communist Party (Italy)
PD	Democratic Party (Italy)
PDS	Party of Democratic Socialism (formerly the Socialist Unity Party)
PIGS	Portugal, Italy, Greece, and Spain (Euro Zone Crisis)
PiS	Law and Justice Party (Poland)
PRC	People's Republic of China

RAF	Royal Air Force (United Kingdom)
RPPS	Polish Socialist Workers' Party
RSDLP	Russian Social Democratic Labor Party (Bolsheviks; Mensheviks)
SA	*Sturmabteilung* (Stormtroopers—Nazi Organization)
SALT	Strategic Arms Limitations Talks/Treaty
SDF	Syrian Democratic Forces
SDI	Strategic Defense Initiative ("Star Wars")
SDS	Socialist German Student Federation
SEA	Single European Act
SED	Socialist Unity Party (East Germany)
SFIO	Socialist Party (France)
SPD	German Social Democratic Party
SR	Socialist Revolutionaries (Russia)
SS	*Schutzstaffel* (Protective detachment—SS Nazi Organization)
STASI	Secret Police (East Germany)
TARP	Troubled Assets Relief Program (United States)
TUC	Trades Union Council (United Kingdom)
UKIP	United Kingdom Independence Party
USPD	Independent Social Democratic Party of Germany
WMD	Weapons of Mass Destruction
WTO	Warsaw Treaty Organization
WTO	World Trade Organization
Y2K	Year 2000

Index

Note: Page numbers followed by *il, n, p, t* indicate illustrations, footnotes, photographs, or tables respectively

Twentieth-Century Europe: 1900 to the Present, Fourth Edition.
Michael D. Richards and Paul R. Waibel.